Private Real Estate Investment

Data Analysis and Decision Making

2nd Edition

Roger J. Brown, PhD
President
IMOJIM Investments
Alpine, California

IMOJIM, Inc.
dba IMOJIM Investments
PO Box 1146
Alpine CA 91903

This book is printed on acid-free paper. <§

Copyright © 2012, IMOJIM Inc. All rights reserved.

No part of this publication may be reproduced or transmitted in any form or by any means, electronic or mechanical, including photocopy, recording, or any information storage and retrieval system, without permission in writing from the publisher.

Permissions may be sought directly from IMOJIM, Inc:, e-mail: permissions@mathestate.com.

LIBRARY OF CONGRESS CATALOGING for First Edition

Brown, Roger J.

Private real estate investment : data analysis and decision making / Roger J. Brown.

Includes bibliographical references and index.

    1. Real estate investment –Decision making. 2. Real estate investment –Planning. HD1382.5 .B764

ISBN for this second edition:

ISBN: 978-0-9850755-1-4

For all information on all IMOJIM, Inc. publications
visit our Web site at www.mathestate.com

Printed in the United States of America
04 05 06 07 08 09   9 8 7 6 5 4 3 2

"Is life mathematics or is it poetry?"

Roger Maguérès

Contents

Acknowledgements   *xii*
Preface to the second edition   1

1. Why Location Matters – The Bid Rent Surface and Theory of Rent Determination..7
    1.1 Introduction
    1.2 Classical location theory
        1.2.1 Notation Guide
        1.2.2 The model
        1.2.3 Example #1 – two competing users in the same industry
        1.2.4 Example #2 – several competing users in different industries
    1.3 Is the bid rent curve linear?
    1.4 Empirical verification
    1.5 An economic topographical map
    1.6 Relaxing the assumptions
    1.7 A window to the future

2. Land Use Regulation 27
    2.1 Introduction
    2.2 Who shall decide – the problem of externalities
    2.3 The important idea of "utility"
        2.3.1 Notation guide
        2.3.2 The model
    2.4 Optimization and comparative statics
    2.5 A graphical illustration
    2.6 Implications
    2.7 A case study in aesthetic regulation
    2.8 Conclusion

3. The "Rules of Thumb" – Threshold Performance Measures 43
    3.1 Introduction
    3.2 Threshold performance measures
    3.3 A general caution
    3.4 The gross rent multiplier (GRM)
        3.4.1 What not to do
        3.4.2 What should be done
    3.5 Capitalization rate (CR)
        3.5.1 The three bad assumptions
    3.6 Capitalization rate and discounted cash flow (DCF) analysis
        3.6.1 Monotonic growth

3.7 The expense ratio and the "honest" capitalization rate
    3.7.1 The normal approach to data
    3.7.2 Questioning the assumption of normality
    3.7.3 The stable approach to data
    3.7.4 Linear relationships
    3.7.5 Linear transformations
    3.7.6 Spurious relationships
3.8 Cash-on-cash (C/C) return
3.9 Price per unit (PPU)
3.10 Other data issues

Appendix

4. Fundamental Real Estate Analysis...73
4.1 Introduction
    4.1.1 The role of computational aids
4.2 Deterministic variables of discounted cash flow analysis
4.3 Single year relationships and project data
4.4 Multi-year relationships
4.5 Sale variables relationships
4.6 The net present value
4.7 Insight into the analysis
4.8 An illustration of bargaining
4.9 Another growth function
4.10 Data issues
4.11 Conclusion

5. Sins of the IRR – What it Will and Will Not Do 99
5.1 Introduction
    5.1.1 Performance measures - why use them at all?
5.2 The reinvestment problem
5.3 The problem of no solution
5.4 The problem of multiple solutions
5.5 The ranking problem
5.6 The scale problem
    5.6.1 Return and scale
    5.6.2 Risk and scale
5.7 The simulation problem
    5.7.1 Foundation
    5.7.2 Multiple roots
    5.7.3 Bias

5.8 Conclusion

Appendix

6. Chance: Risk in General 121
6.1 Introduction
    6.1.1 Objective and subjective risk
6.2 Games of chance and risk bearing
6.3 The utility function revisited
6.4 The "certainty equivalent" approach
6.5 Changing utility functions
6.6 A measure of risk aversion
6.7 Multiple (more than two) outcomes
6.8 The continuous <u>normal</u> case
6.9 Conclusion

7. Uncertainty: Risk in Real Estate 143
7.1 Introduction
    7.1.1 Non-normality – how and where does it fit?
7.2 The continuous stable case
    7.2.1 Stable parameters
    7.2.2 The stable *pdf*
    7.2.3 Stable distribution problems
    7.2.4 Still more distributions?
7.3 Enter real estate
7.4 Determinism
7.5 Determinism and house prices
7.6 Determinism and real estate investment
7.7 Risk and uncertainty
7.8 Rolling the dice
7.9 Real estate - the "Have it Your Way" game
7.10 The payoff
7.11 Data issues
7.12 Conclusion

Appendix

8. The Labor Component of Private Investor Real Estate Returns 187
8.1 Introduction
    8.1.1 The important aspect of time
8.2 Foundation
8.3 Notation guide

    8.4 The no bequests model
        8.4.1 Wealth accumulation prior to retirement
        8.4.2 Wealth accumulation after retirement
        8.4.3 Simulation #1
        8.4.4 Simulation #2
        8.4.5 Simulation #3
        8.4.6 Simulation #4
    8.5 The constant wealth model
        8.5.1 Simulation #5
    8.6 Conclusion

9. Spectral Risk Measures 209
    9.1 Introduction
    9.2 Some recent history
    9.3 The embarrassing problem with portfolios of real estate
    9.4 Spectral risk measure
    9.5 Spectral risk measures for real estate investment
    9.6 Scenario analysis
        9.6.1 Institutional data (NCREIF)
        9.6.2 Non-institutional data (CoStar)
    9.7 Conclusion

10. The Tax Deferred Exchange 225
    10.1 Introduction
        10.1.1 Taxes are less certain for real estate investors
        10.1.2 Variable definitions
        10.1.3 The structure of the examples
    10.2 The base case: Purchase – Hold – Sell
    10.3 Example 1 – A modified growth projection over six years
    10.4 Example 2 – The tax deferred exchange strategy
        10.4.1 Exchange variable definitions
        10.4.2 The value of tax deferral
        10.4.3 Tax deferral as a risk modifier
        10.4.4 The sale-and-better-repurchase strategy: The cost of exchanging
    10.5 Example 3 – Exchanging and "The Plodder"
    10.6 Data issues
    10.7 Conclusion

11. The Management Problem 261
    11.1 Introduction
    11.2 The unavoidable management issue

11.3 The property manager's dilemma
    11.3.1 Is building size really important?
11.4 The property owner's dilemma
    11.4.1 The "No vacancy rate" approach
    11.4.2 Enter the vacancy rate
11.5 Reconciling the two problems
11.6 Data issues
11.7 Conclusion

    Appendix

12. The Lender's Dilemma 285
12.1 Introduction
    12.1.1 Lenders and their rules
12.2 Appraisal techniques
    12.2.1 The capitalization rate approach vs. the mortgage equity approach
    12.2.2 The lender's perspective
    12.2.3 The borrower's perspective
12.3 Irrational exuberance and the madness of crowds
12.4 Bubble theory – How high is up?
    12.4.1 Positive leverage
    12.4.2 The lender as governor
    12.4.3 Resolving the conflict
    12.4.4 Three 2D illustrations
    12.4.5 A challenge in three dimensions
    12.4.6 Endgame
12.5 Data issues
12.6 Conclusion

13. The Private Lender 305
13.1 Introduction
13.2 The "hard money" loan vs. the "purchase money" loan
    13.2.1 The diversification problem
    13.2.2 Other possibilities
    13.2.3 Did we make a loan or did we buy the property?
13.3 The installment sale
    13.3.1 The data inputs
    13.3.2 The client status
13.4 The motivation of the parties
    13.4.1 The buyer

        13.4.2 The seller
    13.5 The installment sale transaction
        13.5.1 Is the seller's financing a good deal for the buyer?
        13.5.2 An NPV test
        13.5.3 An IRR test
        13.5.4 A simple "tax blind" test
    13.6 A prepayment penalty
    13.7 Conclusion

14. The Life Estate as Financing 323
    14.1 Introduction
        14.1.1 Retirement and creative financing
        14.1.2 A life estate
        14.1.3 A zero coupon bond
    14.2 The retiree's dilemma
        14.2.1 The conventional arrangement
        14.2.2 The reverse amortization mortgage
    14.3 Intra-family alternatives
        14.3.1 The income viewpoint
        14.3.2 The larger house viewpoint
    14.4 The remainderman's position
        14.4.1 The income case
        14.4.2 The larger house case
    14.5 Conclusion

15. Real Options 337
    15.1 Introduction
        15.1.1 Real options are different
    15.2 A two-outcome example
        15.2.1 The effect of bad news
        15.2.2 The discount and expectation process
        15.2.3 Option value and the NPV rule
    15.3 The option to redevelop
    15.4 Toward a more complete real option pricing model
    15.5 Conclusion

16. The Economics of Leasing..353
    16.1 Introduction
    16.2 The "Extreme lease"
        16.2.1 The parties
    16.3 A typical ground lease transaction
        16.3.1 The subordination issue

    16.3.2 The option issue
    16.3.3 The cap rate – IRR conflict
    16.3.4 When the option is "in the money"
16.4 Lease termination
16.5 Conclusion

Epilog

ACKNOWLEDGMENTS

When this book is made into a movie and wins an Academy Award, my acceptance speech will be long:

At the end of a project like this there are so many people to thank. I hope I don't leave anyone out. The order of mention is more about chronology than importance for all were vital to my education and intellectual development. All, in some way, made an important contribution to this book.

From my earliest childhood days I was inspired and guided by wonderful math teachers from Sister Fridoline, my first grade teacher through Monty Fones in high school. I was twice blessed when it all had to be done again thirty years later at Penn State. Ed Coulson and Herman Bierens were both patient and talented professors who, in restoring my ancient math skills, gave more of their time than I deserved.

Four people made important contributions to the sort of business understanding one can only obtain in the real world. Chilton and Bryan Jelks provided years of practical guidance outside of real estate. I have Dr. David K. Hostetler and Jim Darr to thank for keeping me on the right track over four decades of real estate practice. For me, these four were Deans of the School of Hard Knocks without whom the knocks would have been a lot harder.

The graduate school part of this quest began in 1992 at San Diego State University under the wise guidance of Bob Wilbur, Andy Do and Milton Chen. In 1995 these fine academics breathed a sigh of relief and handed me off to Ken Lusht and Jeff Sharp at Penn State two superb gentlemen who did their best, given the raw material they had to work with, to finish the job. While at Penn State I was also fortunate to receive vital help at crucial times from Cemile Yavas, Tom Geurts, Jim Jordan, Norm Swanson and Paul Claar. Since I left PSU the help and thoughtful comments of Mike Young, Richard Graff, Colin Rose, Stephen Roulac, Hu McCulloch, Tim Riddiough, Norm Miller, Johannes Ludsteck, Kevin Dowd and Ted Ersek were also appreciated.

The technical aspects of this book, especially the inclusion of very artful *Mathematica* code that produced most of the graphics and many of the technical items on the supplementary electronic files, would not have been possible without the tireless efforts of Marlyn L. Hicks whose clear-headed, agnostic view of mathematics is reflected in every chapter. Marlyn was a wonderful sounding board, a voice of reason never swayed by academic history or politics. A book of this nature needs a real mathematician and Marlyn played that role magnificently.

Tom Zeller, Andreas Lauschke, Bruce Miller, Shenghui Yang, William Rummler and Jesus Hernandez are just some of the very talented *Mathematica* programmers at Wolfram Research who always came through with important assistance when I needed it.

The inspiration for the Risk in Real Estate models of Chapter 6 comes from John Nolan whose help over many years enriched my understanding of the strange world of Stable Distributions. This area in the book also benefited from the long discussions of life, investing, probability and mathematics with Robert Rimmer, MD, who very generously gave of his time, providing important interpretations that may have been missed and also assisting in the *Mathematica* programming. This book benefits from an interactive web site, www.mathestate.com, where many of the routines described in these chapters can be immediately implemented. My thanks to the world famous Cosmo Jones and his more talented sidekick, Chris Sessions for building that site and to Tom Compton and D. Jacob Wildstrom for their help in maintaining it.

My contemporaries in the business world were also very supportive. John Boyle, Terry Moore, Richard Schneider, Chuck Wise and several anonymous reviewers either read portions of the book or provided helpful suggestions. Data provided by the CoStar Group was made possible through the gracious assistance of Craig Farrington. Craig and I spent many a lunch over most of a decade dreaming about new and different ways in which data will be used in future real estate decisions. Pat Barnes and Bruce Howe provided vital data for Chapter Two that made the case study at the end of that chapter possible.

No book ever sees the light of day without a superb editor who believes in the project. Scott Bentley was that person for me. His easy-going manner and always helpful suggestions for the 1st edition made the process a pleasure. Doing without him on the 2nd edition was a struggle.

The first edition was thoughtfully and kindly reviewed by Hugh Kelly and Nick French, for which I am very grateful. I hope their faith in this subject and its author will be continued in the second edition.

Many books leave some innocent soul waiting. No married author ever reaches the end of a process like this without owing yet another un-repayable debt of gratitude to a long-suffering spouse. This author is no different. Without the world's most perfect woman exhibiting the sort of understanding that passes all understanding this book would not exist. Thank you, Bonnie Jean.

Roger J. Brown
Alpine, CA
January, 2012

Preface to the 2nd edition

0.1. Introduction

Before embarking on substantive comments involving content, it is important to warn the reader about the various "lives" this book has enjoyed and how that history influences the choices the reader faces in acquiring this book. The first edition was published by Academic Press in 2005 in print only. The first edition had eleven chapters and was a traditional textbook. The seven years that followed were tumultuous for both the publishing and financial industries, indeed, for the global economy. The second edition, comprising sixteen chapters, updates the subject matter to include unfolding events but also takes on a new, actually three new, looks as it reaches the consumer in 2012.

1. For those who like to hold a book in their hands and turn pages, the 2nd edition is available in print;
2. For those who wish to use various e-readers it is also available in electronic, read-only, format;
3. For those who desire an interactive experience it is available in the Computational Document Format (CDF). To experience this Preface in that format, permitting interactivity, visit www.mathestate.com and click on the "Resources" button.

Your author, while having nearly boundless enthusiasm for the subject, draws the line at writing three different books, one to suit each format. Thus, some compromises are necessary. I must beg the reader's indulgence over these. It has been said many times that it is not wise to try to be all things to all people. My effort here could be criticized accordingly (although I am completely ignoring those who still prefer stone tablets, use quill pens, write on papyrus or get all their information from the little voices in their head). My hope is that, because this preface will be available to all consumers *before* making their decision which version to purchase, readers will be informed and satisfied buyers, having had their expectations conditioned by what appears here.

From a content standpoint, the difference in the versions is nearly none. Anyone buying any version of the full book will get the same information. Those buying the print version will notice no difference in electronic form. It is the CDF version that offers a different experience in that many of the graphics are interactive and permit the reader to change the value of variables and see how the result changes in a particular plot. For those students who wish to work the exercises at the end of each chapter, this interactivity sometimes will be mandatory as some of the problems depend on the reader manipulating data input.

The remainder of the compromises and the consequences the reader must endure involve formatting. In order to produce only one book to fit all applications it was necessary to write the entire book using a software named *Mathematica*, a product of Wolfram Research. This software enhances the author's ability to produce quantitative output in the form of equations, data analysis and graphics. There are many occasions when any particular answer could have merely been typed into the text material. But the ability to produce them using the software within the narrative offers a number of benefits which I hope all readers enjoy.

The result of using *Mathematica* is the occasional disconcerting change in font or style. *Mathematica* uses a different font to distinguish between (a) text, (b) user input, and (c) output from the software (answers in the form of computations, equations or graphics). The reader who does not have Wolfram's free CDF player and does not use the interactive features is requested to tolerate the change in font or paragraph formatting and merely read it as if it were part of the text. Here is an example from Chapter 13:

$$n = -\frac{Log\left[1 - \frac{bal\ interestrate}{pmt}\right]}{Log[1 + interestrate]} \qquad (13.2)$$

Substituting our data into Equation 13.2, we can obtain the amortization period for the seller financing given the payment schedule of the conventional financing.

```
Months required to fully amortize = 283.
```

Notice the change in font from Times New Roman in the text immediately below Equation 13.2 to the next line which is Courier. In the white space between there is code that makes the calculation called for in Equation 13.2 and shows the output in Courier font. This, with much tedious effort, could have been edited for the print version to be one sentence with a single font style. Right or wrong, in the interest of programming efficiency and flexibility in revision, your author has elected to leave the slight discontinuity in style asking the reader to adapt. An advantage is that output computed by the software in which the book was written has a high probability of being correct. Luckily for those without a keen interest in mathematics, the narration of the book is written such that the equations and programming may all be ignored and the "story" remains.

Mathematica also uses "cells" to organize a document. These cells can be thought of as paragraphs in conventional publishing. Indeed, when the cell contains only text that is exactly what each cell represents, a paragraph. But cells can also contain input, output and graphics. Cells can be grouped and the group collapsed to "hide" additional code or detailed exposition. This can result in white space between paragraphs. For the most part all cells with text have been left "open" for all readers. But in the case of a particularly large dataset or very intricate computer code, that material will be "hidden" from the view of the reader under a collapsed cell. Only readers with a full version of *Mathematica* will be interested in the information contained in the closed cells, all others may safely ignore the occasional white space. Those readers who need the actual *Mathematica* code must request it as it is not included in any form of the book.

Here is another example, this time showing code from *Mathematica* input in the first line which is bold Courier, followed by output. Much of the code has been hidden from the reader's view. Occasionally, when the context cannot be misconstrued or the code makes a contribution to the narrative, the code remains. Because the characters "/." are Mathematicaspeak for "given that" the code below says, in words, "take the maximum of b or pv, given data in dataset 1."

```
Max[b, pv] /. data1
258 719.
```

Another useful advantage of *Mathematica* is the ability to update electronic files by either supplementing them with new material or changing material to reflect changing times. Finally, it is much easier to correct mistakes discovered after an electronic version is published than after a paper publisher completes a 2,000 volume print run. I am indebted to those patient readers of the first edition who kindly sent me corrections for the inevitable mistakes that always survive numerous proof readings. Those corrections have been incorporated in the present edition. But as there are five chapters in the second edition that did not appear in the first edition, there has been the obvious opportunity to make gnu mistakes. My hope is that future readers will be as thorough in reporting these as their predecessors have been. If so, corrections may not be made in real time but will be made more quickly than before.

There is one last, nearly imperceptible, advantage for the rare consumer who also owns version 8 or later of the full *Mathematica* software package. The code for all computations and illustrations in the book is available for an additional charge (e-mail contact info at mathestate.com), providing the user with a head start should he wish to modify or expand on the subject matter within *Mathematica*. This will be useful only to researchers or those with a penchant for financial engineering computing applications, clearly the minority of consumers. For everyone else, the companion electronic files in Excel format permit further exploration in a familiar environment.

0.2. Interactivity

The payoff for putting up with the curious result of a book written with a symbolic computing software is the ability to interact with the material. Below, if you have Wolfram's free CDF Player installed (if not the graphic will be static), from Chapter 1, is an example. If you are reading this with Wolfram's CDF Player, drag the slider bars to change the value of variables and change the information in the plot.

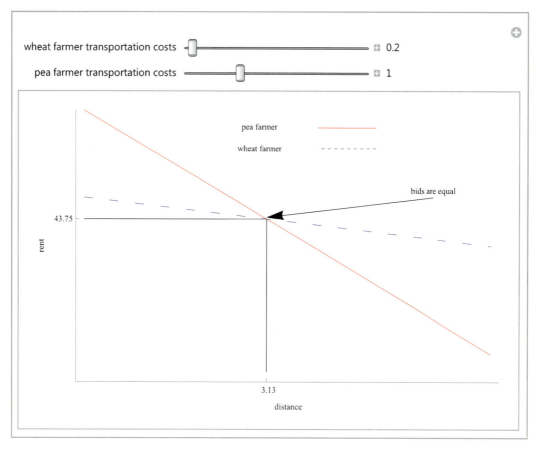

Figure 1.1 Rent at point where bids are equal.

0.3. Who this book is for

This book is designed as a handbook for individual investors in real property, institutional risk managers and as a supplementary text for upper division undergraduate and graduate real estate investment courses. The electronic files included with various chapters (available at www.mathestate.com) contain pre-written code for data analysis tailored specifically to real estate settings. The major thrust is to bridge the gap between theory and practice by showing the reader how to conceive of and implement real estate risk management in the real world.

The study of real estate follows long traditions grounded in Urban Economics and Finance. There is, however an inherent conflict between the twin realities that the finance market is efficient and the real estate market is not. Practitioners in the real world know, or at least act as if they know, that real estate is very different from finance. No investment real estate broker gets up in the morning and does anything even remotely resembling what a stockbroker does. While anecdotal evidence suggests that the two activities are different, until very recently academic theory supporting such a belief has been underdeveloped and has suffered from a lack of data to test hypotheses.

The data are growing around us every day as the industry converts real estate information into digital form. It may be that this will improve real estate market efficiency. It may also lead us to conclude that real estate is different from finance for reasons we previously had not considered.

Three significant ideas motivate this book:

1. Until recently, data on real estate were available only for large, institutional grade properties and its use limited to those who work in that market. Now, robust databases are available for many different types of real estate. For the first time, databases covering private real estate investment have breadth (large number of observations in relatively small geographic areas) and depth (long histories of data covering the same property).
2. Closed-form analytical techniques for risk modeling either (a) have been exhausted and/or (b) because of institutional factors are inapplicable to real estate. Hence, risk modeling using fast, numerically intensive simulation with bounded datasets offers a significant improvement over the present *ad hoc* real estate methods.
3. Considerable recent progress has been made in mathematical software and algorithms that permit one to access, combine and integrate real estate databases in ways that makes possible visual, spatial representations. Such demonstrations are now accessible to a much larger, and at times less sophisticated, audience.

It has been estimated that one-half of the world's wealth is in real estate. A book such as this offers tools to enhance decision-making for consumers and researchers in market economies of any country interested in land use and real estate investment. Empirical risk analysis improves the understanding of markets in general. Real estate is not different in this regard. Each day thousands of bright, entrepreneurial souls arise and make dramatic contributions to our built environment, heretofore without data or database analysis techniques. This book hopes to add a suite of tools that will sharpen their vision and understanding of that process.

0.3.1. Investors

For investors (and all others) familiar with the spreadsheet environment, numerical analysis and sensitivity testing is often done via example for which a spreadsheet is well suited. The use of the tools provided here can enhance the investor's experience by providing better understanding of his advisor's recommendations.

However, all should recognize the inherent limitations of any spreadsheet approach.

1. The use of a spreadsheet implies (but does not require) two dimensions. Certainly the graphics produced by the average spreadsheet program composed of columns and rows model only two variables (what spreadsheet call "3D" are just printing effects, not the introduction of a third variable).
2. Very often spreadsheet use is limited to linear models or models that exhibit non-decreasing functions. These are misleading as the world is neither linear nor do the economic variables in the real world constantly increase.
3. There is a static aspect to spreadsheets that fail to fully consider the time dimensions of any model.

These three limitations are partially overcome by higher mathematics and symbolic computing software that extends beyond spreadsheets. This book employs such software. The reader is urged to develop an appreciation for these advanced tools and recognize the elementary nature of spreadsheet modeling and the complexity such simplification overlooks.

0.3.2. Academic

1. Undergraduate students will find the narrative and examples in the text challenging but manageable without higher mathematics or an understanding of programming. The assumption is that students have had at least a semester of calculus and have for reference a primary real estate investment text.
2. Graduate students with some background in statistics will take the sample data provided and exercise their empirical skills in the context of real estate data limitations. This will enhance understanding of how real estate adds to and fits into the overall economic picture.

0.3.3. Practitioners

1. Lenders and managers of large real estate portfolios, many of whom originate real estate data, will be able to incorporate these tools into their daily real estate risk management activities.
2. The most sophisticated investors and their advisors will use these tools for due diligence in an environment of professional liability and a rising standard of care.
3. Investment real estate brokers in the MAI and CCIM category will find the narrative and illustrations helpful, better explaining investment risk/return tradeoffs to clients.

0.4. A Practical Guide to Investment Real Estate

Perhaps the first manual for the private real estate investor was William Nickerson's How I Turned $1,000 into a Million in Real Estate in My Spare Time based on his real estate investments in the 1930s. Despite the complexities of modern day life, thousands of real estate investors still practice his teachings each day.

This book updates Nickerson's timeless message and elaborates it in a rigorous framework that describes how individual real estate investors make decisions in the 21st Century. Underlying most successful folklore is a sound theory. Private real estate investors follow well-developed and widely respected micro-economic theory in that they are profit seeking, risk averse, utility maximizers. However, their approach differs from that of their brethren in financial assets. Privately owned real estate offers an opportunity to add the value of one's entrepreneurial effort to one's portfolio. Such a process provides an avenue to success quite different from the route taken by the average stock market investor.

After decades of thinking of a database as three comparable sales, real estate investors today suddenly find that they have access to plentiful data. Large datasets light the way to a host of objective ways of viewing real estate. Until now, the thorny issue of risk has been real estate's crazy aunt in the basement, either completely ignored or dealt with subjectively in a variety of *ad hoc* ways. Despite this, over the long run the monetary performance of real estate investments appears to compete favorably with that of financial assets, an outcome that could not have been achieved without addressing risk along the way. However, little analysis of this process exists beyond applying mainstream finance models, often with apologies for how poorly the square peg of real estate fits through the round hole of finance.

Private real estate investment opportunities offer a different kind of risk, a non-linear variety characterized by observations often far from the mean. The persistence of such outliers bespeaks of a need for a new approach to risk. Also, as a result of (1) a fixed supply of land, (2) an adjustment in holding period when needed, and (3) the addition of labor, real estate investors live in a market where the size of their return may be uncertain but the sign is more likely to be positive. With empirical support for the maxim "You can't go wrong in real estate" comes a different view of risk in this unique market.

The goal of this book is, therefore, threefold: First, updating Nickerson's widely respected work, it will apply mathematical rigor to the various homilies and truisms that have characterized private real estate investment for decades. Second, at a time when the industry is digitizing and databases deliver more objective information about the private real estate investment market, it will incorporate appropriate yet innovative ways to use these new data. Third, combining the first two, it will uncover a way of viewing risk in real estate that is intuitively appealing, theoretically sound and supported by empirical evidence.

0.5. What this book is not

As a supplementary text, this book cannot cover in detail the myriad aspects of real estate investment that come before or run along side the need to understand risk and use data. Early chapters lay foundation to some degree but the reader is cautioned not to take the contents of a book this short as exhaustive.

Some fundamentals of probability and statistics are discussed but there is no attempt here to provide what excellent texts covering those subject areas offers. The subtleties of such topics as leptokurtosis, ergodicity and the asymptotic properties of likelihood functions, pervade the subject of statistics. While practitioners can often get by without an intimate knowledge of such things, they exist and should not be ignored. Practical limitations prevent a thorough discussion of these subtleties here.

The illustrations in this book offer guidelines about locating a path, they are not a road map with a certain destination. Indeed the subject of risk and data is about uncertainty. The most a book such as this can offer is a framework for thinking about problems involving uncertainty. Hopefully the illustrations stimulate thinking about how people, property and numbers can be combined in the presence of uncertainty to make good decisions.

Mathematica is a powerful symbolic logic computing software. For some readers, each chapter is in Computational Document Format (CDF). In electronic form it may be viewed with the free CDF Player from Wolfram Research. The reader does not have to own nor does he have to know how to program *Mathematica*. One who does have those qualities may immediately purchase the underlying code and expand on or test the concepts described in this book. There is a balance between displaying too much code and making the narrative unduly complex and showing enough code to provide insight into the computations and results. I have attempted to strike the right balance by "hiding" considerable cold beneath the "cells" making up the *Mathematica* notebook which each chapter represents.

0.6. Organization

This book is written in modular form. The first third (Chapters 1-5) are fundamental, covering the theory of land use and rent determination, the role of government, the basics of investment property analysis and nuances and subtle traps most people overlook. Chapters 6, 7, 8, and 9 cover risk as an abstract concept grounded in probability theory through necessary modifications required to adapt it for real estate. Much of the material in these chapters was written prior to and actually anticipated the global financial problems that followed the events of the mid 2000s. The final chapters are special topics that include tax deferred exchanging, lending, leasing, real options and estate planning.

It is barely overstatement to say that this book is written as a template for one who wishes to "live a life of real estate" from the acquisition to the disposition phase over many decades.

Virtually all chapters, while occasionally referring to other material elsewhere in the book, are stand-alone components. At the reader's option he may purchase only those chapters which are of specific interest. A complete table of contents is available at www.mathestate.com to guide the reader's choice.

0.7. A final thought on purpose

There is an undertone of indifference and occasional hostility between academics and practitioners. At times each side considers the other to be either irrelevant or the enemy. This behavior is not productive. Academics need practitioners mucking around in a messy real world producing observations that in the aggregate provide empirical evidence to support or contradict theory. Practitioners need academics to articulate theory that constitutes a base of knowledge from which to launch successful careers. One of the most ambitious goals of this book is to speak the language of both sides in a way that the separate camps understand each other and appreciate the importance of each other's contribution.

To that end, I counsel patience on the part of practitioners who quickly grow weary of the pedantic formalism of mathematics and on the part of academics who become impatient with examples that may seem superficial and anecdotal.

These sentiments may be summarized in a metaphor from another field. Very few people are interested in the inner workings of the highly mathematical model that sequences the human genome. Even fewer understand it. Similarly, only a few people are interested in models describing the general nature of how real estate markets work. On the other hand, we all have a common and usually strong interest in being healthy. Thus, after the doctor listens very carefully to the patient's description of his symptoms, the patient, otherwise disinterested in biology, listens very carefully as a doctor explains how a particular form of gene therapy may preserve and extend his life. In the spirit of this analogy it may be equally well for academics to observe how real world investors make money as it is for practitioners to learn the mathematics that underlies whatever science there is in real estate investing.

Now let us begin sequencing the genome of real estate investing.

Roger J. Brown
Alpine, CA
January, 2012

Why location matters - The bid rent surface and theory of rent determination

"If you do not rest on the good foundation of nature, you will labor with little honor and less profit"

Leonardo da Vinci (1452-1519) quoted in <u>Mathematics for the Non-Mathematician</u> (Kline, p. 204)

1.1. Introduction

One of the oldest cliches we hear is: "The three most important things in real estate are location, location and location". Most cliches become truisms for good reason. If the value of location is universally acknowledged, there may be some strong underlying theory that can be represented mathematically. That theory is found in the construction of a "bid rent curve". The general notion is that land users "bid" or "offer" to pay rent to land owners based on renters' ability to efficiently use the land. Those who can use it most efficiently will offer to pay the highest rent. If value is based on income, the highest values should occur where land users are willing to pay the highest rent.

In this chapter we will:
- Determine how the market allocates land between consumers;
- Build a model that tells us who will locate where;
- Compute the "Bid Rent Curve", the rate at which rents fall as one moves away from the center of the city;
- Consider how the appropriate use of real estate data permits us to confirm the actual shape of the Bid Rent curve;
- Reach conclusions about another commonly use term in real estate: The path of progress; and
- Discuss how the use of data improves the location decision.

1.2. Classical location theory

Theory predicts that rents (and therefore values) will be highest where economic activity is most intense and productive, hence profitable. Profits are what we observe when land is used efficiently. Therefore, if one land consumer can achieve a greater profitability on a parcel of land than another can, the consumer who can use the land most profitably pays the highest price. Thus efficient outcomes are achieved as property rights in land gravitate to the highest bidder. To illustrate this theory and build a workable model, we make several simplifying assumptions. They are:

- The urban area is monocentric, that is, all activity takes place at the center. There are no suburbs.
- The land is a flat, featureless, uniform plane over which movement is equally possible in all directions. The only variation between different places is the distance from the center of the city.
- No input substitution or scale economies are possible. For instance, you can't substitute cheaper capital for expensive labor; neither can you reduce transportation costs per unit by carrying larger loads.
- Transportation costs are uniform in all directions. These costs are linear in distance based on a cost per unit with no initial fixed cost.
- The urban area contains the textbook competitive market (many sellers, all price takers, identical products, no monopoly, no transaction costs, no economic profits).

These, are admittedly, very restrictive assumptions. We will relax some of them later, but for now this is what is required to establish a baseline understanding of how location relates to value.

1.2.1. Notation Guide:

R = Rent, formally 'Ricardian Rent' after David Ricardo who first observed the nature of rent determination.
π = Economic Profits, assumed in the competitive model to be zero for any individual land consumer.
p = Price of goods produced and sold by land user.
a = Amount of goods sold by the land user.
w = Fixed inputs such as wages, interest, raw materials. This includes managerial profits but excludes rent.
t = Transportation costs, a rate per unit of distance for each unit of product.
μ = Distance from the center of the city in the same units as used for t.

1.2.2. The model:

As always, profits are what are left after subtracting all expenses from revenue, so:

$$\pi = pa - w - ta\mu - R \quad (1.1)$$

Since π, by assumption, is zero, we can move R to the left, leaving

$$R = pa - w - ta\mu \quad (1.2)$$

The above supports the general belief that rent constitutes the residual. That is, land consumers can pay rent in the amount of whatever is left after all other operating costs have been deducted from revenue. For simplicity below, we will take the net income before transportation costs *(pa - w)* as a constant, leaving the result that rent is a linear function of distance.

1.2.3. Example #1 - two competing users in the same industry

We now take two land users, both in the same industry (farming), each with a different product. We assume certain fixed values for the inputs, noting that a pea farmer has higher transportation costs (*t*) than a wheat farmer. In Figure 1.1 we plot rent against distance for each user, noting the difference in the slopes.

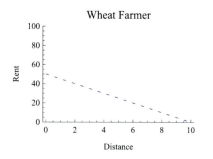 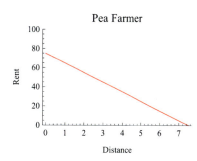

Figure 1.1. Wheat and pea farmers' bid rent curve

By setting rent equal to zero, inserting the fixed inputs for each land user, and solving for μ, we can determine the farthest distance from the center of the city each user can afford to locate. This asks the question: At what distance from the center are all revenues exhausted? Locating outside of that distance would produce negative revenue, an economic consequence that prevents a user from locating there. Notice that, given the inputs, the wheat farmer can afford to locate farther away. Stated differently, the pea farmer MUST locate closer in.

wheat farmer	pea farmer
R = pa - w - taμ = 0	
R:=10*10-50-.5*10μ = 0;	R:=15*10-75-1*10μ = 0
μ = 10 = maximum distance	μ = 7.5 = maximum distance

By assuming an arbitrary value for μ and solving for t we can determine the slope of each party's bid rent curve. Notice that the pea farmer's slope is greater. What does this mean to the way both parties will bid for land closer to the center of the city?

wheat farmer	pea farmer
R:=10*10-50-t*10*10 = 0;	R:=15*10-75-t*10*7.5= 0
t = .5 = slope of bid rent curve	t = 1 = slope of bid rent curve

Placing them both on the same plot is useful at this stage, noting that the point where the curves cross is the point on the land where the bids are equal. Prior to that point the pea farmer is willing to pay the most for the land, beyond that point, the wheat farmer bids more than the pea farmer. Setting the two rent equations equal to each other, inserting the fixed inputs and solving for μ tells us the location on the land of the crossover point. Figure 1.2 shows the point on the land where both parties bid an equal rent and the amount of that rent.

10*10-50-.5*10μ = 15*10-75-1*10μ	μ = 5
R = 10*10*-50-.5*10*5	R = 25

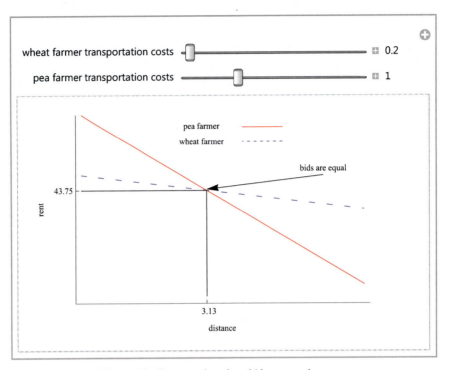

Figure 1.2. Rent at point where bids are equal

A little experimentation with different values for the fixed inputs leaves one with the insight that (in our stylized example) nothing matters but transportation cost. Mathematically, this can be verified by taking the first derivative of R with the quantity produced standardized to 1.

$$\frac{dR}{d\mu} = -t \tag{1.3}$$

1.2.4. Example #2 - several competing users in different industries

Building on this, let us model an entire city with multiple users, each having a different transportation cost. We assume that user classes locate in concentric rings radiating out from the center of the city. The innermost is the central business core of commercial users (*com*), followed by an interior light industrial ring (*indI*), then residential (*res*), a second industrial ring of heavy manufacturers (*indII*) and finally agricultural users (*agr*). Note that transportation costs per unit decrease in the outward direction with each user, resulting in a flatter slope for each curve as we progress outward. The combination of all users on a single graph leads to what is known as the bid rent surface or rent gradient. Note in Figure 1.3 that the largest land mass is taken by residential. Why might that be so?

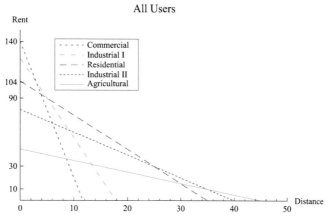

Figure 1.3. Bid rent curves for a city with different land uses

Following our wheat/pea farmer procedure, we can solve for each crossover point. Table 1.1 reflects these values.

	Distance	Rent
com	0	140
com–indI	3.	104.
indI–res	5.	90.
res–indII	25.	30.
indII–agr	35.	10.

Table 1.1. Cross points and rent where land use changes

We can link the crossover points to the change in use on the land by connecting the points to the perimeters of the appropriate circle. In Figure 1.4 you may change the slope of any particular bid rent line and see the change in land devoted to that use.

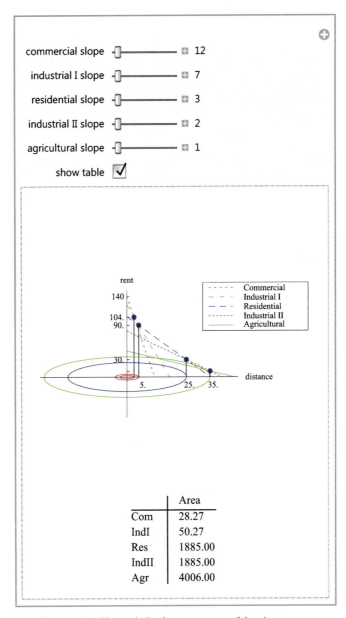

Figure 1.4. Change in land use on a map of the city

A different perspective is provided in Figure 1.5 by placing them all on the same plane.

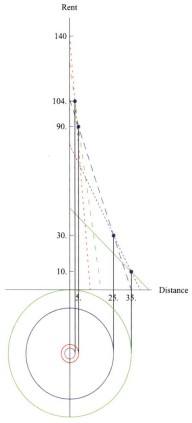

Figure 1.5. Land use mapped on a single plane

The amount of land devoted to each use is dependent upon the size of the circles circumscribing it. Computing the total area of each concentric ring, we see that in this example, land mass devoted to each use generally increases as we move away from the center (Table 1.2) [1]

	Area
com Area	28.2743
indI Area	50.2655
res Area	1884.96
indII Area	1884.96
agr Area	2513.27

Table 1.2. Land mass allocated to different uses

1.3. Is the bid rent curve linear?

Joining the crossover points creates a bid rent surface for the entire city.

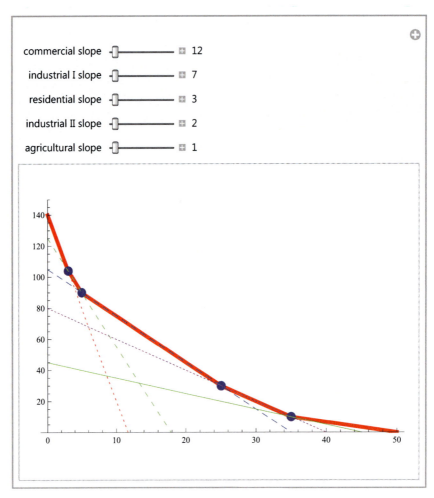

Figure 1.6. Bid rent surface for the entire city

It is clear from Figure 1.6 that multiple classes of users with a sequence of crossover points produce a bid rent *surface* for the entire city that is not strictly linear but appears linear on a piecewise basis. The aggregation of various uses, each with a different transportation cost (and, therefore, a different slope) creates this shape. From this we may speculate that different individual users within any one sector each may also have slightly different transportation costs, and the aggregate of the linear bid rent curves of these different users produce a curve for any specific use that is also not a straight line. Under these conditions one might reasonably assume that the functional form of the bid rent curve for all individual users would be $R = e^{-ax}$ where x is distance from the center of the city, a is a decay rate that may be observed in the market as one moves away from the center and e is the base of the natural logarithm (Figure 1.7).

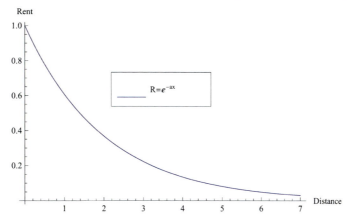

Figure 1.7. A well-behaved, smooth bid rent curve

1.4. Empirical verification

A common method for investigating the relationship between two variables is linear regression analysis. For this, it is useful to convert rent to its natural log. Suppose we collect data on actual rent paid by users along a line in a certain direction moving away from the center of the city (or any high rent point) such as reflected in Table 1.3 below. The first element in each pair is the distance from the center, the second is the rent paid at that point, and the third is the natural log of the rent.

Distance	Rent	LN(Rent)
0	821	6.71052
1	808	6.69456
2	795	6.67834
3	783	6.66313
4	771	6.64769
5	759	6.632
6	748	6.6174
7	736	6.60123
8	725	6.58617
9	714	6.57088
10	703	6.55536
11	692	6.53959
12	681	6.52356
13	671	6.50877
14	660	6.49224
15	650	6.47697
16	640	6.46147
17	630	6.44572
18	621	6.43133
19	611	6.4151
20	602	6.40026
21	592	6.38351

Table 1.3. Rent data

A plot of the distance and rent data in Figure 1.8 shows a nearly linear decay in rent as distance increases.

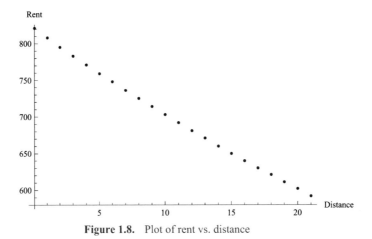

Figure 1.8. Plot of rent vs. distance

Figure 1.9 shows a plot of the data in Table 1.3. Not surprisingly, it appears linear because taking the natural log of a curved function has the effect of "linearizing" the function.

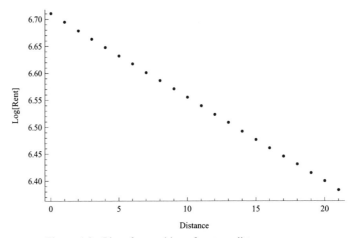

Figure 1.9. Plot of natural log of rent vs. distance

We then fit the regression model:

$$Log[R] = Log[k\, e^{-xd}] = Log[k] - x\, d \qquad (1.4)$$

where k is the regression constant, x is the slope and d is distance from the center. The intercept and slope terms are shown in the regression equation (A complete regression analysis appears among the electronic files for this chapter.):

```
Fitted Model is: 6.71003 - 0.0155191 x
```

	DF	SS	MS	F-Statistic	P-Value
x	1	0.213266	0.213266	1.03289×10^6	1.30516×10^{-48}
Error	20	4.12949×10^{-6}	2.06475×10^{-7}		
Total	21	0.21327			

	Estimate	Standard Error	t-Statistic	P-Value
1	6.71003	0.00018733	35819.3	1.49262×10^{-79}
x	-0.0155191	0.00001527	-1016.31	1.30516×10^{-48}

$$R^2 = 0.999981$$

"Exponenting"[2] both sides of the regression equation produces the conclusion that one may estimate rent based on a fixed intercept multiplied times the base of the natural logarithm taken to an exponent that is composed of the product of the decay rate (as a negative number) and the distance.

Hence, if one is at the center, where distance is zero ($x = 0$) rent is just the intercept: 820.597 On the other hand, if one is ten miles from the center ($x = 10$), the rent is $702.64.

Recall Figure 1.7 and its pronounced convexity to the origin. This noticeable convexity is because the decay rate ($a = .5$) was fairly large. Figure 1.10 reflects the decay rate derived from our regression. As the decay rate is quite small and the range of distance is short, the curve appears linear.

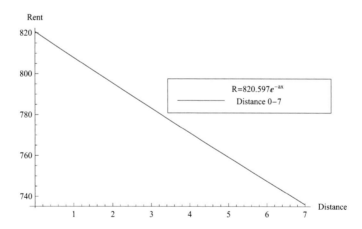

Figure 1.10. Bid rent curve suggested by regression analysis

The same curve in Figure 1.11 is more pronounced over a longer distance.

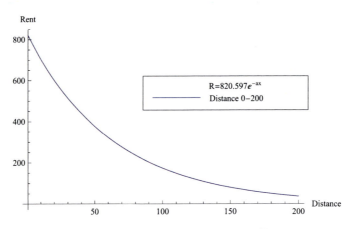

Figure 1.11. Regression bid rent curve over a longer distance

So we see that while the curve is a function of the decay rate, for small decay rates its curvature is only apparent over longer distances.

1.5. An economic topographic map

The world is not flat and neither are its land economics. The story becomes more realistic when one considers the theory in three dimensions. After all, there are an infinite number of directions away from any particular high rent location. One would expect the decay rate to vary in different directions. A stylized version of this uses the trigonometry employed in topography. We need to define a function that not only considers the decay rate away from a high rent area but the direction one travels. The direction-sensitive portion of such a function might look like Equation 1.5:

$$f(\theta) = .5 + 2\left(\sin\left[\frac{\theta}{2} - \frac{\pi}{4}\right]\right)^2 \tag{1.5}$$

The so-called "path of progress" is the direction in which the decline in rent is the slowest, thus the decay rate is the slowest because higher rent is persistent in that direction. In that direction the decline is relatively flat. The opposite case is that of the steepest decay rate. As rents decline fastest, the decay rate is larger in the direction people are not locating.

The three dimensional parametric plot in Figure 1.12 shows the economic topography where $a = .1$. In Figure 1.13, with parameter varying from $a = .01$ to .2 one may simulate the way rent changes as one travels around the land.

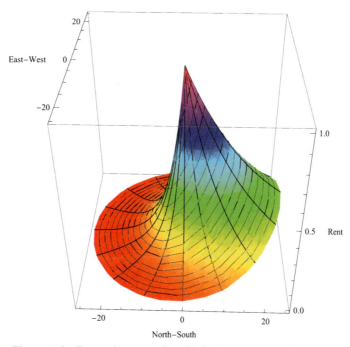

Figure 1.12. Economic topography with fixed parameter "*a*=.1"

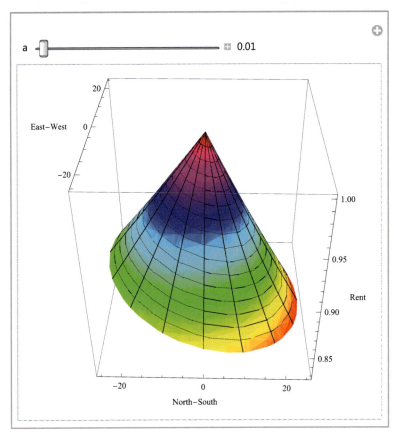

Figure 1.13. Economic topography with parameter "*a*" varying

1.6. Relaxing the Assumptions

All models are only approximations of reality. Unfortunately, we attempt better approximations at the expense of generality. Nonetheless, the exercise of testing the model under more realistic assumptions is useful.

One way to move closer to what we actually observe is to relax some of the assumptions. The first might be the idea that the urban business environment is monocentric. Below in Figure 1.14, we see the potential for two high rent areas in a given market. This representation suggests that the secondary point of high activity might be somewhat flat at the top, representing an economic oasis of activity where rents are generally high in a small area, relaxation of the assumption that the greatest activity takes place at the absolute center. Rotating Figure 1.14 to see the rear of it in Figure 1.15 reveals an area of depressed rent. Clearly there as many portrayals of this conditions as there are different cities on earth.

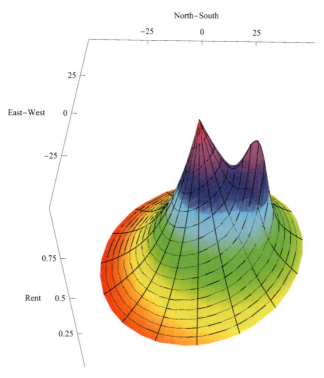

Figure 1.14. Economic topography with two high rent districts

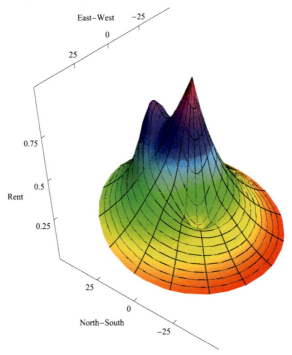

Figure 1.15. Economic topography with depressed rent area

Figure 1.15 could also depict the relaxation of the no transaction costs assumption. Zoning, a constraint on freedom of choice in how one uses one's land, is essentially a transaction cost. If government imposes zoning that prohibits land use in a certain area, the consequence can be higher rent for that use in the area where it that use is permitted. Another explanation for a plot like Figure 1.15 might be non-uniform transportation costs in one direction caused by natural barriers such as a river or mountain that must be crossed. One might also see an impact on the rent gradient as transportation costs differ in directions served by mass transit.

Whether these graphical depictions represent reality is an interesting debate. One can challenge the notion that the market is symmetrical around a point, calling into question whether the most intense activity takes place on a single spot. Clearly, over time "clusters" of similar businesses gather in certain areas. Particular areas become "attractors" for certain kinds of industries. The list of exceptions to the basic theory is long. The primary value of the sort of analysis undertaken in this chapter is to provide a logical framework for location decisions and guide the thoughtful land consumer to a rational choice of location. As one delves more deeply into the exceptions to the general principal one gets closer to what we observe in practice at the expense of a loss of generality. Regardless, with each special case we see repeated the importance distance plays in the decision. Apparent exceptions often just change the place from which we are distant, not the actual importance of distance. Thus the connection between location and distance remains key.

This book will discuss the careful use of data often. In the case of market rents one must be mindful of the fact that no dataset supplants a careful market survey in the local area of a target acquisition. However, as real estate markets become more efficient and data is more robust, the sort of models developed here will assist buyers in "getting up to speed" in an unfamiliar market. Having been instructed by the CEO of an REIT or real estate fund to visit a new city and investigate real estate opportunities there, an acquisition team may first consult data before landing in a market where local players dominate transactions.

Figure 1.16 widens the story further. Using the controls in sequence we see (secondary) the emergence of secondary centers of activity (there need not be three of them and they need not be equidistant from each other) creating new high rent districts away from the center. Using Distance we can adjust the distance away from the center these secondary peaks appear. Using direction we can model the direction, relative to the center, that these new high rent districts appear. Finally, perhaps with the construction of an interstate bypass highway commonly known as a beltway, these "edge cities" agglomerate into a megalopolis ring. The effect is most

pronounced when the controls are operated in sequence and with "secondary" in its extreme right position as the other three are used.

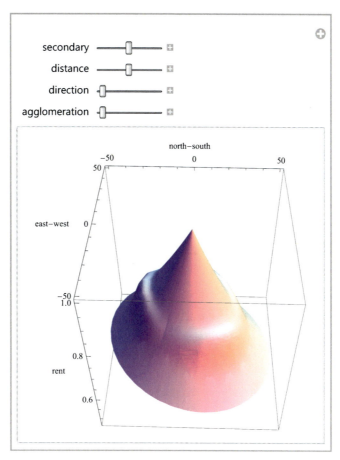

Figure 1.16. Economic topography animated with several features

1.7. A window to the future

Table 1.3 shows rent data collected along a line stretching away from a high rent location. Real estate data always have some location attribute. In the past that attribute was its street address. Later, a zip code was added. Recently longitude and latitude points have been included. Each of these steps moves us closer to a time when the theoretical graphs shown above can be displayed as actual data points and the economic topographical map will represent a real world situation.

Data represent reality and there will be times when reality conflicts with theory. In Figure 1.17 we see a void where a lake, a public park or a block of government buildings might be. In Figure 1.18 we see a number of missing data points throughout, each of which represents a location where rent is not reported. One of these could be owner occupied housing, another a church or a school but some will be where rent is being paid and no inquiry has been made. In time as data collection is more streamlined and coverage more complete the grid will become finer and the picture more complete.

There are a number of excellent data gatherers and providers, some independent firms, some in-house for major real estate companies. It is to these industry support groups we direct a final appeal. As real estate data become more plentiful, observations of rent across the land will become more compact, filling in the grids necessary to describe the actual shape of the bid rent surface. For highly developed countries with efficient markets in financial assets one would expect that real estate data gatherers and providers will deliver not only the raw information but analytics based on that information. For countries with nascent market economies where data collection is just beginning one hopes that those interested in market development will use the models above as templates to guide their database design at the early stages.

Figure 1.17. Economic topography with a void for public area

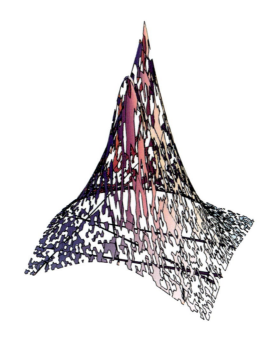

Figure 1.18. Economic topography constructed from simulated data

Endnotes

[1] It is, of course, possible to make a simple supply and demand argument for lower rent for sectors in which more acreage is available.

[2] There is some doubt that "exponenting" is a word. The Oxford English Dictionary does not carry "exponent" as a verb. However, we need a word for the cumbersome statement "using each side of the entire equation, each, as an exponent for the base of the natural log..." For this we press "to exponent" into service.

References

Alonzo, W. Location and Land Use. Cambridge, MA: Harvard University Press.

Geltner, D. M., & Miller, N. G. Commercial Real Estate Analysis and Investments. Upper Saddle River, NJ: Prentice Hall.

Kline, M., Mathematics for the Non-Mathemacian. New York: Dover Publications, Inc.

von Thunen, J. H. (1966). The Isolated State. New York: Pergamon Press.

Problems

1. Using Figure 1.2, change the pea farmer's transportation cost to 1.5. What is the farthest from the center the pea farmer can locate and what rent must he pay at that point?
2. Again using Figure 1.2, move the transportation cost slider for each until the geographic equal bid point is 3 miles from the center. What is the rent either party will pay? Is there more than one combination of transportation costs that will produce the same geographic result? Will the rent result also be the same?
3. Using Figure 1.4, change the agricultural slope from its default to .9. What is the outer perimeter of that land use? Is there more or less land devoted to that use? How much more or less?
4. Again using Figure 1.4, return the agricultural slope to its default (1.0). Assume the government builds a circular bypass freeway around the city at the inner perimeter of the residential area (outer perimeter of Industrial District I) which decreases transportation cost for industrial users. What is the effect on how Industrial District I land will be used? Slide the slope bar to reflect your answer.
5. Using Figure 1.6 move the industrial I slope to the right, reducing the steepness of the slope. What does this say about how much land will be used for that purpose? What other sector or sectors is/are affected? How is/are it/they affected?
6. Again using Figure 1.6, move the sliders to the following values for the slope of each use: commercial - 12; industrial I - 5; residential - 2.9; industrial II - 1.8; and agricultural - 0.9. Note how the shape created by the outer intersections of lines becomes more convex, making the overall shape more uniformly curved.
7. In Figure 1.13 parameter "a" determines the steepness of the decline in rent as distance increases from the center. While moving the slider to the right, increasing the steepness of the decent, note the change in scale on the "Rent axis". When the parameter value is at its leftmost position (0.2) is there a larger or smaller range of rent for the area covered? Is the amount of "high rent district" land more or less than when the slider is all the way to the left?
8. The object in Figure 1.13 is asymmetrical, slightly tilted. Right click, hold and drag the image so that it can be viewed from the top. Notice the length of the lines projected from the center. In which direction is the path of progress?
9. Figure 1.16 permits you to create a variety of shapes which represent urban development. Move the sliders so that three additional areas of business activity appear a short distance from the center. Have the most pronounced of these in the upper left quadrant of the plot. How has the nature of business activity changed from the default position?
10. Figure 1.18 has a number of "voids" where data are missing. If the data used to create Figure 1.18 were drawn from a large metropolitan area, what appearance would you expect the object to have if the data were from a small town in a rural area? Would you expect to see more "voids" or fewer?

2

Land Use Regulation

"We now understand better than before how small groups can wield power in excess of their relative voting strength and thus change the structure of property rights to their advantage, perhaps at the expense of the majority of voters."

Thrainn Eggertsson in Economic Behavior and Institutions p. 62

2.1. Introduction

Chapter 1 dealt with how market participants make land use decisions in their own best interests based *solely* on a combination of revenues and costs together with a distance factor. That discussion naively ignored the regulatory environment. The brief reference to zoning laws at the end of Chapter 1 opens the door for the more involved discussion of how patterns of land use are affected by regulation. This chapter examines land use from the standpoint of the community. If one finds that the bid rent curve in a particular area, rather than having a smooth downward sloping shape, is a series of jagged lines not necessarily pointing in any direction, it may be that market participants are constrained by regulators who have decided what is best for land users regardless of economic considerations. Indeed, one of the harshest criticisms of government planning is that the motives of policymakers are political rather than economic. Thus, land use often proceeds not on the basis of its most efficient use but on the basis of the size and level of protest of vocal groups who have the power to elect or re-elect officials who do their bidding. In this chapter we will

- Introduce the idea of "utility" at the level of a local community operating as a governmental jurisdiction;
- Build and test a model that chooses the proper level of regulation that optimizes community satisfaction;
- Explore the consequences of over-regulation and its affect on other municipal services; and
- Review a case study using actual data in a real setting to illustrate how land users may deal with local government in the face of increased regulatory activity.

2.2. Who shall decide - the problem of externalities

The landscape is littered with spectacular government-inspired land use failures such as Federal housing projects and rent control. But one also observes the occasional successful urban renewal. No conclusion is likely to be reached here, nor is it our purpose to advocate for a specific position. Rather, the goal of this chapter is to provide the reader with (1) a way of thinking about land use regulation and (2) a model to rationally resolve a conflict with a regulatory agency. The chapter will propose a theoretical model that permits one to optimize the conditions of regulation in a general sense. Following that, an actual municipal decision is illustrated with a case study based on real data.

The theory of rent determination advanced in Chapter 1 was developed in a simpler time. Urbanization on a large scale to accommodate a burgeoning population introduces complexities. Observe a transaction between two economic agents, in our case landlord and tenant. Do their choices affect only them? Perhaps they do not.

Economists have a name for the effects transactions have on third parties: Externalities. When I buy a car from a dealer I get a car and the dealer gets my money. A trade has been completed. But when I drive the car I emit pollutants into the air that you breathe. You have been affected by the decision of a car buyer and seller to engage in a transaction to which you were not a party. The transaction imposed a cost on you in the form of soiling the air you breathe. This is known as The Problem of Social Cost.[1] This chapter addresses the social cost issues affecting real estate and how land use is determined in the presence of social costs.

An advanced civilization is a society of rules. To deal with competing interests, cultural differences and the occasional rogue operator we come together as a community to establish what constitutes socially acceptable behavior. The business aspect of society has a set of norms reached through negotiation over many years. The study of this is an active area of research called "Institutional Economics" or "Law and Economics". Academics in this field study the economic consequences of passing laws to regulate human economic behavior. Among the more interesting findings are the unintended consequences of placing barriers in the way of those who would otherwise seek what is best for their own self-interest.

The underlying conflict may be simplified as one in which we must choose between what is good for the individual versus what is good for the community. Part of the debate is: Who shall decide? In economics, institutional factors are constraints on freedom of choice; and the choice we are interested in here is the choice of how land may be used. The unanswered question is: Shall the choice be made by the landowner or the community in which the land is located?

Tariffs and trade agreements govern how commerce crosses international boundaries. Laws prohibiting collusive and coercive activities govern domestic trade at a national level. Our interest lies in local government. For the private real estate investor local land use regulation is a significant aspect of the decision making process. In urban settings it is no overstatement to say that real estate investment success is in large part dependent on an understanding of the regulatory environment in which the local real estate market exists. Whether it is zoning or rent control, real estate investors ignore local politics at their peril.

Several general ideas make this subject important.

First, the unique fixed-in-location aspect that makes real estate different from financial assets provides both stability for investors and a fixed target for policymakers. Businesses that can easily move out of an oppressive jurisdiction restrain policymakers who might otherwise enact ruinous legislation. But the fact that structures are not on wheels and their owners cannot merely roll their buildings across the county line, taking their businesses with them, represents a temptation to local government.

Second, directly affecting residential investment, housing is a politically charged topic. Economists consider housing a "merit good" meaning that part of society has decided that all its members "deserve" a minimum standard of housing regardless of their economic status or ability to pay for it. Out of that mentality arises a host of subsidies, programs, controls and standards designed to shape the market into something that fits the will of a few elected officials, not necessarily market participants.

Third, and often working against the housing issues just mentioned, are the parochial views of the community's established citizenry. Popularized as "NIMBYism,"[2] this manifests itself in the form of local planning groups populated by activists who profess a heightened environmental sensitivity, concern for preservation of "the neighborhood" and who often merely oppose everything that represents change. The unintended consequences of this activity are interesting to study. They can be as benign as imposing a brief delay in obtaining a building permit to extreme outcomes such as litigation that bankrupts a developer pursuing a politically unpopular project.

In a modern city the list of development constraints and regulations is a long one. A builder must comply with the general plan, zoning, minimum lot size, open space requirements, minimum setbacks from lot lines, maximum floor area ratios, building height limitations, grading limitations on slopes, minimum landscaped area, view corridors, off street parking, curb cuts, building codes, fire prevention and suppression regulations, and traffic counts just to name a few. In areas designated as special districts they may also have to deal with architectural and design requirements. Some property owners must get permission to change the color of their building when they repaint it. Charles M. Tiebout (1956) saw a market concept at work for cities. He proposed a model for residential homeowners that views the universe of potential locations as a group of municipalities competing for citizen-taxpayers who "vote with their feet" by moving into communities offering the best (most efficient) mix of services and taxes (benefits and costs) and out of those communities offering less efficient combinations. Thus, under the Tiebout hypothesis, communities that fail to provide services demanded at a market price (reasonable taxes) are punished by an exodus of tax-paying citizens. On the positive, communities that provide high quality services at or below market prices attract tax-paying citizens.

These dynamics influence the choices of commercial land users as well. The recent past has seen a rise in the interest of state and local jurisdictions in being competitive in the regulatory arena. These range from as little as advertising their communities as "business friendly" to as much as offering major tax concessions for many years after construction of a facility.

There is no particular reason to choose for our study one form of land use regulation over another. Zoning, environmental protection or rent control, each has compelling arguments for and against. The method of thinking proposed here is a classical microeconomics approach that leads to the conclusion that the best answer is the one that accomplishes the most good for the most people. One should recognize, however, that the implementation of a *rational* model in a political environment represents a daunting challenge. People are often not rational. Does that mean we should abandon all use of rational models? No, often there is an opportunity to present a well-formed argument to cooler heads. Such an argument can not only be well received, it can carry the day when it is time to vote a project up or down.

There are hundreds if not thousands of examples from the residential field to draw from. Rather than take one of those and its somewhat straightforward analysis, the setting for the analysis here comes from the commercial area. This presents additional challenges that deserve attention, and at the same time illustrates how a somewhat esoteric land use conflict can be modeled.

2.3. The important idea of "utility"

Central to the development of a theoretical model of this type is the use of an abstraction known as "utility", a term economists employ to describe a more general form of happiness or betterment. Our model needs a yardstick that describes the gratification that comes with success and that yardstick is "utility". We can quantify this and with further analysis describe situations that are better or worse in terms of increased or diminished utility. The utility abstraction may seem foreign to non-economists thus the analogy to happiness or betterment. While perhaps ill-defined, most of us know when we are more or less happy or satisfied. Utility is just the word economists use to describe that feeling, nothing more. As we wish to mathematically model this result, "disutility", meaning negative or smaller amounts of utility, translates roughly to unhappiness or less happiness, of course something to be avoided. Clearly, unhappiness is inferior to happiness and thus any mathematical result having a lower value represents a tendency toward unhappiness. Utility is ordinal, not cardinal. That is, the actual number we produce in any calculation has no meaning by itself (unless one believes there is a unit of measure known as "utils"). This frustrates those who have labored to "get the numbers right" in other investment settings by calculating the "right" answer in the form of some specific number. What matters where any number is concerned is *the ranking* of various values of utility computed under differing conditions. Thus, I may know that I am happier than my brother-in-law but I probably would not say that he has a happiness value of 80 unless I was convinced I have a happiness value of, say, 95. (The "happiness" metaphor tends to be stretched rather thin at about this point).

Once we accept the utility abstraction the next step is to construct a way in which utility is achieved. This leads to a "production function" which is nothing more than a "rule" by which people "manufacture" utility. Returning to our happiness metaphor, most readers have heard someone say that our success or happiness is the sum of all of our choices. In such a case the production function or rule we use is merely to add up all the choices (implicitly subtracting the bad choices that may be seen as adding negative numbers) we have made and that determine our happiness.

Such a rule becomes more complex in a real estate setting but nonetheless is still just some sort of rule. The rule we often use for economic choices has two essential properties, both of which are fairly intuitive. First, we assume we are always interested in more happiness thus the utility function is always rising. This is formally known as the property of non-satiation. Second, despite its constant increase, *the rate at which it increases* slows as utility increases. This is formally referred to as diminishing marginal returns, meaning that while we are happier with each new increment of utility we are not as much happier with the next increment as we were with the increment last received.

A silly example may help here. Suppose I love bananas to the point of craving. If, like Groucho, I have no bananas I may be willing to pay quite a tidy sum for a single banana. I would trade money for the utility I receive from eating a banana. Suppose that tomorrow I inherit from my deceased rich uncle a large productive banana plantation providing me an ample supply of bananas. I still have the craving love of bananas but what has changed is what I am willing to trade for yet another banana. Because my utility function for bananas exhibits diminishing marginal returns with increased ownership of bananas, the amount I am willing to pay for another banana when I already have millions of bananas is, although a positive amount due to the non-satiation principle, very small.

However you approach an understanding of it, utility is a useful abstraction for considering the cost and benefits of different choices we face. The reader is encouraged to find a comfort level with this abstraction as it is one we will return to again in this book.

With the free market lessons of Chapter 1 in mind we proceed with the counter example: Political land use determination.

2.3.1. Notation guide:

A	=	advertising
q	=	tax rate
U	=	utility
M	=	municipal services
Env	=	environmental protection
S	=	sales volume
α	=	proportion of utility arising from citizens' preference for environmental regulation, $0 < \alpha < 1$
$1-\alpha$	=	proportion of utility arising from citizens' preference for non-environmental regulation community services
β	=	citizens' negative utility from the appearance of advertising
γ	=	merchants' productivity of advertising $\gamma > 0$
A_0	=	the maximum imaginable amount of advertising possible – full saturation, full coverage by any measure, an amount beyond which it is impossible to go.

2.3.2. The model

Suppose a community wishes to protect the environment (Env), specifically the *visual* environment, by regulating the commercial advertising (A) of local businesses. We assume that community retail merchants advertise via outdoor signage. Regulation comes in the form of restricting the height, size, mass, design, shape, illumination, position, color, copy, etc. of signs. Resources the community spends on aesthetic regulation reduce scarce resources in the form of tax revenue available for other services the municipality must furnish such as police and fire protection (M). One characterization of the latter would be "hard benefits" rendered by the city to its residents. On the other hand, regulation of the aesthetics of the local visual environment may be termed "soft benefits".

Citizens derive utility (U) from having visually uncluttered or appealing commercial vistas (Env) and from the receipt of municipal services (M). A conflict exists between merchants who wish to maximize advertising to saturation (A_0) and residents who wish to regulate signage as close to zero as possible. A trade-off exists because the reduction of advertising brings about the related but not exactly equivalent reduction of municipal income from taxes. Tax revenue is a function of (1) sales which, in turn, are a function of advertising; and (2) property values. As property values are, through rent, an indirect a function of sales, we impound all tax effects into the sales tax and ignore for simplicity the dual source of municipal revenue. Thus, the city's tax revenue must be allocated between paying for the soft benefits afforded by aesthetic regulation and the hard benefits of non-aesthetic-regulation municipal services.

The city derives its income from taxes levied on sales (S) at a tax rate (q) set exogenously by the State. Merchants who employ signs to advertise their businesses to passing consumers generate sales, in part, on the basis of the productivity (γ) of their advertising, which is related to characteristics of the individual signs such as size, height, etc. One of the ways the city may regulate advertising (A) is by reducing the efficiency (γ) of signs by restricting their characteristics.

The city must maximize utility (U) by choosing the *correct* amount of allowable advertising ($A*$). All other variables are exogenous.

The city derives revenue from sales taxes levied on sales generated by businesses. Businesses depend on advertising to promote sales. The following expression describes sales, S, as a function of advertising, A, where γ represents the productivity of advertising:

$$S = A^\gamma \tag{2.1}$$

The following expression describes municipal services (M) in the form of an annual budget wherein revenue is derived from taxing sales (in the interests of simplicity property taxes are not considered here even though increases in sales increases property values and therefore property taxes):

$$M = qS \qquad (2.2)$$

Citizens find advertising objectionable and have a production function (rule) for environmental protection (*Env*) based on their disutility of advertising:

$$\text{Env} = (A_0 - A)^\beta \qquad (2.3)$$

The disutility is subtle. The term "*A*" must be viewed as "allowed advertising". The controversy surrounds the difference between the maximum amount of advertising, (A_0), and that which is allowed, *A*. Merchants want *A* to be as high as possible, as close to full saturation, (A_0), as they can get. This makes the term ($A_0 - A$) approach zero. Residents want *A* to be as low as possible, making the difference between the maximum and the allowed advertising ($A_0 - A$) as large as possible. The condition $A = 0$ may be viewed as "full regulation", the case of no advertising allowed. Plotting Env, in Figure 2.1, the term ($A_0 - A$), for an arbitrary value of (A_0) and two different values of β against *A* shows that the amount of environmental protection (Env) residents achieve falls with the increase of *A*. The exponent β indicates the intensity with which residents derive utility from the ($A_0 - A$) term thus determines *the rate* at which *Env* falls with the rise in *A*.

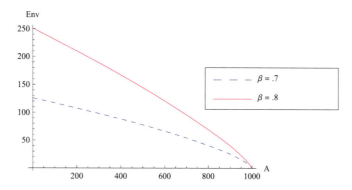

Figure 2.1. Decline in Env with different β as advertising rises

The utility function describes the total utility that citizens receive from (1) municipal services and (2) environmental protection in the form of aesthetic regulation. The following expression describes that utility, *U*, as a variant of a Stone-Geary production function where α is the citizens' preference for Environmental Regulation ($0 < \alpha < 1$):

$$U = \text{Env}^\alpha M^{(1-\alpha)} \qquad (2.4)$$

Note in the output above that the first term is environmental Protection (*Env*) and the second term is municipal services (*M*). We wish to maximize this function. It is mathematically helpful and common practice to take the Log of both sides of the utility function.[3]

$$\text{Log}[U] = \alpha\beta \text{Log}[A_0 - A] + (1 - \alpha)(\gamma \text{Log}[A] + \text{Log}[q]) \qquad (2.5)$$

2.4. Optimization and comparative statics

Comparative statics allows us to examine how the model output changes with changes in the inputs. This is accomplished by taking the partial derivative of the logged function. Because Log[utility] is monotonically increasing in utility we will sometimes discuss the change in utility even though it is the log of utility that we actually differentiate. The partial derivative of utility *with respect to tax rate* describes how utility changes with changes in tax rate. Taking the partial derivative of Log[u] w.r.t. q produces a positive sign, indicating that as tax rate rises, utility rises :[4]

$$\frac{\delta \text{Log}[U]}{\delta q} = \frac{1-\alpha}{q} \tag{2.6}$$

The partial derivative of utility *with respect to advertising* is our real interest. This describes how utility changes with changes in advertising. Taking the partial derivative of Log[u] w.r.t. A produces:

$$\frac{\delta \text{Log}[U]}{\delta A} = \frac{\alpha \beta}{A - A_0} + \frac{\gamma - \alpha \gamma}{A} \tag{2.7}$$

We want to know the value of A at which the community achieves the optimal (most) utility. Setting the above equal to zero creates an implicit equation

$$\frac{\alpha \beta}{A - A_0} + \frac{\gamma - \alpha \gamma}{A} = 0 \tag{2.8}$$

Transferring the second term on the left to the right hand side of the equation sets marginal cost equal to marginal benefit. We know that optimality is achieved in economic settings such as this when marginal cost equals marginal benefit.

$$\frac{\alpha \beta}{A - A_0} = \frac{\alpha \gamma - \gamma}{A} \tag{2.9}$$

Solving for optimum A in Equation 2.8 results in an unambiguous solution for A^*, the optimal amount of allowed advertising:

$$A^* = \frac{A_0 (\alpha - 1) \gamma}{\alpha (\beta - \gamma) + \gamma} \tag{2.10}$$

Remember the ordinal nature of utility. If we achieve an optimum this represents a "peak" utility, the highest possible. All change from that point must be in a direction resulting in diminished utility. Thus, to test the model for optimality, we are only interested in the sign of certain derivatives.

Comparative statics performed on this expression below have the correct sign. Increases in γ, the productivity of advertising, shifts the marginal benefit curve outward and results in increases in optimal advertising, as expected. Increases β, the disutility for advertising, shifts the marginal cost curve inward and results in decreases in optimal advertising (recall that $0 < \alpha < 1$ is what makes the numerator in both expressions negative). These expressions constitute the dilemma the city finds itself in when it reduces the efficiency of advertising or experiences an increase in disutility for advertising.

$$\frac{\delta A^*}{\delta \gamma} = -\frac{(\alpha-1)\alpha\, A0\, \beta}{(\alpha(\beta-\gamma)+\gamma)^2} \tag{2.11}$$

$$\frac{\delta A^*}{\delta \beta} = \frac{(\alpha-1)\alpha\, A0\, \gamma}{(\alpha(\beta-\gamma)+\gamma)^2} \tag{2.12}$$

We also have an intuitive result for the derivative of A^* w.r.t α. Increases in α represent an increase in the community's *preference* for environmental regulation over the other forms of municipal services. The negative derivative indicates that an increase in α decreases advertising from the optimal.

$$\frac{\delta A^*}{\delta \alpha} = -\frac{A0\, \beta\, \gamma}{(\alpha(\beta-\gamma)+\gamma)^2} \tag{2.13}$$

Below is the second derivative of utility with respect to advertising. As both numerators are negative, the second derivative is negative, indicating that we have a global optimum. (This is not surprising because all functions are strictly convex).

$$\frac{\delta^2 \operatorname{Log}[U]}{\delta A^2} = \frac{(\alpha-1)\gamma}{A^2} - \frac{\alpha\beta}{(A-A0)^2} \tag{2.14}$$

2.5. A graphic illustration

To create graphics that illustrate this process we define the marginal benefit and marginal cost as functions for plotting the marginal benefit and marginal cost curves for advertising.

We can insert arbitrary values for dependent variables to produce numeric answers for marginal benefit and marginal cost. Keep in mind that these numbers don't mean anything until we have others for comparison.

Plots of marginal benefit and marginal cost against advertising in Figure 2.2 indicate the functions have the expected classical shape but the x axis is not intuitive as the marginal benefit is falling with increased advertising. Recall this is from the utility maximizing perspective of the community, not the merchants.

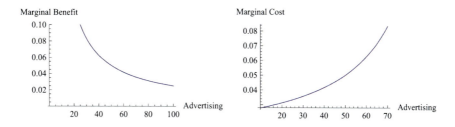

Figure 2.2. Marginal Benefit and Marginal Cost of Advertising from community perspective

The intersection of marginal cost and marginal benefits curves in Figure 2.3 marks the optimal advertising, which in turn maximizes utility for the community.

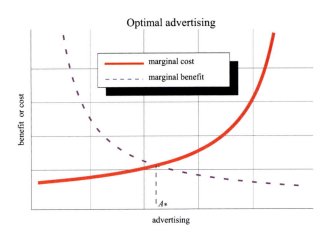

Figure 2.3. Optimal advertising at the intersection of marginal benefit and marginal cost

Figure 2.4 shows how a decrease in γ moves the marginal benefit function in toward the origin and an increase in β moves the marginal cost function in and up in a northwest direction (dashed lines represent the new functions). Note that both movements are away from optimality.

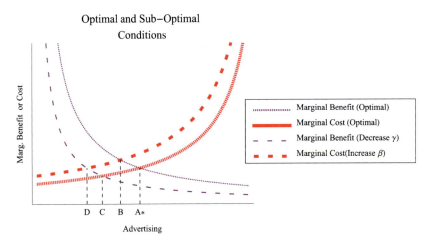

Figure 2.4. Change in advertising from the optimal with changes in γ and β

A^* is optimal advertising where utility is maximized. B is the result of increases in β (such as election of a city council member hostile to business) moving the marginal cost curve inward while marginal benefit curve does not change. C is a reduction of γ (resulting from a vote of the city council to increase regulations by reducing sign size, height, etc.) leading to a downward shift of the marginal benefit curve with the marginal cost curve unchanged. D is the most drastic result (the new city council member influences an even more draconian level of regulation) where β is increased *and* γ is lowered at the same time. At D allowed advertising is the farthest from optimal, thus utility is the lowest of the four.

Below we show the changes separately.

First show the effect when the city lowers γ and therefore the marginal benefit of advertising falls.

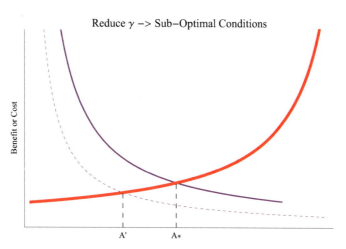

Now to show the effect of raising β:

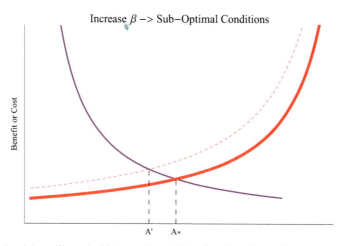

Recalling that the optimum is the "peak", we illustrate this by making utility a function of advertising.

$$U = \left((A0 - A)^\beta\right)^\alpha (q\, A^\gamma)^{1-\alpha} \tag{2.15}$$

As mentioned previously, regulation of commercial signage usually comes in the form of reducing some physical aspect of it. We can view that as modifying the sign ordinance so as to improve public vistas (*Env*) at the expense of the efficiency (γ) of advertising. Thus, advertising is implicitly limited by reducing γ.

Table 2.1 provides a set of arbitrary values for all variables that produce a numeric A^*. Note the value for γ.

α	β	γ	A_0	q
0.5	4.1	3.1	100	0.07

Table 2.1. Numeric values for illustrating optimization of utility

Inserting the values above into Equations 2.10 produces a numeric value for A^* of 43.0556. Using that answer and the same variables above in the Utility Function, equation 2.4, produces 358,071 for Utility, a number that will gain meaning when compared with an alternative.

Locating 358,071 on the plot in Figure 2.5 shows that indeed utility peaks at that value. Notice the importance of domain and range values with changes in parameters. Remember also that the actual values have no meaning except in reference to other values calculated the same way. The importance of the general model is that it achieves an optimum for all combinations of numerical values given the parameters. What we are interested in is what happens when equilibrium is disturbed. Assume you are considering a certain community for locating your business. You find the present condition (equilibrium for our purposes) of sign regulation as plotted in Figure 2.5. How does a change in the political landscape change your decision to locate? How does it change the fortunes of market participants? How does that change of fortune affect other business owners' decision to locate in the community? Taking aesthetic regulation as just one example of the restrictions on freedom of choice imposed by government, what would you expect the aggregate effect of numerous restrictions to be?

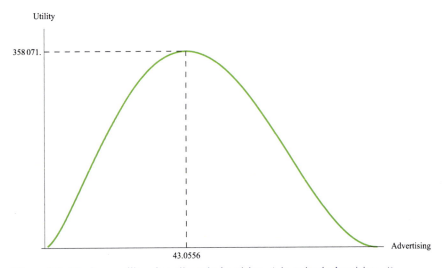

Figure 2.5. Maximum utility when allowed advertising, A, is optimal advertising, A^*

A reduction in the value of γ from the 3.1 shown in Table 2.1 to the value 2.3 results in a reduction in both allowed advertising to 35.9375 and, as expected, utility to 82,218, as shown in Figure 2.6.

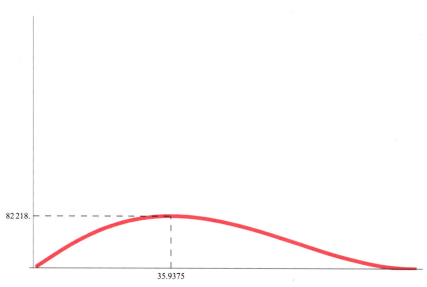

Figure 2.6. Utility when allowed advertising is reduced

Combining the last two plots in Figure 2.7 shows the cost, in terms of lost utility, of reducing the effectiveness of advertising, γ. It is this argument that may persuade the one vote an investor needs from the local council. If the vote is close and swing vote is rational this argument may only need to ring true with that one member.

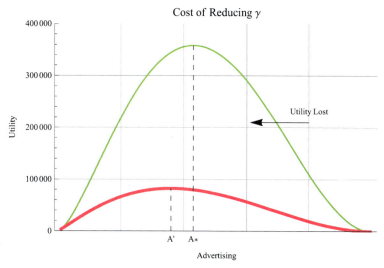

Figure 2.7. Comparison of optimal and sub-optimal advertising and its effect on utility

Figure 2.8 demonstrates how utility falls continuously with reduction in permitted advertising from optimal advertising. Utility, U, changes with the changes in (1) allowed advertising, A, (2) the efficiency, γ, of advertising and (3) *community disutility* for *Env*, β. The effect on utility of a change in allowed advertising is greatest when the efficiency is highest. This is reasonable as the merchants lose more and tax revenue falls more.

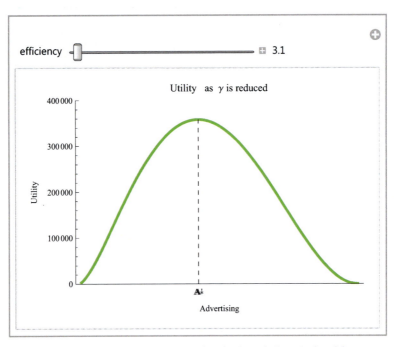

Figure 2.8. Reduction of optimal utility with reduction of allowed advertising

2.6. Implications

The implications of this exercise should be clear:

1. People make decisions on the margins. Marginal analysis is a very powerful tool for measuring the net effect of a trade-off between two alternatives. Many, if not all, economic choices between two alternatives may be modeled on a cost-benefit basis provided one makes plausible assumptions about how people generate well-being, happiness or utility.
2. Any item on the list of development constraints mentioned in the introduction to this chapter could be substituted for the one illustrated here. The aggregate of all such constraints, if applied by a heavy handed legislative body, can operate as a strong disincentive to entrepreneurial activity in a community.
3. Arguments for change and arguments for preservation are often equally persuasive, especially when couched in an emotional framework. Alternatively, a balanced, methodical approach to resolving these issues is preferable when rational people of good intent must agree on how change is to be implemented.

2.7. A case study in aesthetic regulation

The developer who appears at the City Council meeting waving his arms and talking about utility functions runs the risk of having security escort him to just outside the City Hall property line. The power of the general result above is often lost in the day-to-day implementation of policy. What follows is an example of how the thinking described above may be employed to construct a good argument in a specific case.

The fact situation involves an independent hardware store in a municipality in California. The store has been in the same location for over fifteen years. The Excel worksheet that accompanies this chapter provides a detailed historical record of sales for the past five years. The store is located in a commercial project of approximately 22,000 square feet, of which the store itself comprises 40% of the area available for lease. The remaining 60% is leased to other tenants at approximately the same rental rate as the hardware store. A 30-foot high "pylon-style" interior illuminated sign occupies a spot on the perimeter of the project. The owner/operator of the store is not only a long standing and admired member of the local community; he holds an undergraduate degree from West Point and a Masters in Business Administration from Columbia University. Local city officials respect his integrity and business acumen such that any estimate he might be required to make of the impact of city regulatory action on his business would be viewed as factual and well reasoned rather than self-serving.

Municipal revenue is generated from three sources. Local governments in California receive 1) a portion of state sales taxes equal to 1% of sales generated within their jurisdiction; 2) 12.8% of property taxes received by the County; and 3) a variety of grants-in-aid, revenue sharing, assistance, subventions and pass-throughs from the State. Tax revenue generated from the hardware store operation over the past five years from first two of these sources are calculated from the sales data and also shown in the Excel worksheet.

The city is too small to maintain its own police department. Therefore, the city contracts with the county Sheriff's Department for police protection. The contract calls for four patrol units, seven days per week with relief; two traffic units (one five days per week and one seven days per week); 2.39 units of "Special Purpose Officer" (vice, homicide, etc.) for a total annual cost of $1,245,761 including all overhead, vehicles, uniforms, and benefits.

The county uses a computer aided dispatch system which tracks the exact time a unit is actually operating in a contract city. If a unit is called out of the area to assist on a priority call in an adjacent area not covered by the contract, that "time out" is tracked and not billed. From this information, the county estimates a "beat factor" for billing quarterly and to assist the contract city in budgeting. The beat factor is based on the total number of working minutes per year for the entire force. The beat factor multiplied times the cost times the number of units results in the amount billed for the specific service. Insurance is billed separately. The contract detail is as follows:

SERVICE TYPE	PER UNIT	BEAT FACTOR	NET	# UNITS	TOTAL
PATROL	$ 249,753	0.7452	$ 186,116	4	$ 744,464
TRAFFIC - 5 DAY	$ 140,950	0.9487	$ 133,719	1	$ 133,719
TRAFFIC - 7 DAY	$ 197,329	0.9487	$ 187,206	1	$ 187,206
SPECIAL PURPOSE	$ 72,463	1.0000	$ 72,463	2.39	$ 173,187
INSURANCE					$ 7,185
ANNUAL GRAND TOTAL					$ 1,245,761

A conflict exists between the municipality and the property owner over the existing 30-foot pylon sign. As part of a city beautification effort, the city passed a sign ordinance limiting the height of commercial signs to eight feet. The ordinance provided for an amortization period, which has now passed, and the city has ordered the sign removed. Presently existing parking requirements prevent dedicating any more land to the sign structure. If this were not so, its shorter replacement could be installed on a gently rising landscaped berm elevated above parking lot grade as is common in new developments. As it is now, vehicles may park adjacent to the sign. Because adjacent parked cars would block its visibility, the practical effect of the ordinance limiting sign height on this site to eight feet is to eliminate nearly all of the commercially beneficial use of the sign.

To simplify the calculation we make the following assumptions:

1. The sales revenue of the hardware store per square foot is representative of square foot sales revenue for the entire project. Therefore, sales and municipal revenues for the entire site are calculated by "grossing up" the sales from the hardware store.
2. The hardware store's owner estimates sales will drop 25% if the sign is removed or replaced by a sign structure conforming to the new ordinance. This reduced revenue estimate is presumed to apply to other tenants equally.
3. There are approximately forty (40) signs remaining in the city affected by the sign ordinance. Because 1) this project is one of the larger projects among these sites, 2) not all projects experience the parking conflict which exacerbates the problem for this site, rather than a multiple of 40, one-quarter of the multiplier effect, a factor of 10 rather than 40, is applied to arrive at the total citywide effect of enforcing the ordinance on all non-conforming signs.
4. No cost of administration or litigation is considered. No cost of removal and replacement of the existing signs is considered.
5. No municipal revenue from the state other than sales tax is considered, although the financial health of the tenants and the landowner affects state income tax revenue and, therefore, the share of state grants to cities.

6. The maximum loss to the businesses is captured by the estimated 25% decline in revenue. This assumption may not hold in practice as many businesses operate at margins that would not accommodate such a sales decline. These businesses would fail, expanding the loss of municipal revenue to include the 75% expected to remain. No synergistic effect is considered. That is, the fact that the hardware store is the "anchor tenant" for this property and its fortunes have a large impact on the satellite stores is not considered.
7. Property tax revenue is uniform throughout the sites affected. This is unlikely because of California's Proposition 13, which indexes assessment and property tax levies on random transfers of title. However, the annual effect during the historical period for this site is small. As this property has been under the same ownership for nearly 20 years, the property taxes are uncharacteristically low. Relaxing this assumption would result in an increased cost of the enforcement calculation because other sites undoubtedly have transferred more recently and have higher assessments.
8. No consequential economics are considered. The site employs approximately 50 people. No calculation is made for loss of income by those who would be laid off due to a decline in sales, nor is the economic base multiplier applied to lost sales in order to approximate total community revenue loss.
9. Residual effects such as the decline in property values due to reduction in rental income (required if sales volume dropped) are ignored. These are presumed to be offset by claims of increased value brought about by the elimination of visual blight occurring with the removal of the sign. This assumption is very hard to justify for commercial property, as values are so heavily dependent upon rental income.
10. The contract with the County for police services is expected to continue as written for the foreseeable future without alteration. No change in demand for service or rate at which service is charged is contemplated.

Most of the above assumptions are generous in favor of the regulatory interest.

If, using the data and the above assumptions, the hardware store represents a normal sample of city retail activity and the coming five years would otherwise produce the volume shown for the past five years, the annual decline in municipal revenue would approximate $22,400 from the site in which the hardware store is located. Expanding that by a factor of ten to represent the entire city, the approximate annual cost of reducing the size and visibility of commercial signs is $224,000. This figure is roughly equal to 18% of the annual cost of police protection under the county contract.

The cost of the county contract is based on the number of patrol units, a "beat factor", and the number of days squad cars are provided to the city. Assuming that the city does not wish to institute a specific tax for payment of police services, any of these variables can be adjusted downward to allow for the income loss traceable to aesthetic regulation under the sign ordinance. A number of possibilities exists, only three of which are:

1. One of the four patrol units can be eliminated;
2. The beat factor can be manipulated to require patrol units to spend less time within city limits;
3. In combination with other adjustments, week-end traffic patrol could be eliminated at a savings of $56,379 per year (the difference between 5 day and 7 day coverage).

Any of the components of the police protection can be valued in "aesthetic units". Assume that weekend traffic patrol is valued by the hour. The $56,379 cost for weekend coverage becomes $1,175 for a 48-hour period. In the case of our example, the loss in revenue associated with one sign ($22,400 per year) is equal to 19 hours of weekend police protection rendered weekly for one year.

So the operative question becomes, do the citizens of this city prefer one unit of aesthetic value in the form of the removal of an oversized commercial sign or 19 hours of police protection during the weekend?

This illustration represents one of an infinite possible combination of benefits and costs that may be argued successfully in a regulatory setting. Although the mathematical elegance of the abstract model we started with is less apparent in the example, the thinking behind it remains one of optimization in the presence of constraints. Budgets are limited and resources are scarce meaning that choices must be made. The general form of the model always reduces to a discussion of how costs and benefits are to be managed in a way that bring about the most good for the most number. In actual practice there is much opportunity for field adjustment. The spreadsheet provided in the electronic files may be used to "tweak" the analysis in various ways. Suppose the 25% loss in sales is unconvincing. Change it to the number relevant to your circumstance and you have a different answer. Perhaps your regulatory issue is not signage but lot line set-back distance or floor area ratios. These, too, lend themselves to an optimization problem, one of the most widely respected decision tools in and out of the business world.

2.8. Conclusion

The impact of governmental decisions at all levels cannot be ignored. At the local level the effect of restrictions on value may be positive or negative. The sign of effects for the short run may differ from the sign of the long run effects. Land users and policymakers must strike a balance between the competing interests represented in the private economic market and the market for public services and lifestyle. This chapter presents just one example of many. It is estimated that 80% of the decisions made by the typical Southern California City Council are land use decisions. In effect this makes local politicians the largest real estate agent the city. How well they do their job depends in part on how well they understand the consequences of their decisions. Good government arises from an informed citizenry. The tools of this chapter may be employed to shed light on a process that is vital to real estate investing.

Endnotes

[1] Coase, R. H., "The problem of social cost," The Journal of law & Economics 3: 1-44 (1960).

[2] NIMBY = "Not In My Back Yard."

[3] Maximizing the Log of the function also maximizes the function because the Log is monotonic and convex for all positive log bases.

[4] This ignores the interplay between taxes and the level of sales which is not our story.

References

Cheung, S. N. S. (1970). The structure of a contract and the theory of a non-exclusive resource. Journal of Law and Economics, 13, 49-70.

Coase, R. H. (1960). The problem of social cost. Journal of Law and Economics, 3, 1-44.

Costonis, J. J. (1982). Law and aesthetics: A critique and a reformulation of the dilemmas. Michigan Law Review, 80(3), 355-461.

Demsetz, H. (1967). Toward a theory of property rights. American Economic Review, 347.

de Soto, Hernando. The Mystery of Capital: Why Capitalism Triumphs in the West and Fails Everywhere Else. New York. Basic Books.

Dukeminier, J. J., Jr. (1955). Zoning for aesthetic objectives: A reappraisal. Law and Contemporary Problems, 20, 218-237.

Eggertsson, Thrainn. Economic Behavior and Institutions. Cambridge, UK. Cambridge University Press.

Ely, James W., Jr. The Guardian of Every Other Right. Second ed. New York. Oxford University Press.

Manne, Henry G., ed. The Economics of Legal Relationships, Readings in the Theory of Property Rights. New York, West Publishing Company.

Meiselman, A. (1985). The regulation of outdoor advertising: Balancing freedom of speech and aesthetics. Annual Survey of American Law, 671-697.

Posner, R. A. (1998). Economic Analysis of Law (5th Ed. ed.).Aspen Law and Business.

Tiebout, Charles M. (1956). A Pure Theory of Local Expenditures, The Journal of Political Economy, 64(5), 416-424.

Titman, S. (1985). Urban Land Prices Under Uncertainty. American Economic Review, 75(3), 505-514.

Williams, S. F. (1977). Subjectivity, expression, and privacy: Problems of aesthetic regulation. Minnesota Law Review, 62, 1-58.

Problems

1. Using Figure 2.8 slide the efficiency from the default (optimal) of 3.1 to 2.1 and note the lost utility. Using data from Table 2.1 and Equations 2.4 and 2.10, compute the new, smaller, utility. What is the lost utility under the new efficiency value in percentage terms?
2. You are a community activist interested in civic beautification. Next week you will attend and speak at the meeting of the local planning board where you will advocate for a reduction in visual blight by eliminating large commercial signs. You are aware of the utility optimization argument which will be advanced by opposing business owners wishing to retain their signs in current form. Fashion cogent arguments in opposition using quantitative values and different assumptions input into the model discussed in this chapter. Show how you will prevail over the other side's argument with your computations.

3

The Rules of Thumb - Threshold Performance Measures

"Pluralities non est ponenda sine necessitate" (approximately: *"Keep it simple, stupid"*)

<u>**William of Occam**</u>, c. 1280-1349

3.1. Introduction

This chapter deals with the initial measures used in the field to decide if one wants to collect more information and perform further analysis on a real estate investment opportunity. We will also demonstrate how the analysis of data can enhance decision-making. The availability of plentiful data for privately owned real estate investments is relatively new. As with any new tool, using it to full advantage depends on using it correctly. Rules of thumb, having their place in the acquisition of individual properties, can also play a role in data analysis. In that role one can reach preliminary conclusions about the market in which the target acquisition competes.

In this chapter we will

- Look closely at the real estate equivalent to ratio tests used in corporate finance;
- Make the connection between the simple one-year snapshot measures and the more elaborate multi-period analysis methods;
- Suggest ways that data can be used to improve the value of rules of thumb;
- Perform tests on data to determine the validity of representations made by real estate professionals and investors in the field; and
- Introduce the effect that extreme values have on data analysis

3.2. Threshold performance measures

Rules of Thumb are short cuts. They are for the "tire kicking" stage of a search for a property. They give quick-and-dirty answers. As such, they ignore many important aspects of investing. Thus the answers provided can easily be wrong. But we must start somewhere. Rules of thumb are important for two reasons. First, real estate information is costly and the decision to pursue more information on one project precludes devoting more time to another, possibly more profitable, pursuit. The wise use of data can improve the value of threshold measures and increase search efficiency. Second, the smallest income properties often trade in the market solely on the basis of threshold measures. Thus, the decision to purchase a duplex might be based entirely on its gross rent multiplier. The investor who never purchases more than four units may never encounter the more sophisticated tools such as net present value or internal rate of return that we will encounter in the next chapter.

The model we will use is shown below. The reader may benefit from comparing this model to financial statements used in generally accepted accounting procedures (GAAP). Note the similarities. The first three lines may be considered a simple balance sheet, the remainder an income statement.

Balance Sheet	MV	Market Value
	(LN)	(Loans)
	EQ or DP	Equity or Down Payment
Income Statement	GPI	Gross Potential Income
	(VAC)	(Vacancy)
	EGI	Expected Gross Income
	(EXP)	(Expenses)
	NOI	Net Operating Income
	(DS)	(Debt Service)
	BTCF	Before Tax Cash Flow
	(TAX)	(Income Tax Consequences)
	ATCF	After Tax Cash Flow

Figure 3.1. Basic Income Property Model

There are two main differences between accounting identities for corporations and those for real estate investments.

1. <u>Financing</u>. Corporate bond financing usually calls for a series of payments of interest only followed by a large single payment of principal. Generally, real estate loans payments include principal and interest. Thus, it is common to include amortization in the debt service shown on a real estate investment operating statement. The corporate line item "Earnings Before Interest and Taxes (EBIT)" is replaced by Net Operating Income (*NOI*) in the real estate income statement. Of course, these are general rules and exceptions apply for both cases.
2. <u>Taxes</u>. Not shown below is the detail associated with Income Tax Consequences. Included in that detail is a depreciation deduction, something that has special implications for real estate investment. Although we will incorporate these details in the model in Chapter 4, the reader is urged to consult a basic real estate investment text to become acquainted with these details before proceeding.

There are seven common rules of thumb, five of which primarily concern investors, the other two concern lenders. In a later chapter we will show how the interests of these two parties can merge. This chapter is devoted to examining the investor measures. In Part III we look more carefully at the lender measures.

The five investor rules are:

1. **GRM** = gross rent multiplier, the result of dividing gross potential income into the value ($\frac{\text{Value}}{\text{GPI}}$)
2. **Expense Ratio** = expense ratio, the result of dividing operating expenses by expected gross income $\left(\frac{\text{Exp}}{\text{EGI}}\right)$. Some prefer the gross potential income as the divisor;
3. **CR** = capitalization rate, the result of dividing net operating income by the value $\left(\frac{\text{NOI}}{\text{Value}}\right)$;
4. **C/C** = cash-on-cash return, the result of dividing after-tax cash flow by the equity or down payment $\left(\frac{\text{ATCF}}{\text{Equity}}\right)$. In some cases a before tax cash-on-cash return is desired in which case it is the BTCF that is divided by the equity or down payment.
5. **PPU** = price per unit, the result of dividing the value of the property by the number of units $\left(\frac{\text{value}}{\text{units}}\right)$. The denominator varies with the type of property. For instance, residential income properties use dwelling unit; commercial property may use either square foot or front foot.

The two lender rules are:

1. **LTV** = loan to value ratio, the result of dividing the loan encumbering the property by the value $\left(\frac{\text{Loan}}{\text{Value}}\right)$;
2. **DCR** = debt coverage ratio, the result of dividing net operating income by the loan payment $\left(\frac{\text{NOI}}{\text{DS}}\right)$.

Figure 3.2 provides a summary of six of the rules. Sample calculated values are provided. The computed value shows on the line for the variable appearing in the numerator of the ratio and an "X" on the line for the variable that is the denominator.

				Investor				Lender	
				GRM	Exp Ratio	CR	C/C	LTV	DCR
Balance Sheet	MV	Market Value		7.14		X		X	
	(LN)	(Loan)						70%	
	EQ or DP	Equity or Down Pmt					X		
Income Statement	GPI	Gross Potential Income		X					
	(VAC)	(Vacancy)							
	EGI	Expected Gross Income			X				
	(EXP)	(Expenses)			40.3%				
	NOI	Net Operating Income				8.00%			1.43
	(DS)	(Debt Service)							X
	BTCF	Before Tax Cash Flow							
	(TAX)	Income Tax Consequences							
	ATCF	After Tax Cash Flow					8.70%		

Figure 3.2. Rules of thumb

3.3. A general caution

The main weakness of all rules of thumb is that they argue for a simple, often linear, relationship between variables. Note that three of the four investor measures involve the property value. The most common reason for using *any* analysis tool is to determine the appropriate value one should pay for an asset. Rearranging the equations to solve for value in each we have:

Value = $NOI \frac{1}{CR}$ = $GPI (GRM)$ = # Units (PPU)

In each case the presumption is that we know one variable (net or gross income or number of units) and if we just had the "magic bullet" in the form of the "right" capitalization rate, *GRM* or *PPU* we could make a simple multiplication to arrive at value. This is naive to say the least. Few things in life are linear. Few things as complex as a real estate investment can be explained with a single variable. Yet the market persists in using these tools.

Let's take them one at a time, examining their strengths and weaknesses.

3.4. The gross rent multiplier (*GRM*)

An important feature of this rule is its accuracy. Both of its components, price and rent, are usually reported correctly. There is little opportunity for or benefit to manipulation of gross income by sellers or their brokers because a minimum due diligence prior to sale uncovers the actual rent the tenants pay. The significant drawback of *GRM* is that, as a "top line item" it does not consider the ingredients that go into other rules of thumb that use numbers closer to the bottom line. Contrasted with the capitalization rate which is based on *net* operating income that considers a property's expenses, *GRM* assumes all buildings have the same expenses. Two buildings with the same *GRM* and the same income will have the same value. But what if the owner of Building A includes furniture or utilities in the rent and the owner of Building B does not? A real estate investor should remember what business he is in. He is in the business of renting enclosed space resting on a parcel of land. He may also be in the "side" business of renting furniture but that is a different business with different income and cost dynamics. If you doubt this, compare the useful life of the building to the useful life of furniture in those buildings.

Presumably one acquires utilities from the utility company at the same price the tenant could. Providing utilities should be viewed as a non-profit "pass through" arrangement where the owner merely operates as a conduit for tenant utility payments. Including this pass through in income that is used for calculating value distorts the value unless a downward adjustment is made in the *GRM* for buildings offering paid utilities.

Does this render the *GRM* totally ineffective? No, it just must be used appropriately. One should be sure that services provided to tenants are consistent throughout all buildings upon which the same *GRM* is to be used. Other expense indicators such as age should be considered and further adjustments in the *GRM* should be made accordingly.

One can maximize the use of *GRM* as an accurately reported field in a database. Let's take a look at how we might use the reported *GRM* for a reality check on the market in general.

To the buyer's complaint that the seller's price is too high, it is common for sellers to claim that rents are low and the buyer need only raise the rent to make the property pay off at the price the seller offers. In general, tenants may be presumed to stay if rent increases are small and leave if they are large. Our interest is in knowing how much of a rent increase is too much, causing turmoil in the building in the form of costly turnover and vacancy. One way to approach this is to assume we know a *market equilibrium* gross rent multiplier. This is the *GRM* at which most buildings provide a "normal" cash flow at "normal" rents and a "normal" return under "normal" financing terms.

We use data for the sale of 700 apartment buildings ranging between five and 100 units in size during the period between April and October, 2001 in Los Angeles.[1] Included are the Price, *GRM* and building size in square feet (*SF*) for each sale. We display only the first six lines of the data to get a feel for what it looks like.

Area	Price	Date	Age	SF	Units	GRM	CR
4	825 000	04/02/01	30	13 780	16	7.12	0.0982
4	2 450 000	04/03/01	36	28 846	32	7.98	0.0851
2	1 250 000	04/03/01	36	7094	10	11.61	0.0582
1	337 500	04/03/01	61	4452	8	5.58	0.1129
3	2 200 000	04/03/01	30	28 284	40	6.67	0.0975

Table 3.1. Los Angeles Apartment Data

These data gives us our first opportunity to inquire into how a particular real estate market works. One definition of market rent is the rent at which a building is fully occupied or as close to that as is considered healthy. "Healthy" means that vacancy is neither zero or excessively high. "Normal" vacancy of 4-5% due to market frictions (job change, births, deaths, etc.) that cause turnover is to be expected at market rent. Owners are interested in market rents to determine whether the actual (contract) rents for the building under consideration are at market.

3.4.1. What not to do

Tempting though it is to let the data tell us the market *GRM*, we must resist that urge. It is true that *Mathematica* can provide, in Table 3.2, several measures of central tendency...

Mean	HarmonicMean	Median	Max	Min	Variance	StdDev
7.85691	7.47772	7.53	13.43	4.01	3.14458	1.7733

Table 3.2. Measures of Central Tendency for Los Angeles Apartment GRM Data

...and we could, without ever leaving the comfort of our office, conclude that we know the market *GRM* from one of these measures. But which do we choose? In fact, there are very good reasons not to rely on any of them. The use of data should not replace but rather supplement field work, in this case a good market survey in the property's immediate neighborhood. The best way to determine market *GRM* is by knowing the market, its participants, the time in which the data were collected and whether at that time it was a buyer's or seller's market.

3.4.2. What should be done

We can generate some additional information based on the data we have. Combining price, GRM and SF provides monthly rental price per square foot. Since

$$GRM = \frac{\text{price}}{gpi} \Longrightarrow gpi = \frac{\text{price}}{GRM}$$

and

$$\frac{gpi}{sf} = \text{annual rent per square foot of building.}$$

Therefore, the average monthly rent per square foot for all buildings is $0.91

Having average rent per square foot is somewhat helpful. But Los Angeles is a big area. We still should conduct a rent survey close to our subject property. We then know if rents in our neighborhood are above or below the general Los Angeles area and can inquire as to why this is so. We then compare neighborhood rents to our subject property to determine what sort of rent change is desirable or feasible.

We are interested in an equilibrium *GRM*. That is, we want to know *the equilibrium of the ratio* of value to gross income. We will assume that a thorough rent survey has been performed at various points in time in the past and compared to sale prices at those times. Characteristics of buyers' and sellers' markets were matched with those different times and the experience and judgment of the analyst tells him that 7 is the equilibrium *GRM* for the area. One way of expressing equilibrium is to say that when the market is *neither* a buyers' nor a sellers' market the *GRM* is 7. There must be such a time because markets transition from being buyers' markets to sellers' markets over time and at some time there must be a point when the tide changes. It is at that point the market can be said to be in equilibrium. At those times buyers and sellers, *as a group*, may be viewed as indifferent between owning the property or the cash the property value represents. The qualifier "as a group" is important. At any given time in all markets we observe transactions and each of these mean that an individual buyer valued property more than cash and the corresponding seller valued the cash more than the property. Market equilibrium is a somewhat cerebral concept. Appreciating it requires blocking out what one may know about specific transactions and considering the overall market as a functioning entity. One must make the transition from deal maker to market analyst to maximize the value of real estate data.

Returning to our scenario, we have a market with an average *GRM* (recall the mean calculated above) in excess of what we believe to be the equilibrium *GRM*. This suggests a seller's market because despite the fact that the income may not represent a good return (another definition of equilibrium is when prices offer a good return) for the price, buyers still buy. Many a buyer has told his broker that he will buy "whatever makes sense" or "whatever pencils out". This is buyer's vernacular for the idea of equilibrium. In a seller's market deals don't "make sense" or "pencil out" from the buyer's perspective. But if transactions take place anyway that often means sellers are telling buyers "rents can be raised" and buyers believe them.

Discounting future rent increases is not new. Nor is it entirely an artifact of seller's markets. Even when prices do not "lead" the income, buyers imagine increasing their income as soon as possible. Our interest is in getting a feel for the risk involved in accepting the seller's assertion that rents can be raised. One way to do this is to derive a measure that places the rent raise requirement in some perspective.

There are two ways to own, at an equilibrium *GRM*, a property offered by the seller at a price above equilibrium *GRM*. One is to buy it at a lower price, a price that represents an equilibrium *GRM*. This ALWAYS works. But we have concluded that this is a seller's market so we assume that is not an option. The other way is to raise rent immediately after purchase. It turns out that there is a simple formula based solely on actual and equilibrium *GRM* that tells us the increase in rent that will drive the *GRM* down to equilibrium. We define the required rent raise, *rrr*, as a percent of present rent:

$$rrr = \frac{GRM_A}{GRM_E} - 1 \qquad (3.1)$$

Where GRM_A is the actual *GRM* and GRM_E is the equilibrium or normal market *GRM*.

We can separate those properties priced over equilibrium from the entire list to find out how many there are. Not surprisingly, they constitute more than half. The number of properties over equilibrium is 434, and average *GRM* of properties over equilibrium is 8.89802.

We can also determine the average rent raise needed to bring this property to our equilibrium *GRM* of 7. Throughout the Los Angeles area prices indicate that on average rents for this building must be raised 27.11% to bring it into equilibrium. [2]

Suppose we found three properties located near one another that happen to be #200, #210 and #220 on our list. Table 3.3 shows that one only requires a 6.4% rent raise and one requires a 30% increase to bring it to equilibrium. All else being equal we would first investigate property #210. If a broker brought us #220 we would want to know what is so superior about it that we should consider it, given the fact that rent must be raised more to justify its price. Of course *rrr* is sensitive to how much below the market a property's rent actually is. It might just be that property #220 *is* the best deal. We must always be mindful of the fact that it is necessary to investigate each individual property. It's real estate: There is no substitute for a site inspection.

Property #	rrr
200	0.249
210	0.064
220	0.300

Table 3.3. Three individual properties from the Los Angeles data

Plotting the required rent raises for all properties priced over equilibrium, we see that *rrr* ranges up to nearly 100% meaning that rents must double on some properties to justify their price, given our assumption about equilibrium.

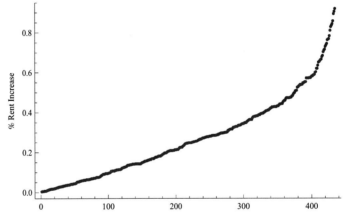

Figure 3.3. Plot of *rrr* necessary for properties above equilibrium GRM

The slope of the curve in Figure 3.3 above 60% *rrr* indicates that there are 29 sellers, or 6.68% of the total, on fishing expeditions that will likely return to the dock empty handed.

Combining data (Figure 3.4 uses data for San Diego, CA) with mapping software we can place each property on a map, color coding the properties in a way that presents grades of required rent raise as shown in the legend to the right. A major benefit to this is that we can quickly select which property to visit first. It is the one that doesn't fit in with the others (circled).[3]

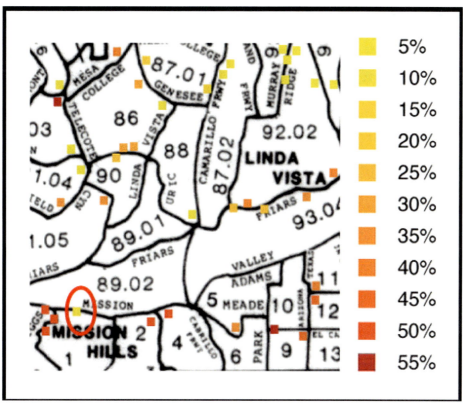

Figure 3.4. Properties requiring rent raises to achieve equilibrium

Among the smallest properties the use of *GRM* dominates as a rule of thumb. But as property size increases the favored threshold measure is capitalization rate, to which we now turn.

3.5. Capitalization rate (CR)

The second question most commercial investment brokers ask about a property is "What is the cap rate?" This rule of thumb improves on the *GRM* because the income used for its calculation is the net income after vacancy and expenses. In the market for large properties where tax exempt institutions purchase property for all cash, this measure is quite useful. Imagining the property as a parking place for cash, the capitalization rate constitutes the interest rate the property earns debt free as if it were a bank account. Naturally, the bank account analogy is limited. Investment property capitalization rates are typically much higher than interest rates paid by banks for reasons that should be apparent.

3.5.1. The three bad assumptions

Capitalization rate history is intertwined with the income approach to appraisal which indulges in the fiction that all properties are acquired in a tax free environment without the use of debt. Capitalization rate ignores financing and tax effects (something we will do as well later in this chapter). This is far less true for individuals than it is for institutions. However, there is something more troublesome at work here. Capitalization rate also requires one to accept three assumptions:
- Income is perpetual
- Income is unchanging
- Risk is unchanging

All of these assumptions are virtually *guaranteed* to be wrong. Little exists in perpetuity and change is inevitable.

The mathematical derivation of the capitalization rate is as follows: Start with the simple notion that value, v, is a function of this period's income, Inc, and a discount rate, $r \subset [0,1]$, operating to reduce the present value of this period's income - assumed to be unchanging over time - with each successive replication in future years. Therefore:

$$v = Inc + \frac{Inc}{(1+r)} + \frac{Inc}{(1+r)^2} + \frac{Inc}{(1+r)^3} + \ldots + \frac{Inc}{(1+r)^n} \tag{3.2}$$

Multiply both sides by $(1+r)$ to get

$$v(1+r) = Inc + \frac{Inc}{(1+r)} + \frac{Inc}{(1+r)^2} + \frac{Inc}{(1+r)^3} + \ldots + \frac{Inc}{(1+r)^{n-1}} \tag{3.3}$$

Factor out the Income on the right to get

$$v(1+r) = Inc\left(1 + \frac{1}{(1+r)} + \frac{1}{(1+r)^2} + \frac{1}{(1+r)^3} + \ldots + \frac{1}{(1+r)^{n-1}}\right) \tag{3.4}$$

The term in the brackets on the right in (3.4) is known as a geometric series (recall that $(1+r)^0 = 1 = \frac{1}{(1+r)^0}$). Applying assumption #1 above takes n to infinity. The term in brackets in (3.4) may be expressed as

$$\sum_{n=0}^{\infty}\left(\frac{1}{(1+r)^n}\right) \tag{3.5}$$

Such a geometric series converges as n grows without bounds to

$$\frac{1+r}{r} \tag{3.6}$$

Thus, if we substitute (3.5) for the term in brackets on the right side of (3.3) and shorten "Inc" to "i" we get

$$v(1+r) = i\frac{1+r}{r} \tag{3.7}$$

at which point one may divide both sides by $(1+r)$ to cancel them and arrive at

$$v = \frac{i}{r} \tag{3.8}$$

Which is simple capitalization rate.

3.6. Capitalization rate and discounted cash flow (DCF) analysis

Discounted Cash Flow (*DCF*) analysis is not a rule of thumb method and its correct use is taken up at length in the next chapter. However, many practitioners in the field impose assumptions that effectively reduce *DCF* to cap rate. Since *DCF* is often misused in a way that makes it indistinguishable from capitalization rate we shall consider it briefly here.

To begin, we ask: How is Discounted Cash Flow different from capitalization rate? Of course *DCF* explicitly considers after-tax cash flows, taking into account financing and income tax effects. But it is still an income stream. The use of capitalization rate as an appraisal tool in the income approach assumes that all investors and properties have access to identical financing and make decisions in a common tax environment. Under those conditions, the after-debt, after-tax distinction loses its importance.

The usual representation of present value is:

$$pv = \sum_{n=1}^{t} \frac{atcf_n}{(1+d)^n} + \frac{ater_t}{(1+d)^t} \qquad (3.9)$$

Where: *atcf* = after-tax cash flow
ater = after-tax equity reversion (after-tax sales proceeds)
d = discount rate

It is important to recognize that the existence of an *ater* at any specific time *t* is critically dependent upon a future buyer willing to buy the property. Such buyer must have an expectation of future cash flows beyond time *t*. He must also have an expectation of his own *ater*, which requires yet another buyer, who then expects still more future cash flows and still another buyer at the end of his time horizon, and so on until the perpetuity assumption is restored. Collapsing all the expectations of this sequence of buyers into one results in the following equation. Note the similarity of (3.10) to (3.5).

$$ater_t = \sum_{n=t+1}^{\infty} \frac{atcf_n}{(1+d)^n} \qquad (3.10)$$

Therefore one may, under the assumptions above, ignore a sale for the present investor (and all future investors) and, in the interest of generality, conclude that

$$pv = \sum_{n=1}^{\infty} \frac{atcf_n}{(1+d)^n} \qquad (3.11)$$

If *atcf* is *Inc* and *d* is *r* (3.11) expresses the same concept as (3.2).

3.6.1. Monotonic growth

BUT, you say, income grows over time.

It is true that income *changes* over time. Wishful thinking compels us to hope that the change is always positive. Such hopefulness is at the core of subjective valuation. However, even if long term growth is positive, there is no more justification for believing in monotonic (constantly) increasing income than there is to believe in unchanging income. In a way, income reflecting constant, unchanging growth is just a special case of unchanging income.

An example of monotonic growth is the compound interest function (Figure 3.5). A plot of this function is smooth, orderly, certain and deterministic. Despite the claims of many a real estate broker, it is unlikely to be realized from most real estate investments.

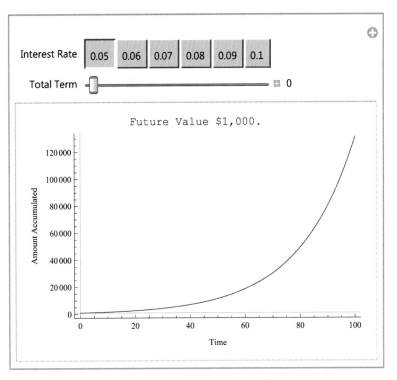

Figure 3.5. The compound interest function

Suppose we assume a "growth factor", g, that is to be applied to each year's income to produce the subsequent year's income.[4] We then reach a value, V_s, subscripted with an s for "subjective", that appears thus:

$$V_s = \frac{cf}{(1+d)} + \frac{cf(1+g)}{(1+d)^2} + \frac{cf(1+g)^2}{(1+d)^3} + \frac{cf(1+g)^3}{(1+d)^4} + \ldots + \frac{cf(1+g)^{n-1}}{(1+d)^n} \tag{3.12}$$

As we will shortly see, this merely changes the result in the denominator to be the difference between d and g.[5]

Notice that the infinite series above converges below to a simple solution that appears much like equation (3.8) taking $cf = i$ and $d-g = r$.[6]

$$v_s := \sum_{t=0}^{\infty} \left(\frac{cf(1+g)^t}{(1+d)^{t+1}} \right) = \frac{cf}{d-g} \tag{3.13}$$

If we set the equation for v in (3.8) equal to the equation for v_s in (3.13), use $cf = i$ and solve for each of g, d and r we find they have simple arithmetic relationships:

$v == v_s$ becomes $\frac{i}{r} = \frac{cf}{d-g}$, therefore if $i = cf$,

$g = d-r$
$d = g+r$
$r = d-g$

Alternatively, if we make i and cf unitary (because they are scalar) and provide arbitrary but reasonable values for d and r we can set v equal to v_s and solve for g, demonstrating that each r used in capitalization rate methodology has an implicit g. For instance, using a discount rate of .13 and a capitalization rate of .09 produces an implicit growth rate of .04.

The point of the exercise above is that little new is learned by *DCF* modeling when monotonic growth is assumed. So it appears that early critics of *DCF* were right when they complained that no project recommended by cap rate methodology would be rejected after *DCF* analysis provided that the growth rate applied to *DCF* cash flow was appropriate (meaning that it was the same as that implied in the cap rate). So the question becomes: Under what conditions is *DCF* a useful, if not superior, analytical tool? This is the subject of the next chapter.

3.7. The expense ratio and the "honest" capitalization rate

We will now provide a look at the use of data to analyze capitalization rates from the perspective of expense ratios with an eye to determining when a capitalization rate may be relied on.

We opened the *GRM* discussion saying that there is little manipulation of the input variables. While true for *GRM*, this is not so for capitalization rate. Bragging rights about selling a building at a high price are often denominated in capitalization rate terms. But capitalization rate is a function of the property's net income. Net income is further dependent on the accurate reporting of expenses. This is problematic in datasets for a number of reasons:

- Sales of property in some jurisdictions result in reassessment for property taxes so the seller's property tax expense can vary widely from the buyer's.
- It is in the seller's interest to minimize expenses so to show net income in the best light. While the buyer may have recast the property's income for his own purposes, his analysis and the capitalization rate it produced usually are not reported.
- Some brokers merely report last year's expenses which may or may not be representative of a stabilized year of operation.
- Reserves are often not included, as they should be, in the expenses shown on property listed for sale.
- Management style, self-management and agency issues all play a part in the construction of an expense schedule.

One might argue that such a list precludes reaching what is sometimes called "an honest net income", thus an honest capitalization rate. This argument, while at times persuasive, must not be considered fatal. Indeed, there is enough uncertainty in all phases of real estate investment to make this argument at every turn. The question becomes: If we have large numbers of reported expenses, can we learn anything about the accuracy of expense information impounded in capitalization rates from those large numbers?

Recognizing that cap rate makes value a function of net income...

$$Value = \frac{Net\ Operating\ Income}{Capitalization\ Rate} \tag{3.14}$$

...and net income in turn is a function of vacancy and expenses...

$$Net\ Operating\ Income = Gross\ Potential\ Income - Vacancy - Expenses \tag{3.15}$$

...leads us to simplify the difference between gross and net income as...

$$Net\ Operating\ Income = Gross\ Potential\ Income\ (1 - evr) \tag{3.16}$$

Where evr = expense and vacancy rate ($0 < evr < 1$). Rearranging the value equation, recalling that $GPI = \frac{Val}{GRM}$, and substituting our simplifying assumption produces:

$$Capitalization\ Rate = \frac{\frac{Val}{GRM}(1 - evr)}{Value} \tag{3.17}$$

Given that value and gross income are accurately reported, this makes the "honest" cap rate we yearn for a function of the expense and vacancy rate chosen.

Further rearrangement, gives us an equation for *evr* that is dependent on only two variables, both commonly found in reported sales of investment property: The *GRM* and the capitalization rate of which one, *GRM,* is more reliable than the other. In reconciling these two rules of thumb we can gain some additional insight.

$$evr = 1 - caprate\, grm \qquad (3.18)$$

One should be cautioned that, mathematically, it is possible for *evr* to be negative. However, in real estate it can never be less than zero. Should a negative *evr* be calculated by (3.18) from observations in a dataset it *virtually must* result from misreporting of either or both the Capitalization Rate or *GRM*. A moment's thought about what it would mean for an apartment building to sell for ten times its gross income AND at a 13% cap rate will convince you that such things do not occur in nature. In Equation 3.19 we solve for *GRM* in terms of the other variables.

$$grm == \frac{1 - evr}{caprate} \qquad (3.19)$$

GRM is always greater than 1 (all buildings in first world countries sell for more than their annual gross income) and capitalization rate, the reciprocal of a positive real number, must always be greater than zero and less than 1. Thus, the only way for both sides of the above equation to be greater than 1 is for the numerator of the ratio on the right to be greater than its denominator. Since *evr* is a rate that, by definition is a positive number between 0 and 1, 1-*evr* must be a number between 0 and 1. For the whole right side of (3.19) to be greater than one, 1-*evr* must be larger than the capitalization rate.

3.7.1. The normal approach to data

Let's look at a dataset of 1000 actual apartment sales that took place in the San Francisco area between October, 1996 and September of 2001. Each observation shows the area, price, date sold, age, building size in square feet, number of units, Gross Rent Multiplier, and Capitalization Rate. The dataset is named "expdata" and the first five observations are displayed below

Area	Price	Date	Age	SF	Units	GRM	CR
5	880 000	09/21/01	94	2100	6	11.24	0.0697
5	1 075 000	09/21/01	48	5302	9	8.07	0.0918
1	920 000	09/19/01	0	5502	6	10.6	0.0603
5	1 000 000	09/14/01	42	5368	8	14.56	0.0546
5	1 150 000	09/07/01	50	5200	8	8.87	0.0835

Table 3.4. First five observations in San Francisco data

Using (3.18), we can combine the cap rate and *GRM* to create a list of expense and vacancy ratios. It is useful to look at the range of the *evr* observations in evrlist and plot them.

```
Minimum = 10.43%

Maximum = 59.1824%
```

Most practitioners in sunny California would agree that expenses of 59.18% of income for an apartment building are at least unusual if not unlikely. Likewise at the other extreme, expenses of 10.43% are probably understated. We need to adopt a healthy suspicion about the extreme observations. A plot of an ordered list shows, as always, a few extreme observations but the majority of the

observations are between 25% and 45%

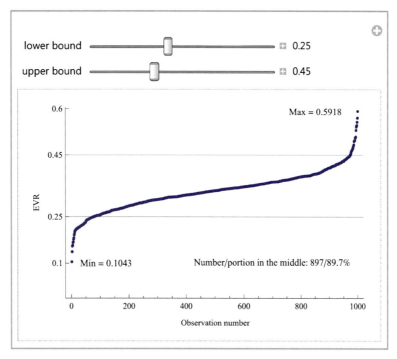

Figure 3.6. Plot of ordered list of *evr*s

The histogram in Figure 3.7 provides a visual way to see the discrete distribution of grouped *evr* data.

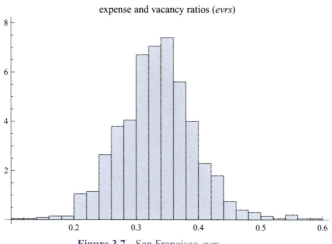

Figure 3.7. San Francisco *evr*s

Measures of central tendency, shape and variance are shown in Table 3.5.

Location statistics	
Mean	0.333921
Harmonic mean	0.322032
Median	0.334293
Mode	0.319379
Dispersion statistics	
Variance	0.00370466
Standard deviation	0.0608659
Range	0.487524
Mean deviation	0.046557
Shape statistics	
Skewness	0.221308
Excess kurtosis	1.07313

Table 3.5. Descriptive statistics for San Francisco *evr* data

Notice that the values above include measures of something known as "tail behavior". One is skewness, the measure of how much the distribution is *not* symmetrical. The other is excess kurtosis, a measure of the thickness of the tails. These are important features of the distribution that are "non-normal". We will return to these later.

Our data are a sample. We know its shape but we do not know the shape of the distribution of the population from which the sample was drawn. Assuming (naively) for the moment that the sample of expense ratio observations are from a population of expense ratios that are distributed normally, we can create a probability distribution function (*pdf*) for such a distribution from its first two moments, the mean and the variance. We then plot these over a range equal to three standard deviations away from the mean.

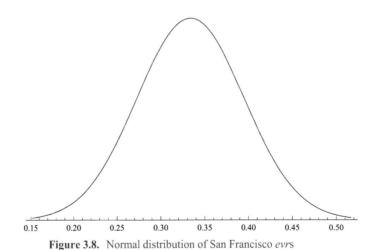

Figure 3.8. Normal distribution of San Francisco *evr*s

With the above we can assess the probability that any specific reported expense ratio will occur. To do this we use the cumulative distribution function (*CDF*) and ask, simply, how much of the probability mass resides below some specific point?[7] For instance, suppose we are interested in knowing the probability that the building we are investigating has an expense ratio of 25% or less. One indication of this is that portion of the data having expenses ratios at or below that figure. The answer the *CDF* produces is plotted on the *pdf* in Figure 3.9. We must keep in mind that the illustrations and computations shown below are dependent on our assumption that all *evr*s are normally distributed.

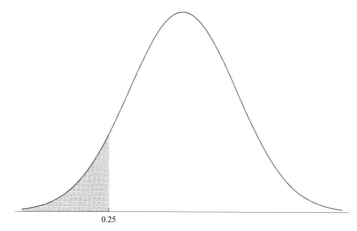

Figure 3.9. Portion of *evr* observations at or below 25%

Earlier we plotted the data as an ordered list and concluded that most of the expense ratios were in the range of 25-45%. This is confirmed by the *pdf* in Figure 3.10 showing most of the probability mass in that range.

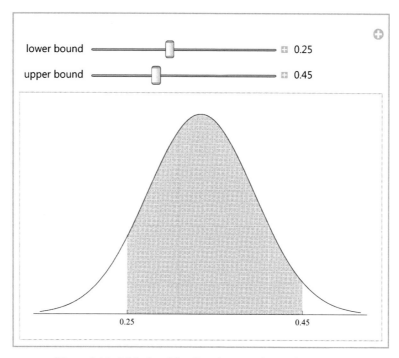

Figure 3.10. Majority of San Francisco *evr* observations

Often we want to put a number to our conclusions about probability. The common phrase "What are the chances of that?" is vernacular for the more formal "How much of the data is below that [certain point]?" Table 3.6 shows several examples in which the *evr* on the left is matched with its respective probability on the right.

evr	P(evr)
0.25	0.0839818
0.3	0.288662
0.35	0.604179
0.4	0.861185
0.45	0.971748
0.5	0.99682

Table 3.6. Probability of certain *evr* observations

Table 3.6 shows that 99.7% of our *evr* observations are at or below 50% while only 8.4% of them are at or below 25%. Thus, about 91% of them are between 25% and 50%. If we are given a capitalization rate that is based on an *evr* of 30% we see from the Table 3.6 that only 28.9% of the buildings have an *evr* that low or lower. From this we can make an assessment of the reliability of the capitalization rate. But how reliable is the model we employed to make this claim?

3.7.2. Questioning the assumption of normality

Before continuing it is useful to take a step back and ask a broad question: Why do we use data and statistics? Used properly they help us peer into the unknown. The unknown may be the way a market works - something we cannot see because it is not directly observable. The unknown may be the future, something we can't see because we haven't arrived there yet. Either way, we hope that samples are representative of the population from which they are drawn, thus approximating the unknown we hope to see or predict.

A frustrating reality of using data that affects practitioners in the field is that data never predicts a specific outcome for a specific act like buying a particular property. If helpful at all it enables us to more accurately predict the mean of a large number of repeated trials of the same act. Recall that earlier in this chapter we counseled a "healthy suspicion about the extreme observations". This advice applies both to specifics where we believe there is something wrong with a reported data point and, more generally, to the way extreme observations affect our ability to predict the mean. Extreme observations are known in statistics as "outliers", [8] meaning that they lie at a point that is far(out) from the mean. Such outliers have an affect on the mean that exceeds their relative importance to the entire distribution.

Let us now address the "non-normal" issue. The assumption of normality is often convenient but also often troublesome. We already suspect that the distribution is <u>not</u> normal because normal distributions are symmetrical (skewness = 0) and have "skinny" tails (excess kurtosis = 0). Neither is the case for these data as Table 3.5 shows. Skewness and heavy tails are indications of outliers in the sample. Our concern is that outliers are common in this process (market) and that this sample is drawn from a population that has a similarly skewed and fat-tailed shape.

There are many tests for normality. We shall use one known as the Jarque-Bera (JB) test. The statistic produced by his test has a chi-squared limiting distribution with two degrees of freedom. Provided the sample is large enough to emulate the asymptotic properties of its limiting distribution one rejects the hypothesis of normality if the JB statistic exceeds 5.99. The J-B Test Statistic for *evr* data is 57.4658, Thus, the JB test statistic has us rejecting the null and suggests that the *evr* data is not normally distributed.

Another important question is whether the variance is finite. That is, does the second moment exist, a requirement for normality? There is a large and growing literature on infinite variance models and extreme value theory that goes beyond the scope of this book. A partial list of references appear at the end of this chapter. Below, using the Granger-Orr (1972) test for infinite variance we find that the sample variance may converge to a finite number. If the graph in Figure 3.11 pointed up at the right end this would indicate an infinite variance for the sample, suggesting that the normal assumption is incorrect. But we do not have that condition so we reserve judgment for the present.

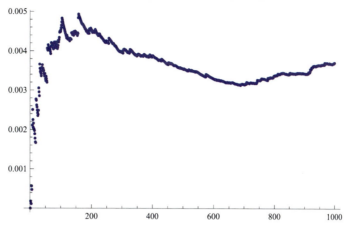

Figure 3.11. Granger-Orr graphical running variance test on *evr* data

The assumption of normality imposes a set of strong conditions. Notably, because the normal distribution is constructed from only its first two moments (meaning that it is a two parameter model dependent only on its mean and variance) the assumption of normality *requires* one to ignore skewness and heavy tails. Thus, to believe in the probability estimates in Table 3.6, one must believe that the world from which the data are drawn is symmetrical, has thin tails and a finite variance. In essence, the assumption of normality can be like a set of blinders. It rules out the presence of outliers, or more dangerously, blocks the presence of outliers from view. Relaxing the normality assumption permits a larger view the unknown world we wish to see.[9]

3.7.3. The stable approach to data

It happens that the normal distribution is a special case of a family of stable-Paretian (SP) distributions. The expansion of our discussion into stable distributions offers a way to estimate probabilities when extreme values are allowed. The assumption of normality distorts our view of the data away from its actual shape.

Comparing the expense ratio probabilities first given in Table 3.6 with those estimated under the SP hypothesis, in Table 3.7 we get a different view of how likely a certain building expense ratio is. In this case the normal assumption about the population produced probability estimates fairly close to those if one makes a non-normal stable assumption. This is fine when the distribution is close to normal but many distributions are not, leaving the opportunity for considerable estimation error.[10]

evr	normal probability	stable probability	difference
0.25	0.0839818	0.0737426	0.0102392
0.3	0.288662	0.282799	0.00586302
0.35	0.604179	0.61979	−0.0156108
0.4	0.861185	0.874215	−0.0130299
0.45	0.971748	0.969922	0.00182616
0.5	0.99682	0.99154	0.00527964

Table 3.7. San Francisco *evr* probabilities under different assumptions about the distribution

We can also plot the stable probabilities on quantile plots where deviations from the diagonal line at the ends are further indications of tail behavior. The left plot shows how far the tails are from normal. The right plot show how far the actual data are from the theoretical quantiles of a distribution having the stable parameters we estimated.

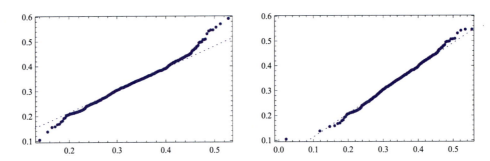

Figure 3.12. Quantile-Quantile Plots comparing data to normal (left) and theoretical stable distributions

Let's change tactics and deal with dataset under the assumption that it was drawn from a population having a stable distribution that is not normal.

Paying careful attention to the tails of the distribution, notice the similarity in the shape of the histogram of the actual data to the shape of a plot of the stable *pdf*. Again, focusing on the tails, contrast that with the assumption of normality made earlier as shown in the far right plot below. The assumption of normality distorts our view of the data away from its actual shape. Note how *pdf* of the stable distribution matches the histogram better than the normal distribution does in Figure 3.13.

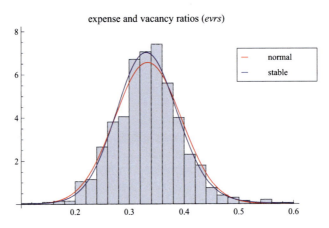

Figure 3.13. *evr* histogram, theoretical norm and stable *pdf*s from data parameters

The estimated stable parameters (reported again for reference below) included an α that was close to the normal (where $\alpha = 2$, more about this in Chapter 6). This is why our normal assumption produced estimated probabilities reasonably close to those calculated with parameters from our stable fit (See Chapter 6 for further discussion of how stable distributions may be used for real estate data).

α	1.89403
β	0.399657
μ	0.334158
σ	0.0402889

But let's assume we encounter a dataset in which α is considerably below 2. α is an exponent in the characteristic function of the SP distribution so small movements can make a big difference. We now create a dataset of 1000 observations for such a market using a random number generator and repeat our tests. We assume this market has an $\alpha = 1.5$, leaving other parameters the same. The Granger-Orr plot indicates that the variance is infinite.

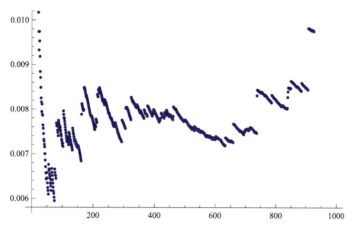

Figure 3.14. Granger-Orr graphical running variance test on random data with $\alpha \approx 1.5$

Of course this finite sample has a mean and a variance. We can create the familiar bell-shaped plot of the normal distribution that would be suggested by only the mean and variance of the random data. Superimposing it over the histogram of the actual data is instructive. As you change the value of alpha from the incorrect value toward its correct value notice the change in the tails of the *pdf*.

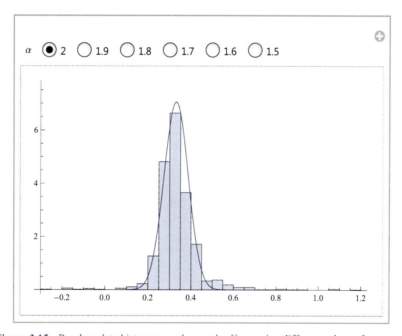

Figure 3.15. Random data histogram and normal *pdf* assuming different values of α

While the change in Figure 3.15 is not overly dramatic, calculating the probabilities both ways and computing the difference shows the magnitude of the error traceable to the normal assumption. The simple conclusion is that as α falls away from 2 (the normal case) and the tails become heavier the magnitude of the error increases. In Table 3.8 imagine you represented to your client that the probability of a 25% *evr* was 20% based on the assumption of normality when in fact it was under 10%, clearly an unacceptable error, perhaps bordering on negligent misrepresentation.

quantile	normal probability	stable probability	difference
0.25	0.206312	0.0942532	0.112059
0.3	0.36871	0.325277	0.0434326
0.35	0.55912	0.657359	−0.0982388
0.4	0.736552	0.854324	−0.117772
0.45	0.867952	0.930251	−0.0622988
0.5	0.945287	0.959817	−0.0145304

Table 3.8. Random data probabilities under different assumptions about the distribution

3.7.4. Linear relationships

In the general caution at the beginning of this chapter we cast doubt on rules of thumb based on their linear nature. This admonition carries over to the analysis of data. There is a very practical reason for a natural dependence on linear models - they offer tools that are considered "tractable", a term that mathematicians use to mean manageable. However, manageable does not necessarily mean realistic or even correct. There are a number of opportunities, using linear models common to most spreadsheet programs, to either dazzle a client with numbers that argue for a spurious relationship or data mine to the point of disproving a claim that is in fact true. Time and space do not allow a full elaboration of these traps, such being left to econometric texts. However, since we have a dataset at hand, let's use it to provide several examples of suspected relationships and look a bit closer at their true nature.

3.7.5. Linear transformations

Linear transformations involve subjecting each observation to either the addition or subtraction of a constant or the multiplication by a constant (which, if in the form of a reciprocal can turn into division). Many times these manipulations are harmless and permissible. Here is an example.

Suppose that we know that vacancy in the market from which our *evr* data were drawn was 4% during the time in question. We can remove this from *evr* to leave us with just the expense ratio. Note that this does not change the shape of the distribution, it only moves the range down 4% in Figure 3.16. This is a "shift" of the distribution along the *x*-axis. One of the important and useful properties of stable distributions is that they retain their shape under linear transformation.[11] Subtracting a constant from each observation as we have done here is a form of linear transformation. As long as the value of the constant is known such an adjustment can be made and all the conclusions reached earlier still hold.

	evr	exp ratio
Max	0.591824	0.551824
Min	0.1043	0.0643

Table 3.9. Extreme Observations for *evr* data and expense ratio data

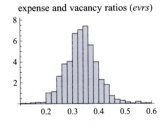 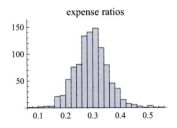

Figure 3.16. Histograms for *evr* data (left) and expense ratio data (right)

3.7.6. Spurious relationships

One might claim that property characteristics influence the expense ratio. A reasonable example of this would be a claim that older buildings have higher expenses. This suggests that expense ratios increase as property age increases. Since building age is in our dataset we can plot these in Figure 3.17 for an initial indication of a relationship.

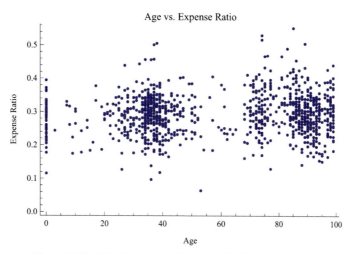

Figure 3.17. Plot of expense ratio against building age

It doesn't look like there is much in the way of a relationship there. Do owners of these buildings just charge higher rents to offset the higher expenses? Likewise in Figure 3.18 there seems to be little relationship between our two size measures, building square footage or number of units, and expense ratios.

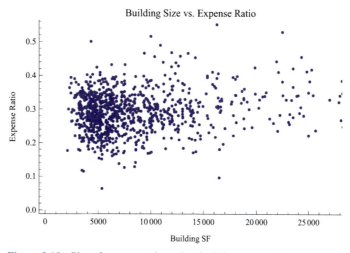

Figure 3.18. Plot of expense ratio against building square footage

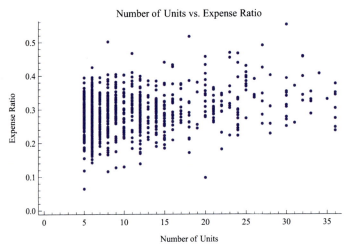

Figure 3.19. Plot of expense ratio against number of units

There might be a weak inverse relationship between *GRM* and expense ratios (Figure 3.20). However, intuition and the weakness of the relationship in the plot does not recommend pursuing this.

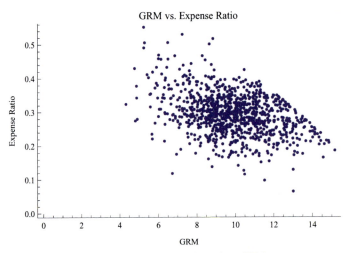

Figure 3.20. Plot of expense ratio against *GRM*

Each of the foregoing have tested and discarded a relationship based on a graph of the data. Later, while considering the Price Per Unit (*PPU*) rule of thumb, we will extend the investigation of a suspected relationship to regression analysis.

3.8. Cash-on-cash (*C/C*) return

Arguably, Cash-on-Cash Return (*C/C*) is the best of the first year measures because, if we are talking about after-tax cash-on-cash return, both debt payments and taxes are considered. In all types and sizes of properties market participants value the cash-on-cash measure. Some even prefer it over multi-period models because it requires no estimation of future income.

Unfortunately, for all its value it is the least observable. Because terms of debt rarely appear and income taxes never appear in datasets, we have only theory on which to rely. The data to confirm any theory we may construct are sparse at best. This rule of thumb and its related theory will be dealt with in connection with our discussion of lender issues in Chapter 12.

3.9. Price per unit (*PPU*)

Perhaps the simplest question asked is: "How much per foot?" or "How much per acre?" Many people buy certain property types based on whether its price is appropriately scaled to its size. Some people spend considerable time reviewing sales and offerings to determine what price per unit the market supports. Table 3.10 shows the average price per unit for our two cities.

We have suggested that purchasers of smaller properties tend to make decisions based on rough measures of investment value. One could also argue that as one buys larger properties there are economies of scale involved, more dwelling units per land unit, and more sophisticated parties. Thus, one might expect the price per unit to decline as property size increases. These are known as "testable hypotheses". That is, if we collect data associated with such assertions we can test their validity. Below we compute the average price per unit from our two datasets, noting that prices in San Francisco were higher than those in LA. (Caution is advised as the SF data were gathered over a five year period and the LA data were gathered over approximately the last six months of that same period. Here we faced a difficult choice. Because the comparison is between two markets of different size there are fewer sale observations over the same period of time in the smaller market. Nonetheless, it is desirable to compare datasets of approximately the same size.)

Mean price per unit in Los Angeles	71,936.
Mean price per unit in San Francisco	118,847.

Table 3.10. Price per unit in Los Angeles and San Francisco

Below in Table 3.11 we divide the San Francisco data into approximately half using >10 units as "large" to learn that people apparently do pay more for smaller units.

	# of Sales	Average Price
Large SF	424	103,901.
Small SF	576	129,849.

Table 3.11. San Francisco price per unit by size category

The same appears to hold for the LA data (Table 3.12).

	# of Sales	Average Price
Large LA	343	63,550.
Small LA	357	79,992.

Table 3.12. Los Angeles price per unit by size category

On the surface, it appears we are correct in our theory about small properties and price, but this merely suggests a relationship between two groups of data. Does this relationship hold generally? A plot of the San Francisco data indicate a weak negative relationship between unit price and building size. We see fewer large buildings in the higher price per unit range. But how strong is the relationship in general? As we shall see, it is not very strong at all.

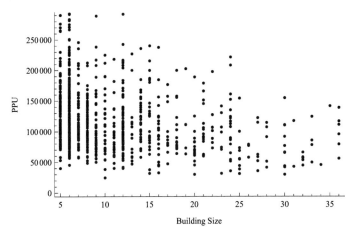

Figure 3.21. San Francisco price per unit vs. building size

Regression analysis is a process that attempts to specify a rule, known as a functional relationship, which governs the connection between two variables. Univariate analysis, which we have performed here, involves a single variable, building size. Ordinary Least Squares (OLS) Regression finds the "least squares" line that purports to describe how price per unit "functions" as building size grows. The weakness of the relationship as seen in the plot (Figure 3.21), together with the low T-Statistic and R-Squared values in the regression analysis (Table 3.13) suggests that there is no relationship in this case. The low F-Statistic suggests that the model does not apply. Another interpretation of this is that most of the model behavior is captured in the intercept, meaning that we are little better off using the conditional probability suggested by OLS than we would be using the unconditional mean for prediction. All of this is to warn the reader that when using the sort of easy data analysis provided in many popular spreadsheet packages one must be careful to interpret the results correctly.[12]

$$\text{Model Fit is } 119\,205. - 20.2564\,x$$

$$\text{Standard Error of the Coefficients are } \begin{matrix} 1792.87 & \text{Intercept} \\ 15.8767 & \text{Units} \end{matrix}$$

$$\text{Parameter T Statistics are } \begin{matrix} 66.4885 & \text{Intercept} \\ -1.27586 & \text{Units} \end{matrix}$$

$$\text{Parameter P values are } \begin{matrix} 6.27746745280 \times 10^{-369} & \text{Intercept} \\ 0.202302 & \text{Units} \end{matrix}$$

Parameter Confidence Intervals are

	Lower 95%	Upper 95%
Intercept	115 687.	122 724.
Units	-51.412	10.8991

Number of observations are 1000
Adjusted R Square is 0.000628054
R Squared is 0.00162843
Standard Error is 55 967.4

ANOVA Table

	DF	SS	MS	F-Statistic	P-Value
x	1	5.10401×10^9	5.10401×10^9	1.62782	0.202302
Error	998	3.12922×10^{12}	3.13549×10^9		
Total	999	3.13432×10^{12}			

Table 3.13. Regression of San Francisco value on number of units

If higher prices for small properties are persistent across time and other markets, we can say it is not because of the number of units in the building. This raises more questions: Do higher prices result from a larger land component? One can test for the significance of the price per unit difference, given lot size. Separate from the small building value question, these data can be used to investigate other matters. Are there economies of scale? One can relate expense ratio to size via a closer examination of price per unit. Is there a time component? Price per unit as a function of the date sold can give some insight into pricing trends.

3.10. Other data issues

Many excellent texts cover statistics in depth. We close this chapter with some red flags that require further study.

One should exercise care when comparing a continuous variable such as expense ratios to a discrete variable such as number of units. There are also problems when one variable is constrained as expense ratios are to [0,1] differently than the other such as age $[R_+]$. These issues also cause problems in a regression context, something discussed in the Appendix to Chapter 6.

Sample size is a factor in data analysis. We arbitrarily chose a random sample of data from a larger dataset for the above illustrations. Taking the entire dataset or just a larger sample could improve our conclusions. This dataset is drawn from a large area for which we have several subsets based on location. A reductionist view would have one analyzing the data from each subset. What would your expectation be about data drawn from an area in Los Angeles near the ocean versus an area in Central LA? An expansionist view would collect data from other cities and compare them. What would your expectation be about expense ratios in Los Angeles vs. Minneapolis? San Francisco vs. Madrid, Spain?

The San Francisco dataset covers a long period of time. There is little reason to believe that expense ratios are time dependent. On the other hand, local building code and zoning laws together with market demands can affect the level of services landlords offer tenants. The price of these services - in a free market - is impounded into the rent. Expenses as a portion of rent will change with these factors. Price-restricted markets, those with rent control such as San Francisco, may show a decline in expense ratios as the cost of services are transferred to tenants because landlords cannot recover those costs in the rent.

One intuitively promising idea is that expense ratios are related to clientele occupying the unit. To the extent that area serves as a proxy for this we could compare the "Area" field to the expense ratio data to see if there is a relationship. Although this is possible in *Mathematica*, other statistical software packages do a better job of this. One should remain neutral about the outcome of any such study. Recall that we postulated earlier that expense ratios should increase with age and that was not supported by the data!

The use of stable-Paretian models is relatively new. The tools we have at the present may be considered crude when compared to those available for normal distributions. Often we must rely on visual/graphic tests that do not provide strong conclusions. Current active research in the area of heavy tails deserves watching carefully. Small comfort that it is, at present the only thing we can say for certain is that the assumption of normality may very often produce measurement errors. Therefore, the investigation of other aspects of the distribution, however flawed, has probative value and should not be ignored.

One last time we must be reminded that, regardless of how good the data and the models become in time, there is no magic bullet here. We still have to rely on a careful inspection of the property itself to be confident about a certain expense ratio or capitalization rate for that particular property. Remember that data do not supplant good fieldwork at the site, it only provides context about the market in which the property competes for tenants and investors. It is the general understanding of the market that comes from data analysis. Such understanding is the foundation for successful "buy" and "sell" decisions relating to individual properties.

Endnotes

[1] This and most other data described in this book was furnished by CoStar. As of the Fall of 2011 CoStar could be located on the Internet at http://www.costar.com/

[2] because $rrr = \frac{8.89802}{7} - 1 = 0.2711$

[3] The graphic is a census map. The numbers on the map are census district numbers and do not affect any calculation.

[4] Note that if $g = 0$ in Equation 3.12 you have the assumption of unchanging income in Equation 3.2.

[5] It also requires d and g to be different from each other so that the denominator is not zero and introduces a host of problems if d is less than g, problems we will not address here. Note also that if $cf_n = cf_0(1 + g)^n$, then $\sum_{n=1}^{t} \frac{cf_n}{(1+d)^n}$ becomes $t*cf_0$ when $g = d$ because the $(1 + ?)^n$ terms cancel.

[6] This is the "Gordon Growth Model" in finance.

[7] For a review of the way the probability distribution function and the cumulative distribution function are related, see Appendix to this chapter.

[8] We are taking liberties here. The word "outlier" has a stricter meaning to statisticians, indicating an observation that is in error. We will use "outlier" and "extreme value" interchangably, ignoring the distinction for the moment. We become a little more formal in Chapter 7.

[9] This section intended to introduce ideas about non-normality using as an example expense and vacancy rates (*evr*). The alert reader will immediately recognized that since *evr* data is, by definition, bounded strictly positive ($0 < evr < 1$), such data can never be normally distributed. This, while true, does not change the importance of critically examining data that might be normal to determine if in fact it is normal.

[10] The estimation methodology was first developed by Prof. John P. Nolan of the Mathematics and Statistics Department of American University in Washington, DC. As of the Fall of 2011 Dr. Nolan could be reached at Robust Analysis, Inc.

[11] This shape preserving quality includes additivity and requires common alpha values. That is, neither linear transformation nor adding together many random variables with the same alpha change the shape of the distribution. These properties are important to the theoretical notion that value is affected by many bits of information arriving randomly which, in aggregate, move value up or down.

[12] One should know that simple OLS regression produces incorrect coefficient estimates in the presence of non-normal stable data. An excellent source for this, including a real estate dataset as an example is McCulloch (1998).

References

Adler, Robert J.; Feldman, Raisa E., and Taqqu, Murad S. A Practical Guide to Heavy Tails: Statistical Techniques and Applications. Boston, MA: Birkhauser; 1998.

Corgel, J. B. , Ling, D. C., & Smith, H. C. (2001). Real Estate Perspectives: An Introduction to Real Estate (4th ed.). New York, NY: McGraw-Hill.

Granger, C.W.J. and D. Orr, "Infinite Variance" and Research Strategy in Time Series Analysis. Journal of the American Statistical Association, 1972. **67**(338): p. 275-285.

McCulloch, J. Huston. Linear Regression with Stable Disturbances. Adler, Robert J.; Feldman, Raisa E., and Taqqu, Murad S., Editors. A Practical Guide to Heavy Tails: Statistical Techniques and Applications. Boston, MA: Birkhauser; 1998; pp. 359-376.

Nolan, John P. "Maximum Likelihood Estimation and Diagnostics for Stable Distributions". [Working Paper]. 1998.

Nolan, John P. "Numerical Calculation of Stable Densities and Distribution Functions". Communications in Statistics - Stochastic Models. 1997; 13(4):759-774.

Nolan, John P. "Parameterizations and Modes of Stable Distributions". Statistics and Probability Letters. 1998 Jun; 38(2):187-195.

Nolan, John P. "Univariate Stable Distributions: Parameterization and Software". Adler, Robert J.; Feldman, Raisa E., and Taqqu, Murad S., Editors. A Practical Guide to Heavy Tails: Statistical Techniques and Applications. Boston, MA: Birkhauser; 1998; pp. 527-533.

Problems

1. There are several reasons cash on cash return is difficult to analyze in aggregate form. Why is data for this measure so difficult to obtain?
2. How does corporate accounting in finance differ from real estate investment accounting?
3. Using Figure 3.5 increase the rate and the time to change the shape of the curve. Does its general shape (constantly increasing) seem plausible? What do changes in the variables in this plot say about risk as time and rate increase?
4. Figure 3.6 Shows the number of observations between arbitrary lower and upper bounds of *evr* data. As you change the horizontal grid lines the number of observations in the middle changes. What does this say about the probability of the building you are analyzing having its *evr* located between the two lines?
5. Change the bounds for Figure 3.10 to the same values you chose for Figure 3.6. Elaborate on your answer to the previous question.
6. The histogram in Figure 3.15 has a barely imperceptible bar at the far lower right near the *x* axis which represents at least one extreme value. How does this relate to reducing the value of α to 1.5?
7. If the R Squared value for the regression summarized in Table 3.13 been .75 rather than the value shown, how would that have changed your opinion of the value of the model?
8. Navigate to the Capitalization Rate Probability page on the Wolfram Demonstrations Project site. Select San Francisco and note the probability. Change the city to Chicago and note the change in probability. Why might the probability change in that direction when moving between those two cities?

Appendix - Connecting the *CDF* and the *pdf*

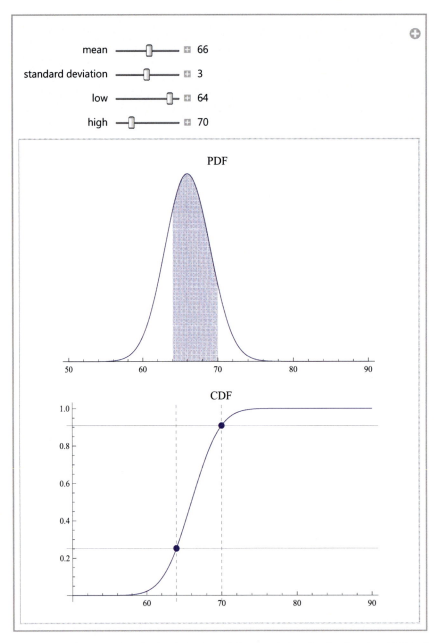

The probability density function (*pdf* - upper plot) is the derivative of the cumulative density function (*CDF* - lower plot). This elegant relationship is illustrated here. The default plot of the *pdf* answers the question, "How much of the distribution of a random variable is found in the filled area; that is, how much probability mass is there between observation values equal to or more than 64 and equal to or fewer than 70?"

The *CDF* is more helpful. By reading the axis you can estimate the probability of a particular observation within that range: take the difference between 90.8%, the probability of values below 70, and 25.2%, the probability of values below 63, to get 65.6%

The calculations here are based on the normal distribution, which is completely determined by its mean and standard deviation. Changing these values changes the result of probability estimates. Change the values to mean = 67.8, std dev = 2.3, low = 50 and high = 70. You can see that the chance of seeing a value at or below 70 is approximately 81%. There is no need to subtract as in the default view because the lower bound of 50 is presumed to have a zero probability.

4

Fundamental Real Estate Analysis

"Compound interest is the eighth wonder of the world."

Attributed to *Albert Einstein* and others

4.1. Introduction

There are a number of excellent real estate analysis programs for practitioner use in "numbers crunching". Essentially, these are variant forms of spreadsheets that perform *numerical* analysis. A simple Excel version of such a program is included with the electronic files for this chapter to provide the reader with a fully elaborated example in a familiar context. Programs such as these all perform the same basic tasks, usually offering different menus of reporting and printing options to dress up the appearance of the analysis for use with clients. In this chapter we will:

- List all the relevant variables required to perform a complete multiperiod discounted cash flow analysis of a real estate investment;
- Perform that analysis, computing various performance measures, including net present value and internal rate of return;
- Demonstrate the interdependencies between the variables;
- Set up a series of scenarios based on the variables for simple risk evaluation via sensitivity testing; and
- Introduce ways in which data may be used to further understand the process.

4.1.1. The role of computational aids

Much of the heavy lifting of this chapter is done by *Mathematica*. Technical computing software performs a different function than spreadsheet programs. It can, and we will, make any numerical calculation that can be done by a spreadsheet program. The primary value of the *Mathematica* approach is to perform *symbolic* analysis. That is, rather than operating on the numbers of a specific real estate project, it solves for the relationships between the variables used in the mathematics to reach the conclusions that drive business decisions for *all* projects. In that, *Mathematica* (a) offers the ability to solve almost any equation for almost any variable, thus providing a more general view of the process not tied to any particular investment, and (b) permits one to look behind spreadsheet icons at their inner workings to more fully understand the total process.

There are several good reasons for employing the power of Mathematica:

- Understanding general rules permits one to draw on that knowledge when encountering exceptions, when addressing more complex problems and when using data. Simply stated, there are a few rules that virtually always work. The deductive reasoning behind those rules is expressed in symbols and equations. Familiarity with those symbols and equations leaves one with an understanding of *why* good business decisions *are* good business decisions.
- The market is competitive. Principals and brokers compete for the best deals. Many decisions must be made very fast. Although spreadsheets are ubiquitous, in a competition between two parties one of whom knows only how to click on an Excel icon and the other knows what is happening behind that icon, the latter is able to react more swiftly, avoid fundamental errors and perhaps consummate better transactions.
- The use of data can be tricky. The old saying "You can prove anything with numbers" is only true for a loose definition of "prove". The analyst who is well grounded in the theory of real estate and its underlying mathematics is able to separate the proper use of data from the improper. Understanding symbolic analysis is how one becomes well grounded in theory.
- We can observe sale prices and, to some extent, extrapolate returns investors achieve. Risk is another matter, much harder to observe. Behind every sale observation in our database are two parties, a buyer and a seller. These players engaged in a negotiation arriving at the price we see in our data. Inherent in that negotiation was an evaluation of the risk attendant to choices made by each party. We are curious about how that process works. It is useful to understand risk/return trade-offs each party must make to reach agreement on price.

Mathematica does the job we need done here, but with all powerful software one must use it only where appropriate. Below we will see that *Mathematica* can do things that are trivial or even silly. *Mathematica* is agnostic about the appropriateness or usefulness of its conclusions. It, like all software, is merely a tool in the hands of the user. *Mathematica* is a powerful tool, so powerful that it will ALWAYS return the right answer. But the real power in the hands of a careful user is *Mathematica*'s ability to guide the user to asking the right questions. Very often when an answer generated by *Mathematica* is not the expected answer it is because one has asked the wrong question.

In this chapter, because we are interested in the nuts and bolts, we will keep most symbolic manipulation visible using common abbreviations in the notation. More *Mathematica* syntax and programming statements will be revealed in this chapter than were shown in prior chapters. The non-programmer can safely ignore these. In a later chapter we will create some "modules" that will automate this process. Modules are *Mathematica*'s equivalent of the icons one uses in a spreadsheet program. Once one knows the inner workings of the process - but not before - it is efficient to automate repetitive tasks with modules and icons.

A note about the font style below may be helpful. Throughout this book in general when a variable, such as *noi*, is used in the text it is in italics. But if **noi** is used in *Mathematica* syntax it is bold. Likewise, **data** and **data names** are bold. The occasional exception may be found when a text paragraph containing output is produced by *Mathematica* in which case no font style may be applied. These, sometimes regrettable, formatting issues never affect the meaning of the subject or any computatations.

4.2. Deterministic variables of discounted cash flow analysis

General inputs, rule of thumb measures and other investment performance variable definitions are:

dp	=	down payment, made at $t=0$ and assumed to be Jan 1 of the acquisition year
cf_0	=	initial after–tax cash flow (*atcf*) to be received at the end of year 1
cf_n	=	subsequent year cash flows, compounded annually based on growth rate, g
cr_i	=	'going–in' capitalization rate, the capitalization rate at purchase
cr_o	=	'going–out' capitalization rate, the capitalization rate at sale
r	=	discount rate (when $npv = 0$ this is the internal rate of return)
g	=	growth rate for cash flow, mentioned above
n	=	specific year of the holding period (an iterator in *Mathematica* statements)
k	=	length of holding period (also year of sale, presumed to occur on Dec 31)
grm	=	gross rent multiplier
ppu	=	price per unit
$ccRet$	=	cash on cash return
npv	=	net present value
irr	=	internal rate of return

Operating variable definitions are:

gsi	=	gross scheduled income
vac	=	vacancy
$vacrt$	=	vacancy factor (a rate multiplied times gsi)
egi	=	effective gross income
exp	=	operating expenses
$exprt$	=	expense factor (a rate multiplied times egi)
noi	=	net operating income (debt free cash flow)
$btcf$	=	before–tax cash flow

Financing variable definitions are:

ltv	=	loan–to–value ratio
dcr	=	debt coverage ratio
ds	=	debt service (usually paid monthly but often annualized)
i	=	interest rate (per payment period – if monthly, then i = annual interest/12)
$initln$	=	initial loan balance
t	=	time period in payment periods over which the loan is fully amortized(if monthly, then t = years over which loan is amortized $*12$)
bal_n	=	balance at end of period n
int_n	=	interest paid over the 12 months prior to n

Income tax variable definitions are:

tx	=	income tax consequences
$txrt$	=	ordinary income tax rate
$txbl$	=	real estate taxable income
$basis$	=	income tax basis ($dp + initln - accdepn$)
$land$	=	allocation of tax basis to land (given as a percent of total value)
$depr$	=	annual depreciation
$dprt$	=	depreciation rate

Equity reversion (net after-tax sale proceeds) variable definitions are:

sp	=	sale price calculated as $\frac{noi_{k+1}}{cr_o}$
accdp	=	accumulated depreciation
cgtx	=	capital gains tax ($cg * cgrt$)
cg	=	capital gain ($sp - basis - sc$)
cgrt	=	capital gain tax rate (assumed to be a flat percentage of gain)
recaprt	=	tax rate on depreciation recapture
sc	=	sale costs ($scrt * sp$)
scrt	=	sale cost rate
endbal	=	balance of loan outstanding at the time of sale
ppmt	=	prepayment penalty on loan
er	=	after–tax equity reversion ($sp - sc - endbal - ppmt - cgtx$)

4.3. Single year relationships and project data

Relationships between the variables *for a single first year* are as follows:

```
vac = gsi * vacrt;
egi = gsi - vac;
exp = egi * exprt;
noi = gsi - vac - exp;
```
$ds = 12 \left(i / \left(1 - 1 / (1 + i)^t \right) \right) \text{initln};$
```
btcf = noi - ds;
grm = (dp + initln) / gsi;
ppu = (dp + initln) / units;
dcr = noi / ds;
ltv = initln / (dp + initln);
basis = dp + initln;
depn = (basis - (basis * land)) * dprt;
```
$bal_{12} = ds / 12 \left(1 - 1 / (1 + i)^{t-12} \right) / i;$
$int_t = ds - (initln - bal_{12});$
```
txbl = noi - int_t - depn;
tx = txbl * txrt;
cf0 = btcf - tx;
cri = noi / (dp + initln);
ccRet = cf0 / dp;
```

Figure 4.1. First year relationships between the variables

As an example of a specific project, details are entered below in a list of rules named **"data"**. These match the companion Excel worksheet provided.[1]

Down payment	375 000	Interest rate (monthly)	0.00916667
Gross scheduled income	200 000	Initial loan balance	875 000
Vacancy rate	0.1	Loan term (months)	360
Expense rate	0.35	Hurdle rate for *npv*	0.13
Tax rate	0.35	Holding period	6
Depreciation rate	0.0363636	Sale cost rate	0.075
Land component	0.3	Capital gain rate	0.15
Going–out cap rate	0.0936	Recapture rate	0.25
Growth rate	0.03	Prepayment penalty	0
		Number of units	22

Table 4.1. Input data for sample project

Important: There are two *Mathematica* input conventions that appear repeatedly. First, the convention " /. " may be read as "given that". It is used to insert values from the data into any equation for the limited purpose of that particular computation. Second, the symbol "→" preceding a numerical value given a variable means that value is a "rule" to apply to the variable for the specific computation only.

For example, below we see

```
{cri, grm, ppu, ccRet, dcr, ltv} /. data
```

which may be read as: "provide a list of values for **cri**, **grm**, **ppu**, **ccRet**, **dcr**, and **ltv** *given the values in* "**data**". When formatted and evaluated the syntax above produces the list shown in Table 4.2.

Also, the syntax

```
gsi → 60 000
```

means that for the purpose of the present calculation the value of **gsi** is 60,000.

The relationships defined above handle the simple "rule of thumb" tests applied to first year performance discussed in Chapter 3.

Cap rate	0.0936
GRM	6.25
PPU	56 818.2
After–tax C/C	0.0554981
dcr	1.17007
ltv	0.7

Table 4.2. Rule of thumb values for sample project

We can also compute the monthly loan payment and first year after-tax cash flow. Note that since *ds* is defined as an annual amount we must divide out the 12 to obtain the monthly payment.

```
The monthly loan payment is: $8,332.83
The first year after-tax cash flow is: $20,811.78
```

Figures 4.2 and 4.3 show Excel output for first year inputs and computations

Basic Analysis		02/29/12			MARKET VAL		1250000	100.0000%	
Chapter 4 Base Example			GR RENT MULT	6.25	LOANS		875000	70.0000%	LTV
			PRICE/UNIT =	56818	MV EQUITY		375000	30.0000%	
	# UNITS	22							
			EX. LOANS	BALANCE	MO PMT	INT RATE		CONSTANT	TERM
ASSESSED LAND VALUE		300000.00	1ST MTG	875000.00	8332.83		11.00%		360.00
ASSESSED IMPVMT VAL		700000.00							
% LAND		30.00%							
% IMPROVEMENTS		70.00%							
BASIS CODE =		1.00							
	1250000.00	ACB @ ACQ							
GROSS POTENTIAL INCOME		100.00%		200000.00	RENT SCHED	AVG RENT		RENT	#UNITS
LESS:VACANCY		10.00%		20000.00	1 BR 1 BA		550.00	5500	10
EXPECTED GROSS INCOME		90.00%		180000.00	2 Br 1 Ba		750.00	3750	5
LESS: EXPENSES					2 Br 2 Ba		850.00	3400	4
TAXES (% VALUE)		0.00%			3 Br 2 Ba		1250.00	3750	3
INSURANCE		0.00%						0	
UTILITIES		0.00%			Laundry		266.67	267	
JANITORIAL		0.00%							
LANDSCAPING		0.00%			TOTAL			16667	22
SUPPLIES		0.00%			AVERAGE				
REPLACEMENTS		0.00%							
HVAC		0.00%							
MAINTENANCE		0.00%							
PROF MGT. @ _%		0.00%							
CAM REIMBURSEMENT		0.00%							
ACCUMULATED EXP		35.00%	63000.00		REQUIRED RATE OF RETURN				13.00%
					PROJ NOI CHANGE				3.00%
TOTAL EXPENSES		35.00%		63000.00	GOING OUT CAP RATE				9.36%
NET OPERATING INCOME				117000.00					
MARKET VAL CAP RATE		9.36%							

Figure 4.2. Input and first year operations for sample project

NET OPERATING INCOME				117000		
LESS: LOAN PAYMENTS		FIRST YEAR ONLY:				
INTEREST			96055			
PRINCIPAL			3939			
TOTAL DEBT SERVICE & DCR			99994	-99994		1.170
CASH FLOW BEFORE TAXES				17006	17006	4.53%
PLUS: PRIN PAYMENT				3939		
SUB-TOTAL				20945		
LESS: DEPRECIATION						
	LIFE =	27.5 YEARS				
	LAND =	375000				
ANNUAL DEP'N DEDUCT				-31818		
RE TAXABLE INCOME				-10874		
INCOME TAXES		TAX BRACKET=35% COMB S&F		-3806	3806	
AFTER TAX CF					20812	5.54981%

Figure 4.3. Input and first year operations for sample project

4.4. Multi-year relationships

For a multi-year projection we need computations spanning the years of the holding period.

For instance, we need a method for expressing each end-of-year loan balance. Figure 4.4 displays functions that produce metrics for various years.

$$\text{bal}[n\_] := \frac{ds}{12} \, \frac{1 - \frac{1}{(1+i)^{t-n*12}}}{i} \, ;$$

$$\text{cf}[n\_] := \text{noi} \, (1+g)^{n-1} - ds - \text{yrtx}[n];$$

$$\text{int}[n\_] := (ds \, /. \, \text{data}) - (\text{bal}[n-1] - \text{bal}[n]);$$

$$\text{netop}[n\_] := \text{noi} \, (1+g)^{n-1};$$

$$\text{yrtx}[n\_] := \left(\text{noi} \, (1+g)^{n-1} - \text{int}[n] - \text{depn}\right) * \text{txrt}$$

Figure 4.4. Multi-year relationships between the variables

Below is the output of a module that produces an amortization table for the loan.

n	Payment	Interest	Principal	Balance
1	8332.83	8020.83	311.996	874 688.
2	8332.83	8017.97	314.856	874 373.
3	8332.83	8015.09	317.743	874 055.
4	8332.83	8012.17	320.655	873 735.
5	8332.83	8009.24	323.595	873 411.
6	8332.83	8006.27	326.561	873 085.
7	8332.83	8003.28	329.554	872 755.
8	8332.83	8000.25	332.575	872 422.
9	8332.83	7997.21	335.624	872 087.
10	8332.83	7994.13	338.7	871 748.
11	8332.83	7991.02	341.805	871 406.
12	8332.83	7987.89	344.938	871 061.

The ending balance of the loan (**endbal**) is simply the balance at the end of the holding period, **k**

```
endbal = bal[k] /. data
```

843 381.

We also need information about how much interest is paid each year, which is a function of the debt service, the beginning of year balance and the end of year balance on the loan. While we are at it, we also create a table showing each year's interest that we name "**intpd**"

```
intpd = Table[int[n] /. data, {n, 1, k /. data}];
TableForm[intpd]
```

96 055.4
95 599.6
95 091.1
94 523.7
93 890.7
93 184.4

We can "pick out" any specific year of interest paid, for instance here is year 3 interest paid.

```
intpd[[3]]
```

95 091.1

We often assume that income grows by some rate over the holding period. Here, for simplicity, we assume the unlikely case of monotonic growth in a fixed unchanging percentage each year. "**netop**" calculates the NOI for any specific year, n, of the holding period. Notice that **netop** is a function not a variable name. A function is indicated by [**var_**] where **var** is the variable upon which the function is dependent for its value. We cannot use the name "**noi**" because it is already in use as a variable name for occasions when we wish to use it in a dataset. **netop[k]** is the net operating income for year **k**, the final year.

> **netop[k] /. data**
>
> 135 635.

A multi-period projection requires variables whose values change over the holding period. If, as we do here, the change in value is simple compounded annual growth, the convention is to compound the value from the day of purchase. Compounding of cash flows, however, is offset one year. The idea is that an investor on January 1 makes a decision to purchase based on his expectation of the income to be received at the end of the year. Thus, cf_1 is the initial cash flow to be received at the end of year one. The first year of compounding is 12 months later at the end of year two, hence only *n-1* years of *compounded cash flows* occur during the investor's holding period. This has repercussions when considering the equity reversion at the time of sale. Value compounds for the full *n* periods. The rationale is that at the time of sale, the next investor anticipates the end-of-year income (to be received 12 months after his acquisition) in making his acquisition decision. So the first investor collects the first cash flow without any compounding and *n-1* years of compounded cash flows but receives the benefit of *n* years of compounded cash flow because he prices the property for sale on the basis of *n* compounded cash flows. Figure 4.5 displays the sample project in spreadsheet form, having used the equations shown in Figure 4.4 with the input data from Table 4.1.

BEGINNING OF YEAR --->	1	2	3	4	5	6	7	8
END OF YEAR --->	0	1	2	3	4	5	6	7
VALUE	1250000	1287500	1326125	1365909	1406886	1449093	1492565	1537342
LOANS	875000	871061	866667	861764	856294	850191	843381	835784
EQUITY	375000	416439	459458	504145	550592	598902	649184	701559
GROSS SCHED INCOME		200000						
LESS:VACANCY & CREDIT LOSS		20000						
EFFECTIVE GROSS INCOME		180000						
LESS: EXPENSES		63000						
NET OPERATING INCOME		117000	120510	124125	127849	131685	135635	139704
CAPITALIZATION RATE		9.36%	9.36%	9.36%	9.36%	9.36%	9.36%	9.36%
NET OPERATING INCOME		117000	120510	124125	127849	131685	135635	139704
LESS: INTEREST PMTS		96055	95600	95091	94524	93891	93184	92396
LESS: DEPRECIATION		31818	31818	31818	31818	31818	31818	31818
RE TAXABLE INCOME		-10874	-6908	-2784	1507	5976	10632	15489
NET OPERATING INCOME		117000	120510	124125	127849	131685	135635	139704
LESS: TOTAL LN PMTS		99994	99994	99994	99994	99994	99994	99994
BEFORE TAX CASH FLOW		17006	20516	24131	27855	31691	35641	39710
INCOME TAX EFFECT		3806	2418	974	-528	-2091	-3721	-5421
AFTER TAX CASH FLOW		20812	22934	25106	27328	29599	31920	34289

Figure 4.5. Multi-year projections for sample project

We need a function that defines the after-tax cash flow in any given year. With that we can compute any specific year's cash flow (here we calculate cash flow from year #3, given the data. Note that, when rounded, this matches the third number in the last line of Figure 4.5).

> **cf[3] /. data**
>
> 25 105.7

We need to be able to calculate the annual income tax consequence of owning the property. Below we create a function to do this, assuming growing income, fixed interest on the loan and straight line depreciation. The illustration is for Year #3 income tax due. We use a different format to reflect dollars and cents and the accounting convention for negative numbers. Also, note that the sign convention differs between Excel and *Mathematica*. Below the value is shown as a negative number. The same amount in Figure 4.5 (third number in the second to list line) is shown as a positive. The answer does not change because subtracting a negative number is the same as adding.

```
Style[AccountingForm[yrtx[3] /. data, {5, 2}], Red]
```

(974.38)

4.5. Sale variables relationships

Relationships between the variables affecting the sale of the property at the end of the holding period are shown in Figure 4.6:

$$sp = \left(noi \, (1+g)^k\right) / cro;$$
$$cg = sp - sc - basis + accdp[k];$$
$$cgtx = (cg - accdp[k]) * cgrt + accdp[k] * recaprt;$$
$$sc = scrt * sp;$$
$$er = sp - sc - cgtx - endbal - ppmt;$$

Figure 4.6. Sale variable relationships for sample project

We need a way to determine the amount of depreciation deduction taken through any specific time period. This is needed for the annual tax consequence and to determine cost basis at the time of sale so that the capital gain amount may be calculated. Here is the accumulated depreciation for the project life, through the end year, **k**.

```
accdp[n_] := depn * n
accdp[k] /. data
```

190 909.

The alert reader will note we have taken some liberties with one computation. At this stage we provide a simplified approach to capital gain tax rates, assuming they are "flat" and applied to the entire gain. In fact, IRS regulations as of 2011 tax the gain at different rates depending on how long one owns the property.[2] Also, capital gain tax on that portion of the gain created by taking depreciation deductions is levied at a different "recapture" rate. Congress tinkers endlessly with the tax code and tax rates. Making precise tax computations is best done at the time of any particular analysis. The goal here is to be general and a flat capital gain tax serves that purpose.

For most of the history of capital gain taxes the important issue has been the spread between ordinary income tax rates and capital gain tax rates. To the extent that the latter is lower than the former, US tax policy rewards the long term ownership of depreciable assets by allowing taxpayers to convert ordinary income, otherwise taxed at a higher rate, to capital gain income that will be taxed at a lower rate. Figure 4.7 displays the after-tax consequences of a sale in each year of the holding period.

BEGINNING OF YEAR --->	1	2	3	4	5	6	7
END OF YEAR --->	0	1	2	3	4	5	6
VALUE	1250000	1287500	1326125	1365909	1406886	1449093	1492565
LOANS	875000	871061	866667	861764	856294	850191	843381
EQUITY	375000	416439	459458	504145	550592	598902	649184
ACCRUED DEPRECIATION		31818	63636	95455	127273	159091	190909
SALE COST PERCENT:							
7.50%		96562	99459	102443	105516	108682	111942
B-TAX SALES PROCEEDS		319876	359999	401701	445076	490220	537242
BASIS CALCULATION:							
GROSS SALE PRICE		1287500	1326125	1365909	1406886	1449093	1492565
ORIGINAL COST		1250000	1250000	1250000	1250000	1250000	1250000
LESS DEPRECIATION		-31818	-63636	-95455	-127273	-159091	-190909
PLUS COST OF SALE		96562	99459	102443	105516	108682	111942
OTHER BASIS ADJUST							
ACB AT SALE		1314744	1285823	1256989	1228244	1199591	1171033
CAPITAL GAIN		-27244	40302	108920	178642	249502	321532
REAL GAIN		-59063	-23334	13466	51370	90411	130623
TAX RATE	15.00%	15.00%	15.00%	15.00%	15.00%	15.00%	15.00%
RECOVERY RATE	25.00%	25.00%	25.00%	25.00%	25.00%	25.00%	25.00%
TAX		-905	12409	25883	39524	53334	67321
REVERSION CALCULATION:							
B-TAX SALES PROCEEDS	0.00	319876	359999	401701	445076	490220	537242
TAX		905	-12409	-25883	-39524	-53334	-67321
AFTER TAX EQ REVERSION		320781	347590	375818	405552	436886	469921

Figure 4.7. Sale computations for sample project

With these in place we can calculate the after-tax equity reversion, **er**. Given the data in Table 4.1 we get the same result in the lower right corner of Figure 4.7.

    er /. data

    469921.

4.6. The net present value

In order to determine net present value we need a function, Equation 4.1, that iterates each annual cash flow, takes the present value of each, sums these, adds the total to the present value of the after-tax equity reversion (**er**) and subtracts the initial investment (**dp**)

$$npv = \sum_{n=1}^{t} \frac{cf_n}{(1+r)^n} + \frac{er_t}{(1+r)^t} - dp \qquad (4.1)$$

Figure 4.8 displays the results of Equation 4.1 for the sample project. The lower right corner matches the *Mathematica* result

```
npv /. data
```
-47353.3

	BEGINNING OF YEAR →	1	2	3	4	5	6	7	YIELDS	NPV
	END OF YEAR →	0	1	2	3	4	5	6		
GPI										
EGI										
NOI		-250000	117000	120510	124125	127349	131685	1516258	11.3087%	
BTCF		-375000	17006	20516	24131	27355	31691	572883	11.9799%	
ATCF		-375000	20812	22934	25106	27328	29599	50841	10.1146%	-47353

Figure 4.8. Net present value and IRR computations for sample project

We certainly went to a lot of trouble only to learn that the property has a negative net present value. For our sample project this means its return does not support its cost of capital. Therefore, the potential buyer/investor will reject the project. Simply stated, a negative *npv* means this project is a bad deal from the buyer's perspective.

4.7. Insight into the analysis

Above we referred to the variables as "deterministic" because we can *determine* the outcome - the *npv* - by choosing particular variables.[3] The outcome changes every time the values of the variables change. With any change in the nominal value of a variable we explicitly *cause* a change in return, as measured by the *npv*. But there is usually also a corresponding *implicit* change in the risk. Understanding the inner workings of the variables provides an explicit view of risk and insight into the bargaining process. Seeing dependencies at the general level allows us to ask "if-then" type questions about the entire process, not just about a single acquisition.

To illustrate the concept of dependency in a very simple case, we look at the deterministic inputs that affect the gross rent multiplier. We know this equation as:

$$grm = \frac{value}{gross\ scheduled\ income} \qquad (4.2)$$

Hence it would seem that **grm** is simply dependent upon two variables, the value and the gross income. *Mathematica* sees it differently. Because value is defined above as a combination of two other deterministic variables, when evaluating the expression "**grm**" *Mathematica* considers and displays not only the variables in the equation above but the variables which are the antecedent primitives that make up value.

grm

$$\frac{dp + initln}{gsi}$$

So we see that, given how we have defined the variables, three things determine the **grm**, not the two we originally thought.

grm is too simple to illustrate the full benefit of *Mathematica*. One can easily see what determines **grm**. More difficult and complex examples exist at the other extreme. When we look at what affects after-tax cash flow, cf_0, we find a really ugly equation that incorporates all of the inputs leading to this output.

$$cf_0 = -txrt\left(-dprt\left(-land\left(dp + initln\right) + dp + initln\right) - exprt\left(gsi - gsi\,vacrt\right) + gsi\left(-vacrt\right) + gsi - \frac{12\,i\,initln}{1 - (i+1)^{-t}} - \frac{initln\left(1 - (i+1)^{12-t}\right)}{1 - (i+1)^{-t}} + initln\right) - exprt\left(gsi - gsi\,vacrt\right) + gsi\left(-vacrt\right) + gsi - \frac{12\,i\,initln}{1 - (i+1)^{-t}} \quad (4.3)$$

Ugly as the (4.3) may seem, it is really nothing more than a fairly long algebraic equation. One could, with some difficulty, construct such an equation from the formulae underlying the cells of a spreadsheet program.

Sometimes we can gain more useful insight by giving fixed numeric values to some of the variables. This has the beneficial effect of eliminating some of the variables as symbols in favor of constants. *Mathematica* further simplifies these constants by combining them where possible. It makes sense to substitute real numbers for those variables out of the owner's control. For instance, income tax rates, depreciation rates and land assessments are handed down by government. Taking part of the data from our list, below we reproduce Equation 4.3, providing temporary rules for tax rates and land assessments, thereby reducing the number of symbolic variables to cap rate, loan amount, interest rate, expense and vacancy rates and the gross scheduled income in Equation 4.4.[4] Do these affect cash flow? They certainly do and the owner has some influence on them.

$$cf_0 = -0.35\left(-0.0225806\,dp + exprt\,gsi\,(vacrt - 1) - gsi\,vacrt + gsi - \frac{12\,i\,initln\,(i+1)^t}{(i+1)^t - 1} - \frac{initln\left(1 - (i+1)^{12-t}\right)}{1 - (i+1)^{-t}} + 0.977419\,initln\right) + exprt\,gsi\,(vacrt - 1) - gsi\,vacrt + gsi - \frac{12\,i\,initln\,(i+1)^t}{(i+1)^t - 1} \quad (4.4)$$

Suppose we have already decided to purchase the property or we already own it. Under those conditions we may know the income, loan details and expense and vacancy factors. Inserting these values as numbers shows us that our cash flow is related to some constants and the interest rate. This permits us to consider explicitly the risk of variable interest rate loans. We also get a feel for the meaning of what is sometimes referred to as "positive leverage". Using capitalization rate > loan constant as the definition of positive leverage, we know that if leverage is positive then cash flow must be positive. (If you don't know that you have just discovered an important reason to use symbolic analysis). As the last constant term in Equation 4.5 is the net operating income, the aggregate of everything before that term must be smaller than that number for cash flow to be positive. This is, of course, critically dependent on the interest rate.[5]

$$cf_0 = \frac{10\,500\,000\,i}{\frac{1}{(i+1)^{360}} - 1} - 0.35\left(\frac{10\,500\,000\,i}{\frac{1}{(i+1)^{360}} - 1} + \frac{875\,000\left(1 - \frac{1}{(i+1)^{348}}\right)}{\frac{1}{(i+1)^{360}} - 1} + 963\,774.\right) + 117\,000. \quad (4.5)$$

Here we calculate the going-in capitalization rate, cr_i. Then, by varying the loan interest to a rate above and below the cap rate we show first negative leverage then positive leverage, this time using capitalization rate > interest rate as our definition. Note the difference in cash flow in Table 4.3.

$cr_i = .0936$	
int=.09	cf_0 = $26,652.30
int=.095	cf_0 = $28,921.20

Table 4.3. Initial cash flow with loan interest above and below the capitalization rate

Another awful looking equation, 4.6, is what goes into the witches brew we call the equity reversion. Note that since the loan is assumed to be paid off at the time of sale, the equation contains a constant, the final loan balance. This would only be a constant when the loan is a fixed interest rate loan. If the loan carried a variable rate of interest an equation would replace the constant.

$$er = \frac{1}{cro} \big(cro\,((dp + initln)\,(cgrt + dprt\,k\,(land - 1.)\,recaprt) - 1.\,ppmt - 843\,381.) + \\ gsi\,(g + 1)^k\,(cgrt\,(exprt\,(scrt\,(vacrt - 1.) - 1.\,vacrt + 1) - 1.\,scrt\,vacrt + scrt + vacrt - 1.) + \\ exprt\,(-1.\,scrt\,vacrt + scrt + vacrt - 1.) + scrt\,(vacrt - 1.) - 1.\,vacrt + 1) \big) \quad (4.6)$$

The capital gain is a little more accessible. Note below that it is, not surprisingly, quite dependent on the going-out capitalization rate.

$$cg = -\frac{1}{cro}\big(cro\,(dp + initln)\,(dprt\,k\,(land - 1) + 1) + (exprt - 1)\,gsi\,(scrt - 1)\,(vacrt - 1)\,(g + 1)^k\big) \quad (4.7)$$

If we are interested in what drives before-tax cash flow, Equation 4.8 shows that it is, of course, heavily dependent on the loan terms and net operating income.

$$btcf = (exprt - 1)\,gsi\,(vacrt - 1) - \frac{12\,i\,initln\,(i + 1)^t}{(i + 1)^t - 1} \quad (4.8)$$

A look at the variables that influence the tax consequence is the result of subtracting the symbolic expression for before-tax cash flow (**btcf**) from the symbolic expression for after-tax cash flow (**cf0** in the initial year). Note the recognizable components in Equation 4.9. The large term inside the parentheses multiplied by the tax rate is the taxable income from operating the property. Inside the parenthesis we see the components of real estate taxable income. If you stare at it long enough you will see the components of the net operating income, the interest deduction and the depreciation deduction.

$$-txrt\bigg(-dprt\,(-land\,(dp + initln) + dp + initln) - \\ exprt\,(gsi - gsi\,vacrt) + gsi\,(-vacrt) + gsi - \frac{12\,i\,initln}{1 - (i + 1)^{-t}} - \frac{initln\,(1 - (i + 1)^{12-t})}{1 - (i + 1)^{-t}} + initln\bigg) \quad (4.9)$$

Returning to an exceedingly simple term, as we learned in Chapter 3, the **noi** (or debt-free-before-tax annual cash flow) is really only a function of the gross income and two rates, vacancy and expenses.

$$noi = (exprt - 1)\,gsi\,(vacrt - 1) \quad (4.10)$$

Of course the debt service, **ds** (the annualized monthly loan payment) is a function of the interest rate, the term and the amount borrowed. Note the constant 12 multiplies out the monthly factor. This is necessary because **data** provide the interest rate and amortization period in monthly form.

$$ds = \frac{12\,i\,initln}{1-(i+1)^{-t}} \tag{4.11}$$

Some readers will recall the Ellwood tables. The equations underlying these are easily provided. Equation 4.12 is the factor from Elwood table #6 - the payment necessary to amortize a dollar. To produce this we divide out the 12 in our annual debt service equation and make `initln` equal to 1.

$$payment\ factor = \frac{i}{1-(i+1)^{-t}} \tag{4.12}$$

For museum curators and those who still own Ellwood tables, inserting numeric values for i and t produce one of the numbers found in the tables. This same number is more usually found with a hand calculator with financial function keys. Using $i = .10/12$ and $t = 360$, Equation 4.12 returns a monthly payment for a loan of $1.
[Note that the "%" symbol refers to the immediately prior input in the *Mathematica* notebook].

```
% /. {i → .1 / 12, t → 360}
```

0.00877572

When contemplating a VIR loan it can be a useful exercise is to ask what happens to cash flow if interest rates rise. In Equation 4.13 note the last term, the fraction with the "`i`" variables in it. Of course this term is monthly debt service (all the other variables sum to `noi`). Remembering what a negative exponent in the denominator means, we observe this function rising with rising interest rates. The entire term is negative so as it gets bigger, `btcf` grows smaller.

$$btcf = -exprt\,(gsi - gsi\,vacrt) + gsi\,(-vacrt) + gsi - \frac{12\,i\,initln}{1-(i+1)^{-t}} \tag{4.13}$$

Some equation decomposition is not helpful. Suppose the vacancy increases. What does this do to after-tax cash flow? Notice below it affects only part of the equation for first year cash flow. This is not too helpful as that term is also multiplied by the tax rate, something that has nothing to do with vacancy.

$$cf_0 = -txrt\left(\frac{1}{(i+1)^t - 1}\left(dp\,dprt\,(land-1)\left((i+1)^t - 1\right) + initln\left(dprt\,(land-1)\left((i+1)^t - 1\right) - (12\,i+1)(i+1)^t + (i+1)^{12}\right)\right) + (exprt - 1)\,gsi\,(vacrt - 1) + initln\right) + exprt\,gsi\,(vacrt - 1) - gsi\,vacrt + gsi - \frac{12\,i\,initln\,(i+1)^t}{(i+1)^t - 1} \tag{4.14}$$

We have covered just a few examples showing how insight into the process can be gained by dissecting the equations in component parts and looking at dependencies. Symbolic analysis is rather sterile and too abstract for some. Let's combine the approach taken above with the example and see how it may be applied in practice.

4.8. An illustration of bargaining

Most of the foregoing examples all have to do with isolating one deterministic variable. Does the change in one variable affect another? What about interest rates and capitalization rates? Vacancy and expenses? Are these related? Yes, they are. How about gross income and vacancy? What happens when two of these change? Let's take a simple example. When rents increase vacancy should also increase. Below we see they both affect net operating income. The key question is: how much of the increase in vacancy will neutralize the increase in income. This is the sort of thing that sensitivity testing does. We are interested in knowing how sensitive tenants are to rent increases. Will a small increase cause an exodus of tenants?[6] Assuming we are a potential buyer for the property in our example, and using the required rent raise (*rrr*) idea introduced in Chapter 3 we will look at how this process enters into the negotiations with the seller.

We will assume our building is in a market where the equilibrium *grm* is 6. We know the *grm* for our building is 6.25. We see that the building is, not surprisingly, offered for sale above the equilibrium *grm*. One cannot blame the seller for trying. Recalling the Mathematica function from Chapter 3, *rrr*, that tells us what rent raise is necessary to bring the acquisition to equilibrium and inserting the data for our project and our market-based rule for equilibrium *grm*, we compute the *rrr* and find that our required rent raise is 4.17%. After a careful rent survey in the neighborhood, we conclude that the tenants will pay the new rent without excessive turnover or increased vacancy. We now must modify our data to consider the higher rents to see what happens to net present value We define a new dataset, just like the first one. The only change is that *gsi* from the original data is increased by the *rrr*, given the equilibrium *grm*. Note that this means the buyer will have to institute an immediate rent raise upon the transfer of title to him to raise annual income to $208,333. Then we ask for the net present value given this new information, which is -10,353.20. Even with this improvement we still do not have a positive after-tax net present value. Something has to change. We believe we have extracted the most out of the tenants in the form of increased current rent. So we make a second change. We assume a higher annual growth rate, 3.25%, on cash flow. This produces a barely positive net present value of $85.

With a positive *npv* we know that the project has an *irr* just above the 13% hurdle rate. But these modifications to the deterministic variables have the buyer taking all the risk. Why? It is the buyer who must raise current rents. It is the buyer who must depend for his required return on a higher future rate of growth. The assumption of a higher growth in cash flow means the buyer is required to raise *future rents faster*.

How might we transfer some of the risk to the seller? The simple answer is to offer a lower price. A buyer refusing to pay a certain price is simultaneously refusing to take a certain level of risk for the reward offered. "**data3**" shows the reduction of down payment,[7] and therefore the reduction in price, necessary to put the project in the positive **npv** range. For this we modify **data1** which has a **gsi** of 1.041667 times the **gsi** of **data** but you will recall retains the original **g** = .03 of **data**.

	data3
dp	360 000
gsi	208 333.
vacrt	0.1
exprt	0.35
txrt	0.35
dprt	0.0363636
land	0.3
cro	0.0936
g	0.03
i	0.00916667
initln	875 000
t	360
r	0.13
k	6
scrt	0.075
cgrt	0.15
recaprt	0.25
ppmt	0
units	22

Note how this change improves first year performance as measured by the rules of thumb in Table 4.4. We have left the loan amount the same. This increases *ltv*, an indication of increased risk, but at the same time *dcr* has increased, an indication of reduced risk. One wonders if these perfectly offset. How we reconcile them to determine if, on balance, the risk is more or less than before will be left for later.

	data3
Cap Rate	0.0986842
GRM	5.928
PPU	56 136.4
After−tax CF	0.0662414
dcr	1.21882
ltv	0.708502

Table 4.4. Rules of thumb for sample project with revised down payment

	data3
npv	3306.97
cri	0.0986842
cro	0.0936
irr	irr

Table 4.5. Performance measures for sample project with modified inputs

Note the *npv* is positive in Table 4.5 but for this to be true capitalization rates must decline over the holding period. This is another risk factor that we will address in a later chapter.

The payoff for undertaking symbolic analysis begins to take shape. The positive *npv* outcome for **data3** says we again have approximately a 13% *irr*. *But is the second 13% irr the same 13%?* By now we should recognize that the two *irr*s, though nominally the same, are in fact not equivalent. It should be evident that the risk of the project must be different under **data3** than under

data2 even though *npv* is approximately zero in both cases and the *irr* is essentially the same.

The internal rate of return is the number that solves Equation 4.1 for *r* when *npv* is set to zero. Mathematicians consider this a problem of finding the 'root' of the equation and both reach the same result, an *irr* of 100.00 irr% for the data that produced the *npv* of $3306.97.

The focus of this discussion as regards *npv* and *irr* has been from the standpoint of the negotiation between two parties over a specific property, what might be termed a "micro" approach. There is a larger, "macro" view that asks the broader underlying question: Where do discount rates come from? Entire books are written in response to this question and is seems an injustice summarize them in a few phrases, but here is a way of thinking about them that fits in our context. In general, discount rates are the aggregate of all the negotiations that take place every day with all the buyers and sellers in a market. They encapsulate the combined expectations of a large number of people who compete with one another to acquire business opportunities that have uncertain outcomes. During times of positive business conditions characterized by solid growth, low inflation, high employment, low interest rates, discount rates will be lower than they are during the opposite times of negative macroeconomic news when buyers demand more compensation in the form of higher discount rates for undertaking risk when the horizon is comparatively dark.

The foregoing was but one of many tradeoffs that can occur to keep the return constant. The Wolfram Demonstrations Project and the Problems Section for this Chapter each provide an omnibus tool called "The Price-Terms Tradeoff" which measures how changes in any input or any number of inputs affect return

4.9. Another growth function

The above, quite standard *dcf* analysis, implies a fixed holding period terminating in a taxable sale. This assumption will be relaxed, in part, in future chapters. The above model also depends on the unrealistic assumption that the change in income and value over the holding period is constant and positive. Not only is this unlikely because of variable economic conditions, the successful "add labor" strategy we will discuss in Chapter 8 suggests that, due to the owner's active management, the property could undergo a dramatic transformation in the early years, resulting in a rapid change in value in those years, after which slower, "normal", appreciation takes place. To represent this we choose a modified logistic growth function, **val[n_]**, that exhibits two phases of value change, an early entrepreneurship phase with high appreciation, followed by a stabilized "normal" appreciation phase. Note that the dependent variable, *n*, means that value is dependent time. But the specific functional form of **val[n_]** is chosen such that the change in early years is different from changes occurring in later years.

$$val(n) = \frac{lc}{1+e^{-af*n}} + g*n \quad (4.15)$$

It is helpful to examine this function a little closer. Let us focus on the first term in Equation (4.15). Note that as *n* grows larger the second term in the denominator approaches zero making the entire denominator approach unity; hence the entire term approaches the numerator as a limit ($n \to \infty$). Thus the value selected for the numerator, which we can call the logistic constant ("**lc**"), is the answer to the question "how high is up" in the near term. It is this number that represents the *upper limit* of value improvement over the short run due to entrepreneurial effort in the early years of the holding period. In the field this is sometimes known as "upside" or "value added" potential. Figure 4.9 illustrates how value changes over ten years. Figure 4.10 displays alternatives using different values for **lc** keeping the denominator the same.

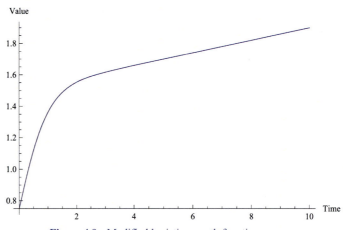

Figure 4.9. Modified logistic growth function

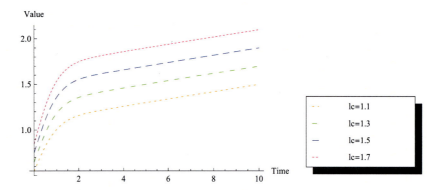

Figure 4.10. Various values of **lc** for modified logistic growth function

We now focus on the second constant in the first term of (4.15). It appears in the denominator operating on n, the acceleration factor ("`af`"). This answers the question "how fast" as it determines how quickly the limit is reached. It may be viewed as the *efficiency* of the entrepreneurial effort. Thus, the larger this constant, the more rapidly the limit is reached. Compare the value of the x axis at the sharp bend for each of the four alternative plots in Figure 4.11.

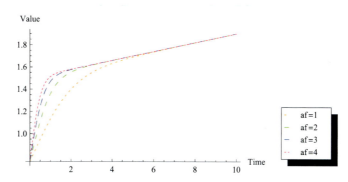

Figure 4.11. Various values of **af** for modified logistic growth function

The last term in the function involves what might be considered "normal" growth ("**g**"), stabilized after the early year "turnaround period".

In Figure 4.12 we compare two entrepreneurs, both in possession of properties with the same upside potential. One is more efficient, having an acceleration factor of 4 contrasted to **af** = 1 for the less efficient owner. The filled area represents the additional growth reaped in the early years for the more efficient owner. The two converge after about six years. But, one might surmise that the more efficient party would not hold the original property for the full six years, choosing instead to repeat the process once or twice in six years.

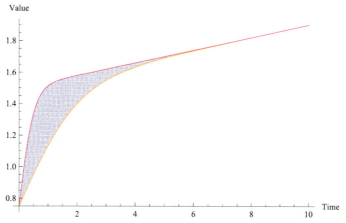

Figure 4.12. Different production functions for gain using different owners having different efficiency

Suppose the acceleration rate is influenced by institutional factors discussed in Chapter 2. We now take one investor as he considers two projects, one with an upside **lc** of 1.2 in a community that allows him to fully exercise his entrepreneurial skills, represented by **af** = 4, relatively unfettered by regulatory interference. A second property has greater upside of **lc** = 1.5 but is located in a community that imposes burdensome regulation constraining his entrepreneurial ability to an artificial **af** = 2. In Figure 4.13 we see the two growth rates do not converge in twenty years. This has implications for communities interested in attracting the real estate equivalent of incubator companies, developers who specialize in urban renewal and infill projects in older neighborhoods that benefit the community by raising the tax base.

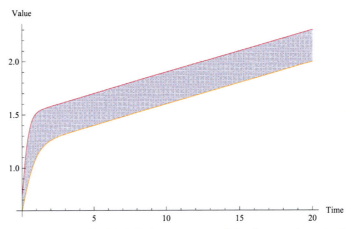

Figure 4.13. Property in different political jurisdictions, one constraining the owner's productive activities

One can smooth out an irregular growth rate to create an average over the holding period. Returning to the original logistic growth function (4.15) with fixed values for **lc** = 1.5 and **af** = 2, value increases just over 60% in the first three years.....

    `val[3]`

  1.61629

...but does not quite double in the first ten years, representing the flattening of the curve in the later years.

    `val[10]`

  1.9

For the sake of comparison we can look at what sort of continuous return would be necessary to produce the same outcome if a constant rate were earned over the same ten years. This involves solving for *r* in Equation 4.16:

$$e^{r10} = 1.9 \tag{4.16}$$

The value for *r* in Equation 4.16, the continuous compounding return, is 6.42%.

Figure 4.14 provides an interactive look at the modified logistic growth function and how various values of **lc** and **af** affect the rate at which capital multiplies.

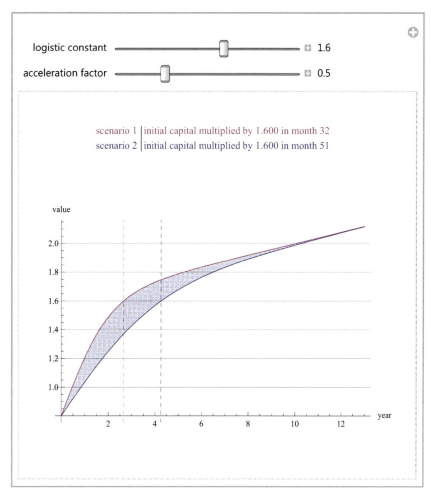

Figure 4.14. A range of possibilities for the modified logistic growth function

4.10. Data issues

In a perfect world (at least for researchers) investors would send in their loan payment coupons and income tax returns to some central data collection agency at the end of each year to be delivered to academics. Alas, we must agree that an imperfect world is a more interesting world. As we may never see after-tax cash flows, we need methods for thinking about how returns are generated in the real estate market. Before developing these methods further it is useful to think of the investment real estate market in a hierarchy composed of three distinct Tiers:

- Tier I constitutes the very small property market. For residential we limit this to properties having four or less dwelling units. Sometimes called the "One to Four Market", this is inhabited by small investors, some of whom live on the property. There are a host of specialized financing programs for this market intended to promote wide distribution of home ownership. The owner-occupancy part of the purchase makes this investment also a consumer good. Indeed, there is some doubt that Tier I contains investment property at all. Finally, due to lack of sophistication, the participants in this market rarely find themselves using anything more advanced than the Rules of Thumb described in Chapter Three. Researchers studying Tier I property are primarily interested in the housing issues. As our interest is in careful and sophisticated analysis of investment property we spend little time dealing with data for Tier I.

- Tier III is institutional size property. Alternatively known as institutional *grade* property, this market is subject to a different size limitation. Because of the cost of raising money and underwriting acquisitions, the players in this market do not acquire small properties. Their interest is in major, sometimes "trophy" but always *large* properties. Although the techniques presented here are applicable to Tier III, it is the different sort of data more recently available that interests us here. Therefore we will not concentrate on Tier III either.
- Tier II property is everything in the middle. For residential, where data are most plentiful, the lower bound of Tier II is defined by the upper bound of Tier I (four dwelling units). The upper bound of Tier II is not so easily found. An informal survey of institutional investors conducted in 1999 suggests that for residential property institutional investor interest begins at 100 units. We shall adopt this to define Tier II residential property as those properties having between 4 and 100 dwelling units.

The data challenges for investment property differ between Tier II and Tier III. Institutional owners are often public companies. They keep and publish detailed records. Accordingly, operating information is plentiful. Many, such as REITs and pension funds, are tax exempt so one may safely ignore the after-debt, after-tax outcomes. The Tier III problem is that sales are infrequent so the equity reversion must be estimated by appraisal. There is a large literature on the distortions, called "smoothing", this causes. Since a major portion of the return is often in the gain on sale, errors in estimating value in mid-holding period can be considerable, leading to errors in estimating returns.

Tier II property has the opposite problem. Purchases and sales by investors in this market produce many publicly recorded transactions but their intra-holding period operational results are out of view.

Such is the imperfect world of real estate investment data. The simple reality this leads us to is that *npv*s and *irr*s are not observable. Therefore, a proxy is required. In our primary interest, the Tier II market, we observe prices and assume that they are driven by income. We further assume, naively, that price is linear in income. That is, whatever return outcomes we observe in price changes are both brought about and supported by an appropriate proportional change in yearly operating income. In later chapters we will see what that means for risk analysis but for now we need only lay the foundation for how price changes can be translated into returns.

Those familiar with high frequency stock market data know the value and usefulness of a time series in which the price of the same asset - a share of stock - is observed repeatedly over short, sequential time periods. As real estate ownership is characterized by long holding periods of irregular length we must find a way to standardize a unit of return.

Consider an investment in a saving account that compounds at an interest rate, r, over time period, n. Such an investment has a future value, fv, at any point in time n of Amount Deposited*$(1 + r)^n$. One can readily see the similarity between the mechanics of this process and those described for capitalization rate in Chapter 3. It is unfortunate that the limitations of data require us to resort to a return metric of this nature for Tier II investment real estate.

What we would like is a real estate equivalent process that can be used for analyzing real estate return data. The mathematical tool we use is the natural logarithm. The unit of return we are interested in is derived from price change.

Recall that $\text{Log}\left[\frac{P_t}{P_{t-1}}\right] = \text{Log}\left[\frac{\text{Today's Price}}{\text{Yesterday's Price}}\right] = \text{Log[Today's Price]} - \text{Log[Yesterday's Price]}$ where "today" is "t" and "yesterday" is a metaphor for "t-1".

If we substitute "Sale" for "Today's" and "Purchase" for "Yesterday's" we get

Holding Period Return = $\text{Log}\left[\frac{\text{Sale Price}}{\text{Purchase Price}}\right]$ = Log [Sale Price]-Log [Purchase Price] which is in ordered time but not specific increments of time. This creates an interval that represents the investor's holding period.

Suppose an asset is purchased for 100 and sold some time later for 200. The log return is

```
Log[200] - Log[100] // N
```

```
0.693147
```

"Exponenting" that return means raising the base of the natural log (a constant with an approximate value of 2.71828 and shown as *e* in most texts) to the power of the log return. Subtracting 1 and multiplying by 100 produces the more familiar percentage return.

```
(e^(Log[200]-Log[100]//N) - 1) * 100
```

```
100.
```

This is the second time in this chapter we have encountered the exponential. When solving for the equivalent continuous compounding return matching a certain modified logistic growth we used the exponential. The continuous equivalent of $(1+r)^n$ is e^{rn}. Thus if one increases the number of compounding intervals, n, to infinity while simultaneously reducing the size of the rate, r, in a similar fashion, in the limit one obtains the continuous compounding return for the same rate.

Real estate markets present a unique problem. For stock market data one can parse a holding period return into even increments because sales of homogeneous assets occur in a continuous auction market. Thus since annual, monthly, weekly or daily stock prices are all available, returns may be expressed over any interval. The example above is slightly less than a 10% per annum return if the holding period was ten years, just less than 20% per annum if held five years, etc.

Real estate investors hold properties for varying lengths of time. Each return observation comes with its own unique holding period. To impose some order on the process we assume that returns, although *realized* at various times separated by differing and often wide intervals, are actually earned in equal daily increments over the holding period. This may seem artificial and certainly represents another sort of "smoothing" problem but some standardization of returns is necessary in order to be able to compare returns and to think about the market as a whole in some coherent way. Patience is recommended at this point. The story is unfolding and later chapters offer additional justification for this approach. We delay until later offering a defense. For now we wish to develop the technical aspects of the methodology.

Our data are 731 repeat sales of buildings between 5 and 100 units covering the period from July, 1987 through September, 2001. Prices and dates of purchase and sale for each building are shown along with the location and number of units. Table 4.6 shows the first five of these.

Area	Sale1	Date1	Sale2	Date2	Units
2	2 600 000	{1993,05,20}	1 530 000	{1995,04,28}	88
2	3 000 000	{1990,08,10}	1 770 000	{1994,07,21}	79
1	2 650 000	{1990,07,12}	1 250 000	{1994,06,30}	78
2	12 200 000	{1989,08,02}	13 800 000	{1990,03,16}	72
2	1 737 500	{1994,06,30}	2 150 000	{1996,05,15}	63

Table 4.6. First five observations of San Francisco repeat sale observations

The first question we can ask is what is the average holding period in days.

Average holding period is 1770.76 days.

Mean daily return over that period is positive, thus the annualized daily return is positive[8]

The mean daily return is 0.0341% and the annualized return is 12.46%

Granted this number does not have a great deal of meaning at this point. Even as an annual return it does not produce a number of the scale needed to attract capital. Do not despair, we shall make good use of this measure and the data that produced it later.

In Chapter 3 we argued, without concluding why, that people may pay higher prices on a per unit basis for smaller properties. This begs the question: If prices are higher are they justified by greater returns? Preserving our convention of considering 10 units or less small and more than 10 units large, it appears that one does obtain a slightly higher return with smaller properties. An Excel file showing these computations is included with the electronic files for this chapter.

The annualized return for small properties is 12.7317%. and for large properties is 12.0162%.

4.11. Conclusion

The real-world analysis of a real estate investment involves many complex variables. All of these, to some degree, change constantly due to market forces. A clear understanding of how deterministic variables affect performance standards permits the analyst to grasp the inner workings of the *npv* function, the consequences of changes in the value of the variables and to place specific prices on those changes as they become bargaining elements in the negotiation.

Using more complex but more realistic growth functions allows one to model outcomes specialized for different types of owners or properties subject to different constraints in different political jurisdictions.

Data opportunities abound. The large quantity of Tier II data now available offers answers to many questions. Here we just scratch the surface, showing the analyst a mere glimpse of what is possible.

Endnotes

[1] Your author has conducted real estate brokerage over four decades and has seen many changes in that time. For instance, while interest rates are at record lows as the second edition of this book is being edited, in 1982 they were at record highs when the US prime rate reached 21.5%. The sample project picks middle ground as an illustration. For the reader willing to make the adjustments, entering current information as required to bring the project current can be a very useful exercise.

[2] A further simplification is the omission of capital gains taxes imposed by various states. Some states have none, some states treat capital gains as ordinary income. While it is pure madness to try to include all of these variations in a book of this nature, these taxes should not be ignored in actual practice. The common phrase "Consult your tax professional before making any decisions about the actual tax ramifications of a particular strategy" will send the average investor to someone with software specifically tailored to the situation under consideration.

[3] Many of the relationships described in this section are dependent on the way our sample project is described. The most general approach would be independent of the construction of any particular example. Our purpose here is to strike a balance between theory and practice by using a stylized example and illuminate its general meaning.

[4] Note that some of the constants combine into other numbers not shown in Table 4.1 because Equation 4.4 has been simplified.

[5] Further analysis, left to the reader as an exercise, will disclose under what conditions our definition of positive leverage is a stronger or weaker constraint than the alternate definition for positive leverage, capitalization rate > interest rate.

[6] Economists call this price elasticity, something *Mathematica* can handle also but is beyond the scope of this work.

[7] In practice it may be that price reduction is shared between loan amount and down payment.

[8] Assuming 365 days in a year.

References

Brown, G. R., & Matysiak, G. A. Real Estate Investment, A Capital Market Approach. Essex, UK: Financial Times Prentice Hall.

Brown, R. J. (1998). Evaluating Future Input Assumption Risk. The Appraisal Journal, 66(2), 118-129.

Messner, S. D., Schreiber, I., & Lyon, V. L. <u>Marketing Investment Real Estate</u>. Chicago, IL: REALTORS National Marketing Institute.

Problems

1. Below you see an elaborate interactive module that permits a large number of permutations to the model this chapter offers. Input as much of the sample project in this chapter as practical, paying close attention to how the performance measures change with input changes.

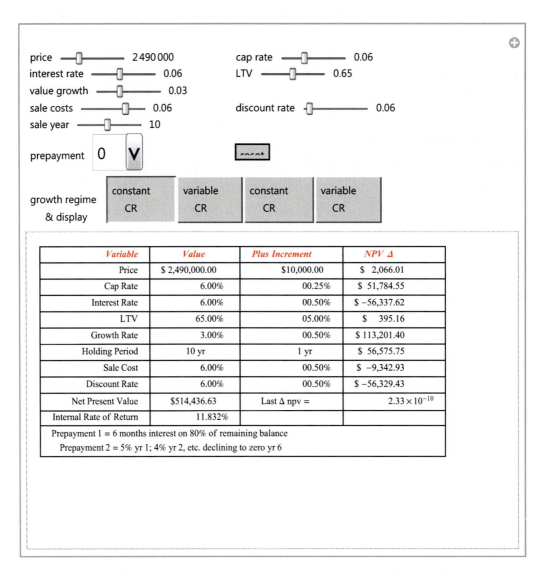

2. Using Figure 4.14, change the sliders until capital in both scenarios is 1.5 times the original. Note the difference in time.

3. Table 4.3 describes the effect positive or negative leverage has on cash flow. Locate the equation or equations among Equations 4.2 through Equations 4.14 that causes this.

4. Data for San Francisco described in Table 4.6 leads us to believe that the average holding period is just less than five years. What would your expectation of total return be if holding period averaged ten years? Do you think your conclusion would change if you picked a different ten year period? How would it change?

5. As suggested in Endnote 1, find an apartment building presently for sale and substitute the marketing information you see into the Excel worksheets provided for this chapter. Make equivalent inputs into the module under Problem #1 above. The results should be identical. What differences between the text illustration and the current market conditions can you identify?

5

Sins of the *irr* - What it will and will not do

"Whom the gods would destroy they first make mad"

Morris Kline <u>Mathematics - the Loss of Certainty</u> p. 273

5.1. Introduction

This chapter chronicles the troubled history of the Internal Rate of Return (*irr*), dissects it and examines how it stands as a decision rule next to Net Present Value (*npv*). At the end of this chapter one might well ask: If there are so many problems, why use *irr* at all? The answer to this questions touches on one of the differences between academia and the real world. Academics like tight, elegant answers. Practitioners like things that work. Academics prefer a decision rule that *always* gives the right signal. Practitioners prefer a tool they can use with clients to close deals. By the end of this chapter we should all be convinced that *npv* is a consistent dependable rule and that *irr* must be used with caution. But nothing in this chapter will deter people from using and occasionally misusing the *irr*. The hope is that this chapter will inform investors and brokers of the shortcomings of the *irr* and contribute to its proper use.

In this chapter we will:

- Describe the real and imagined problems associated with the *irr*;
- Evaluate the limitations of *irr* as a decision tool, comparing it with *npv*;
- Investigate the important idea of convex function and Jensen's Inequality; and
- Provide a number of ways of computing and presenting the *irr* using *Mathematica*.

5.1.1. Performance measures - why use them at all?

At the heart of the problem is the question: What is the investor's goal? Economists believe that it is the maximization of utility, a function of terminal wealth. "Win as much as you can" is the battle cry. There are situations, many of them in fact, in which using either *irr* or *npv* will accomplish that goal. Our interest is in the exceptions, all of which affect the *irr*. When one wishes to maximize terminal wealth one should always choose the highest *npv* as it will make the largest contribution to the goal by adding the most to wealth. Choosing the highest *irr* may or may not accomplish that goal.

In the field, despite its theoretical benefits, *npv* is less than optimal as a tool to counsel clients. A broker may proudly assert that property B has an *npv* $15,657 greater than that of property A but many clients will not understand that. Tell those same clients that property B has an *irr* of 16.4% and property A has an *irr* of 14.45% and the client has a frame of reference in which to make his decision. People are used to considering investments on the basis of rate. Among fixed rate investments, T-Bills of different durations have a higher or lower yield than municipal bonds which have a higher or lower rate than commercial paper which has a higher or lower rate than AAA corporate bonds. Among equity investments, some stocks pay higher dividend yields than others. Include projected growth and certain stocks are expected to outperform a different group of securities, all evaluated on the basis of rate. In short, "rate" is familiar, "net present value" is not.

We would be remiss if we did not remind the reader that both *irr* and *npv* are measures of return. While higher returns imply higher risk, neither *irr* nor *npv*, on their own, says anything explicit about risk. Economists and mathematicians have developed formal risk measurement techniques now in wide use in the financial markets. Many of these have been adapted for use in real estate where it is most appropriate, in the Tier III market. The foundation laid down in earlier chapters focuses on return - how to calculate it, how to use it, how not to use it. This chapter may convince you that real estate investment return calculations can be presented with considerable - some will complain too much - mathematical formalism. Why, you might readily ask, is the subject of real estate risk not treated to the same formal mathematical analysis as return? The reason is that risk measures for private investment in real estate are at best underdeveloped. In the field they are largely subjective and *ad hoc*. The developing and still partly experimental mathematical formality for Tier II real estate risk will be taken up in later chapters. Nonetheless, risk in real estate is real. Everyone knows it exists even if its formal mathematical development is nascent. As we wend our way through the thicket of *irr* problems pursuing the overarching goal of wealth maximization, never far from our thoughts is the intuitive reality that wealth can only be maximized by appropriate *combinations* of returns and risk bearing.

Business is really a simple subject. Three questions need be answered. How much money is earned or lost (a "*what*" question that requires little more than the arithmetic of counting)? When does the money arrive (a "*when*" question that involves the relatively simple process of compounding interest using algebra)? Will the money arrive (an "*if*" question requiring the slightly more but still manageable mathematics of calculus)? Answering those three questions carefully usually leads to a profitable investment experience and the desired consequence of wealth maximization over the long term.

5.2. The reinvestment problem

The least of the *irr* problems is known as the reinvestment problem. The essence of this argument is that during the holding period one is unlikely to be able to reinvest mid-holding period cash flows at the same rate as the projected *irr*. Because they are small amounts arriving at odd times separated by short intervals, practical considerations usually result in the deposit of these funds into a bank account, where they earn a modest interest rate well below the *irr*. As the mathematics behind the *irr* calculation assumes that all intertemporal cash flows are reinvested at the *irr*, the argument is that actual *irr* realizations are lower than those projected. This is a mare's nest for a variety of reasons.

First, for Tier III investors in a portfolio context, the firm constantly seeks projects. It reinvests funds at rates that may fluctuate but need not be substantially lower and indeed may at times be higher than the *irr*.

Second, Tier II investors derive utility from wealth in a variety of ways including spending annual cash flows on consumption goods. The decision to reinvest is part of another discussion called intertemporal consumer choice, the essence of which is the decision to spend now or later. One can argue that utility is at all times being achieved at a rate equal to that which would otherwise be gained from reinvesting cash flows at an acceptable rate or present consumption would be chosen over reinvestment.

Third, even if one wishes to pay homage to the reinvestment rate problem, the problem is one that affects all investors approximately equally. Thus in a competitive market in which bids for investment opportunities are based on slightly flawed *irr* calculations, all such calculations are flawed, all market participants know and accept the computation as approximate.

Fourth, the problem amounts to hair splitting. The *irr* depends on a variety of uncertain inputs. For some size properties something as mundane as the unplanned replacement of a large water heater can move the *irr* by an amount greater than the difference in earnings on cash flows. Focusing on minutiae such as the reinvestment rate difference distracts the investor from anticipating and controlling the more important variation in inputs that can have a much more dramatic effect on overall results.

Fifth, if you must indulge in trivial computations, a simple adjustment in your computer's *irr* algorithm dispatches the problem. If not apparent from the comments thus far, this author considers the problem to be *de minimus* to the point of not bothering to program it into the software included with this book. The reader is cautioned that if competing investors do not also adjust their computations, competing bids for investment properties may routinely be higher and result in missed opportunities.

At the end of this chapter are a variety of references that chronicle the debate about this problem - or as some authors see it non-problem - that occupied practitioners and academics in the late 1970s and early 1980s. Fortunately, most of these authors have gone on to other more important things since then. We will let it rest in peace by not flogging it again here.

5.3. The problem of no solution

Among the difficulties presented by the internal rate of return is that it is possible to reach no solution or more than a single solution. This particular difficulty has been overcome by better programming and faster computing. But for technophiles, here is the cause.

Suppose that for a payment of X now you can buy an investment which will return a given series of payments x_1, x_2, ..., x_n at the end of each year for the next n years. Then the internal rate of return, r, is determined by the solution for r in the equation,

$$\sum_{n=1}^{t} x_n v^n = X, \text{ where } v = 1/(1+r). \tag{5.1}$$

Using the *Mathematica* function **FindRoot** we can obtain a numerical solution as we did in Chapter 4. For example, suppose for an immediate payment of "`initinv`" you can receive the payments shown in the "`data1`" set of values at the end of each year.

```
initinv = 100 000;
data1 = {5000, 7500, 10 000, 8000, 12 000, 11 000, 105 900};
```

We create a polynomial in v, recalling that rules for matrix multiplication require that the length of this polynomial must match the length of the data set,

```
y1 = Table[(1/(1+r))^n, {n, 1, Length[data1]}]
```

$$\left\{\frac{1}{1+r}, \frac{1}{(1+r)^2}, \frac{1}{(1+r)^3}, \frac{1}{(1+r)^4}, \frac{1}{(1+r)^5}, \frac{1}{(1+r)^6}, \frac{1}{(1+r)^7}\right\}$$

The dot product (a special case of the inner product) delivers the polynomial we need...

```
poly1 = y1.data1
```

$$\frac{105\,900}{(1+r)^7} + \frac{11\,000}{(1+r)^6} + \frac{12\,000}{(1+r)^5} + \frac{8000}{(1+r)^4} + \frac{10\,000}{(1+r)^3} + \frac{7500}{(1+r)^2} + \frac{5000}{1+r}$$

Recall that a root is the value for r that makes the function equal to zero. Thus a root is found when the function crosses the x-axis, for which *Mathematica* provides the function, **FindRoot**.

The value of r that makes the sum of **poly1** and the initial investment zero is 0.0833321. If we use that as the hurdle rate for the net present value calculations the *npv* will be 0.

In version 8 *Mathematica* has created some functions for handling this calculation that shortens the code.

```
FindRoot[TimeValue[Cashflow[Join[{-initinv}, data1]], r, 0] == 0, {r, .05}]
```

$\{r \to 0.0833321\}$

The instruction we have used for **FindRoot** has four arguments. The first, r, is the variable for which a value is sought. This is the root of the implicit equation remaining when all is moved to the left hand side leaving zero on the right. The second, $\frac{1}{1.1} = .9090909$ is a starting point, the third and fourth are, respectively the lower and upper bounds of where **FindRoot** is to search for a solution along the x-axis. As we shall see in a moment these last two arguments are not required for this example, but let's continue to get a feel for where the problem lies.

An error message or "no solution" message is generated in some software when the value searched for lies outside of the boundaries of the search. The cure in this case is to widen the boundaries such that you are more likely to include the correct answer.

Plotting the *npv* function against various cost of capital rates in Figure 5.1 discloses the not surprising fact that the *irr* we seek is located where the plot crosses the *x*-axis and *npv* = 0. Note the other extreme where the plot crosses the *y* axis. This is where *irr* is zero. At that point *npv* is the simple difference between the amount invested and the amount received, leading one to the counterintuitive conclusion that the time value of money is zero. The reason this is counterintuitive is that it implies that interest rates are zero. That is, people do not demand payment for waiting. Clearly this does not occur often in first world countries.[1]

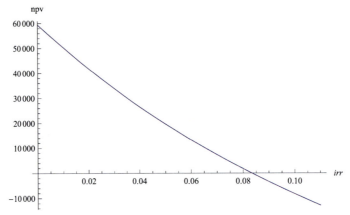

Figure 5.1. Plot of *npv* as a function of *irr*

5.4. The problem of multiple solutions

The *irr* has problems with some sign changes. If there are negative cash flows in the middle of the income stream, there may be more than one answer. To illustrate this, the next series of cash flows below fluctuate in an admittedly unusual way.

$$-\frac{50\,000}{(1+r)^8} - \frac{1100}{(1+r)^7} + \frac{12\,000}{(1+r)^6} + \frac{2500}{(1+r)^5} - \frac{60\,000}{(1+r)^4} - \frac{10\,000}{(1+r)^3} - \frac{7500}{(1+r)^2} + \frac{50\,000}{1+r}$$

Here *Mathematica* can find not only one but two roots for this function, hence there are two "*irr*" values. Note the difference between the 3rd and 4th arguments in red in the { } brackets for each of the two FindRoot routines below. The two routines search along different segments of the *x*-axis, each finding an answer.

    FindRoot[npv2 == 0, {r, .02, .01, .03}][[1, 2]]

0.0245387

    FindRoot[npv2 == 0, {r, .2, .18, .21}][[1, 2]]

0.198262

Why is that? A plot of the *npv* function in Figure 5.2 discloses that it crosses the *x*-axis twice. Each time produces a root that is mathematically correct.

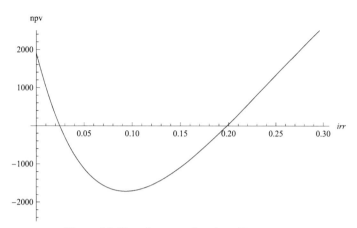

Figure 5.2. Plot of *npv* as a function of *irr*

Note that when the range is very wide, including both roots, *Mathematica* chooses only one of these. **FindRoot** always finds only one, in this case it is the first occurrence of the function crossing the x-axis.

When we merely use **Solve [ ]** we get eight roots, just what we would expect for a polynomial in the 8th degree.

$r \to -1.82446$
$r \to 0.0245387$
$r \to 0.198262$
$r \to 3.7411$
$r \to -1.70119 - 0.880792\ i$
$r \to -1.70119 + 0.880792\ i$
$r \to -0.868529 - 0.897097\ i$
$r \to -0.868529 + 0.897097\ i$

Since we are dealing with a rate of return we are only interested in those roots that represent a positive, real number between zero and one. They are 0.0245387 and 0.198262.

We have illustrated two strictly mechanical problems with the *irr*. The "no solution" problem has a simple programming remedy. The multi-solution problem may be avoided by not using *irr* when there is a sign change in the middle of the flows. When mid-stream negative cash flows cannot be eliminated, one remedy is to set aside sufficient funds at the outset which when compounded forward will service the negative cash flow. This re-opens the reinvestment rate problem in a new light. Does the pre-funding amount compound at the *irr*? Surely not. During the debate over this in the 1970s modifications known as *airr* for "Adjusted *irr*" and *fmirr* for "Financial Management *irr*" were proposed. References at the end of this chapter leave one with the feeling that this later, perhaps last, round of the debate generated more heat than light.

A new breed of nitpickers was born in the age of the computer. To entertain these types an appendix at the end of this chapter provides several different methods for programming *Mathematica* to compute the *irr*.

In the end, however, one has to realize that there are only so many ways you can compound interest. After a number of permutations of $(1 + r)^n$ the question ceases to be interesting and one must accept the fact that nothing really new is being accomplished by further refinements. Taking that position, we now turn to more important and substantive *irr* problems.

5.5. The ranking problem

This problem has to do with mutually exclusive investments. In corporate finance the term used is "Capital Rationing", a fancy moniker that merely means you don't have enough money to pursue all opportunities you identify, so you must choose. Real estate, while also constrained by budgetary issues, introduces its own unique variation to this problem. Consider a piece of vacant land. Local zoning codes may allow development into several uses. Once the land is committed to a certain use there is no turning back. Building out the project involves choosing between mutually exclusive alternatives. We wish to rank them in an order of preference. Under conditions that are discussed below it is possible that *npv* will rank one project higher than the other but *irr* will rank them in the opposite way. Clearly we can't have this. The example that follows is fully elaborated in an Excel file that accompanies this book. Recall Equation 5.1 and suppose for the same immediate payment of "`initinv`" you can finance *either* of the two projects described in Table 5.1, receiving the cash flows shown. Note that the *irr* for the second project is larger. Hence, one would be expected to select the second project.

	cf_0	cf_1	cf_2	cf_3	cf_4	cf_5	irr
Project 1	250 000	25 000	27 500	30 000	32 500	435 000	0.197475
Project 2	250 000	70 000	70 000	50 000	30 000	250 000	0.201224

Table 5.1. Cash flows and *irr* from competing projects

However, suppose further that we have a cost of capital, or "hurdle rate" for *npv* calculations and a decision rule that says we accept all projects with an *npv* over the hurdle rate. Given the individual project data, the *npv* is *dependent on the selected hurdle rate, r.*

Based on the *npv* decision rule and choosing a cost of capital of 18% one would be expected to proceed with Project 1. This contradicts the preferred choice indicated by *irr*. Such a result is troubling.

Project 1 *npv* = 16,101.10 *irr* = 0.197475
Project 2 *npv* = 14,777.50 *irr* = 0.201224

The conflict between the two decision rules can be traced to *the timing and size of the cash flows* and can be analyzed by plotting, in Figure 5.3 for each alternative, the path of *npv* as the hurdle rate increases. Note that the two graphs cross each other before reaching the *x*-axis. What is important is whether they cross before or after the hurdle rate.

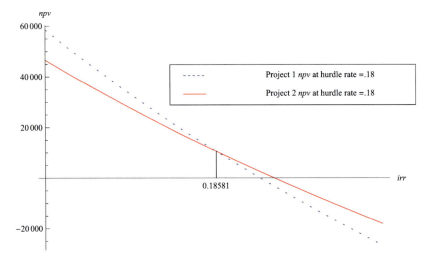

Figure 5.3. Plot of *npv* of two competing projects

In our example the hurdle rate occurs on the *x*-axis *before* the crossover point. Under these conditions, *irr* and *npv* decision rules *always* give conflicting answers. Note, in Table 5.2 that when the hurdle rate is greater than the crossover point, Project 1 has the higher *npv*. After the crossover point Project 2 has the higher *npv*.

Hurdle Rate	Project 1 *npv*	Project2 *npv*
0.14	58 507.3	46 619.4
0.15	47 112.4	38 122.2
0.16	36 267.1	29 996.1
0.17	25 939.7	22 220.8
0.18	16 101.1	14 777.5
0.19	6723.62	7648.26
0.2	−2218.36	816.615
0.21	−10 748.9	−5733.08
0.22	−18 890.6	−12 015.5
0.23	−26 664.6	−18 044.3

Table 5.2. Net present value of two projects at different hurdle rates

What is one to do? At a minimum one must be aware of the location of the crossover point relative to the hurdle rate. If the hurdle rate is known to be below the crossover then one should rely solely on *npv* for the decision. The problem does not exist if the hurdle rate is beyond the crossover point as both decision rules will recommend the same project. An other alternative is to force the hurdle rate to equal the crossover point.

5.6. The scale problem

Related to the problem of ranking is the scale problem. However, this problem goes beyond return and affects how one ranks investments in terms of their *risk*. One wishes to be efficient by selecting investments that maximize terminal wealth. "Efficient" means making investments that not only offer the best return but the best *risk-adjusted* return.

5.6.1. Return and scale

The scale aspects of return are easy to understand. Consider the following question: If offered either a 50% return or a 10% return, which would you choose? The answer to this question appears straightforward - choose the higher return. On the other hand, if you had to choose between investing $1.00 at 50% and getting back $1.50 or investing $10 at 10% and getting back $11.00, which would you choose? Clearly the answers to both questions are now clouded by investment size as revealed by the second question. One can argue that this illustration is unfair because all returns must be compared on the basis of the same investment amount to be meaningful. But there are many real life situations in which this question presents itself.

Let's take a more realistic investment setting. Assume you have $100,000 to invest. You are presented with the choice between a single investment requiring $100,000 offering a 10% return and two investments, one of $80,000 returning 11% and one of $20,000 returning 2%. Ignoring the benefits of diversification in the second alternative and assuming the two alternatives entail equal risk, which would you choose?

The goal is always to maximize terminal wealth. Although the *irr* cannot always be counted on to do this under every set of conditions, simple calculations are all that is necessary to get to the bottom of this problem For example, let

- **inv1** = amount to be invested in a single project
- **ret1** = return on the single project
- **inv2a** = share to be invested in an alternate project that will not use all the funds
- **ret2a** = return on share to be invested in an alternate project that will not use all the funds
- **inv2b** = remaining share after investing in the alternate project that will not use all the funds = 1- inv2a
- **ret2b** = return on remaining share

To test this we create a real-valued data set for the example above and solve for the minimum return we must obtain on the remaining funds in order that the two-project alternative produces the same wealth as the single project alternative. The remaining 20% must yield at least 6% or we invest the entire amount in the 10% project.

```
ret2b → 0.06
```

As the smaller allocation in the second alternative returns less than 6% we choose the single investment alternative.

5.6.2. Risk and scale

The effect of scale on risk is more interesting. Investigating this we uncover an often misunderstood problem relating to how scale affects one's attempt to lower risk by diversification.[2] We need to think about the purchase of an investment offering an uncertain return as placing a bet or buying a lottery ticket. This may appear to lower the lofty pastime of investing to the unsavory habit of gambling. But the pejorative connotation is inappropriate. In a cold, objective light, one can only conclude that an opportunity with an uncertain outcome is still a gamble even if the odds of success are respectably high.

Assume we have a $1,000 bet involving two equiprobable outcomes. One outcome has a payoff of $3,000, the other outcome pays $0. As one can either triple one's money or lose it all, the two percentage returns (*irr*) are, respectively, either 200% or -100%. Taking these percentages as nominal amounts, the dot product of the vector of payoffs and the vector of probabilities is the mathematical expectation.

```
ratebets = {200, -100};
probs = {.5, .5};
meanratebets = ratebets.probs

50.
```

This means that in a large enough number of repeated independent trials we can expect to gain 50% on average (200%*.5 - 100%*.5 = 50%). This would be true *regardless of exactly how many* bets we make so long as the number is high.

In the matter of variance things change as we add bets. Suppose we thought that by increasing the number of bets we would enjoy benefits of diversification and the Law of Large Numbers would work in our favor.

Our interest is in the variation and standard deviation for a population.

$$\text{Population Standard Deviation} = \sqrt{\frac{n \sum x^2 - (\sum x)^2}{n^2}} \quad (5.2)$$

Recall that the variance of a portfolio of assets, each having a separate return and variance is:

$$\sigma^2_p = \sum_{i=1}^{n} w_i^2 \sigma_i^2 + \sum_{i=1}^{n}\sum_{j=1}^{n} w_i^2 w_j^2 \text{Cov}(r_i r_j) \quad (5.3)$$

However, if r_i is independent of r_j (which is the case here), $\text{Cov}(r_i r_j) = 0$ and the second term is zero. Further, because the weights are equal we can set $w_i = \frac{1}{n}$, thus the standard deviation for a "portfolio" of independent equiprobable bets is simply:

$$\sigma(n) = \frac{\sigma}{\sqrt{n}} \quad (5.4)$$

It appears that the benefit of diversification is at work here. Because n is in the denominator (in the *Mathematica* code below the syntax Length[] is *n*, the number of elements in the vector) the standard deviation of returns drops as the number of bets (trials) increases. Returning to our example, the [population] standard deviation of percentage returns for a single bet is (the answer is again in percent terms):

```
stdDevRateBets = √( (ratebets[[1]] - meanratebets)²
                    ─────────────────────────────── +
                          Length[ratebets]

    (ratebets[[2]] - meanratebets)² / Length[ratebets] ) // N
```

150.

Thus, if the standard deviation of a portfolio of independent bets is $\sigma(n) = \frac{\sigma}{\sqrt{n}}$ it would appear one can lower standard deviation by merely increasing *n*. It turns out that this is a fallacy and is only true if one is speaking of percentage returns on portfolios *of equal size*. Once the issue of scale is raised our safe harbor is once again only available when maximizing terminal wealth, a goal measured in dollars, not percent.

Now let's make the same computation, this time applied to the *dollar values* of the potential profits of this single bet with the probabilities unchanged. (Here the rate issues are analogous to *irr*; the dollar issues are analogous to *npv*.)

```
dollarbets = {2000, -1000};
meandollarbets = dollarbets.probs
```

500.

```
stdDevDollarBets = √( (dollarbets[[1]] - meandollarbets)² / Length[dollarbets] +
                      (dollarbets[[2]] - meandollarbets)² / Length[dollarbets] ) // N
```

1500.

Turning to the idea of making multiple bets to reduce our risk, there are two ways to approach this. First, we imagine that such a strategy constitutes constructing a "portfolio" of bets of equal size. The expectation of such a portfolio of *n* bets is the simple sum of the individual expectations

$$E[R(n)] = \$500n \tag{5.5}$$

And the variance (again, because of independence) is the simple sum of the individual variances. But this time we are asking a different question: What is the variance of the *sum of all the returns*? This is a different variance than we computed before, it is the variance of a fixed portfolio of bets.

$$Variance\left(\sum_{i=1}^{n} R_i\right) = n\,\sigma_R^2 \tag{5.6}$$

So the standard deviation of the profits to be made from a portfolio of ten bets *of the same size as the original* is

$$\sigma_R(n) = \sqrt{n\,\sigma_R^2} = \sigma_R\sqrt{n} \tag{5.7}$$

Therefore, because *n* is now a multiplier, in dollar terms the variance of the portfolio *increases* with the number of bets when the size of the bet remains constant.

Returning to our example, let's scale up the stakes, making ten of the original bets, each with equal probability of the same outcome as before.

```
          bets          probs
     {2000, −1000}   {0.5, 0.5}
     {2000, −1000}   {0.5, 0.5}
     {2000, −1000}   {0.5, 0.5}
     {2000, −1000}   {0.5, 0.5}
     {2000, −1000}   {0.5, 0.5}
     {2000, −1000}   {0.5, 0.5}
     {2000, −1000}   {0.5, 0.5}
     {2000, −1000}   {0.5, 0.5}
     {2000, −1000}   {0.5, 0.5}
     {2000, −1000}   {0.5, 0.5}
```

In words, what has happened is that the exposure to risk has been increased by increasing the size of the total bet from $1,000 to $10,000. The dollar amount of the portfolio is ten times the size of the original bet. This is risk pooling, not risk sharing, and it does not accomplish diversification. Both the mean and the standard deviation increase tenfold. Because of the losses attendant to the greater variance, we will suffer a reduction in terminal wealth under this strategy. This, despite the fact that our percent (*irr*) gain or loss and its variance remained the same.

```
multidollarbets = {20 000, -10 000};
meanmultidb = multidollarbets.probs

5000.

stdDevMultidollarbet =
```

$$N\left[\sqrt{\frac{(\text{multidollarbets[[1]]} - \text{meanmultidb})^2}{\text{Length[multidollarbets]}} + \frac{(\text{multidollarbets[[2]]} - \text{meanmultidb})^2}{\text{Length[multidollarbets]}}}\right]$$

```
15 000.
```

Now let's look at how one might approach the scale problem in a different way that actually produces benefits from diversification. Returning to our original example, we had $1,000 to bet. Having shown that making ten $1,000 bets does not reduce variance, let's go the other way and *scale down* by dividing the original $1,000 into ten $100 dollar bets, again each with the same 50/50 probability of losing it all or doubling our money. Note that the only difference is in the denominator of the standard deviation calculation. As expected the standard deviation of dollar outcome drops.

```
     670.82
```

The timeless adage "Diversify by not putting all your eggs in one basket" still applies. What we have shown is that no one ever said "Diversity by putting more eggs in your basket".

We now turn to a final *irr* difficulty that presents a common risk analysis problem to be avoided.

5.7. The simulation problem

Participants in real estate markets rely on a variety of tools to measure risk. Many of these examine potential returns under a variety of "what if?" scenarios. Lacking data for the construction of the kind of market risk measures used in finance, simulation is often an appealing alternative This section examines the limitations of simulating the *irr* for a real estate project, limitations that arise from a bias inherent in using a linear operator with a convex function. The source of this problem is known as "Jensen's Inequality" an insight provided by Johan Ludvig William Valdemar Jensen (1859-1925). Formally this is stated as:

A function, f, is convex in the interval I if and only if the following inequality is satisfied for all $x_1, x_2, \ldots x_n$ in I and for all $\lambda_1 \geq 0, \lambda_2 \geq 0 \ldots \lambda_n \geq 0$ with $\lambda_1 + \lambda_2 + \ldots + \lambda_n = 1$:

$$f(\lambda_1 x_1 + \ldots + \lambda_n x_n) \leq \lambda_1 f(x_1) + \ldots + \lambda_n f(x_n) \tag{5.8}$$

In less technical terms this means roughly that the function of the expection is less than or equal to the expectation of the function when the function is convex (for concave functions the inequality is reversed).

5.7.1. Foundation

Discounted cash flow methodology makes the value of the equity portion of a parcel of income producing real estate equal to the present value (*pv*) of its future income streams, a series of cash flows (*cf*) plus a reversion (*R*) in the form of net sales proceeds. Except for the reversion occurring concurrent with the last cash flow, each of the cash flows occur at different times. All cash flows are discounted at some required rate of return (*k*) below which the investor would not chose to invest. Algebraically, we have:

$$pv = \sum_{t=1}^{n} \frac{cf}{(1+k)^t} + \frac{R}{(1+k)^n} \tag{5.9}$$

It is desirable to have the *pv* function as simple as possible. Equation 5.9 can be rearranged to:

$$pv = \frac{(1+k)^{-n}(cf(-1+(1+k)^n) + kR)}{k} \tag{5.10}$$

With this function we can do several things. For instance we can set it equal to the down payment (*dp*) and solve for cash flow (*cf*) getting the equation for *cf* (Equation 5.11) or reversion (*R*) (Equation 5.12) as a function of all the other variables. Note that one may also solve for *n* (Equation 5.13). Solving for *k* is not possible at this stage.

$$cf = \frac{k(dp(1+k)^n - R)}{-1+(1+k)^n} \tag{5.11}$$

$$R = \frac{cf - cf(1+k)^n + dp\,k(1+k)^n}{k} \tag{5.12}$$

$$n = \frac{\text{Log}\left[\frac{cf - kR}{cf - dp\,k}\right]}{\text{Log}[1+k]} \tag{5.13}$$

We are usually interested in the <u>net</u> present value (*npv*) of the equity portion of a parcel of income producing real estate. This is the extent to which, if at all, the present value of all income streams exceeds the initial outlay or down payment (*dp*) given a prescribed cost of capital or hurdle rate. We wish to develop a function that will produce the *irr*, *k* in this case, from cash flows. We define net present value:

$$npv = \frac{(1+k)^{-n}(cf(-1+(1+k)^n) + kR)}{k} - dp \tag{5.14}$$

In the expressions above there are many variables. To make the process manageable, we create several data sets. Note that the last one, **d5** lacks a value for *cf*. This is to permit later manipulations of the *irr* function we seek.

data 1	cf → 75	n → 10	R → 1000	dp → 600
data 2	cf → 100	n → 10	R → 1000	dp → 600
data 3	cf → 125	n → 10	R → 1000	dp → 600
data 5		n → 10	R → 1000	dp → 600
data 6	k → 0.1	n → 10	R → 1000	dp → 600

Table 5.3. Alternate sets of fixed inputs for *npv*

Suppose that we are interested in a function that, given values for *n*, *R* and *dp*, leaves only *k* and *cf* unknown. Using **d5** for the fixed data inputs we name this function **nd5**, inserting the data from **d5** into our previously defined **netpv**:

nd5 = netpv /. d5

$$-600 + \frac{1000\,k + cf\left(-1 + (1+k)^{10}\right)}{k\,(1+k)^{10}}$$

5.7.2. Multiple roots

As a preliminary step we set **nd5** equal to zero and solve, remembering that it has two unknowns. This intermediate step is named **sk2a** for "solve for *k* with 2 unknowns giving all roots".

sk2a = (Solve[nd5 == 0, k]) // N;

Inserting a value for *cf* into **ska** reduces the number of unknowns to one and produces ten answers, only one of which is positive and real. As sensible *irr*s are positive real numbers, this one is the *irr* we seek.

k → -2.0492
k → 0.193222
k → -1.84822 - 0.617508 i
k → -1.84822 + 0.617508 i
k → -1.32207 - 0.998479 i
k → -1.32207 + 0.998479 i
k → -0.671813 - 0.996313 i
k → -0.671813 + 0.996313 i
k → -0.146576 - 0.608335 i
k → -0.146576 + 0.608335 i

The only positive and real solution for k is: 0.193222

5.7.7. Bias

Where does all this mathematical wizardry get us? The temptation to simulate the *irr* must be resisted. Because the bias grows with the variance, simulation is least effective when it is needed most. The very reason for simulation is to attempt to get some sort of feel for a reasonable expectation in the face of uncertainty. The more the uncertainty, the more simulation is needed. But the more uncertainty the more bias, the less accurate the result of simulating the *irr*. Viewed from the other end, we see that bias drops to zero when variance is zero. Thus, the simulation problem goes away just as the need for simulation also evaporates. When variance is zero there is no bias. There is also no uncertainty and no need for simulation.

Simulation is not a problem with *npv*. The reason is that *npv* is a linear function. At first glance this seems unlikely because the identity for *npv* doesn't look very linear:

$$npv = \sum_{n=1}^{t} \frac{atcf_n}{(1+k)^n} + \frac{ater_t}{(1+k)^t} - dp \qquad (5.17)$$

After all, it has exponents in it!!! What overcomes this is that with *npv* we start out knowing the value of *k*. Since the exponents are merely indices, this means that each denominator is a real number. Returning to our earlier expression for *npv* we us our last dataset, **d6**, adding a crucial input - the hurdle rate.

Applying that data to **netpv** clearly shows that net present value is a linear function of cash flow

$$6.14457\,cf - 214.457$$

Using our simplest example with two cash flows (it will hold for all more complex examples), we notice that the expectation of the *npv* is equal to the *npv* of the expected cash flow. No bias is created by simulation. Jenson is unconcerned with passing a linear operator through the *npv* function as both are linear.

```
expnpv = .5 (npv3 /. cf -> 50) + .5 (npv3 /. cf -> 250)
npvexpcf = npv3 /. cf -> 150
TrueQ[expnpv == npvexpcf]

707.228

707.228

True
```

5.8. Conclusion

This chapter opened with the warning that *irr* might end up as damaged goods. Not so, *irr* used properly has its place. The message is that one may acquire excellent real estate analysis software from a variety of sources. Many of these will perform simulation. Like any other software, its output is only as good as the underlying theory that supports it. For those interested in a short list of do's and don'ts summarizing this chapter, here are antidotes for the seven deadly sins of *irr*:

- Don't worry about the reinvestment problem.
- Be conscious of the range over which your calculator or software "hunts" for an answer.
- If the sign of the cash flow changes in the middle of the stream you have a potential for problems.
- Because *irr* is sensitive to the timing of cash flows one should expect that under those conditions it will sometimes recommend the wrong alternative.
- Scaling returns is sensitive to the amount invested.
- Where the *irr* is concerned, size matters and scale has an impact on risk.
- Avoid simulating the *irr*.

If you are blessed with a willing client it may be well to provide him with a tutorial on *npv*, a decision rule free of all of these problems.

Endnotes

[1] As this edition is being edited interest rates in the US are nearly zero. Many believe this is uncommon and should not be expected to continue. Much market uncertainty and political forces drive such outcomes.

[2] This illustration draws on a famous Paul Samuelson (1963) story

References

Brown, Roger J., Sins of the IRR, Journal of Real Estate Portfolio Management, 2006,12:2, 195-199.

Crean, Michael J., Revealing the True Meaning of the IRR via Profiling the IRR and Defining the IRR, Journal of Real Estate Portfolio Management, 2005,11:3, 323-330.

Jensen, J. L. W. V. "Sur les fonctions convexes et les inégalités entre les valeurs moyennes." Acta Math., 1906, 30, 175-193.

Krantz, S. G. "Jensen's Inequality." §9.1.3 in Handbook of Complex Variables. Boston, MA: Birkhäuser, 1999, p. 118.

Robichek, Alexander A. and Myers, Stewart C., The Journal of Finance, Dec. 1966, 21:4), 727-730.

Robichek, Alexander A. Interpreting the Results of Risk Analysis. The Journal of Finance, 1975, 30:5, 1384-1386.

Young, M. S. FMRR: A Clever Hoax? The Appraisal Journal, 1979, 47:3, 359-369.

Problems

1. You are considering two mutually exclusive projects, each requiring a $250,000 investment and a 5 year time horizon. Project A is a commercial site requiring some tenant improvements and the execution of a new lease in the first year. It is expected to appreciate in value at just under 10% (9.85605% to be exact!) per annum. Project B is a build-to-suit for a special user who will pay high rent in the first year, declining thereafter with no likelihood of renewal at the end of four years. It is expected that the project will then require recycling before it can be sold. The cost of such recycling together with down time is expected to offset any appreciation, permitting merely the recovery of initial capital at the end of the holding period. Cash flows are as shown. At a hurdle rate of 18% compute the *npv* and *irr* for each project.

YR	ALTERNATIVE A			ALTERNATIVE B		
	ATCF	ATER	TOTAL CF	ATCF	ATER	TOTAL CF
0	-250000		-250000	-250000		-250000
1	25000		25000	70000		70000
2	27500		27500	70000		70000
3	30000		30000	50000		50000
4	32500		32500	30000		30000
5	35000	400000	435000	0	250000	250000

2. Test the sensitivity of the *irr* to changes in your assumptions. You have made two critical assumptions. One is the rate of appreciation (growth) in value over the holding period; the other is the income which will be derived during the holding period. Although these are interrelated, you first want to test them separately. Find the growth rate required to equalize the two projects such that the two *irr*s are identical and the *npv*s calculated at that *irr* are identical.

3. Returning to the original growth rate and the original assumptions about change in income after the first year, you wonder what initial lease rate is necessary to again equalize the projects' *irr*s and *npv*s. Assume that there are 5,000 leaseable square feet in the project and that the original assumption was that average first year lease rates would be $5 per square foot per year. What first year rate, holding income and value growth rates constant would, again, make the two *irr*s identical and the *npv*s calculated at that *irr* identical?

4. The graphic below has a slider bar that can be moved to the left where the cash flow range becomes zero. Make that change, remembering that what is being measured on the *y* axis is the bias. What happens to the bias when the cash flow range is zero? When you select the alternate button do you get the same result?

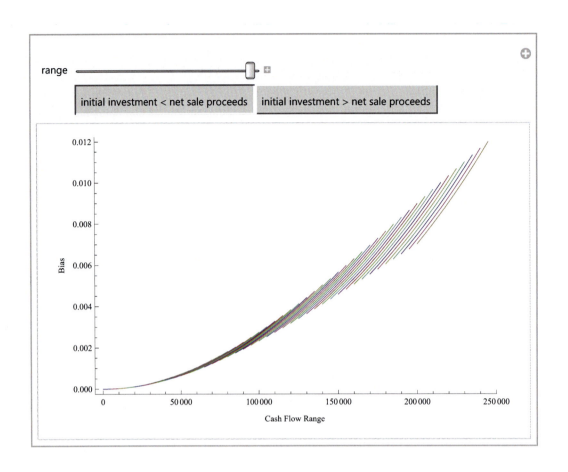

Appendix - Various Ways to Calculate the *irr* using Mathematica

There are several ways to program *Mathematica* to compute the *irr*. For those with *Mathematica* several are illustrated here. All require a dataset of project inputs. We use the data and the input relations employed in Chapter 4.

```
data = {dp -> 375 000,
        gsi -> 200 000,
        vacrt -> .1,
        exprt -> .35,
        txrt -> .35,
        dprt -> 1/27.5,
        land -> .3,
        cro -> .0936,
        g -> .03,
        i -> .11 / 12,
        initln -> 875 000,
        t -> 360,
        r -> .13,
        k -> 6,
      scrt -> .075,
      cgrt -> .15,
    recapturerate → .25,
      ppmt -> 0,
   units -> 22};
```

$$vac = gsi * vacrt;$$
$$egi = gsi - vac;$$
$$exp = egi * exprt;$$
$$noi = gsi - vac - exp;$$
$$ds = 12 \left(\frac{i}{1 - \frac{1}{(1+i)^t}} \right) initln;$$
$$btcf = noi - ds;$$
$$grm = (dp + initln) / gsi;$$
$$ppu = (dp + initln) / units;$$
$$dcr = noi / ds;$$
$$ltv = initln / (dp + initln);$$
$$basis = dp + initln;$$
$$depn = (basis - (basis * land)) * dprt;$$
$$bal_{12} = \frac{ds}{12} \frac{1 - \frac{1}{(1+i)^{t-12}}}{i};$$
$$int_t = ds - (initln - bal_{12});$$
$$txbl = noi - int_t - depn;$$
$$tx = txbl * txrt;$$
$$cf0 = btcf - tx;$$
$$cri = noi / (dp + initln);$$
$$ccRet = \frac{cf0}{dp};$$
$$bal[n\_] := \frac{ds}{12} \frac{1 - \frac{1}{(1+i)^{t-n*12}}}{i};$$
$$endbal := bal[k] \ /. \ data;$$
$$int[n\_] := (ds \ /. \ data) - (bal[n-1] - bal[n]);$$
$$netop[n\_] := noi \ (1+g)^{n-1};$$
$$accdp[n\_] := depn * n;$$
$$yrtx[n\_] := \left(noi \ (1+g)^{n-1} - int[n] - depn\right) * txrt;$$
$$cf[n\_] := noi \ (1+g)^{n-1} - ds - yrtx[n];$$
$$sp = \left(noi \ (1+g)^k\right) / cro;$$
$$sc = scrt * sp;$$
$$cg = sp - sc - basis + accdp[k];$$
$$cgtx = (cg - accdp[k]) * cgrt + recapture;$$
$$recapture = accdp[k] \ recapturerate;$$
$$er = sp - sc - cgtx - endbal - ppmt;$$
$$npv := \frac{er}{(1+r)^k} + \left(\sum_{n=1}^{k} Evaluate\left[\frac{cf[n]}{(1+r)^n}\right]\right) - dp;$$

The matrix method

First we create a list of after tax cash flows which we name "`cflist`". Note that we start with year #1, adding the equity reversion to the last year, which takes some additional manipulation to get **cflist** in the right form. (This is the method employed in Chapter 4).

```
irrdata = data;
partlist = {Table[cf[n] /. irrdata, {n, 1, k - 1 /. irrdata}]};
endcf = {{(cf[k] /. irrdata) + (er /. irrdata)}};
cflist = Join[partlist[[1]], endcf[[1]]]
```

{20 811.8, 22 933.8, 25 105.7, 27 327.6, 29 599.1, 501 841.}

The internal rate of return is the number that solves the following equation for r

$$\sum_{n=1}^{k} \frac{ATCF_n}{(1+r)^n} + \frac{ATER_k}{(1+r)^k} - \text{initial investment} = 0$$

Mathematica considers this a problem of finding the "root" of the equation. Thus we need a polynomial into which we insert the **cflist**. We begin by creating a table that will represent the power series necessary. The variable $v = \frac{1}{(1+r)}$

```
irrtbl = Table[v^i, {i, 1, Length[cflist]}];
irrpoly = irrtbl.cflist;
irrstep := FindRoot[irrpoly == (dp /. irrdata), {v, 1 / 1.1, 0, 1}];
irr := (v^-1 - 1) /. irrstep[[1]];
Print["The irr for this data is: ", irr * 100, "%"]
```

The *irr* for this data is: 10.1146%

A more direct method

Mathematica offers a variety of ways to approach different problems, some more elegant than others. The method above has the advantage of using matrices which may be more familiar to those used to spreadsheet programs. Below is a more straightforward approach that requires better programming skills and requires defining and then clearing the variable *k*. Of course both provide the same answer.

```
k = k /. data; cft = (Sum[cf[n]/(1 + ir)^n, {n, 1, k}] + er/(1 + ir)^k - dp) /. data;
cfs = Solve[cft == 0, ir];
irr = Select[ir /. cfs, Positive[#] &][[1]];
Print["The irr for this data is: ", irr * 100 "%"];
k =.
```

The *irr* for this data is: 10.1146 %

Or, using built in *Mathematica* functions TimeValue and CashFlow, one only must organize the cash flow stream carefully

```
FindRoot[TimeValue[Cashflow[Join[{-dp /. data}, cflist]], r, 0] == 0, {r, .05}]
```

{r → 0.101146}

The module method

A fourth method employs more compact programming style in a module that takes advantage of the dampened Newton iteration that **FindRoot** employs internally. It also begins the search just above 0 resulting in a correct answer for nearly all types of cash flows.

```
Clear[irr]
```

```
irr[p_List,
    t_List, amount_] := Module[{q},
  1/ (q /. FindRoot[p. (q#1 &) /@ t == amount,
        {q, 1.*^-6}]) - 1]
time = Table[t, {t, 1, (k /. data)}];
Print["The irr for this data is: ", irr[cflist, time, dp /. data] * 100 "%"];
```

The *irr* for this data is: 10.1146%

The "package" method

Finally, included in the software that accompanies this book is a *Mathematica* package that contains pre-written routines for calculating both *npv* and *irr*. Below we calculate these measures using the package. Note that the Help Browser description describes options for sequential holding periods including those arising from acquisition via tax deferred exchange, discussed in Chapter 10. Because of concepts developed in later chapters you will notice differences between the data set below and that used in thus far in this chapter. First, the dataset below employs a longfilename convention commonly used in writing *Mathematica* packages. Second, the list of input values is slightly different, allowing greater flexibility to use the ideas presented in Chapter 10. Accordingly, the *irr* computed below is slightly different from that computed above.

```
<< RealEstate`Analysis2011`

base =
  {downpayment -> 375 000,
    initialnetoperatingincome -> 117 000,
    investorincometaxrate -> .35,
    buildingdepreciationrate -> 1 / 27.5,
    landpercentofproperty -> .3,
    capitalizationrateatsale -> .0936,
    monotonicgrowth -> .03,
   logisticconstant -> 0,
   accelerationfactor -> 0,
    interestrate -> .11 / 12,
    initialloanbalance -> 875 000,
    totalamortizationperiod -> 360,
    investorrequiredrateofreturn -> .10,
    terminalyear -> 6,
    sellingcostrate -> .075,
    capitalgainrate -> .22,
  recapturerate -> .22,
    prepaymentpenalty -> 0,
    numberofunits -> 22};
```

? NPV

NPV[data] inputs a list of values as data and computes net present value of an investment property.
NPV[data1,data2,propertynumber,exData] inputs two lists of values as data and computes net present value based on the aggregate results of two properties over sequential holding periods. If propertynumber=1 exData argument may be omitted. If propertynumber=2 exData must be the exchange dataset, the Exchange.m package must be loaded and the CarryoverBasis module must have been evaluated.

NPV[base]

```
127.111
```

? IRR

IRR[data] inputs a list of values as data and computes the internal rate of return for an investment property.
IRR[data1,data2,propertynumber,exData] inputs two lists of values as data and computes the internal rate of return of a sequence of two properties if propertynumber =2. If propertynumber = 1 propertynumber and exData arguments may be omitted. If propertynumber=2 exData must be the exchange dataset, the Exchange.m package must be loaded and the CarryoverBasis module must have been evaluated.

IRR[base]

```
0.100071
```

6

Chance: Risk in general

"Scientific knowledge is a body of statements of varying degrees of certainty - some most unsure, some nearly sure, none absolutely certain."

Richard P. Feynman "The Value of Science" published in <u>The Pleasure of Finding Things Out</u>, Perseus Publishing, Cambridge, MA, 2000, p. 146.

6.1. Introduction

Perhaps one of the most complex notions of the interconnectedness of modern society is the relationship between risk and reward. Each day we take risks of varying kinds. Presumably we evaluate prospects rationally prior to taking risks and decide which risks are "worth it". When we embark on any endeavor with an uncertain outcome we are saying, however casually or informally, that the risk is worth the reward. In so doing we put a *price or value on risk bearing*. We see the price of a shirt in a department store and compare it with the value we place on it before purchasing it. We do the same with investment opportunities. The color, texture, cut, weight, fit and style right down to the buttons of the shirt all play a part in reaching our conclusion that the shirt is or is not worth the price. Likewise, we go through a calculus for accepting or rejecting risky propositions based on a list of criteria we have developed in our minds about what is an appropriate return for the risk involved. This list and the way we process it creates an interesting thought experiment about what part of this calculus is objective, making it truly like a calculus, and what part is subjective making it more like a "feeling" or emotion. The former has properties of known laws of mathematics and physics; the latter is intuition. With only mathematics we can *understand risk*. More is required to *undertake risk*.

This section begins in earnest our investigation of risk. In this chapter we will:

- Address risk more formally than we have thus far;
- Explore the origins of risk as seen through games of chance;
- Re-introduce the utility function, in fact several of them, to illustrate how risk is "priced"; and
- Work through the mathematics of probability and utility for binary outcomes (two results), then multiple discrete outcomes (a few results), concluding with probability in a continuous setting (lots of results).

6.1.1. Objective and subjective risk

The overarching goal of this chapter is to provide context in which to think about investment risk. Embedded in this is the notion of objective and subjective evaluation. It would be nice to clearly separate these. This goal is elusive. If you watch as I flip a fair coin into the air, catch it covered with my hand and then ask you whether it landed heads or tails up, your response is subjective. Whatever you respond must be based on what you "feel" was the outcome. On the other hand, if I flip a coin into the air 1000 times and ask you *over the telephone* approximately how many times it came up heads you could answer without having seen me, the coin, any of the flips or their outcomes. You don't have to "feel" anything about approximately how 1000 trials ended. Elementary understanding of probability tells you *objectively* that in a large number of flips, heads will come up about 50% of the time.

Probability theory, the laws of large numbers and statistics are powerful tools and we shall discuss them briefly here for their applicability to real estate investments. But we must never lose sight of the fact that just as it is impossible to flip a building in the air even once, much less 1000 times, it is impossible to capture all of real estate risk with mathematics. Despite improving our data and the tools we use to analyze it, there will always be a subjective aspect of risk evaluation in privately owned real estate investments. Does this mean that we ignore mathematics when thinking about real estate investment? No, knowledge of mathematical technicalities enhances one's *understanding* of risk bearing. A street-wise appreciation of subjective risk evaluation enhances the *undertaking* of risk. This is an excellent example of the difference between academia and the real world: Understanding risk and profitably taking risk involve very different skills. The challenge we face is combining the two in some useful way. A complicating issue that specifically bears on privately owned real estate investments is the impact of owner management. By this we mean the addition of entrepreneurial skill to the process, not the day-to-day renting, maintaining and accounting functions all of which can be acquired for the payment of wages or commissions to managers. Public financial markets are organized in a way that separates ownership from control. Private real estate investment combines them. The effect of this on the investment result should not be ignored.

Before we take up the thorny issues of risk in real estate we must build a foundation for it from classical risk models that date back centuries. These involve the St. Petersburg Paradox, expected utility theory and the theory of consumer choice under conditions of uncertainty.

6.2. Games of chance and risk bearing

We are interested in learning how people make decisions in the presence of uncertainty. One way to do this is to think about having to choose between certain and uncertain options and how one might put a price on the difference.

The St. Petersburg Paradox (attributed to Daniel Bernoulli in the 1700s) concerns the value of participating in a "fair game". The simplest of these is flipping a coin that has an equal probability of coming down either heads or tails. The game is "fair" in the long run if, each time, one pays a $1 to play and wins $1 plus the return of his bet if he bets tails and the coin comes up tails. In the long run (defined as a series of a large number of equivalent bets) the investor playing this game neither gains nor wins on average. Sometimes we will be ahead, sometimes behind. Some players will win (sometimes a lot), some players will lose.

Let us imagine a different version of the coin flipping game. In this game the prize is paid when the first head appears and the amount of the prize is dependent on the number flips prior to the appearance of the first head. Stated differently, the prize depends on the number of tails that appear in a row. The prize is $2 raised to the power of the number of tails appearing before the first head. Suppose the participant has to pay a fee each round to play. How much should one be willing to pay to enter this game? When one buys an investment with an uncertain outcome (offering different prospective net present values or internal rates of return) we can view the purchase price as a fee to enter the "game" which that investment represents. In Chapter 5 we said that investments are a gamble even if they do not appear on the surface to be games of chance. The mere presence of uncertain prospects makes investments eligible for evaluation in a probabilistic framework.

Table 6.1 demonstrates, for our coin flipping game, how the probability falls as the number of tails before a head appears grows. But at the same time the value of the prize increases. The expected value of the game is the sum of the probability of an outcome times its payoff over all the possible outcomes. The Paradox arises from the fact that, taking n to infinity, the expected payoff is infinite. Thus, one should be willing to pay an infinite amount to play. Yet we observe that people are actually only willing to pay a nominal amount. What explains this?

Here in mathematical symbols using *Mathematica* syntax as input and its related output, is what we just said in words ("Sum does not converge" is *Mathematica*'s way of saying that the sum of the terms cannot be expressed as a finite number).

$$\sum_{n=1}^{\infty} N\left[\left(\frac{1}{2}\right)^n 2^{n-1}\right]$$

Sum::div : Sum does not converge. »

$$\sum_{n=1}^{\infty} 0.5$$

n	p(n)	payoff	p(n) payoff
1	0.5	1	0.5
2	0.25	2	0.5
3	0.125	4	0.5
4	0.0625	8	0.5
5	0.03125	16	0.5
6	0.015625	32	0.5
7	0.0078125	64	0.5
8	0.00390625	128	0.5
9	0.00195313	256	0.5
10	0.000976563	512	0.5
11	0.000488281	1024	0.5

Table 6.1. Probabilities and payoffs in the St. Petersburg Paradox coin flipping game

In addition to the intuitive reasons, here are some graphical illustrations of why rational risk takers would not bet a significant amount of wealth on this game.

First, we show the probability of recovering at least the cost of playing the game assuming one paid $\$2^k$, where k is the number of rounds prior to a success (heads). Below we plot the intersection of the realization of two functions, the payoff = entry cost on the x axis and the payoff probability for each round on the y axis. Recall that the probability that payoff occurs at or after k is $\sum_{n=k}^{\infty} \left(\frac{1}{2}\right)^n$, or 1 - the probability that payoff occurs before k. As we see in Figure 6.1, the more you play (and pay), the lower your chances of recovering your entry fee. This is an unappealing prospect, to say the least.

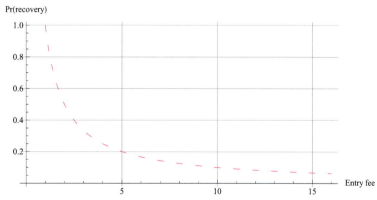

Figure 6.1. Probability of recovery as entry fee increases.

Second, since doubling the payoff of 2^k is $2 \times 2^k = 2^{k+1}$, we can add to the above graph the chance of doubling your money. In Figure 6.2 the probabilities are even lower over the same number of rounds.

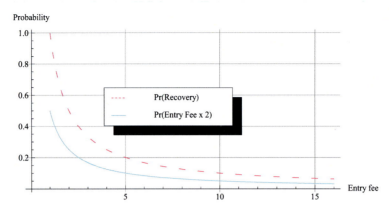

Figure 6.2. Probabilities of recovery and doubling one's money as entry fee increases.

There is another problem with this game. We are concerned that the bank offering this bet cannot take the loss (will go bankrupt) if the payoff becomes too high. To avoid this we limit the number of rounds that may take place. Taking the expected value of a series of different k, each acting as a cap, and comparing it with the expected value of the payoff shows a drastic reduction in expectations, even for a very large bank. This may be seen best in two illustrations. First, all is well if only three rounds are permitted. The maximum Payoff is $8 ($2^3$) and the expected value of that payoff is $2. But dramatic things happen with even a modest number of extra rounds. On the right side of Figure 6.3 we see that a game of 30 rounds still has a small expected value but exposes the bank to a loss of over $1 Trillion.

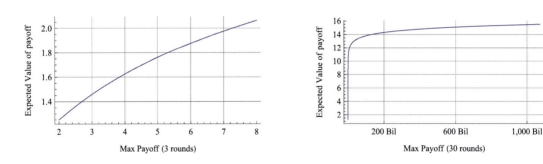

Figure 6.3. Risk of the St. Petersburg Paradox coin flipping game to the sponsor.

So Bernoulli's coin flipping game is hard to justify. Later we question whether real estate investors can *ever* justify a game in which the risk is based on flipping coins.

6.3. The utility function revisited

We first encountered the idea of utility in Chapter Two, using it to indicate conditions under which a community was "better off" depending on how they made choices. There is a natural extension to the individual (some would argue that individual utility is the starting point and the extension is to the community but we won't quibble with such things here). People make choices. Some are good, some are bad. Very often, in fact usually, it is not possible to know in advance whether a choice will turn out to be a good one or not. Models that involve choice under conditions of uncertainty need a way to measure outcome. Utility serves in that capacity, going up or down depending on the success achieved following a given choice.

From a mathematical standpoint there is a practical aspect of utility that involves the illustration of results graphically. Each of the two choices requires an axis. We need a third axis to scale and measure the benefit or cost of any outcome arising from making choices or choosing different combinations of the two choices.

Despite the fact that we grapple with multiple-dimensional problems daily (ask the parent of two children!), the display on a 3D graph can be confusing. In Figure 6.4 one should focus on any point on the vertical axis labeled "Utility". Recall that utility is ordinal, meaning that higher on that axis is better. At any given point on that vertical axis there is a corresponding point on the plane where the combination of two choices intersect to create the value on the vertical axis. For example, on the left of Figure 6.4 a line connects the utility value of 30 with the values 5 and 6 for Choice A and B respectively. Here utility is a function of the product of these two choice values. The rendering on the right of Figure 6.4 is the same plot with a flat plane at utility value = 30 intersecting the utility function at all the points where the two choices may be combined in different ways to produce utility of 30.[1]

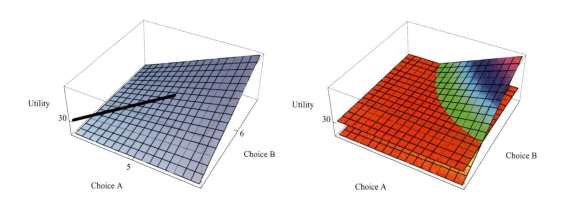

Figure 6.4. Utility as a function of two choices.

While Bernoulli's game may be unappetizing, people *do* take other kinds of risks.[2] To help us deal with what we actually observe in people's actions, we make a critical assumption: People *do not* value each dollar the same. Further, we assume, people place a *diminishing marginal* value on each additional dollar (think about how much an extra $100 means to you and what you imagine an extra $100 means to the average billionaire) Thus, people derive different "utility" from different amounts of money based on how much money they start with. The mathematical way of expressing this is with a curved function to represent people's utility. Figure 6.5 shows several such functions:

Figure 6.5. Several forms of utility functions.

An important and desirable property of any function we might use to illustrate decreasing marginal utility is that the curve of a plot of that function is concave. Of the four curved functions in Figure 6.5, only the first three qualify (the fourth, being convex, represents *increasing* marginal utility). Of the three, the one most often used by economists is the first one, the Log function. Thus, Figure 6.6 illustrates the utility function as the Log of its argument, which is wealth (w) in our case.

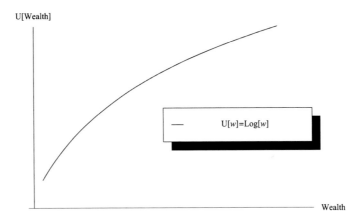

Figure 6.6. Utility as a function of the log of wealth.

In the original game, Bernoulli's series leads to infinity.

$$\sum_{n=1}^{\infty}\left(\frac{1}{2}\right)^n 2^{n-1} = \infty \tag{6.1}$$

Now when we apply Bernoulli's infinite series to the Log of the payoff it converges to a finite number...

$$\sum_{n=1}^{\infty}\left(\frac{1}{2}\right)^n Log[2^n] = 0.693147 \tag{6.2}$$

...which, we confirm by employing it as the exponent of the base of the natural log, is the natural log of 2.

$e^{0.693147}$

2.

This produces a reasonable amount one might pay to enter Bernoulli's game The two assumptions (1) that people maximize the utility of money not money itself and (2) that the utility function is concave, lead us to what is known as the Expected Utility Hypothesis. This is how the paradox is resolved.[3]

Recall from Chapter 2 that the numerical representation of utility had no *cardinal* meaning for the community, rather it was *ordinal* (meaning that its only usefulness is in *ranking* the value of alternatives). This carries over to people and the choices they make about prospects with uncertain outcomes. In a real estate context, most people would view an investment in a true triple-net ground lease beneath a branch of the United States Post Office differently than an investment in an 18 unit apartment building occupied by 75 college students Few would have any difficulty ranking these two in a risk hierarchy. We have purposely chosen extreme alternatives to illustrate our point. One needs a mechanism for thinking about risk in more realistic settings when the alternatives may not be so obvious. For instance, how would we compare two commercial structures, one occupied by a major clothing retailer and another by a major appliance retailer? Or two similar apartment buildings on different sides of the street? Many such opportunities present themselves. They have different risk and while the difference may not be great *there is a difference* and one must be preferred over the other. Our goal in this chapter is to discover a way of ranking risky opportunities in a rational manner. As is so often the case, "rational" means mathematical.[4]

6.4. The "certainty equivalent" approach

The search for a sound way to evaluate risky alternatives leads to an inquiry into how discounts come about. We assume that nearly anything of value can be sold if the price is lowered. Risky alternatives, as "things of value", become more appealing as the entry fee is reduced (because the return increases). The idea that describes this situation well is known as the "certainty equivalent" approach. We ask an investor to choose a point of indifference between opportunities having a certain outcome and an uncertain outcome, given that the price of the opportunity with the uncertain outcome is sufficiently discounted.

Let us use a concrete example to illustrate the concept. Suppose someone has $100,000 and the chance to invest it that provides two (and only two) equiprobable outcomes, one of $150,000 (the good result) and the other of $50,000 (the unfortunate outcome). The certain alternative is to do nothing, which pays $100,000. We want to know what is necessary to entice our investor away from this certain position and into an investment with an uncertain outcome. In Figure 6.7 we see the plot *of utility* of these uncertain outcomes as wealth rises or falls. Note the three points of interest, constituting the original wealth and the two outcomes. Our investor must decide if the gain in utility associated with winning $50,000 is more or less than the loss of utility associated with losing $50,000. The answer is found on the *y*-axis of Figure 6.7.

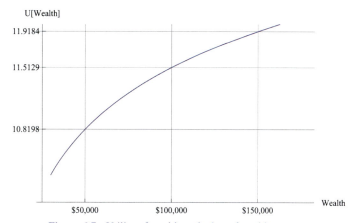

Figure 6.7. Utility of wealth as the log of wealth.

The question of how much to pay for an investment with an uncertain outcome is answered by placing a numerical value on the difference between the utility of the certain opportunity and the utility of the uncertain one. How do we do this in practice? To begin with, notice that the expectation of wealth in this fair game is zero. That is, the mathematical expectation is Beginning Wealth + (probability of gain times winning payoff) - (probability of loss times amount of loss) = zero. Since the outcomes are equally probable, the probability of either event is .5 so we have

Probability		Payoff		Change		Begin Wealth		End Wealth
0.5	x	(100,000) =	(50,000)	+	100,000	=	50,000
0.5	x	100,000 =	50,000	+	100,000	=	150,000
		Expectation	0				100,000

Table 6.2. Mathematical expectation

The graphic representation of this situation is, of course, linear and represents how people who are "risk neutral" view the world.[5] Most people, as we will see in a moment, are presumed to be risk averse. The perspective of the risk neutral party is the reference from which we start to place a value on risk bearing. There are a variety of ways of plotting the risk neutral position, one of which appears In Figure 6.8.

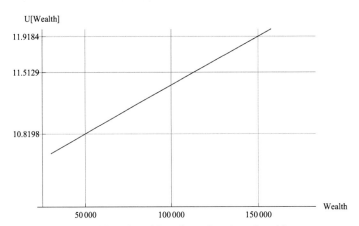

Figure 6.8. Utility of wealth as linear function of wealth.

Notice when comparing the two curves in Figure 6.9 that, relative to the *y*-axis, they both pass through the same points on the *x* axis representing the alternative outcomes. But when they pass through initial wealth they generate different values on the *y*-axis. Figure 6.9 shows the two plots on one graph.

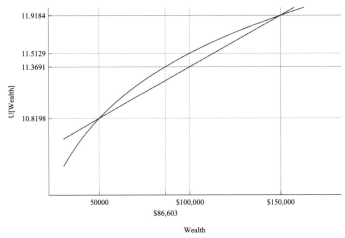

Figure 6.9. Different utility functions for different outcomes.

Note that the difference between the change in utility associated with an increase in one's wealth and the change in utility associated with an equivalent (in nominal terms) decrease in one's wealth shows that the lost utility associated with losing $50,000 is greater than the utility gained by winning $50, 000.[6]

Utility of wealth increase	Utility of wealth decrease
0.405465	0.693147
Utility of Expectation	Expectation of the utility
11.5129	11.3691

Table 6.3. Difference in utilities for gains and losses

The conclusion we reach is that *in order to be compensated for bearing risk,* our investor must be offered the opportunity to pay less than the raw expectation ($100,000) . This is reasonable. Why would someone who already has $100,000 pay $100,000 for a 50/50 proposition knowing that in a large number of trials he will merely breakeven? From the graph above we note that utility for the risky prospect is the same as the utility of the certainty of $100,000 (the "do nothing" position) if the risky opportunity is priced at $86,603. Certainty equivalent is a way of saying that the investor is indifferent between paying $86,603 for the 50/50 opportunity to increase or decrease his wealth $50,000 or having a certain $100,000. How is $86,603 calculated? We know that the expectation of the utility of wealth as shown on the *y* axis of the plot is:

```
certequivW = .5 u[50 000] + .5 u[150 000]
```

11.3691

And we know that number is produced by a function we have chosen **u1[w]** = Log(*w*). Thus, we solve for the known value of *u* by "exponenting" both sides of Equation 6.1:

$$Log[Certainty\ Equivalent\ Wealth] = 11.3691 \qquad (6.3)$$

Doing this to the left side eliminates the Log function and leaves the Certainty Equivalent Wealth as the unknown. Doing it to the right side leaves $e^{11.3691}$ which is easily evaluated using a calculator because *e* is just a number, a constant approximately equal to 2.71828.

$$e^{Log[Certainty\ Equivalent\ Wealth]} = e^{11.3691} \qquad (6.4)$$

$$Certainty\ Equivalent\ Wealth = 86,603.90 \qquad (6.5)$$

The difference between this number and $100,000, the sum of $13,397, is the "discount" the investor applies to the raw expectation, given his specific preference for risk as represented by the shape of his utility function. Stated differently, the discount is the compensation he requires to accept a prospect involving this sort of risk. When a real estate broker asks his client to take money out of a saving account to buy an apartment building it is the discount and its associated prospect of a higher return on the net invested that motivates the buyer to act.

Two final points about this simplified approach are useful. Not only is the concavity of the utility function important, but "how concave" it is matters as we will see in the next section. Additionally, the discount calculated above is a function of not only the *shape* of the utility function but the *spread* of potential returns. Above our investor requires a relatively large discount of more than 13% as a percentage of the amount risked. Below we lower the potential gain or loss to $10,000 and the discount drops to about .5%. The conclusion one might reach is that risk aversion is relative to both one's initial wealth and the portion of that wealth at stake in an uncertain situation. This mathematically supports sage advice that one should not bet more than one can afford to lose.

```
newcertequivW = .5 u[90 000] + .5 u[110 000];
e^newcertequivW;
newdisc = 100 000 - e^newcertequivW
```

501.256

6.5. Changing utility functions

In Figure 6.5, we illustrated three curves that might be taken to represent utility. We chose the first of these, *y* = Log(*x*) and assumed it represented the way investors decide among uncertain alternatives. To emphasize the importance of that assumption, let's choose one of the others. The second one, $y = \sqrt{x}$ is as good as any. We return to our original example but define a new utility function, **u2**:

$$u2[w] = \sqrt{w} \qquad (6.6)$$

Of course if utility of wealth is the square root of wealth, the inverse (wealth in terms of utility) tells us that wealth is the square of utility of wealth. So with this utility function the certainty equivalent utility for our same 50/50 proposition is...

    `certequivW2 = .5 u2[50 000] + .5 u2[150 000]`

    305.453

...which means that the wealth needed to produce that certainty equivalent utility is...

    `certequivW2`^{2}

    93 301.3

...and the discount required to induce the investor to purchase the opportunity is...

    `disc2 = 100 000 - certequivW2`^{2}

    6698.73

...about half of the earlier discount. Therefore, we see that one who employs our second utility function will pay somewhat more (or requires less discount) for the opportunity than our first investor. All of which serves as a warning to choose your utility function carefully.

In practice this becomes an admonition to choose your clients carefully. More specifically, one needs to carefully match the risk of investments offered to clients having the appropriate risk tolerance. Various consumer protection laws governing the standard of care required of investment advisors are based on whether investments are "suitable" for the client. Suitability may be a term of art but it starts with the client's ability to tolerate risk as reflected in his utility function.

Note in Figure 6.10 that when we place a straight line on the plot of our second utility function we notice that the degree of curvature of the new utility function is less than that for our original utility function. This result indicates that our investor with the second utility function is *more risk tolerant* in that he will demand a smaller discount to enter this particular game. The fact that the scale of the *y*-axis is completely different from the prior example serves to reinforce what we have said about numerical utility. We care not about the actual value of utility, only how it is ranked relative to some other choice.

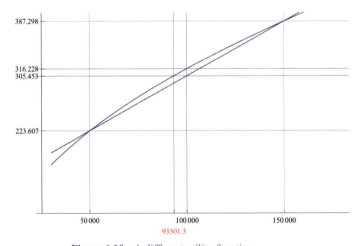

Figure 6.10. A different utility function.

6.6. A measure of risk aversion

Pratt (1964) observed that the degree of curvature in a utility function is a way to measure one's risk aversion (*ra*).[7] How curved a function is can be represented by the negative of the ratio of its second derivative to its first derivative.

$$ra = -\frac{u''[w]}{u'[w]} \tag{6.7}$$

For illustration purposes, it is convenient to have a function that contains a constant we can manipulate to demonstrate this effect, thus for this discussion we employ our third utility function of the three candidates described in Figure 6.5, which we name **u3**

$$u3[w] = -e^{-aw} \tag{6.8}$$

Dividing the second derivative of this function by its first derivative shows that the "coefficient of risk aversion" for this utility function is a constant, *a*. [It should be noted that in general the curvature can change from point to point. The exponential is special in that the curvature is constant. This is another case of choosing a "convenient" mathematical form to model an economic behavioral abstraction.]

$$ra[w] = \frac{\partial_{w,w} u3[w]}{\partial_w u3[w]} = a \tag{6.9}$$

It is this number that determines how risk averse an investor is and what sort of discount he will require to take a particular risk. In Figure 6.11 we take "*a*" to equal 1.

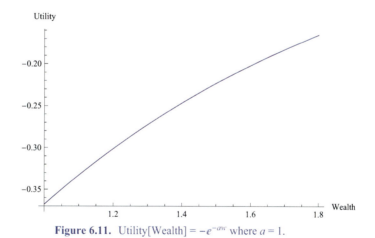

Figure 6.11. Utility[Wealth] = $-e^{-aw}$ where $a = 1$.

Plotting the function with different values for "*a*" we see that the higher the value for "*a*" the more the function curves.

131

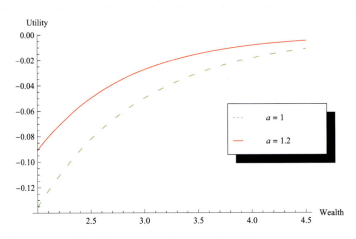

Figure 6.12. Utility[Wealth] $= -e^{-\alpha w}$ where α has different values.

As the coefficient of risk aversion increases the investor becomes more risk averse, his utility function "bows" more and a larger discount is require to entice him into the game.

Here are two examples of discounts required by different investors, each with a different level of risk aversion, as they approach the same investment opportunity. In both cases they start with wealth equal to 3 (feel free to add your own zeros to scale it to whatever level of wealth seems reasonable) and a 50/50 chance of either increasing it to 4 or decreasing it to 2. The "raw expectation" is, of course the original wealth because one half of 2 + 4 is 3. The first investor has a risk aversion of 1.

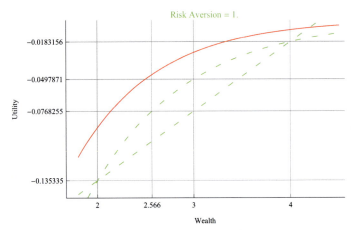

Figure 6.13. First investor with risk aversion = 1.

Figure 6.13 shows that an investor with a coefficient of risk aversion of 1 requires a discount of 3 - 2.566 = .434 as calculated below. The straight line shows risk neutrality as a reference point. We are interested in how risk averse a particular investor is. We see this graphically in the curvature of the line and numerically in the difference between the value at risk neutrality and the value at the price the investor is willing to pay. Imagine two family members, one a 25 year-old and the other the 25-year old's grandparent. Who would you expect to be more risk averse? Given an opportunity to invest in the same project who would you expect to be willing to pay more? It is true that age is not strictly determinative. There are very conservative 25 year olds and some of them may have gunslinger grandfathers. But for the vast majority the analogy is apt.

```
disc1 = 3 - w1;
NumberForm[%, {4, 3}]
```
0.434

Now we consider an investor with coefficient of risk aversion of 1.2 (Recall that *Mathematica* syntax " /.*a*→1.2 " means "given that *a* equals 1.2 for this calculation")

```
exp2 = N[.5 u3[2] + .5 u3[4]] /. a → 1.2
```
−0.0494739

```
w2 = Solve[-a w == Log[-exp2] /. a → 1.2, w][[1, 1]][[2]]
```
2.50526

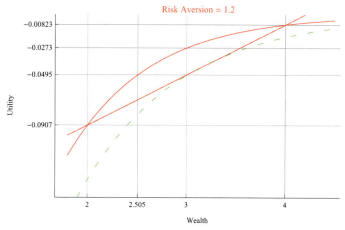

Figure 6.14. Second investor with risk aversion = 1.2.

Figure 6.14 shows that one with a risk aversion of 1.2 requires a discount of 3 - 2.50526 = 0.495, slightly higher (0.06096) than that calculated for the investor with a risk aversion of 1.

A concave utility function means that people value different dollars differently. The coefficient of risk aversion tells us *how much differently* those dollars are valued by different people. This has important implications for the market for uncertain investments. Such a market commands higher prices if populated by people with low coefficients of risk aversion as they require smaller discounts. Figure 6.15 provides the opportunity to adjust the coefficient of risk aversion, noting how different investors would "price" the risk by following the discounted price (on the *x* axis in red) offered under each situation.

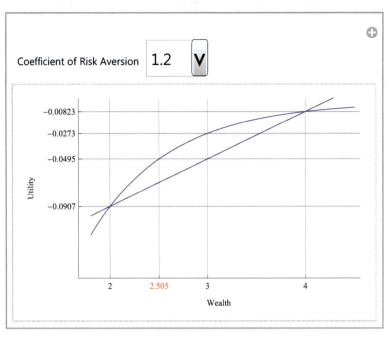

Figure 6.15. A range of risk aversion functions.

6.7. Multiple (more than two) outcomes

Returning to our first utility function (u[w] = Log[w]) we can extend this result to more than two outcomes, each with different probabilities. In Table 6.4 we define some payoffs under different conditions (numbers can represent thousands or millions of dollars to make them more realistic):

	payoffs	probabilities	products
	35.00	0.15	5.25
	65.00	0.25	16.25
	20.00	0.10	2.00
	80.00	0.45	36.00
	95.00	0.05	4.75
sums		1.00	64.25

Table 6.4. Expected value of five payoffs

We then associate a specific probability with each payoff. Note the important fact that they add up to 1. Where did these probabilities come from? Quite simply, we made them up!! (Alert readers will recognize these numbers from the discussion of Jensen's Inequality in Chapter 5). These are *subjective* probabilities, what we think or feel will happen. Objective probability comes, in part, from understanding large numbers representing what *has* happened. Five outcomes is certainly not a large number of possible outcomes, but we are approaching these ideas in increments.

Multiplying the payoffs and the probabilities together and adding them up (the 'dot product' of two vectors in matrix algebra), we arrive at the expectation (note that this is the same as the sum in the lower right of Table 6.4) of 64.25, making the utility, based on our original log utility function, 4.16278. We then compute the utility of each payoff, {3.55535, 4.17439, 2.99573, 4.38203, 4.55388} and take the expectation 4.07608 to conclude, not surprisingly, that the utility of the expectation is greater than the expectation of the utility.

$$U[E(w)] > E[U(w)] \Longleftrightarrow 4.16278 > 4.07608 \qquad (6.10)$$

```
uexp ≥ expu
```
```
True
```

Table 6.5 summarizes the utility calculations above

	U(payoffs)	probabilities	products
	3.5553	0.1500	0.5333
	4.1744	0.2500	1.0436
	2.9957	0.1000	0.2996
	4.3820	0.4500	1.9719
	4.5539	0.0500	0.2277
sums		1.0000	4.0761

Table 6.5. Expected utility of five payoffs

So far we have been working with discrete outcomes matched by given probabilities. Essentially we claim to know the range of possibilities represented by a *discrete* probability distribution. The claim that we *know* these precise probabilities is ambitious to say the least.

6.8. The continuous normal case

The final step for this chapter is to imagine a very large number of possible payoffs and an equally large number of associated specific probabilities. What can one say about those circumstances? The limit of this question is the notion of a probability distribution and the related concept of a probability density function (*pdf*). Recall from Chapter 3 that *pdf*s arise from histograms which are merely ordered groups of outcomes. In this case we assume that we know the result of investing in many buildings (the payoffs) by many investors with different utility functions and coefficients of risk aversion.[8] Properly arranged and processed, such data would produce a *pdf*. Alternatively, if we choose a convenient specific distributional form, we can postulate that a large number of payoffs resulting from an equally large number of associated probabilities would produce outcomes such as those described in Figure 6.16.

Mathematica has a function that specifies a probability density function (when one exists) for a continuous variable when one knows something about the distribution. In our case the variable, *w*, will be different wealth levels arising from undertaking different propositions with uncertain outcomes. The easiest distribution to work with is the normal distribution because it can be completely described if one only knows its first two moments, its mean and its variance.[9] So we assume we know these two parameters, therefore its shape. (Beware: this claim is a little less ambitious than the one we made above in the discrete case but still requires a leap of faith). Equation 6.11 defines the probability density function of the normal distribution when the mean is $1,000,000 and the standard deviation is $200,000

$$pdf_1 = \frac{e^{-\frac{(-1\,000\,000 + w)^2}{80\,000\,000\,000}}}{200\,000\sqrt{2\pi}} \qquad (6.11)$$

Note the second parameter in the *Mathematica* input statement - the standard deviation - is in **color** in the *Mathematica* input line to distinguish it as it will change in a subsequent example.

135

```
pdw1 = PDF[NormalDistribution[10^6, 2 × 10^5], w]
```

$$\frac{e^{-\frac{(-1\,000\,000+w)^2}{80\,000\,000\,000}}}{200\,000\,\sqrt{2\,\pi}}$$

In the case of discrete outcomes the expectation is the result of simply multiplying the outcome times the probabilities and adding up the products as we did in Table 6.4 and Table 6.5. For continuous variables the expectation is the mean. Having the *pdf* we can plot this function and its central moment, the mean, also known as its expectation. The amount of probability mass around the mean but away from the mean represents the variance from our expectation, loosely the probability that we are wrong. Imagine the converse, a certain outcome, something guaranteed to happen without fail. The outcome would ALWAYS match our expectation, there would be no variance and the entire distribution would be the straight line in the middle, a single value. But if an opportunity has uncertain outcomes we must allow for outcomes that do not match our expectations, some better and some worse, that aggregate around the expectation. *So we begin to think about risk in terms of the shape of a function* in which we have a field of possible outcomes sprinkled about a line called the expectation. The distribution is shaped in a way that it "peaks" at one (and only one) point. The area of the field is expressed graphically in Figure 6.16 for the normal distribution as a plot of its probability density function.

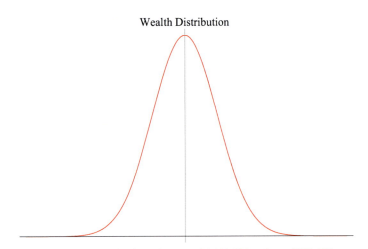

Figure 6.16. Wealth distribution where μ = \$1,000,000 and σ = \$200,000.

Note that the domain is carefully chosen so that the distribution contains mostly positive values. This constraint is for ease of the present exposition with the full discussion of why left for another time (until then we can agree that negative wealth and its related utility does not have a lot of meaning). The integration of the function below shows as much of the probability mass is to the right of zero. [One must accept that ALL normal distributions have negative values. Mathematically one cannot have it any other way. This leads to two observations. First, and most importantly, in a very general sense it speaks of the futility of attempting to reduce risk to zero; second, it points up how the social sciences sometimes must bend mathematics to their purpose].

```
∫₀^(2 × 10^6) pdw1 dw // N
0.999999
```

Alternatively, suppose we had a second game, also having normally distributed outcomes but with different parameters. The critical change is that, while both have the same mean, the second proposition, Equation 6.12, has a larger **standard deviation**:

```
pdw2 = PDF[NormalDistribution[10^6, 2.5 × 10^5], w]
```

$1.59577 \times 10^{-6}\ e^{-8.\times 10^{-12}\,(-1\,000\,000+w)^2}$

Likewise, our second *pdf* covers mostly positive outcomes...

$$\int_0^{2.5 \times 10^6} \text{pdw2 dw // N}$$
0.999968

...and has the same familiar shape...

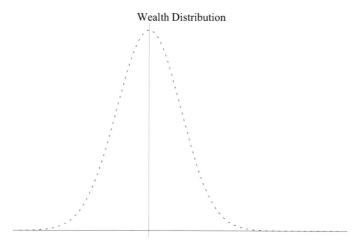

Figure 6.17. Wealth distribution where $\mu = \$1,000,000$ and $\sigma = \$250,000$.

$$pdf_2 = 1.59577 \times 10^{-6} \, e^{-8. \times 10^{-12} \, (w - 1\,000\,000)^2} \tag{6.12}$$

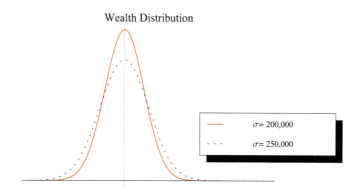

Figure 6.18. Distributions with different standard deviations.

The difference in these shapes means that the spread of outcomes away from our expectation is different, therefore the risk is different. Recall in Chapter 4 we had an investment which modeled in different ways had produced substantially the same 13% *irr*. We postulated that the two *irr*s, while quantitatively the same, were qualitatively different. We pondered how they were different from the standpoint of risk. With the introduction of a probability distribution we move closer to answering that question. We have discussed risk tolerance and utility. We now judiciously combine these ideas with the notion of the distribution's spread, more precisely variance from expectation.

Suppose we have an investor whose decisions about risky alternatives are based on a logarithmic utility function. How would such an investor decide between the two alternatives illustrated in Figure 6.18?

Before we become too tangled in the mathematics let us step back and remind ourselves that the notion of "shape" assists us in understanding risk. It seems that we are interested in both *the shape* of the utility function and *the shape* of the distribution of outcomes. Specifically, we want to know how much area underneath the curve is away from the mean and on what side of the mean. We shall tuck that in the back of our minds for the moment while we wade through some more details.

What follows proceeds on the basis that the reader has some familiarity with transformations of random variables. Transformations can make an otherwise intractable problem manageable. At a minimum, one should know that certain transformations are "shape preserving", thus after transformation the shape of the distribution is the same. The simplest example is a linear transformation, illustrated in Figure 3-16 of Chapter 3, where multiplying a set of values by a constant and/or adding a constant merely rescales and re-centers the distribution. This is how a normal distribution is "standardized" into "standard normal" where the mean is zero and the variance is one. More generally, there are rules for transformations that must be adhered to and certain properties are essential. Numerous references (such as Hogg & Craig, 5th ed. p. 168, et seq) are available to fully elaborate this area. Here is a brief exposition.

A key to transformation is the existence of an inverse, at least over the range of interest. This is easier if there is a one-to-one mapping of set $\mathcal{A}$ onto a set $\mathcal{B}$ as a result of the transformation. By example, suppose we have a random variable y that is a function of x, Thus:

$$y = f(x)$$

But further assume that the inverse function is:

$$x = g(y) = g(f(x))$$

If our interest is the *pdf* of y and we know the pdf of x we can get where we need to go with a transformation

$$pdf_y[y] = pdf_x[g(y)] * |g'(y)|$$

In a later chapter we will encounter an otherwise unmanageable situation in which we are interested in the distribution of utility based on knowing the distribution of wealth. Substituting an appropriate utility function for $g(y)$ and using wealth, w, for x in the above we accomplish desirable results.

Basing utility of wealth on the natural log of wealth is convenient because the inverse of the log function exists (this is also true of the square root function and many others but not all). We can, therefore, express wealth as a function of utility as readily as we can express utility as a function of wealth. Simply w, the inverse of utility, is always exponented utility, $e^{u[w]}$. Also the exponential is, amazingly, its own first derivative, $\frac{du}{dw} = \frac{d}{dw} e^w = e^w = u[w]$. Therefore we can create two lognormal utility distributions from the *pdf*s above. Note that the modes of the utility of wealth as a result of the transformation has moved to the right of their location in the original *pdf*s for wealth.

Returning to the importance of shapes, note that the (normal) symmetry of wealth distribution is lost when operated on by the Log utility function. In Figure 6.19, the plot on the right shows a distinct left skew with the mode to the right of the mean. This is to be expected considering the shape of the utility function.

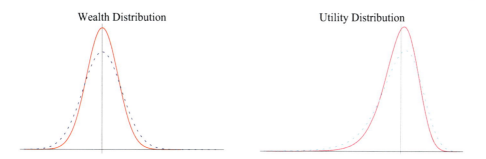

Figure 6.19. The shape of the distribution of wealth and the shape of the distribution of utility of wealth.

In the parametric plot in Figure 6.20 we plot common the intersection of e^{u1} (which you recall is wealth) and the distribution of utility of wealth as utility (u1) changes. This permits plotting utility distribution for our first utility function on a wealth scale.

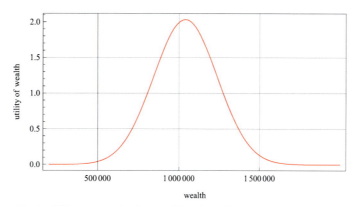

Figure 6.20. Parametric plot of utility of wealth against wealth.

We now combine, in Figure 6.21, two parametric plots showing both distributions on a wealth scale.

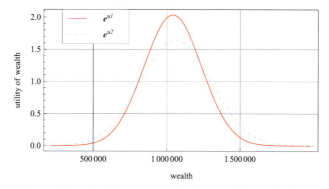

Figure 6.21. Parametric plot of utility of wealth against wealth for two different distributions (portrayals of risk).

The question becomes: Is the investor better off with the investment having the first or second probability distribution? The same Expected Utility Hypothesis that resolved Bernoulli's paradox provides the answer. Remember that the distributions differed only in the variance.

We compute the expected utility of each by integrating the product of the utility function and its probability distribution (this integration is the definition of expectation for continuous variables).

Integrating the functions above is shown below this cell and includes a very small error to consider the fact that we are not including a tiny fraction of the distribution which is negative. The correct output involves creating a truncated *pdf* that specifically precludes negative values and produces the correct expectations you see here:

$$\text{Expected Utility } pdf_1 \quad \text{Expected Utility } pdf_2$$
$$13.7941 \quad\quad\quad 13.7804$$

The result, that the expected utility of **u1** is slightly larger, is intuitively satisfying as one would expect, given identical means and the specific form of the utility function we have chosen, that the distribution having the higher variance (risk) produces less expected utility.

6.9. Conclusion

This chapter lays the foundation upon which we must stand to begin our discussion of risk in real estate. One must appreciate how risk has been dealt with by others to understand how real estate risk differs. Most risk models in finance depend on the classical mathematics of binary probability (coin flipping) and its close cousin, the normal probability distribution. Much ground has been gained on the subject using these models. Important messages to be transferred into our thinking about real estate risk include:

- Utility is a powerful way to express the consequences that arise from making choices;
- By valuing different dollars differently, people make decisions on the margins. It is not average outcomes that count but marginal outcomes;
- The assumption that utility functions are concave is supported by considerable evidence, thus the shape of the utility function bears on the way people evaluate risk;
- A closer look at the shape of utility functions discloses that different people see the same risk differently. Through a bidding process in the market their aggregate behavior determines the price of risky assets;
- Risk is a shape. Specifically, it is the shape of a probability distribution of wealth, a plot of numerous outcomes representing the realization of previously uncertain events; and
- The shape of the transformed probability distribution is related to the shape of one's utility function through the mathematical expectation and the variance.

But, you say, empirical tests of these models have been conducted primarily in the market for financial products. In those markets one can justify using tools based on random outcomes (stock price changes either up or down out of control of the investor).To a good approximation these outcomes may be modeled as continuous. A harsh position might claim that the stock market can be modeled with tools based on gambling because the stock market looks a lot like gambling to some people.

The "some people" who might make this uncharitable characterization are very often real estate investors. At this point they might rightfully ask: "What about us? How should we model risk? These shapes don't look much like our world." These people contend that their market is neither random nor continuous. It may be that it is neither linear nor static (few things are, including the stock market). Accordingly, the risk they face is a very different kind of risk.

It is to those people and their questions that we now turn.

Endnotes

[1] There is a further constraint, provided solely in the interest of exposition, that the maximum value of either choice is 10, hence the minimum to produce 30 is 3.

[2] Not everyone is risk averse and even those who are can be inconsistent. People buy insurance and lottery tickets. The idea of "risk loving" exists but is assumed not be of sufficient importance to affect our discussion here.

[3] Using this reasoning we will shortly develop the idea of risk averse behavior. There is another, less common, resolution using a *convex* utility function. While permitted under the Expected Utility Hypothesis, it implies risk loving behavior, something we observe less frequently than the alternative. The interested student may wish to inquire into the Friedman-Savage utility function.

[4] The reader is urged to be patient with the abstract notion of utility as it is pervasive in economics and in life. It has been observed that even those who don't believe in the expected utility hypothesis *act* as if they do.

[5] Such people are usually not people at all but companies, namely insurance companies having unlimited life and access to capital.

[6] Note the important generality that the utility of the expectation is larger than the expectation of the utility, something that is no surprise to mathematicians who have long known about "Jensen's Inequality" which we discussed in Chapter 5. (This is the converse of the Jensen case in Chapter 5 as this example deals with concave functions and most of our Chapter 5 case involved a convex function).

[7] This is also known as "Arrow-Pratt Absolute Risk Aversion" which may be contrasted with "Relative Risk Aversion" and may be found in most microeconomics texts.

[8] Perhaps a better characterization is investing in the same building a large number of times.

[9] Or the standard deviation, which is the square root of the variance. As the square root transformation is monotonic, it does not matter which is used. The reader is asked to tolerate the rocky motion of moving back and forth between them, something that is unfortunately too common in texts on this subject.

References

Dowd, K. (1999). Too Big to Fail? Long Term Capital Management and the Federal Reserve. Washington, CD: Cato Institute Briefing Paper #52.

Feller, W. (1971). An Introduction to Probability Theory and Its Applications. New York: John Wiley & Sons, Inc.

Hogg, R.V. and Craig, A. T. (1994). Introduction to Mathematical Statistics, 5th Edition. New York: MacMillan.

Lowenstein, R. (2000). When Genius Failed, The Rise and Fall of Long Term Capital Management. New York, NY: Random House.

Nicholson, W. (2002). Microeconomic Theory, 8th Edition. New York: Thompson Learning.

Pratt, J. W. (1964). Risk aversion in the small and in the large. Econometrica 32(1-2). p. 122-136.

Problems

1. Assume you are offered a project requiring a $300,000 down payment. Using Figure 6.15 determine the dollar amount of discount you would require, provided your coefficient of risk aversion is 1.
2. Change the coefficient of risk aversion in Figure 6.15 to another value and compute the discount you would require on an investment offered which requires a capital investment of $500,000, given the coefficient of risk aversion you selected.
3. Using the graphic below, describe an investment that requires a capital outlay. Provide appropriate details for a market offering. Assume there are two investors, one with a risk aversion function which is the log of wealth and one with a risk aversion function of the square root of wealth. Which investor will make the highest offer? How much will that offer be?

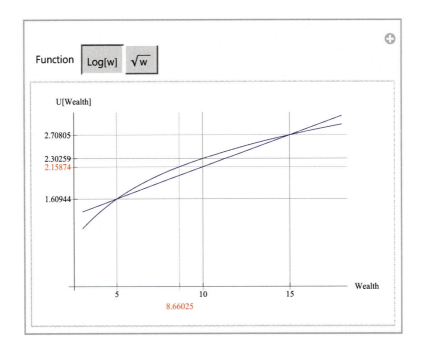

Uncertainty: Risk in Real Estate

"Real Estate is NOT Normal: A fresh look at real estate return distributions"

-- The title of an article by **Michael S. Young** and **Richard A. Graff** published in the Journal of Real Estate Finance and Economics in 1995.

7.1. Introduction

Having laid the foundation for thinking about risk in general terms, our task is the adaptation of these ideas to real estate. At times the fit is quite good. At other times it is quite poor. The discriminating analyst must know which times are which and when to use the right tools.

In this chapter we will:

- Extend the discussion of classical risk to a form more relevant to the market for private (Tier II) real estate investments;
- Explore distributions that may be more useful for Tier II real estate;
- Introduce the concepts of determinism and uncertainty and discuss how those ideas relate to risk;
- Propose an enhancement to classical risk theory that fits private real estate investment; and
- Discuss the way data now available for Tier II property may be used to empirically test the models discussed.

7.1.1. Non-normality - how and where does it fit?

Chapter 6 ended with questions people in the private real estate investment market might pose. It is tempting to claim that the epigram for this chapter makes as much a statement about the participants in the real estate market as about the returns their investments generate. Indeed, much of this book tends toward that sentiment. While it may appear unflattering at first to suggest that individual real estate investors are not normal, a close look may reveal that real estate investors prefer that reputation. The sort of binary, linear behavior suggested by the normal distribution and its progeny, linear regression, may not interest the average real estate investor. It may be that regressing to the mean is not the behavior a real estate investor has in mind when he purchases investment property.[1]

We have to be careful here not to suggest that real estate investors are somehow smarter than their counterparts in the market for financial assets. *Au contraire*, we assume that there is approximately an equal - and small - number of both brilliant and foolish investors in each market. These extreme types are likely separated by a large number of average investors. What we contend in this and subsequent chapters is that the combination of ownership and control in the Tier II market has a greater effect on returns than previously has been thought.

Leaving the comfort of the normal distribution, its symmetry, ease of solution and its accommodation of a linear view of life is not without its drawbacks. If real estate investors wish to claim that theirs is a non-linear, dynamic world they must be prepared to grapple with some daunting mathematical complexity. That is the bad news.

The good news far offsets the bad. The real world of both real estate and finance is complex. There are times when closed form, analytical solutions that are valid across the entire real number line simply elude us. Practitioners recognize this and have developed a number of tools in the field to deal with it. Fortunately, tools such as *Mathematica* provide us with the ability to overcome a number of intractable theoretical problems by using numerically intensive and graphical solutions in a bounded setting. Granted, universality may be the casualty of such approaches but some solution is better than no solution, as any successful practitioner will tell you.

Assume we agree that the real estate market is not normal. The question becomes: Then what is it? If risk in real estate rests on the foundation of risk in general as portrayed in Chapter 6, how does it differ from the view of risk adopted by stock market investors? The simple answer is that no one knows. Study of the Tier II market is relatively new. The first attempts have been to treat it like Tier III, applying the tools of mainstream finance. Our claim is that these tools do not work.[2] The challenge is to find others that do. This book will suggest some appealing alternatives but the reader should be prepared for uncertainty at the end. Many possibilities exist and data are only recently available to test hypotheses. So this chapter and its investigations should be viewed as a journey, not a destination.

7.2. The continuous stable case

7.2.1. Stable parameters

The Normal distribution is popular because it is easy to work with and produces reasonably good estimates in many cases. Unfortunately, its tractability comes at a price - it may distort reality, something we first encountered in Chapter 3. The most noticeable distortion is the requirement of symmetry. Outcomes distributed normally are equally distributed on either side of the mean. Some markets have heavy-tailed return distributions. That is, distributions in these markets contain a sufficient number of observations far from the mean - known as "extremes" - to violate requirements for normality.[3] One such distribution is known as stable-Paretian (SP), "stable" because it is stable under addition (the sum of many such observations added together retains the same shape), and "Paretian" for the Italian economist Vilfredo Pareto (1848-1923) who first observed that some cases in economics have a structural predisposition toward asymmetric heavy-tailed distributions. These kinds of distributions are also often referred to as Levy-stable in reference to the French mathematician Paul Levy (1886-1971) who did major work in this area of probability. We will simply call them "stable distributions."

It is reasonable that the distribution of economic variables might be less symmetrical than variables drawn from biological data. Imagine measuring the height of all the men in a particular area. One would expect to find approximately the same number of men taller and shorter than the average. One would never expect to find a man, say, ten times taller than the average. Would you be surprised to learn that there are people whose incomes are ten times the average? Probably not. In fact, a popularization of Pareto's insight is sometimes referred to as "the 80/20 rule" which claims that 80% of the value of something is the result of 20% of the effort. Keeping with our income metaphor, this suggests that 80% of the income is earned by 20% of the people. Regardless of the actual numbers or their source, the idea is that something out of the ordinary (away from the mean) influences the shape of the tails of the distribution.

Recall from Chapter 3 that the normal distribution is a special case of a stable distribution. Stable distributions are a family containing an infinite number of shapes of which the normal is only one. Knowing this, we see that assuming normality imposes a meaningful restriction on any model.

Stable distributions and the extremes these distributions admit introduce more realism into the discussion but at the price of tractability (the opposite problem we had with the normal). Recent advances in mathematics and the availability of fast numerical computing power allow us to overcome some of the tractability problems. Only a brief discussion of this is appropriate here. The essential problem lies in representing a *pdf*, the key shape we use to describe risk, but something that does not have a closed form for most stable distributions.[4] For the normal case, one can describe its *pdf* in closed form, a term mathematicians use to indicate that it can be written down and that its execution takes a finite number of steps. For all other stable distributions (except two that have little application in finance) one must employ numerically intensive methods to compute a *pdf*. There are several approaches to this, some use mathematical wizardry such as the Inverse Fourier Transform (IFT) and an improper function known as Dirac Delta. These, while fascinating to mathematicians, are not central to our story of risk in real estate so we permit *Mathematica* to do the heavy lifting letting these concepts work in the background to produce the shapes below.

Even though the *pdf* may not exist for most stable distributions, the characteristic function (*ch.f.*) always does. It *is* central to our discussion that the stable *ch.f.* has not two, like the normal, but four parameters.

Why should we go to all this extra effort to use messy distributions? A useful aside may provide both an answer and context. Prior to Markowitz' (1952) path breaking work, investing was a one-parameter model in that investors sought to improve their position ("create utility" if you are an economist or simply "make money" if you are in the Street) by seeking good opportunities that maximized return. Markowitz, by introducing the concept of variance (more specifically covariance) to investing, showed that risk could be managed independent of return, thereby *doubling the number of parameters to be used to examine investment performance*. If one concludes that stable distributions offer more realistic models of risk and provide better estimates, the result is to increase again the number of parameters employed in evaluating risk, this time to three. [5]

To set up our next series of examples, the stable parameters and their ranges are:

α (0,2] The characteristic exponent, a measure of tail thickness, also known as the 'index of stability'
β [−1,1] The skewness parameter, reflecting the distribution's symmetry
δ (−∞,∞) The location parameter, serving a function similar
to but not always the same as the mean for the normal distribution
γ $\mathbb{R}>0$ The scale parameter, a measure of compactness around the center, the stable equivalent of variance

Because stable distributions also retain their shape under linear transformation, the last two may be normalized to, respectfully, 0 and 1 in the usual fashion. Thus the parameters of interest are α and β, both influencing the shape of the distribution. When $\alpha = 2$ and $\beta = 0$ the distribution is normal.

When $\alpha < 2$ the variance as we know it in finance does not exist (or is infinite). This is fatal to most if not all traditional finance models. Covariance, which is key to implementing Modern Portfolio Theory, does not exist when variance does not exist. When $\alpha < 1$ the mean does not exist causing even more serious problems. Fortunately, most finance data appears to have $1 < \alpha < 2$.

7.2.2. The stable *pdf*

To be consistent with Chapter 6 and the Expected Utility Hypothesis we will continue to work with *pdf*s to illustrate how investors maximize expected utility. However, the basic statistical concept is the cumulative distribution function (CDF). The *pdf* is the derivative of the CDF with respect to the random variable. A requirement for a function to qualify as a *pdf* is that it must integrate to 1 (this is an analog to the discrete case where all probabilities must add to 1).

To create a baseline stable example, we illustrate first the normal version of the stable distribution for reference. Note that default settings are $\alpha = 2$ and $\beta = 0$ in this example. The other two parameters, γ and δ may be, respectively, rescaled and shifted without affecting the shape of the distribution. We use $\delta = 10$ to shift the center of the distribution for our exposition here. This places most of the probability mass on the positive side of the real number line.[6]

Figure 7.1 shows two *pdf*s, one having a normal distribution, the other a stable distribution. Change the values for α and β to see how the shape changes when things are not normal.

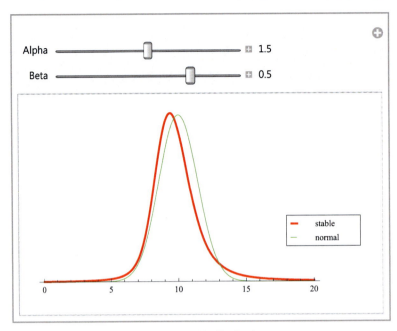

Figure 7.1. Levy-stable distribution

In Figure 7.1, note the additional probability mass for the stable distribution which is outside of the normal. Recall our most general definition of risk is the presence of conditions that permit outcomes away from the "center" of the distribution, where our "expectation" lies. Not only does the stable distribution consider extreme values, it shows how a portion of the risk might move from one side of the distribution to the other. Such knowledge is helpful when the random variable is wealth realization as we would prefer more (farther to the right) to less (farther to the left).[7] Later the random variable is investment return with the distribution centered at zero. In that instance, outcomes to the right are positive returns (gains) and those to the left are negative (losses). Clearly right side behavior is again preferred.

And, of course, what follows is the expectation, which, is δ for the S^1 parameterization (discussed below). Keep in mind that this is the mathematical expectation of the distribution. Because the normal is symmetrical the mean and the mode are the same. For skewed distributions the mean and the mode differ.[8]

    `Expectation[x, x ≈ StableDistribution[1, α, β, 10, 1], Assumptions -> 1 < α < 2]`

10

7.2.3. Problems with stable distributions

We repeat the caution that the use of stable models for real estate is still in its experimental stage. A characterization of risk using the stable model offers an alternative to the normal distribution. But it is not without its drawbacks. One purpose of this book is to open up research to consider *all*, not just stable, non-normal models. In this section we point out some of the special challenges associated with stable distributions. We shall concentrate on two of these:
- The interdependence of the parameters when combined with other functions such as popular and likely utility functions.
- The multiple parameterization problem.

Parameter independence and the use of utility functions

Goals of any theory would include consistency, simplicity and universality. A curious enigma troubles any move from the single stable distribution, the normal, to the broader class of all stable distributions. On the surface it appears that one obtains more universality when one drops the restriction that $\alpha = 2$. And so it is, to a point. But $\alpha = 2$ came with a significant benefit. The only two parameters needed to fully describe the normal distribution, its mean and variance, not only always exist but they are mathematically independent of one another. Such is not the case for the four parameters of non-normal stable distributions. For instance, when $\alpha < 1$ the mean does not exist. The way academic finance has handled this is to assume that finance settings call for $1 < \alpha < 2$. Fortunately, empirical tests usually support this assumption. In finance it is very hard to work with a distribution that has no mean.

When $\beta \neq 0$ the interaction of the parameters can result in very different and sometimes inconsistent results, especially when combined with other functions such as utility functions. The examples provided here are highly stylized. The choice of $\delta = 10$ not only places most of the wealth and utility outcomes on the positive side of the distributions, it affects β. Thus, for a substantial part of micro-economic theory to apply one must assume a specific range of δ values as well as value of $\alpha > 1$. Much of this difficulty may be traced to the combination of heavy tails *and* skewness. Given that the "center" of the distribution is important to prediction, one hopes that a single measure of central location would provide the answer. Alas, such is not the case, as discussed below.

There are interesting and useful mathematical properties of likely (concave) utility functions that work well with the normal distribution. When skewness and heavy tails enter the picture changes in scale and location of the stable distribution affect expected utility in inconvenient ways. So in a sense the move to stable distributions is a move to a broader class of mathematical distributions that nonetheless require certain restrictions on the parameters to be applicable to finance.

Mathematicians are troubled by this. Practitioners are not. Their attitude is: "Life is messy, deal with it!"

The multiple parameterization problem

Another troubling issue is that several parameterizations exist to define the stable characteristic function. Essentially, while all retain the general properties of stable (shape retention under linear transformation, additive, an appeal to the generalized central limit theorem), each is actually a slightly different distribution. Until this point we have used Nolan's S^1 parameterization. A complete discussion of the different parameterizations, their strengths and weaknesses will be found in Nolan's forthcoming book, <u>Stable Distributions, Models for Heavy Tailed Data</u>. For those who cannot wait, Zolotarev (1986) provides similar, if less accessible, information. Nolan recommends the S^0 parameterization for theoretical work in mathematics as it is continuous in all four parameters. The S^1 parameterization is more convenient for work in finance because δ is the mean. Such choices may be troubling, but they are the price paid for more alternatives.

Never a simple matter with stable laws, one would like to seize upon S^1 as the preferred choice because the location parameter, δ, is the mean for S^1. The mean is comforting, a connection with the "normal" past of academic finance. The drawback is that as α falls toward 1 where tails are heaviest and life is most interesting, the mean becomes a poor measure of the "center" of the distribution. Even when the mean is zero, a common normalized condition, the S^1 mode can vary across the entire real number line $(-\infty, \infty)$.

7.2.4. Still more distributions?

Lest the reader conclude that stable distributions represent less than a paralyzing level of complexity, Mittnik and Rachev (1993), using financial asset data, found that the Weibull distribution, Figure 7.2, provided a good fit for non-normal random variates. The simple fact is that normal data are well described by normal distributions, stable data are well described by stable distributions, Weibull data are...(by now one might pick up a pattern here). The message is that statistics offer a bewildering set of choices. There is a huge number of useful distributions out there to explain the universe. Real estate analysts should not be wedded to only one, especially one as restrictive and naive as the normal merely because that has been handed them from the world of finance. The choice of precisely which distribution best describes real estate is yet to be discovered.

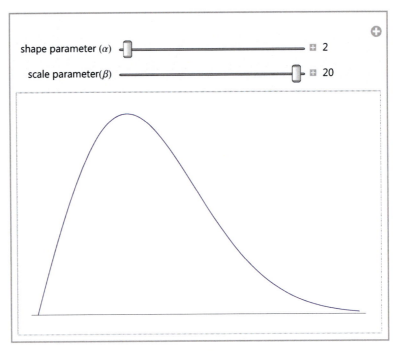

Figure 7.2. Weibull distribution

This is about all the theoretical work in distributions we need do for our purposes. The only lessons we can claim so far are (1) that the shape of the distribution influences how investors choose between risky alternatives, and (2) more robust, non-normal shapes show a wider range of effects than normal shapes. We need to decide how much of this transfers to real estate investing, the subject we tackle in the next section.

7.3. Enter real estate

Analysts of financial assets have evolved a set of advanced risk measures based on the classical theories of Chapter 6. Blessed with copious data, these analysts have been able to subject their theories to a large number of empirical tests. With the advent of plentiful data for real estate, we must be careful not to carelessly borrow these financial models just because they are in place and work elsewhere. Anyone who has owned both real estate and stock knows that the each involve very different risks. We argue that real estate risk is structurally different. Whether that means we abandon classical finance theory in favor of some other remains to be seen.

We have spent a good deal of time on classical risk theory. We ask ourselves if real estate risk is a different kind of risk. In this section we make a distinction between risk and uncertainty, with uncertainty being the broader form, inclusive of more than just classical risk. The idea that real estate could use its own definition of risk may be illustrated with the following metaphor. Taking the coin toss experiment as the epitome of risk, we place it at the left extreme end of a continuum (Figure 7.3) that represents different kinds of uncertainty. At the other end we will place another venture most people recognize involves uncertainty, marriage.

Figure 7.3. A range of uncertainty

An appropriate experiment at this point is to place investing in stock and investing in real estate each on the line above between the two extremes. Those who place stock to the right of real estate have either never owned real estate or never been married.

7.4. Determinism

Before we can discuss uncertainty we need some way to at least approach the unattainable, certainty. One view of uncertainty is a departure from conditions (certainty) under which only one outcome may take place. With this qualitative definition of uncertainty, later we will define risk as a subset of uncertainty having specific characteristics. But for all of this we need a starting point. The starting point might be a kind of measurement that is almost certain, nearly riskless. A mathematical term for such things in general is determinism.

We would like to be certain about things we say. We don't want to make mistakes. We want to be, in the parlance of our digital age, "error free". In some sense this could be taken to mean that we want to reduce to zero the risk of saying something and being wrong. Often we are as close to being as right as possible when we find a mathematical relationship between variables. Among the simplest and *most certain* of deterministic mathematical relationships are *linear* relationships between *physical* objects. When we say something is dependent on something else it is very helpful if the "dependency" is a linear one and it is most convenient if we are talking about physical objects.

A simple example of a linear relationship is the equation for the circumference of a circle, $c = \pi d$. Viewing that as a form of determinism can be helpful. For instance, we can say with absolute certainty that for EVERY circle, if you multiply its diameter by π (an unchanging number, a constant) you will get its circumference. The determinism at work here is: the numerical constant π applied to the diameter *determines* the circumference *every time*.

We can verify this by measuring the diameter and circumference of lots of different circles. When we divide the diameter into the circumference, EVERY time the answer is the same: π. This can be very comforting.
It is also very rare.

To illustrate, we define a function in *Mathematica*:

$$c(d) = \pi d \tag{7.1}$$

Suppose we measure a number of circles, we list them in increasing size (actually we just let *Mathematica* create a table of circle diameters and circumferences where the diameters range from 0 to 50 in increments of 5), as in Table 7.1.

diameter	circumference
0.	0.
5.	15.708
10.	31.416
15.	47.124
20.	62.832
25.	78.54
30.	94.248
35.	109.96
40.	125.66
45.	141.37
50.	157.08

Table 7.1. Dimensions of a number of different circles

We can then plot these on the left of Figure 7.4. It looks like a linear relationship, but is that just luck? One might be able to find a handful of circles that just happen to have π as the value of the ratio of the circumference to the diameter. On the right of Figure 7.4 we plot the function itself (which, of course, we know to be linear) superimposed over the points to see that all the points do indeed fall on the straight line predicted by our theory:

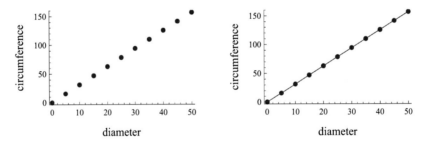

Figure 7.4. Various circles and the function for the circumference dependent on diameter

There are several ways of expressing this outcome. For a calculus approach we can take the derivative of the function and find that the slope of the line is, not surprisingly, π in Equation 7.2.

$$\partial_d c(d) = 3.14159 = \pi \qquad (7.2)$$

Empirical testing of theories involves collecting data and performing statistical tests on them. Applying this to our circle problem in Figure 7.5 we can regress the circumferences (the dependent variable) on the diameters (the independent variable) and find that π is the coefficient, exposing the regression coefficient as nothing more than a slope term. When we "fit" our data to our model (a model that says the observations will all fall on a line with a slope equal to π) we have a *PERFECT* fit. The coefficient of the equation is π. The intercept is at the origin because when the diameter is zero the circumference is also zero. We have empirically tested our theory and found that it fits perfectly. This perfect fit arises from a theory that is *ALWAYS* correct, never deviating when tested in the field.[2]

Circumstances such as these, as we have said already, are rare.

$$\text{Model Fit is } -1.71389 \times 10^{-14} + 3.14159\,x$$

$$\text{Standard Error of the Coefficients are } \begin{matrix} 0 & \text{Intercept} \\ 0 & \text{Units} \end{matrix}$$

$$\text{Parameter T Statistics are } \begin{matrix} -3.12235 & \text{Intercept} \\ 1.69298 \times 10^{16} & \text{Units} \end{matrix}$$

$$\text{Parameter P values are } \begin{matrix} 0.012272 & \text{Intercept} \\ 0 & \text{Units} \end{matrix}$$

Parameter Confidence Intervals are

	Lower 95%	Upper 95%
Intercept	0	0
Units	3.14159	3.14159

Number of observations are 11
Adjusted R Square is 1.
R Squared is 1.
Standard Error is 0
ANOVA Table

	DF	SS	MS	F-Statistic	P-Value
x	1	27141.4	27141.4	2.86619×10^{32}	0
Error	9	0	0		
Total	10	27141.4			

Figure 7.5. Regression of circle circumferences on diameters

In a further analysis we see that residuals (the difference between values predicted by the model and the observed values in Table 7.2) are all zero, meaning that our prediction is always accurate. R squared (the extent to which changes in the diameter explain changes in the circumference) is 1, meaning that 100% of the change in circumference is explained by a change in the diameter. The standard error, sum of squared error and mean squared error are all zero and confidence intervals occupy zero space. All of these are expected in *that rare case* where one variable completely and precisely determines the realization of another in a linear fashion.

Observed Y	Predicted Y	Residuals
0.	0	0
15.708	15.708	0
31.4159	31.4159	0
47.1239	47.1239	0
62.8319	62.8319	0
78.5398	78.5398	0
94.2478	94.2478	0
109.956	109.956	0
125.664	125.664	0
141.372	141.372	0
157.08	157.08	0

Table 7.2. Comparison between observed and predicted circumferences

Regression of circumferences of circles on their diameters is what mathematicians call a trivial result. But it serves our purpose to describe an extreme case of determinism. [It is interesting to add that there is no inconsistency between the brand of determinism we have just demonstrated and Professor Feynman's lament in the epigram for Chapter 6. It is left to the student as an exercise to reconcile these two notions.] From this trivial exercise we launch an ambitious effort to bring the same analysis to real estate.

7.5. Determinism and house prices

We may let a few circles convince us of the theory represented by our circumference function. But things are less certain when you introduce people and their real estate into the equation. For instance, suppose you claim that there is a functional relationship between the square footage of a house and the price at which it sells. The statement might be "Houses in this area sell for $132 per square foot" and has the functional form of Equation 7.3

$$p = 132\,s \tag{7.3}$$

This statement implies that there is a linear relationship between the two variables price (p) and size (s).[10] If true, it would mean that if one knows the square footage of a house one need only multiply it by $132 to get its value. Let's take a closer look at this using a stylized example. Suppose we go out and find ten houses, located close together, that sold in the past month. We record their sizes (in square feet) and their sales price in Table 7.3.

Size(sf)	Price($)
1500	195 000
1750	210 000
1600	225 000
1700	240 000
1900	275 000
1875	285 000
1650	190 000
1810	239 000
1975	249 000
1550	185 000
Average Price	229 300
Average Size	1731 sq ft
Avg Price/sf	132.50

Table 7.3. House sale data

The average price per house is called the "unconditional mean" because knowing it is not conditioned on any knowledge other than the observation of prices. We can compute this without knowing anything about size or any other characteristic of the properties sold. But we do know the sizes. We can compute the unconditional mean of the size variable. This requires knowing nothing about prices. Combining these two helps us focus on whether our $132 per square foot theory is accurate. A pleasant outcome of this example (cleverly rigged by the author) is that the average price per square foot is very close to $132.

OK, let's plot these data and our function and see if it agrees with our theory. We claim that the price of a house, p, is $132 times the number of square feet, s. There may be a linear relationship but it is *far from certain* if our only evidence is the plot in Figure 7.6.

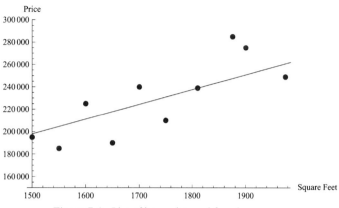

Figure 7.6. Plot of house data and function

The plot doesn't give us a lot of comfort. Only one house actually sold for $132 per square foot and many sold for more or less than $132 psf. Result: the empirical test of our theory about houses being worth $132 per square foot shows that it is less than perfect (most theories are). But "less than perfect" does not mean "useless".

As we did with our circle data, we can fit the data, perform regression, analyze variance and predict prices within confidence intervals, all of which is shown in Figure 7.7. Univariate regression is the process of finding the "conditional mean" in that it helps you predict the mean of one quantity *conditioned on knowing* some other, independent fact about the situation. In this case the fact that we know is the size of each house. But is that fact fully determinative? Note the residuals in Table 7.4, defined as the difference between the observed price and the predicted price. This difference, in a statistical sense, is a measure of the error between what our claim is (that houses sell for $132 per square foot) and what really happens. This sort of thing, while statistically valid, is only partially helpful in guiding an individual property owner to the value of his property.

$$\text{Model Fit is } -79095.6 + 178.16\,x$$

$$\text{Standard Error of the Coefficients are } \begin{array}{ll} 78358. & \text{Intercept} \\ 45.0975 & \text{Units} \end{array}$$

$$\text{Parameter T Statistics are } \begin{array}{ll} -1.00941 & \text{Intercept} \\ 3.95056 & \text{Units} \end{array}$$

$$\text{Parameter P values are } \begin{array}{ll} 0.342328 & \text{Intercept} \\ 0.0042327 & \text{Units} \end{array}$$

Parameter Confidence Intervals are

	Lower 95%	Upper 95%
Intercept	-259789.	101598.
Units	74.1653	282.155

Number of observations are 10
Adjusted R Square is 0.618756
R Squared is 0.661116
Standard Error is 1919.55
ANOVA Table

	DF	SS	MS	F-Statistic	P-Value
x	1	7.18111×10^9	7.18111×10^9	15.6069	0.0042327
Error	8	3.68099×10^9	4.60124×10^8		
Total	9	1.08621×10^{10}			

Figure 7.7. Regression analysis of house price and size data

Observed Y	Predicted Y	Residuals
195000.00	188145.00	6855.04
210000.00	232685.00	−22685.00
225000.00	205961.00	19039.00
240000.00	223777.00	16223.00
275000.00	259409.00	15590.90
285000.00	254955.00	30044.90
190000.00	214869.00	−24869.00
239000.00	243375.00	−4374.67
249000.00	272771.00	−23771.10
185000.00	197053.00	−12053.00

Table 7.4. Comparison between observed and predicted house prices

Compare the output in Figure 7.7 with the regression output of the circle example in Figure 7.5. The R squared for the house price regression is only 66%, residuals are non-zero, standard errors are positive and the confidence intervals are positive. All of this states the obvious: relying on price per square foot as an indicator of value is less than perfect. From this we conclude that in a more complex world determinism rarely exists and the rule is uncertainty. Diameter *completely* determines the circumference of *all* circles. Size *only partially determines* the price at which a house sells. The positive standard errors of the residuals measure how much our theory is wrong for particular houses. The 34% "unexplained" part encompasses the non-size characteristics that determine value. The effects of these characteristics are embedded in the error terms. This suggests that our $132 theory of house prices based on the single variable (size) and a linear relationship is simplistic, something any home buyer or seller knows.[11]

Despite being less than perfect, we press on. Data analysis does not always lead us directly where we want to go. The process involves many partial glimpses of the truth and the rare epiphany. Letting the numbers talk to us enlarges our understanding about how a process works. The constant reconciliation of objective outcomes based on the numbers with our subjective reasoning based on field experience is a big part of the value of the data analysis exercise. The artful use of both the objective and the subjective leads to a risk measure for real estate that is elaborated further in Chapter 9.

7.6. Determinism and real estate investment

The above examples include the case (a) where a definite, constant linear relationship (the diameter and circumference of a circle) *surely exists* between two variables, or (b) where a suspected linear relationship (house size and price) *may exist* between two variables. We now complicate this by examining relationships between variables in an investment context.

Recall the General Caution of Chapter 3. The capitalization rate rule of thumb claims that value is a function of income and that the functional relationship is

$$V(I, CR) = \frac{I}{CR} = I \frac{1}{CR} \qquad (7.4)$$

where V is Value, I is (net operating) Income and CR is the capitalization rate. The essence of this argument is that one may compute the value of property by multiplying its net income by the reciprocal of the capitalization rate. This is a linear relationship. But there is the added complication that we must choose between income and capitalization rate, both of which influence value, to decide which is the dependent variable and which is the conditioning coefficient or slope term. In the market both income and capitalization rate vary. They may vary independently of each other or the way they vary may be connected. Let's create a value function, (v[ ]) that is dependent on both variables, income (*inc*) and capitalization rate (*cr*). The dependence on income is linear; the dependence on capitalization rate is inverse, non-linear.

Our function is indifferent. When both income and rate are given, it produces a value

```
v[10000, .1]
100000.
```

But notice in Table 7.5 the range of values we get when income is constant and capitalization rate varies between, say, 7% and 12% in increments of 1%. Also, notice the range when we hold capitalization rate constant and vary income between $9,500 and $12,000 in increments of $500.

Income constant at $10,000		Cap rate constant at 10%	
Cap rate	Value($)	Income($)	Value($)
0.07	142 857	9500	95 000
0.08	125 000	10 000	100 000
0.09	111 111	10 500	105 000
0.1	100 000	11 000	110 000
0.11	90 909	11 500	115 000
0.12	83 333	12 000	120 000

Table 7.5. Investment property values, income and capitalization rates

Table 7.6 contrasts the difference between the case where the value of π was π or $132 was always $132 and the case of investment value.

Circles	Houses	Investments
c=πd	p=$132/sf	$V = \frac{I}{CR} = I \frac{1}{CR}$

Table 7.6. Three Theories

Suppose we collect some apartment property sales. Each has a sales price and a net operating income, therefore each has a cap rate. (Actually, in Table 7.7 for convenience we just re-use the list of house sizes, dividing each by 20,000 to produce a set of numbers that are scaled like capitalization rates.)

0.075
0.0875
0.08
0.085
0.095
0.09375
0.0825
0.0905
0.09875
0.0775

Table 7.7. A collection of observed capitalization rates

Recall that in Equation 7.3, the theory of price, p, is based on a single number ($132). The function, v, we use for our theory about investments involves the reciprocal of a rate, $\frac{1}{cr}$, by which we multiply income. The rate is not only variable but as we will see is a composite of several other variables. Our claim is not just that some specific constant number times income produces value but one of a (suitably scaled) set of different numbers multiplied times income constitutes value. Here we have three opportunities to be wrong : We may be incorrect about the shape of the function (it may not be linear). We may be incorrect about the value we pick from the set of capitalization rates we use as the multiplier. Finally, we may incorrectly estimate the income to be collected from the property. Although these sorts of errors may also plague the house example, the opportunity for capitalization rate error goes beyond measurement error.

What is different in the investment context is that the multiplier, $\frac{1}{cr}$, implicitly introduces a number of other variables into the equation. Arguably, capitalization rates are a kind of interest rate, affected in many of the same ways that interest rates are affected.[12] Specifically, there is a curious three-way connection between interest rates, capitalization rates and inflation. These forces are implicitly in our thinking when we use capitalization rate. Note the composition of the interest rate, i. It is a combination of the real rate (r), the default risk ($dfrt$), and inflation expectations ($inflexp$).

$$i = r + dfrt + inflexp \qquad (7.5)$$

One may reasonably conclude that real estate capitalization rates (cr) are composed of the interest rate (i) and a real estate risk premium ($rerp$) to compensate for lack of liquidity, non-systematic site-specific real estate risk and other risks peculiar to real estate investment.

$$cr = i + rerp \qquad (7.6)$$

Substituting Equation 7.5 and Equation 7.6 into Equation 7.4, we can now decompose the value-based-on-income-capitalization function to find that the right side of Equation 7.4 is actually made up of several components.

$$\frac{I}{CR} = \frac{inc}{dfrt + inflexp + r + rerp} \qquad (7.7)$$

The curious part is that investors may discount future expected rent increases in such a way that expected inflation may, while a positive number itself, indirectly exert negative pressure on capitalization rates. This is reason to doubt a simple relationship between the value of investment real estate and its capitalization rate.

Let's look at a dataset of 500 actual apartment sales that took place in the Los Angeles area between May and October of 2001. Each observation shows the price sold, net operating income and capitalization rate. The dataset is named "**aptdata**" and the first five observations are displayed.

Value	Income	Cap Rate
419 000	32 514	0.0776
2 100 000	148 050	0.0705
675 000	44 078	0.0653
490 000	31 507	0.0643
1 325 000	82 813	0.0625

Let's begin by assuming that value is dependent on the correct selection of a capitalization rate. This makes $\frac{1}{cr}$ the coefficient of income in our theoretical relationship. We create a set of matched pairs from these data where the x variable is capitalization rate and the y variable is price. This dataset is named **crpr**.

The equation of the least squares regression lines described by the *Mathematica* function LinearModelFit for regressing value on capitalization rate is shown in Table 7.8 (and matches the output provided by Excel for the same data on the electronic files included for this chapter).

	Equation	R-squared
Regress value on cap rate	$2.77739 \times 10^6 - 1.9146 \times 10^7 \, x$	0.0254441
Regress value on income	$-108\,848. + 13.6603\,x$	0.962347

Table 7.8. Two investment property regression equations and R-squared values

The sign of the coefficients make sense. One expects that value would decline with increases in the capitalization rate and that it would increase as income rises.

But, finding the R squared of the first regression leaves us with little confidence that the choice of capitalization rate explains the variation in value. Hence we should be careful about claiming that a certain capitalization rate of x will, given income, produce a correct value of y. With an R-Squared this low, one wonders if knowing capitalization rate gives us very much information at all about value. What is the problem here? This is an example of model misspecification. We have assumed that the relationship between value and capitalization rate is linear. Given that the coefficient is $\frac{I}{cr}$ it is clear that the relationship is non-linear, thus the use of *linear* regression is in error.[13]

On the other hand, when we use net operating income as our independent variable we get a very high R squared. Variation in income explains nearly all of the variation in value. (Perhaps that is why we call it "income property"). Performing the same tests for the gross rent multiplier (*grm*) is an exercise left to the reader.

A plot of the data in Figure 7.8 shows a much stronger relationship between price and income than between price and capitalization rate.

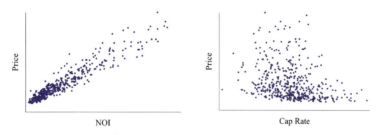

Figure 7.8. Scatter plots of price against income and cap rates

In addition to the non-linearity problem, there is another reason that our first regression of price on capitalization rate is an incorrect approach. It is important when regressing one variable on another that both may vary across the same range. Price and Income vary only across the entire range of positive real numbers. Thus, regression of price on income is proper. The capitalization rate in developed countries varies only between 0 and 1. This is another example of why wrong conclusions may be reached when one begins with a flawed model.

Determinism is a strong claim. Professor Feynman surely was thinking of the physical sciences. The social sciences bear an even heavier burden of proof when a claim is made for linear relationships. Opportunities for error abound. Risk is everywhere and very little is certain.

7.7. Risk and uncertainty

Let's add to our coin toss-marriage graphic (Figure 7.3), this time associating risk with the left side and uncertainty with the right in Figure 7.9. An appeal is again made to the reader's experience or observation to appreciate this enhancement.

Figure 7.9. Uncertainty Continuum.

Knight (1921) described the difference between risk and uncertainty as the former being a subset of the latter. Imagine that uncertainty is the universe of everything that can go wrong as shown by the large circles in Figure 7.10. Further, allow the small darker circle to represent that portion of uncertainty subject to measurement via an *a priori* probability distribution. The distinguishing characteristic of risk is that *it can be estimated* if one has sufficient data and a proper model.

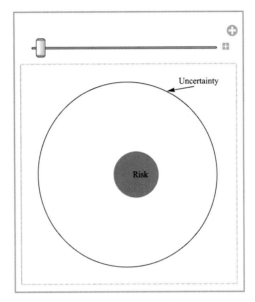

Figure 7.10. Risk and uncertainty

Figure 7.10 makes no point about scale. We do not suggest that we know what portion of uncertainty constitutes risk. Slide the slider bar to the right to increase the risk component of uncertainty. We might say that we tend more toward determinism when risk constitutes a larger portion of uncertainty. That is, we have a better chance of being right the more we can measure our probability of error. But as Professor Feynman reminds us, uncertainty is always there regardless of how good we are at defining and measuring risk. So no matter how large we make the small circle it is always smaller than and contained in the larger circle.

An important limitation of data and the value it adds to the decisionmaking process is that it only helps us assess risk - those variates that are observable, subject to measurement and eligible for repeated, independent experiments. Notwithstanding this limitation, there are numerous opportunities to investigate these and understanding them can add much to one's understanding of the market. But business decision making, as distinguished from the comparatively straightforward study of risk, involves directly addressing uncertainty, the mathematics for which are limited at present.

In privately owned real estate the line between risk and uncertainty may not be so well defined as in Figure 7.10. It is hard to tell where one ends and the other begins. What we have begun here is not just a discussion of how and if real estate return distributions have heavy tails. We question the idea that there is a bright line distinction between risk and uncertainty. It may be that the transition is continuous as in Figure 7.11. If so, the gray transition area may represent the risk inherent in those investments that involve personal risk management by the owner. Just as in Chapter 4 we postulated that growth rates such as the modified logistic could be specific to different owners, it may be that real estate risk varies according to the *probabilities influenced by the owner*. Some owners with stronger entrepreneurial skills may affect the gray area in Figure 7.11 differently than owners less adroit at operating their real estate investments.

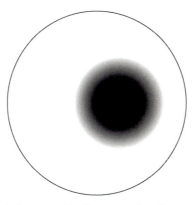

Figure 7.11. A fuzzy transition between risk and uncertainty

To further understand how individual real estate investors deal with this problem, let's appeal to another example from classical probability theory, rolling dice. This exercise has useful similarities to the coin toss example but offers some additional features that we will use to advantage in explaining risk in private real estate investing. An underlying assumption about the coin is that it is a so-called "fair coin", meaning that there is an equal probability that it will fall with either side up. Another assumption, perhaps too obvious to mention earlier, is that the edges of the coin are too thin to permit the coin to land on and remain on any surface other than its two opposing sides. Also unstated but implied is the fact that the person flipping the coin may not influence the outcome. Dice permit us to relax these assumptions to better understand private real estate investment risk. A significant benefit of the dice example will be to move the discussion away from gambling and into the idea of the owner adding entrepreneurial management to influence the probability of any particular outcome.

7.8. Rolling the dice

A natural extension of the two-outcome case of a coin flip is a "many-outcome" case of the roll of a "fair die" or a pair of "fair dice". We may think of a die as a square coin that starts out with two "sides" between which we insert mass to permit it to land, in addition to either "side", on any of four "edges". If all sides and edges are the same size, that is they have the same surface area, each side has an equal opportunity to land and remain on the table when thrown. Thus, the "fair" die, a cube with six equal sides, is a more complex and differently shaped version of a coin.

It is important to remove the pejorative aspect of this discussion by pointing out that "fair" does not mean "virtuous" or "positive" and the contrary, "unfair", does not mean "evil" (despite the fact that the term "loaded dice" has come to mean "cheating"). In our context "fair" means nothing more than the fact that all outcomes have an equal chance of occurring.[14]

Let's take a closer look at the probability behind throwing a pair of "fair dice". First, we recognize that there is a bounded set of eleven outcomes, the integers between 2 and 12. There are six *different* outcomes possible for each die, each with an equal, one sixth, chance of occurring. Thus the probability mass function (*pmf*) for a single die is:

$$pmf = \{\frac{1}{6}, \frac{1}{6}, \frac{1}{6}, \frac{1}{6}, \frac{1}{6}, \frac{1}{6}\} \tag{7.8}$$

This game of chance looks like Table 7.9 and Figure 7.12[15]

Table 7.9 shows the fractional and decimal representation of probabilities for each of the eleven outcomes. Note that there is some duplication.

Outcome	Pr(Outcome)	Pr(Outcome)
2	$\frac{1}{36}$	0.0277778
3	$\frac{1}{18}$	0.0555556
4	$\frac{1}{12}$	0.0833333
5	$\frac{1}{9}$	0.111111
6	$\frac{5}{36}$	0.138889
7	$\frac{1}{6}$	0.166667
8	$\frac{5}{36}$	0.138889
9	$\frac{1}{9}$	0.111111
10	$\frac{1}{12}$	0.0833333
11	$\frac{1}{18}$	0.0555556
12	$\frac{1}{36}$	0.0277778

Table 7.9. Outcomes and probabilities for a pair of fair dice

A plot of the probabilities is also helpful. It is no accident that the shape In Figure 7.11, which began as a flat, uniform distribution begins to vaguely resemble the shape of the normal distribution, but the discussion of why is outside the scope of our effort here.

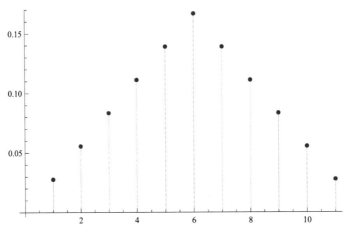

Figure 7.12. Plot of dice probabilities

So far all we have done is construct the probabilities associated with a set of outcomes more numerous (six versus two) and more complex (different values for the side that lands facing up) than a coin toss. However, these outcomes, provided the dice are "fair", are purely probabilistic. Known laws of combinatorics govern the probability of success a game based on rolling dice. At this stage we merely roll the dice and note how often certain combinations appear in a large number of rolls. One might reasonably surmise that an investment "game" in which the player has no opportunity to influence the outcome would be governed by similar laws. Stock market investors using various theories based on market efficiency and random walks often model price behavior in their markets based on these laws.

We argue that private real estate investing is different not only because of the items on everyone's list of reasons why real estate differs from financial assets but because investors may, by combining ownership and control, influence the outcome.[16] Thus, for real estate investors the probability described thus far may apply differently. Continuing with our dice example we will show how such a game might be played.

Let's change the game so that we favor two outcomes by shaving one side of the dice. The result is that, *relative to the remaining sides*, two sides (the shaved one and the side opposite the shaved one) have a greater surface area than the remaining four "edges" thus a greater chance of landing down (with the opposite side up). Mathematically, this amounts to removing some of the probability from four sides and adding it to the shaved side and its opposite. Hence the *pmf* for a pair of thusly modified dice becomes:

$$pmf_{mod} = \left\{ \frac{1}{6} + \frac{\delta}{3}, \frac{1-\delta}{6}, \frac{1-\delta}{6}, \frac{1-\delta}{6}, \frac{1-\delta}{6}, \frac{1}{6} + \frac{\delta}{3} \right\} \tag{7.9}$$

where $\frac{\delta}{6}$ represents the probability removed from each of four of the sides and added to the sides affected by the shaving. Each die is now the shape on the right in Figure 7.13.

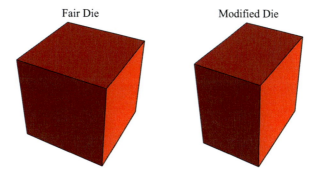

Figure 7.13. Die having different shapes

In Figure 7.14 we see that probability removed from the center of the distribution is added to the tails. The red circles represent probabilities for the modified die with the original probabilities shown as the blue disks.

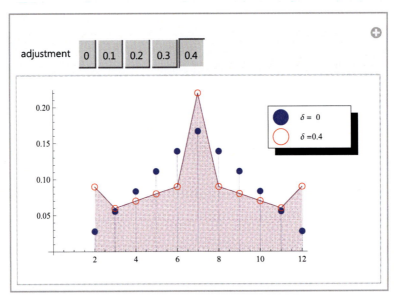

Figure 7.14. Moving probabilities to the tails by modifying dice

A table further contrasts the probabilities for the normal dice and the modified dice for the case where, for instance, $\delta = .3$.

$\delta \rightarrow 0$	$\delta \rightarrow .3$
0.0277778	0.0711111
0.0555556	0.0622222
0.0833333	0.0758333
0.111111	0.0894444
0.138889	0.103056
0.166667	0.196667
0.138889	0.103056
0.111111	0.0894444
0.0833333	0.0758333
0.0555556	0.0622222
0.0277778	0.0711111

Table 7.10. Difference between probabilities for a pair of fair dice and a pair of modified dice

In Equation 7.9, pmf_{mod}, δ is a percent and is constrained between [0,1]. Note in Equation 7.10 that as δ approaches 1, the point where so much shaving takes place that our cube only has two sides, the probabilities return to those of flipping a square (and fair!) coin.

$$pmf_{\delta \rightarrow 1}\left\{\frac{1}{2}, 0, 0, 0, 0, \frac{1}{2}\right\} \tag{7.10}$$

7.9. Real estate - the "Have it Your Way" game

The modification on the right side of Figure 7.13 was relatively straightforward, having changed the "fair" dice in a way that increased probability on the "ends" and decreased it on the "sides". This resulted in a symmetrical change in the probabilities. But there is nothing cast in stone about how we might modify dice. It is entirely possible that dice could be "engineered" asymmetrically such that the modification affected one side by taking from the remaining five sides. *Mathematica* allows us to model this and calculate its probabilities. Imagine that area on each of the four "edges" is gradually and uniformly rearranged such that the distance between each of four corners on the side previously shaved move apart and the four corners of the side opposite the previously shaved side move closer together by a like amount (keeping the volume constant). The four "sides" of the die become isosceles trapezia while the two "ends" remain square but one is smaller than the other. One such die looks like the one in Figure 7.15 where the sides are tapered from an end that is 1 x 1 to an end that is .4 x .4. In order for the landing probabilities of such a die to depend solely on the relative area of its sides we must assume that the die is statically and dynamically balanced about its center.[17]

Figure 7.15. An engineered die

Area	Probability
0.16	0.0503286
0.504777	0.158779
0.504777	0.158779
0.504777	0.158779
0.504777	0.158779
1	0.314554

Table 7.11. Area and probability of each side landing for engineered die

Table 7.11 shows the area of each side and the probability that a particular side will come to rest against the table, given the assumptions of about the balance properties. The probability for a particular side is the ratio of the surface area of a particular side to the total area of all sides. The *pmf* then becomes the list in Equation 7.11, all of which add to 1, as they should.[18]

$$pmf_{skew} = \{0.0503286, 0.158779, 0.158779, 0.158779, 0.158779, 0.314554\} \qquad (7.11)$$

Our list of probabilities for the deformed dice, Equation 7.11 for the present example, and the functions that produce these lists assign probabilities in the order of ascending payoff. We assume in any given list the far left probability is that for rolling the lowest score (1 for a single die, 2 for a pair) and the far right probability is that for rolling the highest score (six for a single die, twelve for a pair).

This produces the maximum benefit to the player by placing the highest point count on the smallest end, the one most likely to come to rest facing up. The player therefore makes two adjustments. One is the degree of taper and the other is the way the pips are arranged on the different sides. Figure 7.16 shows a graph of probabilities of all the possible outcomes when two dice are tapered as shown in Figure 7.15 and the pips arranged in the fashion as described above.

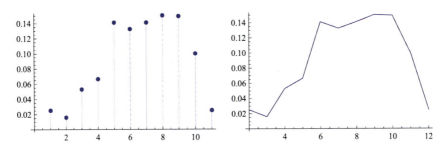

Figure 7.16. Plot of probabilities of engineered die

We see probability more pronounced on the right compared to the symmetrical conditions we previously had. This is because we have modified the object to increase the chance it will land on a particular side.[19]

Figure 7.17 permits the reader to choose the taper and number of rolls of an engineered die, noticing the probability of each side and the distribution when rolling a pair of dices shaped as selected. The default values are those we have used in the example above.

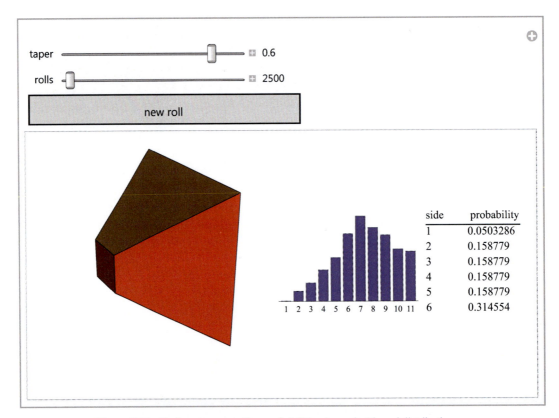

Figure 7.17. Various tapers on dice, probabilities for each side and distribution

7.10. The payoff

We now consider ways in which an investor, if he had the chance, would influence the shape of the dice and placement of the pips in order to enhance his prospects. As usual, the measure we use to judge the prospects of each alternative is expected value. Expected value involves the usual two simple steps. First, multiply the probabilities times the payoff. Second add up the results. The simplest form, the flip of a fair coin where heads pays $1 and tails pays $0, has an expected value of $0.50 because

$$.5 * \$1 + .5 * \$0 = \$0.50 \tag{7.12}$$

The reason we introduce permutations of tapered the dice and differently arranged pips is to introduce real world complexity into the equation. The connection to real estate investing is that the player can exert entrepreneurial effort to change the shape of his real estate (the dice) and influence the outcome. Many variations are possible. The dice can be eight sided with uniquely sized areas, etc. We must put some limits on the exposition, however. The assumptions we make about the taper, the fixed volume, the balance properties are of course restrictive but they are not as restrictive as the original set of "fair" dice and far less restrictive than coin tossing. The important point is to illustrate - however imperfectly - how risk blends with uncertainty in real estate investing by showing some but never all of the ways in which the player might influence the outcome.

To complete our story we assume a simple game in which the payoff is $1 for each pip facing up after a pair of dice is thrown. It is useful to keep in mind that specifying the number of pips on the large end means specifying the higher probability that number of pips will end up resting on the table. The fact that opposite sides of die always total 7 tells us the number of the pips that face up.

Recall the shape for unmodified, so-called "fair dice". We can produce that using our probability mass function. Note in Figure 7.18 how the shape of the *pmf* for our engineered die, as in Figure 7.15, differs from that for an unmodified die.

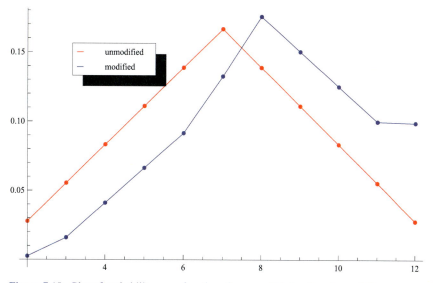

Figure 7.18. Plot of probability mass functions for unmodified and engineered dice

We can create an <u>e</u>xpected <u>r</u>eturn for <u>t</u>apered <u>d</u>ice function, ertd, to calculate the expected return. For the case where the dice are cubes the expected return is in the center of the distribution where the highest probability occurs, a roll of 7 as shown in Equation 7.13. (Note that this function merely takes the dot product of the vector of probabilities and the payoffs. This is the matrix equivalent of multiplying the probabilities times the payoffs and adding them up.)

The function, *ertd[taper]*, depends further on *pd3[lep,taper,n]* which specifies <u>l</u>arge <u>e</u>nd <u>p</u>ips (*lep*), the number of pips on the large end of the die. The combination of these functions produces the expected return for throwing a pair of dice having *lep* value of 1, meaning that the large end of the die has only one pip. With a zero taper we have conventional, fair, dice which have an expected value of 7, the result of Equation 7.13.

```
ertd[taper_] := Table[pd3[1, taper, n], {n, 2, 12}].Range[2, 12];
ertd[0]
7.
```

$$ertd[taper] = ertd[0] = 7 \qquad (7.13)$$

However, in Equation 7.14, if one pays $7 to enter the game one has an expected payoff in excess of the entry fee if the dice are tapered as in Figure 7.15.

$$ertd[taper] = ertd[.6] = 8.32112 \qquad (7.14)$$

The expected return for unmodified die is $7. Suppose the entry fee (investment) required to enter the game is $7.20. One would not be willing to enter the game unless one was convinced he could modify the die with a taper such that the expected return is larger than the entry fee. In Table 7.12 we show the *net* return to various degrees of taper after payment of a $7.20 entry fee.

Taper	Net Gain
0.	-0.2
0.1	-0.0247771
0.2	0.16835
0.3	0.38021
0.4	0.610839
0.5	0.858937
0.6	1.12112
0.7	1.39103
0.8	1.65832
0.9	1.90799
1.	2.12051

Table 7.12. Net gain at various tapers given an initial investment of $7.20

One could easily conclude that someone had to go to a lot of *work* to modify dice in such a way as to produce this outcome. That becomes the important point of this section and the central theme of the next chapter. The change in the dice was not done to somehow nefariously rig the odds. The modification is done with full disclosure and in full view of all. Suppose that the player *conditioned* his entering the game on his being allowed to modify the dice. The *work* involved in changing the odds can be viewed as the addition of entrepreneurial labor, a common occurrence in private real estate investing. The payoff (net present value) to the entrepreneur is the net gain resulting from subtracting the entry fee (initial investment) from the expected return (present value).

Suppose that the smallest side of the dice represents the chance of a positive return on a real estate investment. One might surmise that an investor would, if he were allowed to, spend considerable time making the opposite side as large as possible by adjusting the taper as much as he could!! This really is not as outlandish as it may seem at first. Our modern society contains numerous examples of people expending considerable effort to "get the odds just right" in order to produce profits. Las Vegas and Atlantic City are good examples. So are the gaming casinos that dot the landscape of Native American lands. One can hardly open a box of cereal, turn on the television or check e-mail without being bombarded with offers of chances to win something. Each of these are situations in which probabilities have been calculated very carefully so that the house wins in the long run. Investment real estate may be seen as such an opportunity. In its simplest form the owner of a rented single family dwelling *becomes the house*. Clearly the separation of ownership and control renders such a discussion moot for stock market investments. Imagine buying 100 shares of Microsoft and appearing on Bill Gates' doorstep announcing cheerily, "Hi, I just bought some of the company and I am here to help!" Investors in private real estate enter that market so that they can influence the outcome by their entrepreneurial effort.[20]

Modified dice illustrate what may happen when ownership and control are efficiently combined. Mathematically the result is an interesting combination of determinism and probability. While the outcome is still probabilistic the probabilities are *determined* by the way the dice are modified. An owner of investment real estate chooses that market so that he can exert influence over the outcome. Certainly he would like to influence the return, but at the same time he hopes to influence the risk. In his market he has an opportunity to manage some of the uncertainty of his investment.

7.11. Data issues

At the end of Chapter 4 we introduced a repeat sale model for analyzing Tier II return distributions using a small ($n = 731$) San Francisco dataset. Numerically intensive analysis tools require large datasets. Below we import a dataset composed of 4877 observations of Tier II apartment building repeat sales in the Los Angeles area over the 15-year period from January, 1986 through October, 2001. Following Young and Graff (1995), returns were regressed against zip codes as dummy variables to separate the location component of the return. Residuals were collected from the regression. According to Young and Graff the residuals represent site-specific (non-location) risk. The dataset has two elements for each observation, the raw return and the residual from the regression. As the shape for each is virtually identical we will work only with the return series and leave as an exercise the equivalent analysis for the residuals.

After reading in the data file, viewing the first few observations, isolating the return series and reporting the number of observations, maximum and minimum, we plot the sorted data, noting there are no gaps in Figure 7.19.

Returns	Residuals
−0.00458584	−0.0140007
−0.00289829	−0.0138034
−0.00179665	−0.0138021
−0.00167854	−0.0137846

n	4877
Max	0.2849
Min	−0.00458584

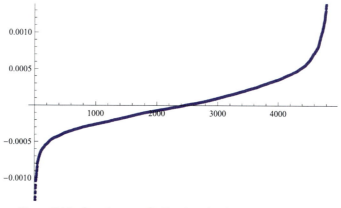

Figure 7.19. Sorted returns for Los Angeles data (n=4877)

Using Nolan's S^1 parametrization (it is left as an exercise for the reader to conclude that the S^0 parametrization produces the same estimates for α, β and γ) and maximum likelihood estimation (MLE) we fit the data and find that it has a heavy right tail.

$$\alpha \to 1.62711$$
$$\beta \to 0.695005$$
$$\mu \to 0.0000732967$$
$$\sigma \to 0.000228383$$

Table 7.13. MLE stable fit of Los Angeles Returns

Plotting the data in Figure 7.20 we see the long right tail.

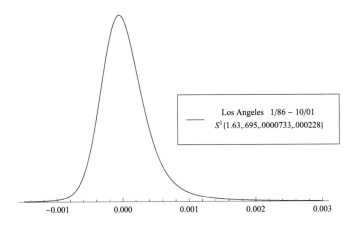

Figure 7.20. Plot of Los Angeles returns (n=4877)

We convert the daily returns to annual to arrive at a meaningful value for $\hat{\delta}$. As δ is the mean for S^1, we note the average annual appreciation rate over these 15 years in Los Angeles as about 2.68%. This serves as a proxy for overall return as after tax cash flows and the benefits of leverage are not observable in presently available data.

$$\mu \to 0.026811$$

Tests conducted on similar data for San Diego, San Francisco, Chicago, Las Vegas, Phoenix, Tucson and Orange County, CA produce similar results. Below are returns from 9 cities in four states comprising 11,275 observations reflecting $\hat{\alpha} = 1.543$ and $\hat{\beta} = .487$.

	$\hat{\alpha}$	$\hat{\beta}$	$\hat{\gamma}$	$\hat{\delta}$
9 Cities (n = 11275)	1.54332	0.486659	0.000216603	0.000136544
Chicago (n = 781)	1.02971	0.707732	0.000147478	0.00240412
California (n = 9034)	1.59129	0.578385	0.000215479	0.000102666
Px,Tuc,LV (n = 1460)	1.19417	0.196651	0.000165812	0.000259807

Table 7.14. Stable parameter estimates for nine cities in four states

The individual states (Las Vegas has been included with Arizona data) also have heavy right tails. With approximately 80% of the observations coming from California it is not surprising that the California parameters are very close to the parameters for the total dataset. Plotting the distributions in Figure 7.21 shows the now familiar heavy right tails.[21]

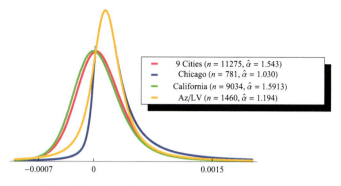

Figure 7.21. Plot of stable *pdf* for nine cities in four states

7.12. Conclusion

In this chapter we have built a case for using non-normal probability distributions to examine and perhaps explain privately held real estate returns. This requires demanding mathematics but the challenge is manageable using *Mathematica*. Such distributions permit a more robust view of the variation investors face. We have provided a theoretical foundation for non-symmetrical distributions based on owner involvement in the operation of the investment. The positive influence the owner exerts, on average, appears to locate more probability mass on the right. Whether this supports the common claim of practitioners that "you can't go wrong with real estate" is unclear.[22] Other explanations for right skewed distributions exist. Owners may simply extend their holding periods until they have a positive result, something we will discuss at length in Chapter 10. Regardless of owner influence, the fact that land is fixed in supply and communities restrict its use a little more each day could explain heavy right tail return behavior.

We may debate the reason, but few argue that real estate investment is not like investing financial assets. Tier II property demands owner involvement.[23] A final use of our arrow graphic in Figure 7.22 returns us to our earlier metaphor, this time contrasting the sort of risks inherent in stock market investment and those involved in real estate.

Figure 7.22. Fully elaborated uncertainty continuum

Probabilities associated with concepts on the left may be modeled with classical statistics, involve a separation of ownership and control, and depend on forces that are not easily influenced by any specific investor. Probabilities associated with concepts on the right are the result of combining ownership and control (we strain the marriage analogy a bit here), thus are affected by the addition of labor.[24] That addition confounds the accurate computation of both return (the compensation for labor is mixed with the compensation for risk bearing) and risk. It involves a human element, something we all agree involves uncertainty.

Resorting to the generic meaning of risk, clearly the narrowly defined risk on the left of our arrow graphic is different from the broader version on the right.[25]

Having done what we can to explain real estate risk using classic probability models improved by stable laws,[26] in the next chapter we will look into the human motivations of owners. We hope to get a glimpse of why some people self-select into the real estate investment market instead of the market for financial assets.

Endnotes

[1] The term "regressing to the mean" is part of the foundation of basic statistics. In the biological sciences there are many examples of systems regressing to the mean.

[2] We must add these applications are largely the earlier form of the tools. Forced by recent events, the field of finance, in and out of academia, has more recently recognized that non-normal conditions exist. They have also had plentiful data with which to examine the ramifications of this. Tier II real estate, lacking such data, has had to make do with the more rudimentary tools of finance.

[3] As distinguished from "outliers" which is the name often used for extreme observations that arise from errors in the data.

[4] Some texts take the position that stable *pdf*s are "undefined" or do not exist. This is technically not true. Mathematicians have found ways of handling the problem of definition. It is describing them analytically and working with them in practice that is elusive.

[5] Under the right conditions both the normal and stable distributions have the same first parameter, the mean.

[6] Given that negative wealth has no meaning.

[7] Indeed, if one believes utility theory, investors not only prefer but *require* return distributions have this shape.

[8] It is tempting to draw comparisons between the simple, two-parameter normal case of the stable distribution and the more robust four-parameter non-normal stable case. Such comparisons are misguided. Non-normal stable outcomes depend on all four parameters.

[9] We have used regression in earlier chapters. Regression is the Boy Scout knife of statistics. It is often used and perhaps as often misused. A complete discussion of regression may be found in any number of excellent texts. In this chapter we use the built in *Mathematica* functions. This is the equivalent of using icons in Excel. Because we feel it important that readers be aware of the underlying mathematics of regression, Appendix A provides a fully elaborated example in which all the usual results of regression and analysis of variance are derived using the matrix algebra required to reach them. An Excel version is among the electronic files for this chapter.

[10] It is true that size can be a proxy for other variables such as quality and amenities. For purposes of the exposition, we wish to focus solely on size for the moment.

[11] Mathematicians will object with the casual use of "linear", a term that has a specific and precise mathematical meaning. There is a thread of "linear", however tenuous it may be, that links binary outcomes, the normal distribution and linear regression. We do take liberties here and sometimes indulge in a metaphorical use of "linear" as meaning "unduly simplistic".

[12] This could be challenged as one could argue that capitalization rate is more like a dividend yield rate. The purpose here is to broaden the subject to various rates of returns that attract capital to one investment over another.

[13] The fact that the relationship is between value and *the inverse* of the capitalization rate is important because it is non-linear, but in this particular case regressing value on the reciprocal of the capitalization rate do not produce meaningfully different results.

[14] This is a loose definition. To mathematicians the definition of "fair" is more precise. Their view is: as the number of trials, n, approaches infinity the expected value converges to a finite number.

[15] It is important not to further complicate this illustration by assuming we are playing craps, a game with a set of rules designed to favor the house. At this stage we merely roll the dice and note how often certain combinations appear in a large number of rolls.

[16] This example is a modification of one drawn from Mathematical Statistics with *Mathematica* by Colin Rose and Murray Smith, Springer-Verlag, 2002. As of the Fall of 2011 the Internet link where the reader may obtain this excellent text and software was http://www.mathstatica.com/.

[17] This means, roughly, that both the first and second moments of mass distribution are equal with respect any axes through the center. Allowing for other than this in our story introduces a nasty physics problem dealing with the other means of "loading" dice, adding weight to one side, that goes well beyond our needs here.

[18] The *pmf* in Equation 7.11 is for a pair of dice shaped like the one in Figure 7.15

[19] The reader may notice a connection between the probabilities under these conditions and markets in which distributions are heavy right tailed.

[20] Some would argue that this merely "contaminates" the return calculation by combining returns to labor with returns to capital. Regardless of the merit of this comment, the point here is that the aggregate return to both exceeds the sum of the two returns due to the combination of ownership and control.

[21] One must not conclude from this that individual datasets, each with stable distributions, when pooled necessarily produce a distribution that is stable. This would only be the case if all pooled distributions had the same value of α.

[22] At a minimum this is overstatement. The fact that left tail observations exist means that some investors did not fare well. One could postulate that higher leverage contributes to such outcomes. This is an interesting research question that awaits an answer.

[23] Although Tier III may also require it, the involvement is less personal, usually through agents. Such a process fails to offer the same level of critical information to the Tier III owner.

[24] Don't try this at home. Few would argue that marriage involves the addition of labor. The marriage analogy breaks down about now. The purpose of this comparison is to distinguish very simple probabilities associated with simple systems from the uncertainties associated with complex systems.

[25] While this discussion has concentrated on a "labor added" theme to explain positive skewed tails, many other uncertain issues can cause tail behavior, not all of which are positive. The introduction of terror risk to so-called "trophy properties" represents a sobering uncertainty with left tail implications.

[26] Some of the stable parameter estimations were produced by Stable.exe, a Fortran package written as a MathLink for Mathematica by Professor John P. Nolan. It is not included with the electronic files for this chapter. As of the Fall of 2011 this package could be obtained from Professor Nolan at http://www.robustanalysis.com/. Additional useful information, software and interactive material extending this subject may be found at www.mathestate.com.

References

Adler, R. J., Feldman, R. E., & Taqqu, M. S. (1998). A Practical Guide to Heavy Tails. Boston, MA: Birkhauser.

Benninga, S., & Wiener, Z. (1998). Value-at-Risk (VaR). Mathematica in Education and Research, 7(4), 1-7.

Brown, R. J. (2000). Risk and Private Real Estate Investments. The Journal of Real Estate Portfolio Management, 10(2) 113-127.

Graff, R. A., & Webb, J. R. (1997). Agency Costs and Inefficiency in Commercial Real Estate. Journal of Real Estate Portfolio Management, 3(1).

Greene, William H. (2002). Econometric Analysis, 5th Ed., Upper Saddle River, NJ: Prentice Hall.

Knight, F. H. (1964). Risk, Uncertainty, and Profit. New York: Augustus Kelley.

Lusht, K. M. (1988). The real estate pricing puzzle. AREUEA Journal, 16(2), 95-104.

Mandelbrot, B. (1963). The Variation of Certain Speculative Prices. Journal of Business, 36(4), 394-419.

Markowitz, H. M., "Portfolio Selection", The Journal of Finance, 7(1), March, p. 77-91

McCulloch, J. H. (1998). Linear Regression with Stable Disturbances. R. J. Adler, R. E. Feldman, & M. S. Taqqu (Editors), A Practical Guide to Heavy Tails (First ed., pp. 359-376). Boston, MA: Birkhauser.

McCulloch, J. H. (1986). Simple Consistent Estimators of Stable Distribution Parameters. Communications in Statistics: Simulation and Computation, 15(4), 1109-1136.

Nolan, J. P. (1998). Maximum Likelihood Estimation and Diagnostics for Stable Distributions. [Working Paper].

Nolan, J. P. (1997). Numerical Calculation of Stable Densities and Distribution Functions. Communications in Statistics - Stochastic Models, 13(4), 759-774.

Nolan, J. P. (1998). Parameterizations and Modes of Stable Distributions. Statistics and Probability Letters, 38(2), 187-195.

Nolan, J. P. (In Press). Stable Distributions Birkhauser.

Nolan, J. P. (1998). Univariate Stable Distributions: Parameterization and Software. R. J. Adler , R. E. Feldman, & M. S. Taqqu (Editors), A Practical Guide to Heavy Tails: Statistical Techniques and Applications (pp. 527-533). Boston, MA: Birkhauser.

Peters, E. E. (1996). Chaos and Order in the Capital Markets. New York, NY: John Wiley & Sons, Inc.

Roulac, S. E. (1995). Implications of Individual Versus Institutional Real Estate Strategies. A. L. Schwartz Jr., & S. D. Kapplin (Editors), Alternate Ideas in Real Estate Investment (pp. 35-58). Norwell, MA: Kluwer Academic Publishers.

Young, M. S. , & Graff, R. A. (1995). Real Estate is Not Normal: A Fresh Look at Real Estate Return Distributions. Journal of Real Estate Finance and Economics, 10(3), 225-259 (1995).

Zolotrev, V. M. (1986) One Dimensional Stable Distributions Providence, R.I.: American Mathematical Society.

Problems

1. Using Figure 7.1, change the values for alpha and beta to reflect those associated with the Los Angeles data in Table 7.13. The shape will approximate Figure 7.20. What is the major difference and why?
2. Examine Figure 7.6 and the surrounding text describing how it was created. What variables are omitted? Of these, which do you believe would improve the model by having the points fall closer to the line?
3. Figure 7.10 shows risk as a portion of uncertainty. Using the insurance industry as context, pick two different risks and decide which one constitutes the greater portion of uncertainty. For instance, since considerable data exist for drivers in cars it is relatively easy for insurance companies to set premia for insuring automobile risk, so one would expect that the risk portion of the uncertainty in that market would be comparatively large. On the other hand, insurance policies that guarantee an 18 year old who enters college will graduate does not exist (why?) so the risk portion of uncertainty is relatively small. Describe the two risks you chose and why the risk/uncertainty portions are what they are.
4. Change the adjustment (taper) in Figure 7.14 to reflect normality. How has the risk changed? How has the uncertainty changed?
5. Assume the default values for Figure 7.17 are the correct ones for real estate investment. Pick another investment that is not real estate and change the values to reflect what you believe is a reasonable way to modify risk to attract capital. Then, assume the default values for Figure 7.17 are for commercial real estate. Pick another sector (apartments, office, industrial, land) and change the values again to match that market. Explain how you arrived at the values you chose in each instance.

Appendix - *Mathematica*, Excel, Regression, and Matrix Algebra

Introduction

The purpose of this appendix is to look inside the regression process so that the reader may see the computations required to produce regression output. There are a variety of different ways to present many particular results. This appendix derives results several ways to illustrate the different presentations. Readers should not view regression output as computer magic. Enhanced understanding comes with knowing the equations and the calculations that take place when one clicks on an icon or executes a regression command. (Even greater understanding comes from understanding the formal proof of these equations, something that exceeds the scope of this work).

This material draws heavily upon two sources. One is Econometric Analysis, 5th Ed., by William H. Greene. The other is *The Classical Regression Model*, lecture notes of Prof. Herman J. Bierens, http://econ.la.psu.edu/~hbierens/index.htm, of the Economics Department of the College of Liberal Arts at The Pennsylvania State University.

The example we use here elaborates the univariate case of Chapter 7 involving house prices and sizes. The model is of the following form

$$y_i = \alpha + \beta x_i + \epsilon_i, \quad i = 1,\ldots,n$$

Where:

- y = the regressand or dependent variable to be explained
- x = the regressor or independent variable offering explanation
- α = intercept term where the function crosses the y axis (when $\beta x_i = 0$)
- β = coefficient to be estimated indicating the effect of x on y in the form of a slope
- ϵ = error or disturbance term

The model is estimated under the following assumptions

1. The model is in the correct functional form, in this case linear;
2. $E[\epsilon_i] = 0$ for all i, that is the mean of the disturbance terms is zero;
3. $\text{Var}[\epsilon_i] = \sigma^2$, a constant, for all i, the property of homoscedasticity;
4. $\text{Cov}[\epsilon_i, \epsilon_j] = 0$ if $i \neq j$, meaning the error terms are independent of each other, not correlated with each other;
5. $\text{Cov}[x_i, \epsilon_i] = 0$ for all i and j, meaning that the regressor and the disturbances are uncorrelated.

Although not strictly required, it is very common to further assume

6. $\epsilon_i \sim N[0, \sigma^2]$, meaning that the error terms are normally distributed with a zero mean and a variance of σ^2.

Assumptions #3 and #4, if they hold, mean that the data are independently and identically distributed, referred to as "iid". The idea is that the error term is the sum of many small effects that are individually unimportant, random, both positive and negative. Assumption #2 assumes that the sum of these have a zero effect on the system.

Assumptions #4 and #5 are hard to maintain for real estate. For instance, #4, the non-autocorrelation assumption, assumes that there is no relationship between the error terms. Much financial data have evidence of autocorrelation. Also, as valuation in real estate sales usually depend on recent sales of nearby properties, correlation may result. There are tests to adjust results to consider autocorrelation and heteroscedasticity but these are beyond the scope of this primer.

For reasons found deep in probability theory, if data are distributed normally it is by definition independent. Thus, Assumption #6 is common. The point is that while normality is not required, independence is and when you assume normality independence comes with it. In several places in the text we question the validity of this assumption for real world data. It is mathematically convenient nonetheless.

It is our purpose here to consider the regression process in a critical way. Regression is very good for a host of purposes. The general notion of conditional probability underlying regression is a powerful concept. But like all tools it must be viewed in terms of its limitations and used correctly. To the extent assumptions cannot be maintained results will be distorted. Conclusions based on distorted results obtained under incorrect assumptions can be wrong.

A note about notation: Convention in most texts is to represent algebraic equations in standard font and matrix algebraic symbols in **BOLD** and sometimes upper case. This conflicts with the *Mathematica* convention of user defined variables being lower case and the capitalization of *Mathematica* built-in variable names and routines. To replicate the convention in most texts the *Mathematica* convention may be violated at times.

This appendix is provided to only to show the calculations underlying regression output, not interpret or explain the output. For interpretation the reader is referred to Greene or any of the many fine econometric or statistics text books that cover regression.

The Data

Using our House Price example as familiar input, here is the same information we saw in Chapter 7:

```
ydata = {195 000, 210 000, 225 000, 240 000,
    275 000, 285 000, 190 000, 239 000, 249 000, 185 000};
xdata = {1500, 1750, 1600, 1700, 1900, 1875, 1650, 1810, 1975, 1550};
houses = Transpose[{xdata, ydata}]
```

$$\begin{pmatrix} 1500 & 195\,000 \\ 1750 & 210\,000 \\ 1600 & 225\,000 \\ 1700 & 240\,000 \\ 1900 & 275\,000 \\ 1875 & 285\,000 \\ 1650 & 190\,000 \\ 1810 & 239\,000 \\ 1975 & 249\,000 \\ 1550 & 185\,000 \end{pmatrix}$$

We need the y values arranged as a vector named **Y**

```
Y = Transpose[{Transpose[houses][[2]]}]
```

$$\begin{pmatrix} 195\,000 \\ 210\,000 \\ 225\,000 \\ 240\,000 \\ 275\,000 \\ 285\,000 \\ 190\,000 \\ 239\,000 \\ 249\,000 \\ 185\,000 \end{pmatrix}$$

We create a matrix (**X**) composed of a vector of 1's for the intercept (alpha) and vectors for each of the independent values (x_i). Vector length of **X** must match that of **Y**.

```
X = Transpose[{Table[1, {10}], Transpose[houses][[1]]}]
```

$$\begin{pmatrix} 1 & 1500 \\ 1 & 1750 \\ 1 & 1600 \\ 1 & 1700 \\ 1 & 1900 \\ 1 & 1875 \\ 1 & 1650 \\ 1 & 1810 \\ 1 & 1975 \\ 1 & 1550 \end{pmatrix}$$

We sometimes need the independent variables in the form of a vector that we will name "size".

```
size = Transpose[{Transpose[X][[2]]}]
```

$$\begin{pmatrix} 1500 \\ 1750 \\ 1600 \\ 1700 \\ 1900 \\ 1875 \\ 1650 \\ 1810 \\ 1975 \\ 1550 \end{pmatrix}$$

For equations developed below we need to set values for n (number of observations) and k (the width of **X**, one more than the number of independent variables). This makes **X** an $n \times k$ matrix (10 x 2 in our example).

```
n = Length[Y]; k = Length[Transpose[X]];

Print["The X matrix is ", n, " x ", k]

The X matrix is 10 x 2
```

Descriptive Statistics

We will compute two descriptive statistics, the mean and the variance for each variable.
The mean may be computed using *Mathematica*'s function or directly

Here is the mean of Y produced by *Mathematica*'s built-in function

```
Mean[Y][[1]]

229 300
```

Using $\frac{\sum_{i=1}^{n} y_i}{n}$ we get the same answer. This time we name the result for future use

$$\mu_Y = \frac{\text{Plus @@ Y}}{n}[[1]]$$

229 300

We follow the same procedure for the independent variables

```
Mean[X[[All, 2]]]
```

1731

$$\mu_X = \frac{\text{Plus @@ X}}{n}[[2]]$$

1731

Here are two presentations arriving at the same sample variance of the size vector, the sum of the squared differences between individual values of the independent variables and the mean, all divided by n-1.

This is *Mathematica*'s automated output

```
N[Variance[size]][[1]]
```

25 137.8

To produce it using an equation we must define $\overline{X}$, a vector of the mean of **X** having a length equal to **X**

```
X̄=μ_X*Table[i,{i,n},{i,1}];
```

This is the algebraic version, $\frac{\Sigma(x-\bar{x})^2}{(n-1)}$

$$\frac{(\text{Plus @@ } (\text{size} - \overline{X})^2)[[1]]}{n-1} // N$$

25 137.8

The mean and the variance are known as, respectively, the first and second moment of the distribution. Other useful measures are skewness and kurtosis, the third and fourth moments of the distribution. These, if significant, represent a deviation from normality because a normal distribution has a skewness of zero (it is symmetric) and an excess kurtosis of zero (it has light tails). Our Y data have a slight skewness and lighter than normal tails.

```
Skewness[Y] // N
Kurtosis[Y] - 3 // N
```

{0.231227}

{-1.14215}

Regression

Preliminary calculations, matrices and the normal equations

Crucial to the regression process is the creation of some special matrices.

For instance, the dot product of $X^T X$ must be a non-singular matrix. This means the $X^T X$ matrix must have an inverse. This property leads to a unique solution of the minimization problem required to solve for the least squares estimators.

```
Transpose[X].X
```

$$\begin{pmatrix} 10 & 17\,310 \\ 17\,310 & 30\,189\,850 \end{pmatrix}$$

The above creates a matrix with the sum of the squares of the individual vectors in X on the diagonal and the sum of the values of the independent variable on the off diagonal. Note that this also produces the coefficients of the "normal equations". These are simultaneous equations which, when solved, produce the estimated a and b of the regression. The two equations in two unknowns, a and b, are shown as equations (7.15) and (7.16).

$$\sum_{i=1}^{n} y_i = n\,a + \left(\sum_{i=1}^{n} x_i\right) b \quad (7.15)$$

$$\sum_{i=1}^{n} x_i\, y_i = \left(\sum_{i=1}^{n} x_i\right) a + \left(\sum_{i=1}^{n} x^2{}_i\right) b \quad (7.16)$$

Let's unravel this notation one term at a time.

On the left hand side of equation (7.15), the sum of the dependent variables (observed house prices), $\sum_{i=1}^{n} y_i$ is

(Plus @@ Y)[[1]]

2 293 000

n is simple enough. Note that it is the upper left term in the $X^T X$ matrix.

n

10

The upper right and lower left (off diagonal) terms in the $X^T X$ matrix is the sum of the independent variables (size of houses), $\sum_{i=1}^{n} x_i$. This is the coefficient of b on the right hand side of equation (7.15).

(Plus @@ size)[[1]]

17 310

Moving to equation (7.16), the term on the left hand side, $\sum_{i=1}^{n} x_i\, y_i$, is the sum of the product of each house price and its size

(Transpose[Y].size)[[1]][[1]]

4 009 490 000

On the right side of equation (7.16) we again encounter the term in off-diagonal of the $X^T X$ matrix, the sum of the independent variables (size of houses), $\sum_{i=1}^{n} x_i$. This time it is the coefficient of a.

(Plus @@ size)[[1]]

17 310

Finally, the lower right element in the $X^T X$ matrix, the sum of the square of the size of each house, $\sum_{i=1}^{n} x^2{}_i$ is the coefficient of b in equation (7.14).

(Transpose[size].size)[[1]][[1]]

30 189 850

Inserting the values we have found for the terms in equations (7.15) and (7.16) produce two equations in two unknowns.

$$2293000 = 10\,a + 17310\,b$$
$$4009490000 = 17310\,a + 30189850\,b$$

These can be combined into a pair of equations using *Mathematica*'s Solve function to find the values for the a and b unknowns.

```
Clear[a];
Solve[{(Plus @@ Y)[[1]] == n a + b (Plus @@ size)[[1]], (Transpose[Y].size)[[1]][[1]] ==
    (a (Plus @@ size)[[1]] + b (Transpose[size].size)[[1]][[1]])[[1]]}, {a, b}]
```

$$\left(a \to \frac{400\,949\,000}{1731} \quad b \to -\frac{4\,030\,700}{2\,996\,361} \right)$$

Students are often confused by the different notation styles used to present equations and mathematical identities. One usually learns algebra and its symbols and then "graduates" to matrix algebra and its notation form. In time one recognizes the similarities between the two styles and moves easily between them. Until that time one may endure much frustration.

For instance, the regression equation may be expressed in matrix notation as

$$Y = X\beta_i + \epsilon \tag{7.17}$$

Where the symbols stand for vectors and matrices.

In general, above we have used both methods to present the normal equations and solve for their two unknown coefficients. This is easy enough when there are only two equations and two unknowns. But algebra becomes unwieldy in the multivariate case when the number of independent variables exceeds one. The multivariate case involves multiple coefficients (b_i, $i = 1 \ldots n$) to allow for many independent variables (such as not only the size of the house but the size of the lot the house is on, the number of bedrooms, etc.). This results in a system of many unknowns with an equal number of equations that is too cumbersome for the algebraic format. Matrix algebra streamlines the notation in the multivariate case.

Above we said that the $X^T X$ must have an inverse. $(X^T X)^{-1}$ is the inverse of $X^T X$.

```
N[Inverse[Transpose[X].X]]
```

$$\begin{pmatrix} 13.3442 & -0.00765117 \\ -0.00765117 & 4.42008 \times 10^{-6} \end{pmatrix}$$

Here are two ways *Mathematica* "picks" the lower right corner term. We name the second one "LwrRt" for later use in forming the t-statistic for the estimated beta coefficient

```
N[Inverse[Transpose[X].X]][[2, 2]]
```

4.42008×10^{-6}

```
LwrRt = N[{0, 1}.Inverse[Transpose[X].X].{{0}, {1}}]
```

$\{4.42008 \times 10^{-6}\}$

The product of the inverse matrix and X^T also produces a matrix. Using that matrix and the **Y** values produces a vector of parameter estimates (a and b) for the regression:

```
N[Inverse[Transpose[X].X].Transpose[X]]
```

$$\begin{pmatrix} 1.86742 & -0.0453722 & 1.1023 & 0.337186 & -1.19305 & -1.00177 & 0.7 \\ -0.00102104 & 0.0000839816 & -0.000579031 & -0.000137023 & 0.000746994 & 0.000636492 & -0.00 \end{pmatrix}$$

The parameter estimates are the solutions to a minimization problem. We present them as a vector, $\hat{\theta} = \begin{pmatrix} \hat{\alpha} \\ \hat{\beta} \end{pmatrix}$. The elements in this vector should be compared with values for a and b reached with the normal equations above and values for the Model Fit of Figure 7.7 of Chapter 7.

The matrix algebra equation for the parameter estimate vector is $\hat{\theta} = (X^T X)^{-1} X^T Y$

θ̂ = N[Inverse[Transpose[X].X].Transpose[X].Y]

$$\begin{pmatrix} -79095.6 \\ 178.16 \end{pmatrix}$$

Mathematica puts these in the form of a regression equation using the function "Fit"

Fit[houses, {1, x}, x] // TraditionalForm

$178.16 x - 79095.6$

Mathematica also uses LinearModelFit to produce an object that can be used for a variety of diagnostics, listed below

lmf = LinearModelFit[houses, {1, x}, x]

FittedModel[$-79095.6 + 178.16 x$]

Here are all the diagnostics available from LinearModelFit

lmf["Properties"]

{AdjustedRSquared, AIC, ANOVATable, ANOVATableDegreesOfFreedom, ANOVATableEntries, ANOVATableFStatistics, ANOVATableMeanSquares, ANOVATablePValues, ANOVATableSumsOfSquares, BasisFunctions, BetaDifferences, BestFit, BestFitParameters, BIC, CatcherMatrix, CoefficientOfVariation, CookDistances, CorrelationMatrix, CovarianceMatrix, CovarianceRatios, Data, DesignMatrix, DurbinWatsonD, EigenstructureTable, EigenstructureTableEigenvalues, EigenstructureTableEntries, EigenstructureTableIndexes, EigenstructureTablePartitions, EstimatedVariance, FitDifferences, FitResiduals, Function, FVarianceRatios, HatDiagonal, MeanPredictionBands, MeanPredictionConfidenceIntervals, MeanPredictionConfidenceIntervalTable, MeanPredictionConfidenceIntervalTableEntries, MeanPredictionErrors, ParameterConfidenceIntervals, ParameterConfidenceIntervalTable, ParameterConfidenceIntervalTableEntries, ParameterConfidenceRegion, ParameterErrors, ParameterPValues, ParameterTable, ParameterTableEntries, ParameterTStatistics, PartialSumOfSquares, PredictedResponse, Properties, Response, RSquared, SequentialSumOfSquares, SingleDeletionVariances, SinglePredictionBands, SinglePredictionConfidenceIntervals, SinglePredictionConfidenceIntervalTable, SinglePredictionConfidenceIntervalTableEntries, SinglePredictionErrors, StandardizedResiduals, StudentizedResiduals, VarianceInflationFactors}

Each of which can be separately researched. Example (follow link): AIC

The LinearModelFit object can be represented in standard form by wrapping it with "Normal"

houseFit = Normal[lmf]
TraditionalForm[%]

$-79095.6 + 178.16 x$

$178.16 x - 79095.6$

We pick the intercept and the parameter estimate, each, out of the vector of estimated parameters, $\hat{\theta}$, and name them for later use.

a = {1, 0}.$\hat{\theta}$

{-79095.6}

b$_1$ = {0, 1}.$\hat{\theta}$

{178.16}

Before continuing, it is important to relate all of this to the SP distribution issues. A central purpose of regression is to predict the conditional mean. For our example that is the average house value *conditioned upon knowing some other fact*, in our case the size of the house). This prediction is dependent on the accurate estimate of β, shown as the value of b_1 above. After performing the regression, our claim is that the value of a house goes up by $178.16 for each added square foot. This is only correct if we have correctly estimated the mean itself. Outliers, as we have said, have a significant affect on the mean. Thus, if the assumption of normality is violated by significant outliers in the distribution the estimated regression coefficient(s) are distorted. For an excellent and quite technical explanation of this situation using a real estate example see McCulloch (1998) described in the References for Chapter 3.

Residuals

The regression report in Table 7.4 of Chapter 7 is reproduced here for comparison to the results below.

RESIDUAL OUTPUT

Observation	Predicted Price	Residuals
1	188145.0	6855.0
2	232685.0	-22685.0
3	205961.0	19039.0
4	223777.0	16223.0
5	259409.1	15590.9
6	254955.1	30044.9
7	214869.0	-24869.0
8	243374.7	-4374.7
9	272771.1	-23771.1
10	197053.0	-12053.0

Mathematica will also perform the above as part of diagnostics and analysis for lmf

n	Predicted Price	Residual
1	188145.	6855.04
2	232685.	-22685.
3	205961.	19039.
4	223777.	16223.
5	259409.	15590.9
6	254955.	30044.9
7	214869.	-24869.
8	243375.	-4374.67
9	272771.	-23771.1
10	197053.	-12053.

The values predicted by the model, our estimated house values $\hat{Y}$, are the product of the vector of independent variables and the vector of parameters, $\hat{Y} = \hat{X}.\hat{\theta}$

$\hat{Y}$ = X.$\hat{\theta}$

$$\begin{pmatrix} 188\,145. \\ 232\,685. \\ 205\,961. \\ 223\,777. \\ 259\,409. \\ 254\,955. \\ 214\,869. \\ 243\,375. \\ 272\,771. \\ 197\,053. \end{pmatrix}$$

Our model is expected to differ from reality. The regression residuals, the error terms, are the result of subtracting the predicted values ($\hat{Y}$) from the actual (Y) values.

The equation for the error terms is $\epsilon = Y - \hat{Y} = Y - X\hat{\theta}$

```
ϵ = Y - X.θ̂
```

$$\begin{pmatrix} 6855.04 \\ -22\,685. \\ 19\,039. \\ 16\,223. \\ 15\,590.9 \\ 30\,044.9 \\ -24\,869. \\ -4374.67 \\ -23\,771.1 \\ -12\,053. \end{pmatrix}$$

Notice these are the same as the residuals

```
resids
```

{6855.04, -22 685., 19 039., 16 223., 15 590.9, 30 044.9, -24 869., -4374.67, -23 771.1, -12 053.}

Analysis of Variance

From Figure 7.7 of Chapter 7 we reproduce for reference the analysis of variance table.

ANOVA

	df	SS	MS	F	Significance F
Regression	1	7181109658	7181109658	15.6069079	0.004232704
Residual	8	3680990342	460123792.8		
Total	9	10862100000			

Mathematica will produce the same ANOVA table, parts of which we will derive individually below.

```
LinearModelFit[houses, {1, x}, x]["ANOVATable"]
```

	DF	SS	MS	F-Statistic	P-Value
x	1	7.18111×10^9	7.18111×10^9	15.6069	0.0042327
Error	8	3.68099×10^9	4.60124×10^8		
Total	9	1.08621×10^{10}			

We need a vector, $\overline{Y}$ in which each element is the mean of Y

```
Ȳ = μ_Y * Table[i, {i, n}, {i, 1}];
```

The sum of the squares of the regression (known both as SSR and $b^2 S_{xx}$) is $(\hat{Y} - \overline{Y})^T (\hat{Y} - \overline{Y})$.

```
SSR = Transpose[Ŷ - Ȳ].(Ŷ - Ȳ)
```

(7.18111×10^9)

The Sum of the Squared Errors (SSE aka $\Sigma[\epsilon_i^2]$)

```
SSE = Transpose[ϵ].ϵ
```

(3.68099×10^9)

The total sum of squares (known either as SST or S_{yy} or $\Sigma(y_i - \hat{y})^2$) is the dot product $(Y - \overline{Y})^T (Y - \overline{Y})$.

```
SST = Transpose[Y - Ȳ].(Y - Ȳ)
```

$(10\,862\,100\,000)$

The Mean Square of the Regression (MSR) is the Sum of Squares of the Regression (SSR) divided by the degrees of freedom for the regression (k-1).

```
MSR = SSR / (k - 1)
```

(7.18111×10^9)

The Mean Square of the Error terms (MSE) is the Sum of the Squared Errors divided by the degrees of freedom for the errors.

```
MSE = SSE / (n - k)
```

(4.60124×10^8)

The F-test for model utility (F-statistic) is the result of dividing the MSR by the MSE

```
F = MSR / MSE
```

(15.6069)

The Parameter Table

From Figure 7.7 of Chapter 7 we reproduce for reference the parameter table of the regression output. This provides, in addition to parameter estimates, the standard errors, t-statistics and p values for each estimate.

	Coefficients	Standard Error	t Stat	P-value
Intercept	-79095.58434	78357.96111	-1.009413507	0.342328491
Size	178.1603607	45.09751892	3.950557923	0.004232704

Mathematica's parameter table produces the same information. We will compute these individually for the independent variable only.

```
LinearModelFit[houses, {1, x}, x]["ParameterTable"]
```

	Estimate	Standard Error	t-Statistic	P-Value
1	-79095.6	78358.	-1.00941	0.342328
x	178.16	45.0975	3.95056	0.0042327

The standard error of the b coefficient uses SSE and the square root of the lower right element in $(X^T X)^{-1}$. We will shortly see that the term on the left, Sqrt[SSE/(n-k)], is also known as the Standard Error of the regression, S.

S_{b_1} = Sqrt[SSE / (n - k)] * Sqrt[LwrRt]

(45.0975)

The t-stat for the b coefficient test of the null hypothesis that $\beta = 0$ is the ratio of the coefficient to its standard error. This is sometimes referred to as a "signal to noise ratio". Depending on the asymptotic properties of the distribution we view the size of this measure as a level of confidence that the value of our estimator did not occur by chance. A large value indicates that our coefficient provides more "signal than noise"

$\hat{t}_{b_1}$ = (b_1 / (S_{b_1}))[[1]][[1]]

3.95056

Summary Output

Finally, the Summary Output below is provided from Figure 7.7

SUMMARY OUTPUT

Regression Statistics	
Multiple R	0.813090489
R Square	0.661116143
Adjusted R Square	0.618755661
Standard Error	21450.49633
Observations	10

The sum of the squared differences between X and $\overline{X}$ (known both as S_{xx} and as $\Sigma(x_i - \overline{x})^2$) is the product $(x - \overline{x})^T.(x - \overline{x})$.

S_{xx} = Transpose[size - $\overline{X}$].(size - $\overline{X}$)

(226240)

There are several ways to compute the R^2 value. the first is to have *Mathematica* compute it as an option in the Regression Report.

LinearModelFit[houses, {1, x}, x]["RSquared"]

0.661116

R^2 is the ratio of the sum of the squared regression to the total sum of squares.

Rsqd = SSR / SST

(0.661116)

Or it is 1 minus the ratio of the sum of the squared errors to the total sum of squares.

1 - (SSE / SST)

(0.661116)

Or it is the product of the estimated coefficient, b_1 and the ratio of the sum of the squared differences between **X** and $\overline{X}$ and the total sum of squares, $b^2 S_{xx}/S_{yy}$ or $b^2 S_{xx}/SST$

```
(b₁²) * Sxx / SST
```

(0.661116)

R^2 is also the square of the correlation coefficient

```
N[Correlation[xdata, ydata]^2]
```

0.661116

The standard error of the regression (S) is the square root of the ratio of the SSE to the degrees of freedom (n-k):

```
S = Sqrt[SSE / (n - k)]
```

(21 450.5)

Notice that the square of S is also the Mean Squared Error

```
TrueQ[S² == MSE]
```

True

The standard deviation of the observed Y values, s_y, may be computed by *Mathematica*'s StandardDeviation function or as the square root of the ratio of the total sum of squares to (n-1).

```
StandardDeviation[ydata] // N
```

34 740.5

```
Sy = N[Sqrt[SST / (n - 1)][[1]][[1]]]
```

34 740.5

It is, of course, also the square root of the variance.

```
Sqrt[Variance[ydata]] // N
```

34 740.5

Dividing the square of s_y into the square of the standard error of the regression and subtracting the result from 1 gives the adjusted R^2:

```
LinearModelFit[houses, {1, x}, x]["AdjustedRSquared"]
```

0.618756

```
adjRsqd = N[1 - (S² / Sy²)]
```

(0.618756)

Alternate presentations

Here are some other ways to use *Mathematica* to display regression output.
We can produce all the output options at once.

```
LinearModelFit[houses, {1, x}, x][{"ANOVATable", "ParameterTable",
  "SinglePredictionConfidenceIntervalTable", "DurbinWatsonD", "FitResiduals"}]
```

$\left\{\begin{array}{l|lllll} & \text{DF} & \text{SS} & \text{MS} & \text{F-Statistic} & \text{P-Value} \\ \hline x & 1 & 7.18111\times 10^9 & 7.18111\times 10^9 & 15.6069 & 0.0042327 \\ \text{Error} & 8 & 3.68099\times 10^9 & 4.60124\times 10^8 & & \\ \text{Total} & 9 & 1.08621\times 10^{10} & & & \end{array}\right.$,

	Estimate	Standard Error	t-Statistic	P-Value
1	−79 095.6	78 358.	−1.00941	0.342328
x	178.16	45.0975	3.95056	0.0042327

Observed	Predicted	Standard Error	Confidence Interval
195 000	188 145.	24 792.4	{130 974., 245 316.}
210 000	232 685.	22 513.8	{180 768., 284 602.}
225 000	205 961.	23 260.2	{152 323., 259 599.}
240 000	223 777.	22 540.9	{171 798., 275 756.}
275 000	259 409.	23 753.4	{204 634., 314 184.}
285 000	254 955.	23 416.	{200 958., 308 952.}
190 000	214 869.	22 792.1	{162 310., 267 428.}
239 000	243 375.	22 777.8	{190 849., 295 900.}
249 000	272 771.	25 044.4	{215 019., 330 524.}
185 000	197 053.	23 932.5	{141 865., 252 241.}

, 1.84186, {6855.04, −22 685.,

19 039., 16 223., 15 590.9, 30 044.9, −24 869., −4374.67, −23 771.1, −12 053.}}

We can name the errors and predicted values in separate lists and plot them together to get a visual look at whether there is a relationship such as bigger errors for larger predictions.

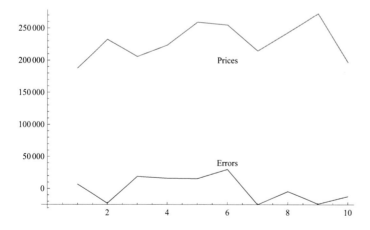

8

The Labor Component of Private Investor Real Estate Returns

"If we restrict ourselves to models which can be solved analytically, we will be modeling for our mutual entertainment, not to maximize explanatory or predictive power."

Harry M. Markowitz commenting on Microscopic Simulation of Financial Markets by Levy, Levy, and Solomon (2000)

8.1. Introduction

Suppose that private (Tier II) real estate investment return distributions exhibit non-normal, stable distributions having so-called "fat tails". Further, suppose that these fat tails are skewed right. What might explain this? Anecdotal evidence and intuition suggests that a portion of real estate returns observed in this market is attributable to the investor's entrepreneurial effort. In the field this concept is sometimes referred to as "sweat equity" or "value added". Technically this constitutes an addition of labor, implicitly a non-cash but valuable additional contribution of human capital to the investment. If the private real estate market is dominated by investors who self-select into this market because they have the ability or time to enhance their investment, and if the addition of this time and effort increases returns, this would contribute to the explanation of a fat right tail. By studying investor returns we hope to uncover a return generating process. Chapter 7 offered an empirical argument for such a process. This chapter further explores the "add labor" theory.

In this chapter we will:

- Discuss how the addition of labor enters into the return equation;
- Build a two-part model of investor behavior where real estate investment decisions are a labor trade-off rather than a portfolio trade-off;
- Perform simulations to illustrate how the model works; and
- Attempt to find a natural point in time where real estate investing is supplanted by investing in financial assets.

8.1.1. The important aspect of time

The model developed here includes considerable real world complexity. Academia has not yet explained why people invest in individual parcels of real property. The reason for this may be traced to the fact that no model yet proposed offers an analytical solution. This obstacle, often fatal in academia, does not constrain actors in the market. Much of what practitioners do each day is trial and error in a messy real world environment. This chapter, while perhaps not yet a formal theory, may be the best if not the only way to approach the subject.

Our model is a dynamic model. This means it is dependent on time. We argue that investors divide their time not only between real estate and other pursuits but divide their lifetimes into pre- and post-retirement periods. Dynamic models require differential equations, mathematical constructs that offer difficult challenges. Most differential equations have no solution. It is interesting to note that one of the most famous results of finance, a Nobel Prize winning one, employs a differential equation. It happens that a physics equation describing the way heat diffuses has a solution that Fisher Black, Myron Scholes and Robert Merton used to create the widely known Black-Scholes Option Pricing Model.[1] Our description of the labor component of real estate returns will also use differential equations. Unfortunately for us we will not be able to solve those equations in closed form. Rather, we will simulate them over a reasonable range and illustrate probable outcomes. Very often model builders must choose between mathematical tractability and reality. We have chosen the latter.

8.2. Foundation

The simple static model of labor supply (Killingsworth, 1983) holds that one chooses between work and recreation. To the extent one works for an employer and receives wages, the static model assumes that one earns money, permitting one to purchase goods and services, all of which are consumed in the same period. If one chooses recreation rather than work, enjoying leisure, the implicit price of leisure is the forgone consumption goods one may have gained by working. The theory claims that most people enjoy a mix of work (consumption goods) and recreation.

Acknowledged in the simple static model is that fact that an agent may have or acquire along the way non-human assets, property in the form of bank accounts that pay interest or stock that pays dividends. The agent's reservation wage (the wage below which he refuses to work) is affected by the amount of property income. The natural conclusion is that "coupon clippers" cannot be hired because their marginal substitution of wages for leisure is too high due to the fact that income from their non-human assets provides their creature comforts without the necessity of a job or an employer.

Adding real estate introduces daunting complexity. It is common for labor theorists to use financial assets as property, but when the source of property income is *real* property, interesting things can and do happen. The important distinction is that the investor may impact the productivity of his investment in real assets. Effort applied to the operation and management of the asset can change the income from the property and, therefore, the outcome of the investment.[2]

When the investor adds his labor to property he owns there are several new considerations.[3]
- The time for that labor must come from somewhere. In the simple model all time was devoted to work and leisure. Given a fixed amount of time available, real estate investment activity much take from one or the other.
- The election to work on property to improve its income introduces a third choice variable in the utility function.
- The addition of the owner's labor normally represents a positive value, increasing property income *over time*. Hence, the model has a time dimension. This leads to the modeling difficulties common to a dynamic setting.
- Any model must provide for an efficiency factor to allow for differing skills among real property owners. Presumably, investors self-select into this market based on some real or imagined ability to successfully operate their acquisition. Those with particularly good skills should enjoy improved results as a consequence of greater talent. Those misjudging their abilities or simply lacking what it takes should have marginally lower returns and be washed out of the market in sales to more efficient agents.[4]

A host of other, smaller, considerations must be incorporated. The challenge is to make the model simple enough to be as elegant and universal as possible, yet include the vital, often complicating, factors necessary to make it realistic. It is reasonable to assume that the investor enters the real estate investment market only after amassing enough wealth to overcome the down payment barrier. It is also assumed that the investor has a retirement goal measured by (a) accumulated dollars of capital to produce income; and (b) age. In fact, the argument here is that one of the reasons the investor chooses real estate is *to accelerate the date of retirement to an earlier point in life*. The choice of real estate evidences the individual's belief that this acceleration is more likely or more rapid when that asset is held and over which some measure of control may be exercised.[5]

These real world assumptions introduce more differences between ours and the traditional labor model. In labor supply theory it is assumed that the length of economic life is measured by the time between the day the agent first enters the job market, perhaps after graduating from school, until death. Our model assumes that (1) *investment* economic life begins at the time real estate is purchased.

This is presumably *after* some period of pre-investment wealth accumulation, time that begins upon entry into the labor force and ends when capital for a down payment has been acquired;[6] and (2) that some retirement date prior to death, a critical factor in the agent's plan, exists. This retirement date is variable and based, in part, on the investor's efficient operation of his real estate. This, of course, means that the time spent working for an employer and the time (retirement) following that working period are both variable but still sum to the whole of investment economic life as defined here.

The matter of bequests must be addressed. One method, which might be quaintly referred to as "the die broke scheme", assumes bequests = 0. That is, all wealth is consumed during one's lifetime. The alternate extreme, for which competing monikers might be "the live forever scheme" or more likely "the leave a rich wife scheme", forbids any capital erosion. In this second version a constraint on wealth is imposed such that only earnings are consumed after retirement while capital remains intact. Neither of these extremes is terribly realistic and something in between is what we observe in practice. As always some simplifying assumptions are appropriate so we will concentrate our effort on the zero bequest and constant wealth cases.

Special note must be made of the efficiency factor. This is the productivity of the investor's entrepreneurial effort (how good he is at it) applied to his rental property. It produces a reward that acts like (but is not) a wage rate. Unlike wages sometimes behave, property returns are neither constant nor do they monotonically increase over time. The vagaries of property ownership and income, like self employment, introduce uneven motion. There are economies of scale, discontinuities and variation, all differing over time, which affect how much the investor makes on any particular property over any specific holding period. A useful characterization, but still an oversimplification, would be to call the property return function the average rate at which the residual claim is rewarded over the holding period. This reward is only in part for time spent. It is also a reward for bearing the *uncertainty* associated with the residual claim.

It is important to note that the efficiency factor does *not* represent property management ability but talent in the larger matters of strategy, timing and entity management. This is not to say that the investor might not also choose to do his own property management. He may also choose to do his own plumbing. Presumably these decisions will be determined by any comparative advantages he may have in these areas. No assumption is made that he MUST hire vendors for these tasks or that he is necessarily better able to perform them. The primary purpose of the efficiency factor is to represent the payoff to the residual claim arising from the global coordination of the entire venture, of which property management, maintenance, etc. are all a part but do not, in the aggregate, represent the whole of what is required to own and successfully operate real property.

8.3. Notation guide

A considerable amount of notation is involved. This is brought about in part because of the complexity of a dynamic model and in part because of the way in which *Mathematica* processes symbols. Because *Mathematica* has difficulties with subscripts in functions we use the subscripts in the narrative and we sometimes use similarly appearing, but not subscripted, characters in the *Mathematica* code.

$W0$	=	initial wealth, assumed to be > 0 because of the down payment barrier imposed by real estate investing
wg	=	wage rate during time employed
t	=	time (t_0 is beginning of real estate investment period)
T	=	total time working and retired (t_w+t_r)
H	=	exogenously determined portion of one's time devoted to working at a job
L	=	leisure time, assumed to be > 0 (at least some time must be spent sleeping)
t_{w0}	=	beginning point of working years
t_w	=	working (pre−retirement) years
t_r	=	retirement years
c_w	=	consumption during time working
c_r	=	consumption during retirement
r	=	interest rate or rate of return over time
p	=	exogenously given prices
S	=	portion of time devoted to working on real property investments, the time remaining after H and L
ρ	=	efficiency of time spent working on real property investments, a measure of entrepreneurial ability
α	=	preference for consumption over a base amount, assumed to be $0 < \alpha < 1$
β	=	preference for leisure over a base amount, assumed to be $0 < \beta < 1$
γ	=	preference for time retired, assumed to be $0 < \gamma < 1$
uf	=	utility function of the form $u(x,y,z) = x^\alpha y^\beta z^\gamma$ with $\alpha+\beta+\gamma=1$

We assume that all wealth and excess earnings are invested in real estate in all time periods.

$w0$	=	boundary condition in the differential equation representing wealth accumulated at the point of retirement
ww_1	=	differential equation solved to produce w_1
w_1	=	wealth accumulation function for pre−retirement years
w_2	=	wealth accumulation function for retirement years
$wr1$	=	the differential equation we solve to produce the function that accumulates wealth during retirement
$tr1$	=	total retirement period, a variant of t_r needed to rearrange some terms
st	=	solution of the retirement time variable in terms of the other variables in the function produced by the differential equation
scw	=	solution of the consumption while working variable in terms of the other time variables
$dv(x)$	=	data version(x) necessary to create the graphic objects $frho$ = the function of rho (ρ) that employs the data, the utility function and its partial derivatives
ds	=	partial derivative of the utility function with respect to S
dtw	=	partial derivative of the utility function with respect to time working
tws	=	a function used to produce a graphic object using the arguments ρ and c

The approach is to demonstrate the two extremes. First we work out the no bequests model, describing the daredevil who earns precisely enough money to enable him to retire for the exact remainder of his physical life. Second we show the constant wealth model, representing the investor who, hoping to live forever, accumulates enough wealth to support an infinite life.

Clearly reality is somewhere in between...

8.4. The no bequests model

Initially we assume that our investor only wishes to provide for himself during his lifetime and cares not about leaving a bequest to his heirs.

8.4.1. Wealth accumulation prior to retirement

Equation 8.1 is the wealth accumulation function, $w_1(t_w)$, during working years, a continuous process beginning after our investor enters the work force, a time when sufficient wealth has been accumulated from other sources to meet the down payment requirement for a real estate investment. Note that $w_1(t_w)$ is the solution to the differential equation ww_1, the instantaneous wealth production process. In w_1 you will note that time, t, becomes a specific period of one's life, time working, t_w

$$w_1(t_w) = \frac{1}{S\rho}\left(-c_w\left(-1 + e^{\frac{S t \rho}{1+S}}\right)p(1+S) + \left(-1 + e^{\frac{S t \rho}{1+S}}\right)H(1+S)wg + e^{\frac{S t \rho}{1+S}}S W0 \rho\right) \tag{8.1}$$

Although differential equations can appear daunting, a bit of decomposition can help understand it. The first derivative of a function measures instantaneous change. A differential equation (and *Mathematica*'s DSolve[ ]) asks the question: Suppose I know what the derivative looks like, what is the function that, upon differentiation, would produce that derivative?

The derivative, $w_1'[t_w]$, of the wealth production function, $w_1[t_w]$, describes how wealth is accumulated instant-by-instant on a continuous basis. This derivative is composed of two parts

$$\frac{\delta w_1(t_w)}{\delta t} = w_1[t]\rho\frac{S}{(S+1)} + wg\,H - c_w\,p \tag{8.2}$$

The right side, $wg\,H - c_w\,p$, merely describes the daily accounting of going to work at a job and collecting wages ($wg\,H$) which are then applied to paying bills ($c_w\,p$). If the net of these is positive wealth accumulates (saving), if it is negative wealth deteriorates (consumption).

The term $w_1[t]\rho\frac{S}{(S+1)}$, is central to our story. It shows how the application of our investor's labor affects his real estate investments.

Recall that $w_1[t]$ begins with, $w_1[0] = W0$, a non-zero number by definition. Thereafter we assume that the investor possesses not only sufficient funds for a down payment but aptitude for and ability to operate his property. This ability, which varies among different investors, is represented by a positive number, ρ, which is modified by the portion of one's time, S, devoted to real estate investment management. S appears in the equation in a functional form, $\frac{S}{(S+1)}$, that represents marginally decreasing returns to added S. This is a common assumption in labor analysis and elsewhere. People are less efficient as they exert more labor and become tired. Figure 8.1 illustrates three arbitrary values of ρ. Applied to any given amount of wealth, $w_1[t]$, these produce differing but positive results.

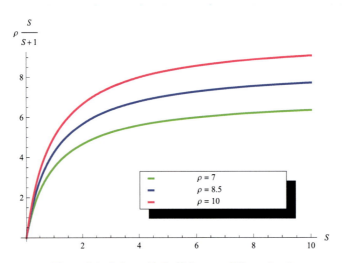

Figure 8.1. Labor-added efficiency at different levels

The notion that any and all effort applied to the operation of real estate always produces a positive result is doubtful. Our model applies primarily to those who have self-selected into real estate because of their predilection for operating their investments. It is not hard to imagine others who mistakenly choose real estate, discover they do not like it or learn they cannot do it and leave the market, probably selling to someone who fits our model. Departing investors are presumed to be short-term owners. Our model is for the long-term real estate investor who resides in this market because he finds it profitable and to his liking.

8.4.2. Wealth accumulation after retirement

Another differential equation, 8.3, is required for wealth following retirement. This is also a function of time and its derivative, Equation 8.4, is the instantaneous wealth production function, $w_2'(t_r)$, for retirement years.[7]

$$w_2(t_r) = \frac{c_r p - c_r e^{r\,tr1} p + e^{r\,tr1} r w0}{r} \tag{8.3}$$

$$\frac{\delta w_2(t_r)}{\delta t} = w_2(t_r) - c_r p \tag{8.4}$$

Note that the right hand side of Equation 8.4, $w_2[t_r] - c_r p$, is again in two parts. The right side, $c_r p$ is retirement consumption. In retirement there are no wages, thus no accumulation or savings aspect arising from labor at a job. The remaining term, $w_2[t_r]$, must produce all required income from wealth accumulated prior to retirement, $w_2[0] = w0$, adjusted by any post retirement return, r, on that wealth.

Substituting Equation 8.1 for the boundary condition in Equation 8.3, we then set the result to zero and solve for $tr1$. Thus we define st, the solution for time in the implicit function $w_2 = 0$. Note that the boundary condition, $W0$, is w_1, the wealth accumulated prior to retirement. We are interested in solving for *the time retired*, $tr1$, in terms of all the other variables (Equation 8.5). To meet the "no bequests" assumption this answers the question "how long does it take for wealth to reach zero?" This occurs at T, the end of time and the conclusion of our investor's life.[8] We name this solution, $tr1$, for future use as the length of retirement.

$$tr1 = -\frac{1}{r}Log\left[1/(c_r\,p\,S\,\rho)\left(c_w\left(e^{\frac{St_w\rho}{1+S}}-1\right)p\,r(S+1)-\left(e^{\frac{St_w\rho}{1+S}}-1\right)H\,r(1+S)\,wg+S\left(c_r\,p-e^{\frac{St_w\rho}{1+S}}r\,W0\right)\rho\right)\right] \quad (8.5)$$

The length of retirement, *tr1*, is critical because the investor is presumed to derive utility from increased retirement time. As suggested earlier, an important motive for choosing real property as an investment is the possibility of positively influencing the outcome. This model accounts for that positive influence by reducing time working for an employer, therefore increasing retirement time. Presuming that the agent has a disutility for working for an employer, the sooner retirement can occur, the better. The investor's problem is now one of maximizing the utility function in equation 8.6 where the variables follow the notation given earlier and the constants (900 minimum consumption and .25 minimum non-working time) represent base minimums. These constants may be viewed as subsistence in each case so that the agent values consumption and leisure only over the minimum required to sustain life.[9]

$$\underset{(L,S)}{Max}\,uf(c_w,L,t_r) = (c_w-900)^\alpha (L-.25)^\beta (t_r)^\gamma \quad (8.6)$$

Using *tr1* as t_r, we are now in a position to conduct some simulations to explore how well our model fits reality.

As expected, a model composed of differential equations and many variables admits no closed form analytical solution. Instead, we employ bounded *numerical* solutions and create graphics of reasonable dimensions to simulate how the model behaves. This is in lieu of the conventional comparative statics (as we used in Chapter 2) permitted by analytic methods. Simulation, while suboptimal in meeting the usual standard for theory, becomes the best one may do in this case. Graphics produced by simulation allow no more than three variables. To accomplish this we assume plausible but fixed values for a number of parameters. The result is a graphic showing how different combinations of three of the most critical variables produce different optimum utility. The variables chosen for the graphic are not the choice variables and the graphic is not a conventional optimization exercise. Rather, it depicts ranges of optimal utility that may be achieved under different conditions. The three important variables used in the simulations below are the efficiency factor (ρ), working years (t_w) and the portion of one's time devoted to real estate ownership activities (*S*), the latter two both being functions of ρ. The intuition is that persons of varying skill levels devote different amounts of time to maximizing their real property investments while also working for an employer with the result that they retire from employment at different times in their lives.

8.4.3. Simulation #1

The first set, **dv1**, of data values, shown in Table 8.1, is provided for the first simulation.

The first simulation demonstrates how different combinations of time working t_w, rental owner efficiency, ρ, and time spent operating rentals, *S*, produce different optimal utility. We need a function of ρ, which will be named "*frho*". This is created in several steps.

1. Define the value of t_r as *tr1*, using the data in **dv1** as fixed inputs.
2. Using the fact that t_w and t_r total *T*, solve for consumption in working years, c_w, in terms of *S*, t_w, ρ and the parameters fixed by **dv1**. That function is then named c_w.
3. Define leisure, *L*, as the portion of waking time (itself a fraction of total time) left after working for an employer, *H*, and working on real estate, *S*.
4. Assume the agent derives utility from (a) consumption in working years (recall that consumption during retirement is part of *tr1*) over a fixed level of subsistence; (b) leisure over a fixed minimum; and (c) years in retirement, t_r.
5. Define a utility function, *uf*, with those variables in the form $u(xyz) = x^\alpha y^\beta z^\gamma$ where $x = c_w-900$; $y = L-.25$; and $z = t_r$. Exponents represent relative preferences, and are assumed to be, each, $\subset (0,1)$, exhibiting diminishing marginal returns. Also, $\alpha + \beta + \gamma = 1$.
6. Find partial derivatives of the utility function with respect to *S* and t_w naming them, respectively, *ds* and *dtw*.

Note in Table 8.1 a value for *T*. This represents the maximum time capital will last. This is not a natural lifespan. Rather it is an individual's investment lifespan. Assuming one does not enter the workforce and begin investing in real estate until one is at least

20, when $T = 60$ natural age is 80.

T	α	β	γ	c_r	p	r	wg	H	W0
60	0.1	0.4	0.5	1200	20	0.07	120 000.	0.25	50 000.

Table 8.1 Fixed parameter values for simulation #1

Inserting values from Table 8.1 into equation (8.5) we reduce the number of variables in *tr1*. Using the fact that $t_w + t_r = T$ we can solve for c_r in terms of variables already in *tr1*. Knowing that $L = 1 - H - S$ completes what we need for the utility function, *uf*. Table 8.1 specifies values for α, β and γ so we are now ready to make the calculations needed for simulation. We take the first partial derivative of the utility function with respect to S and t_w, set them equal to zero and solve for optimal utility using a number of different values of ρ, t_w, and S. Figure 8.2 reflects the graph of optimal utility, given the data in Table 8.1, showing how optimal utility changes with changes in the critical variables. Note that time working prior to retirement, $t_w(\rho)$, decreases with higher values of ρ and/or S.

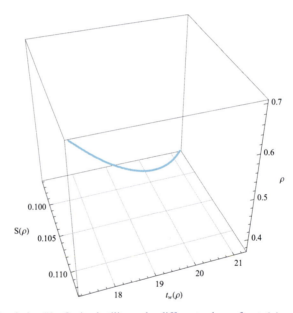

Figure 8.2. Simulation #1 - Optimal utility under different values of ρ, $t_w(\rho)$ and $S(\rho)$

To review, Figure 8.2 plots the values of S, and t_w, each as a function of ρ which yield optimal utility when all other parameters are fixed by **dv1** in Table 8.1. Optimal utility occurs when the first derivative of the utility function is set to zero. Note that, given these fixed parameters, optimal utility increases with smaller amounts of time working, t_w, presumed to be the agent's goal. This occurs, as hoped, when ρ, $S(\rho)$ or combinations of them increase.

Table 8.2 displays values used to create Figure 8.2. Note that the points for the lower right hand rear corner of the graph are on the first line in the table and the last line shows the points for the upper left forward corner.

ρ	$t_w(ρ)$	$S(ρ)$
0.375	21.2433	0.0961118
0.4	20.826	0.0987225
0.425	20.4329	0.100959
0.45	20.0618	0.102885
0.475	19.7104	0.104552
0.5	19.3772	0.106002
0.525	19.0603	0.107268
0.55	18.7586	0.108376
0.575	18.4707	0.10935
0.6	18.1956	0.110206
0.625	17.9323	0.110962
0.65	17.68	0.11163
0.675	17.4377	0.11222
0.7	17.2049	0.112743

Table 8.2 Selected points from Figure 8.2

8.4.4. Simulation #2

Using a slightly different dataset, **dv2**, for fixed parameters, the value of two of the variables is changed to see how the plot changes. For the present H remains fixed at .25, the change is in one of the exponents in the utility function. Increasing $γ$ indicates a greater preference for retirement time, suggesting the investor gains utility by retiring earlier in life (expressed by shorter time working, t_w). Because $α + β + γ = 1$ increasing $γ$ means decreasing something else. We choose $β$.

The procedure for creating *frho* is the same except the new data, **dv2** from Table 8.3, are employed.

T	α	β	γ	c_r	p	r	wg	H	W0
60	0.1	0.2	0.7	1200	20	0.07	120 000.	0.25	50 000.

Table 8.3 Fixed parameter values for simulation #2

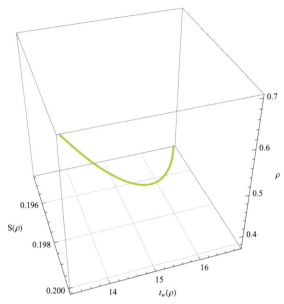

Figure 8.3. Simulation #2 with $\beta = .2$ and $\gamma = .7$

Figure 8.3 is the plot of our second simulation. It looks nearly identical to Figure 8.2 and it is except for the range on the axes. The exponents representing relative preference, α, β, and γ, are highly abstract. When γ increases at the expense of β optimum utility occurs along the same range of ρ but along a broader range of S, with working years consistently lower. Hence, when one prefers greater retirement time (as evidenced by a higher γ) and takes from leisure time (by lowering β) he can reduce time working over the relevant ranges of S and ρ. Those who might refer to such a person as a "workaholic" may wish to rethink this accusation. Such investors just prefer to organize life in a way that concentrates larger effort in early years to allow for less effort in later years. Thus, like the fable of the ant and the grasshopper, the investor willing to forgo some leisure early in life is able to retire sooner.

Table 8.4 displays values used to create Figure 8.3. Again, the points for the lower right hand rear corner of the graph are on the first line in the table and the last line shows the points for the upper left forward corner.

ρ	$t_w(\rho)$	$S(\rho)$
0.375	16.8842	0.19454
0.4	16.5004	0.195789
0.425	16.1402	0.196799
0.45	15.8013	0.197612
0.475	15.4816	0.198264
0.5	15.1793	0.198783
0.525	14.8929	0.199191
0.55	14.621	0.199506
0.575	14.3624	0.199743
0.6	14.116	0.199913
0.625	13.8808	0.200027
0.65	13.656	0.200094
0.675	13.4408	0.200119
0.7	13.2347	0.20011

Table 8.4 Selected points from Figure 8.3

Figure 8.4 displays plots of optimal utility for both datasets on the same graph for comparison purposes.

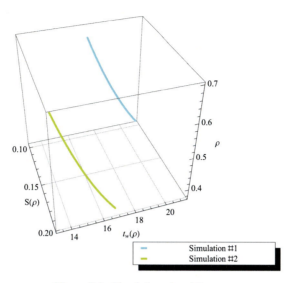

Figure 8.4. Simulations 1 and 2

8.4.5. Simulation #3

Returning to the original values for β and γ in **dv1**, in **dv3** we change the assumption of fixed (25%) percentage of work time to a different fixed percentage, 15%. This could be the result of semi-retirement from one's job or changing to part-time employment. The procedure for creating *frho* is repeated using the new data, **dv3** in Table 8.5.

T	α	β	γ	c_r	p	r	wg	H	W0
60	0.1	0.4	0.5	1200	20	0.07	120 000.	0.25	50 000.

Table 8.5 Fixed parameter values for simulation #3

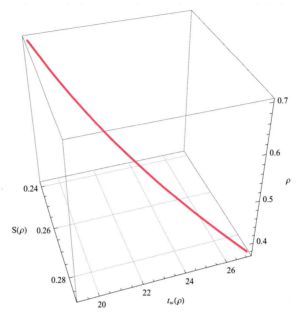

Figure 8.5. Simulation #3 with H = 15%

ρ	$t_w(\rho)$	$S(\rho)$
0.375	27.0852	0.287647
0.4	26.1397	0.282013
0.425	25.2798	0.276822
0.45	24.4935	0.272024
0.475	23.7711	0.267575
0.5	23.1043	0.263438
0.525	22.4865	0.25958
0.55	21.9119	0.255972
0.575	21.3758	0.252589
0.6	20.8741	0.24941
0.625	20.4033	0.246415
0.65	19.9603	0.243588
0.675	19.5426	0.240913
0.7	19.1477	0.238379

Table 8.6 Selected points from Figure 8.5

Again, combining the plots is instructive. The last plot indicates that, because more time is devoted to leisure as *H* declines (because *L* = 1 - *H* - *S*), *ceteris paribus*, years spent working prior to retirement increases. Beyond lowering the percentage share of time that goes to working, the model does not distinguish years spent working less than full time.

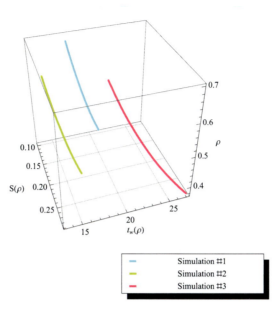

Figure 8.6. Simulations 1, 2 and 3

As t_w and s are functions of ρ Figure 8.7 shows how these change with ρ (t_w is divided by 100 to permit it to scale closer to the plot of $S(\rho)$). As one might expect, with an increase in management efficiency, ρ, less time, S, is required to attend to real estate duties. Time working, t_w, also declines with increased management efficiency. The intuition is straightforward: the better one is at operating one's rentals the less time it takes and the earlier one retires.

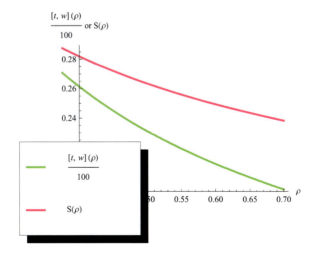

Figure 8.7. Efficiency measures on ρ - Changes in $S(\rho)$ and $t_w(\rho)$ with changes in ρ

8.4.6. Simulation #4

One can easily claim that retirement time is dependent on maintaining a frugal post-retirement lifestyle. To illustrate this we take a different approach that fixes ρ, then calculates S, t_w, as functions of c_r.

T	α	β	γ	ρ	p	r	wg	H	W0
60	0.1	0.4	0.5	0.7	20	0.07	120000.	0.25	50000.

Table 8.7 Fixed parameter values for simulation #4

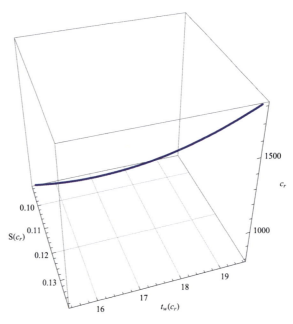

Figure 8.8. Simulation #4 - t_w and S as functions of c_r assuming fixed ρ

Figure 8.8 describes a person with a given, constant level of wealth management efficiency. He may increase consumption during retirement by either working longer at his job (delaying retirement) or by spending more time working on his rentals. The factor of interest here is the relative efficiency or the productivity of spending effort at one's job vs. working on one's real estate. Neither this model nor its graphic depiction above addresses this, but one can see that there are many different ways to approach the problem.

c_r	$t_w(c_r)$	$S(c_r)$
900	15.4205	0.0916943
1000	16.0848	0.0997158
1100	16.6749	0.106654
1200	17.2049	0.112743
1300	17.6854	0.11815
1400	18.1242	0.122999
1500	18.5278	0.127385
1600	18.901	0.131382
1700	19.2478	0.135047
1800	19.5716	0.138427

Table 8.8 Selected points from Figure 8.8

8.5. The constant wealth model

Alternatively, the agent may prefer to leave behind whatever estate he amasses during working years, spending only income during retirement. This problem is simpler. In fact, if retirement consumption and retirement return are both known, it is straightforward to calculate the required wealth and from that determine the time necessary to spend working.

To make the problem more interesting we assume that real estate investment continues into retirement. This means that there are two ways the retiree may spend his post working days - leisure or working on his property. This model defines some new terms

S_r	=	portion of time during retirement devoted to working on real property investments, the time remaining after L_r
L_r	=	leisure during retirement
ur	=	utility function during retirement, a function of the form $u(x,y)=x^\varphi y^\omega$, where $x = c_r$ and $y = L_r$
drs	=	partial derivative of utility with respect to S_r
sru	=	portion of time spent working on real estate when utility is maximum (given certain data)
cru	=	retirement consumption when utility is maximum and real estate time is sru (given certain data)
wwe	=	required wealth available at retirement given cru, sru and the data

One effect of this is to replace r in the no bequests model with $\rho \frac{S_r}{S_r+1}$, the function that leaves the investor's entrepreneurial abilities a factor after retirement. It is probable that as the investor ages he will "slow down" with age and become less willing or able to attend to property matters. At some time $\rho \frac{S_r}{S_r+1}$ should drop to r, indicating that the owner's efforts are no longer adding to value in excess of those available from non-real estate passive investments bearing a predetermined return. This would be a signal to sell property.

Equation 8.7 is the utility function that describes this investor's problem

$$\underset{(S_r, c_r)}{\operatorname{Max}} ur(c_r, L_r) = (c_r)^\varphi (L_r)^\omega \tag{8.7}$$

8.5.1. Simulation #5

We begin with the differential equation, $w_2[t_r]$, that leads to the retirement years wealth producing function, $w_2'[t_r]$, again substituting $tr1$ for t in Equation 8.8

$$w_2(t_r) = \frac{e^{\frac{S_r tr1 \rho}{1+S_r}} S_r w0 \rho - c_r \left(e^{\frac{S_r tr1 \rho}{1+S_r}} - 1\right) p(S_r + 1)}{S_r \rho} \tag{8.8}$$

$$\frac{dw_2(t_r)}{dt} = w_2(t_r) \frac{\rho S_r}{S_r + 1} - c_r p \tag{8.9}$$

The next step is a simplification of the above that retains the initial conditions in the rate of change of wealth. Even though the rate of change of wealth will be zero (the obvious case when wealth is constant) in this model, it is useful to define the rate of change of wealth in terms of the initial conditions. Taking the partial derivative of $w_2(t_r)$ with respect to $tr1$, we solve for a named c_r, consumption during retirement. This is done by fixing the rate of change of post-retirement wealth at zero. Another obvious consequence of this is that post-retirement consumption must equal returns from $w0$.

$$c_r = \frac{S_r\, w0\, \rho}{p\,(1 + S_r)} \qquad (8.10)$$

In Table 8.9 we show data values during retirement, **dvr**, that are assigned for simulation, definitions are provided for leisure during retirement, L_r, utility during retirement, ur, and its partial derivative with respect to S_r, the time spent working on property during retirement.

ρ	φ	ω	p
1	0.1	0.9	2

Table 8.9 Fixed parameter values, **dvr1**, for simulation #5

Assuming that one amassed sufficient funds to retire, we ask for the optimal portion of time spent on real estate after retirement by setting the partial derivative equal to zero and solving for S_r.

Given the data in **dvr1** that produced *drs1*, our agent would spend 9.233% of his time on his real estate during retirement. The same result is obtained when the technique of setting *w0* in *drs* to an arbitrary value is used.

Given the data in **dvr1** that produced *drs1*, our agent would spend 9.233% of his time on his real estate during retirement. The same result is obtained when the technique of setting *w0* in *drs* to an arbitrary value is used.

To determine what wealth is necessary to provide consumption during retirement we solve for c_r in terms of wealth at retirement, *w0*, to obtain a function providing a constant factor which when multiplied times retirement wealth produces consumption income. This factor is the cash flow rate on accumulated wealth.

```
cru = (c_r /. dvr1) /. S_r → sru[[1, 2]]
```
```
0.042262 w0
```

We can then 'back in' to the amount of wealth required, given a certain level of consumption. Suppose one wishes to have an annual income of $60,000, then the capital needed to produce the requisite income given the return is: $1,419,714.

As expected, consumption available during retirement is a rising function of wealth.

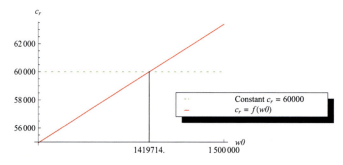

Figure 8.9. Consumption as a function of wealth

A plot of utility, in Figure 8.10, based on time spent on real estate S_r, and initial retirement day wealth, $w0$, shows that under the specified conditions optimum utility is primarily dependent on S_r with the optimum where we previously calculated it at just over 9%.

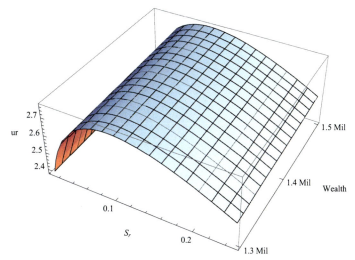

Figure 8.10. Utility during retirement as a function of S_r and w0

Returning to the idea mentioned at the beginning of this section, as one grows older during retirement, the March of Time erodes one's efficiency and/or patience with the ownership of property. The result is that the output of the return function that influences utility in retirement, something we might now call effective return, $er = \rho \frac{S_r}{S_r+1}$, drops in value as less time or skill is devoted to real estate. The natural conclusion of this is that at some time the attraction of passive investments begins to compete favorably with real estate.

In Figure 8.11 effective return is declining with various combinations of lower ρ and S_r to a point that it drops below the cash flow rate provided by *cru* above (the flat plane in Exhibit 8.11). One considers selling if competing returns on the reinvested after tax sale proceeds are at or above the real estate cash flow in *cru*.

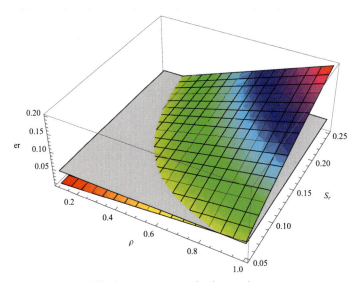

Figure 8.11. Effective return vs. passive income instruments

Let's define an effective return function, *er*, dependent on ρ and S_r, and plot various values for it in Figure 8.13. Working from right to left, returns decline as time shortens or ability erodes.

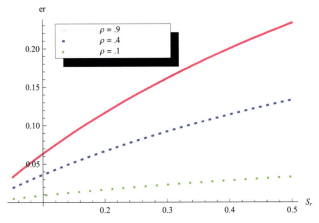

Figure 8.12. Effective return over a range of S_r for various values of ρ

The last two illustrations are merely mathematical/graphical expressions of the aging process playing itself out over an investment career. Late in life most Tier II investors succumb to the rigors of property ownership and operation, turning to management-free investments for a more complete retirement. While these may at first thought sound like offerings of the securities market, let's reserve judgment for a bit. In later chapters we will encounter familiar and comfortable real estate-oriented strategies that offer the investor a passive safe harbor in the most golden of his later years.

8.6. Conclusion

If the investor adds efficient labor in order to accelerate retirement, he influences his return by making *r* in Equation 8.11 larger.

$$r = \frac{P_t}{P_{t-1}} \tag{8.11}$$

Different agents exhibiting different levels of efficiency in real property ownership self-select into the private real estate investment market. These agents experience different right tail investment return outcomes depending on the time they devote to their property, the real estate market during their tenure, their length of ownership, their operational efficiency, the demands of an outside employer, the length of their life and a host of other realistic game-of-life conditions.[10] *Mathematica* can be coaxed into creating a broad range of simulations illustrating these outcomes. Those shown in this chapter offer a mere beginning once the concept is established.

The value of a theory is its expression, in a compact and elegant form, of a rule that has universal value. The most desirable form is an equation that (a) is true across the entire real number line $(-\infty, \infty)$ and is thus universal; and (b) submits to the rigorous proof and comparative statics possible when expressed in a closed analytical form. The labor exposition advanced here is sorely lacking on both points. Some would argue that the empirical demonstration of fat tails provided in Chapter 7 should follow rather than precede a chapter on theory. The order was deliberate. The empirics provide strong evidence for a *positive* claim of fat tails. A strong theoretical argument providing a *normative* explanation is at present dependent on demonstrative simulation rather than proof.[11]

On the other hand it has been said that economics is just common sense expressed mathematically.[12] The idea that sweat produces equity is common sense. The idea that such equity shows up in real estate returns is logical. The idea that most people seek a comfortable and early retirement is not much in doubt. The failure of the labor-added argument to rise to a formal theory may lie in the large number of variables required to describe this particular game of life. That does not make the argument less real. Further work with Lord Occam's razor may make the problem more mathematically tractable but the problem then described may be less real than what actual investors experience.

In 1952 when Professor Markowitz propounded Modern Portfolio Theory it was indeed fortunate that he tackled the mathematical explanation of the value of diversification. He modeled the time-worn saw: "Don't put all your eggs in one basket" with the tool of choice in 1952, a #2 lead pencil. In this chapter we have explored diversification's converse: "Put all your eggs in one basket, *but watch that basket*!" Doing so has required computing power not dreamed of fifty years ago.

The news for research in this area is mixed. Data for testing the hypothesis proposed herein is unavailable and likely to remain so until real estate investors begin punching time clocks. One can only speculate from anecdotal evidence that labor included in Tier II returns explain heavy right tails. Disappointing though this may be, with the ideas proposed here researchers may someday develop a suitable proxy to test and from which they may draw inferences.

An appropriate criticism of this effort would be to trivialize it as merely the "work harder" model. One could charge that this story is no different than one in which an agent works two jobs, his regular job and a part time job. Such comments fail to grasp subtleties. Yes, one who has two jobs probably works harder. However, an added dimension exists when the second job represents an opportunity to transition out of the employed labor force into a form of self-employment.

The second job, like many others, may initially involve menial tasks such as showing and leasing space, doing minor repairs, etc. Horatio Alger fables of the boy who starts in the mail room and ends up running the company brighten corporate folklore. Fewer stories exist in which the boy *begins by owning the company* and yet that is exactly what happens routinely in the Tier II market. When researchers view the building as the firm a new perspective emerges. In a sense Tier II property is the "family farm" of an urbanized society where market skills are handed down from generation to generation. Figure 8.13 takes another look at the model we used in Chapter 3, suggesting that a real estate investor is the general manager, owner and operator of a small business.

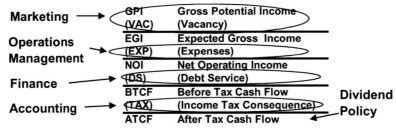

Figure 8.13. The building as the firm

Tier II activities hold lessons that extend beyond the study of real estate:

- The field of finance may wish to re-think the transition from uncertainty to risk. In corporate settings venture capitalists undertake a form of uncertainty prior to the firm offering shares to the public and becoming subject to "normal" risk analysis. Other than the plottage gained by assembling adjoining property, there appears little chance for our Tier II investor to "grow" into a larger, more sophisticated investor the way industrial giants appear to grow. Later chapters may suggest otherwise. It may be that Tier II is a sort of training ground in uncertainty and studying that market provides valuable insight into a previously shadowy area.
- There is an approach to this problem using option theory. Dixit and Pindyke (1994) offer a method using the Bellman equation to solve a dynamic optimization problem under uncertainty. That methodology would focus on the option to retire as its central theme. This may represent a useful simplification without loss of considerable reality.
- Management academics complain of the ill-formed definition of entrepreneurship. It may be that research built on surveys of entrepreneurs could be enhanced by studying the entrepreneurship required of Tier II investors. Such a study would go beyond surveys. Tier II properties should be viewed as "entrepreneurial objects" traded by a certain investor type. Observing what people do usually offers more powerful explanations than recording what they say.
- International policy academics studying emerging capitalist societies may want to consider the importance of wide dispersion of land ownership in the form of small parcels in the hands of many citizens as a means to "train" a society in the ways of capitalistic behavior.
- At the end of Chapter 1 we suggested how nascent international real estate data providers might organize their efforts to anticipate demand. It may be that international educational institutions could better place real estate in their curriculum before it ossifies among the politics and budgets of academic finance. It is not clear that real estate is a subset of finance. There may be a cross-disciplinary role for real estate, especially Tier II real estate, to play. There may be lessons for economics, management and finance in Tier II activities.

One final illustration emphasizes the point. In numerous observations of repeat sales of Tier II real estate it appears that the number of units in the building in the second sale often differs from the number of units in the first sale. If the number of units increase in a statistically meaningfully way more often than they decrease, several questions arise. Is the increase due to owners recognizing that income can be increased by converting a larger unit to two smaller units? Is this income-increasing activity a finance issue? Is it entrepreneurship, therefore a management issue? It is a response to housing shortage, therefore a housing economics issue?

Perhaps it is some of all three.

Endnotes

[1] It is interesting to note that the misuse of this idea played a significant role in two major financial crises, one in 1998 when Long Term Capital Management collapsed, the other in 2007-? involving the subprime mortgage lending mess. Many have written about this with strong criticism of relying on models which assume life is distributed normally. The author first wrote about this in 1999.

[2] The simplest example is purchasing a small apartment building, making improvements that increase income and therefore increase value.

[3] This list could be applied to one's home, a real estate parcel in the Tier I market, but often the motivation is less economic and more oriented to personal matters.

[4] A large literature holds that property rights gravitate to the highest bidder, presumably the one who can make the most efficient use of them.

[5] There are, of course, factors out of the investor's control such as general inflation, interest rates and global economic changes. These are out of the control of one who invests in financial assets as well. The point is that *some* of the site specific factors relating to real estate are controllable where none are in the case of financial assets.

[6] This can be a very short time if one is to believe the "nothing down" infomercials that appear on late night television.

[7] Equation 8.3 makes a crucial substitution of *tr1* for *t*, the reason for which will become clear shortly.

[8] Macabre as it may seem, in this model it also fixes the date of death.

[9] This functional form is chosen in part for convenience. The simpler, general, two period model, $U(C, L) = U(C_1, L_1) + U(C_2, L_2)$, was attempted. However, given the constraints, the second order condition for this model contains variables that must have known values to confirm that the Hessian matrix of the function is negative definite. Our problem suffers similarly and we overcome it by specifying these values in advance and then conducting simulations.

[10] This is consistent with Markowitz' (1991:b.5) advice regarding modeling the individual investor: "In sum, I encourage readers with requisite skills to try building and using realistic game-of-life simulators; and editors to look kindly on the publication of their results."

[11] I leave it to purists to provide a bright line distinction between simulations that demonstrate a concept under bounded conditions and theories blessed with formal proof.

[12] The author first heard this from N. Edward Coulson. Similar observations have no doubt been made by other scholars.

References

Bellman, R., & Cooke, K. L. (1968). <u>Modern Elementary Differential Equations</u>. New York, NY: Dover Publications, Inc.

Black, Fischer; Myron Scholes (1973). "The Pricing of Options and Corporate Liabilities". Journal of Political Economy 81 (3): 637–654.

Dixit, A. K. and Pindyke, R.S. (1994). <u>Investment under Uncertainty</u>. Princeton, NJ: Princeton University Press.

Farlow, S. J. (1982). <u>Partial Differential Equations for Scientists and Engineers</u>. New York, NY: Dover Publications, Inc.

Killingsworth, M. R. (1983). <u>Labor Supply</u>. Cambridge, UK: Cambridge University Press.

Markowitz, H. M., (1991). "Foundations of Portfolio Theory", Journal of Finance, 2, p. 469-77.

Merton, Robert C. (1973). "Theory of Rational Option Pricing". Bell Journal of Economics and Management Science (The RAND Corporation) 4 (1): 141–183.

Roy, A. D. (1951). Some Thoughts on the Distribution of Earnings. <u>Oxford Economic Papers, 3(2), 135-146</u>.

Utz, W. R. (1967). A Short Course in Differential Equations. New York, NY: McGraw-Hill, Inc.

Problems

1. An investor buys a duplex with a one bedroom, one bath unit and a three bedroom, 2 bath unit that has a combined monthly rent of x. After work and on week-ends he converts the larger unit into two units, one a two bedroom, one bath unit and the other a two bedroom, one bath unit. After the conversion the combined income of all three units is $1.5x$. Find the variable among the list in the Notation Guide that represents his time spent on the conversion project.
2. Two investors each buy a duplex and convert them as described above. One investor spends y time on the project and improves the income from x to $1.5x$. The other investor spends $.75y$ time on his building and improves the income from x to $1.7x$. This is an example of a difference which is described by which variable in the notation guide?
3. An investor works days for the US Postal Service and hates his job, a different investor is a middle manager for a large automotive manufacturing firm and loves his work. They separately decide to acquire a rental property and apply their efforts in managing it. How will their preferences (α, β, γ) be different?
4. Figure 8.11 is reproduced below. As you move the slider to the right what is the effect on an investor's willingness to own and operate real property investments? Choosing two different combinations of time spent, efficiency and alternative return, for which combination is he more likely to sell?

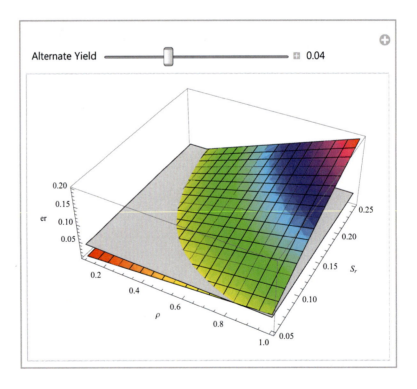

9

Spectral Risk Measures

"Only a combination of theory and practice can produce profitable technology"

Edgar E. Peters, Chaos and Order in the Capital Markets, 2nd ed. p. 40

9.1. Introduction

Public consciousness of how extreme events affect everyday life began with the failure of Long Term Capital Management (LTCM) in the fall of 1998. Ten years later, the cascade of events following the collapse of Lehman Brothers in late 2008 brought most of whoever remained ignorant of terms like "risk management", "heavy tails" and "outliers" into the fold. Today a crisis-weary public has reason to question whether everything is "normal".

Academics have long doubted that risk is fully explained by the scale parameter of classical statistics. Exculpatory language throughout the securities industry includes the constant refrain that "past performance is no guarantee of future results." Beyond the street vernacular, for most of half a century scholars and mathematicians have formally questioned historical frequency as a basis for prediction.

At the heart of the controversy is a discussion of the nature of risk and how it should be measured. Those advocating a purely objective measure appeal to the empirics for evidence. In an opposing camp, subjectivists point to the success of their intuition.[1] The former have Markowitz; the latter have Warren Buffett. Neither offers evidence that may be replicated perfectly.

We opened Chapter 6 with remarks about subjective and objective risk evaluations. In this chapter we explore a more rigorous approach with a goal of common ground where peace may be made between these two warring factions. The battle has been waged valiantly in the market for financial assets. For real estate the search for a proper risk measure is, or should be, virgin territory.

In this chapter we will

- Introduce the foundation for a so-called "coherent risk measure";
- Describe a particular set of utility functions that model an investor's aversion to risk;
- Construct a tool which become the spectral risk measure for real estate investment; and
- Test the model with two sets of data;

9.2. Some recent history

From the ancients throwing astragalus bones until Pascal, Fermat and Bernoulli's formalism of probability as a mathematical endeavor, practically every era has seen an attempt to properly describe, measure or manage risk. Our era is no exception. Throughout the second half of the 20th century denizens of the stock market dominated the subject for the benefit of university finance departments (academics would have it the other way around but we won't quibble about that here).

With the advent, at the end of the 20th century, of worldwide securitization of assets and international banking, the focus became "systemic risk". This asked the somewhat unmanageable question: "What is it that could bring down the entire financial system?" Bankers became latter-day risk management explorers in their search for the answer to this question. The Bank for International Settlements formed the Basel Committee on Bank Supervision which propounded the so-called "Basel Accords".[2]

The Basel Accords are a regime of banking and finance stabilization efforts that have seen a number of generations. The first, Basel I, was developed in 1988, Basel II was published in 2004 following long and tortuous negotiations and was still in the adoption stage when the financial crisis of 2007-08 arrived. Basel III was touted as a "comprehensive set of reform measures designed to strengthen the regulation, supervision and risk management of the banking sector.[3]

Tumultuous times in the real world accompanied the architects of the Basel regime. A full-on international crisis was triggered by the collapse of LTCM in 1998.[4] Academic work proceeded on a parallel path. Three years earlier Young and Graph (1995) published their pathbreaking article suggesting heavy-tailed probability distributions precluded the use of conventional finance methodology for real estate. Almost concurrent with the LTCM debacle Artzner, Delbaen, Eber and Heath ("ADEH" 1997, 1999) introduced Coherent Measures of Risk.[5] The work of ADEH was conducted in a banking setting and motivated by weaknesses of the popular risk metric, Value-at-Risk (VaR), which had been in common use by financial institutions following Basel I.

VaR may be viewed as a sort of "stopping mechanism" which purports to tell a financial institution how far is too far with respect to risky behavior.[6] The idea is to simulate a large number of outcomes, create from them a probability distribution and choose a point which, if the distribution form is correct and the point was exceeded, would make the institution insolvent. In Figure 9.1 we show the risk at the left extreme of the distribution. The line shown on the left tail of the distribution (right side of Figure 9.1) is the stopping point. Assume that all the transactions and possible market movements are simulated. Assume further that the institution wants to be sure that it reserves sufficient capital to withstand losses 99% of the time. The distribution is such that 99% of the outcomes will occur to the right of -3 (red line in plot on right side of Figure 9.1). The bank reserves capital for all of those events with the understanding that such reserves will be inadequate only once in 100 days.

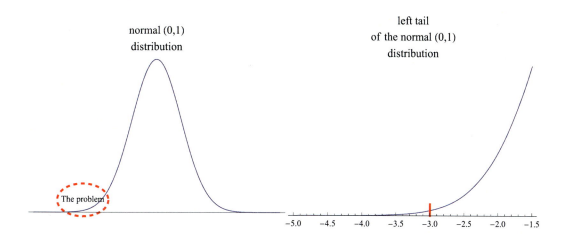

Figure 9.1. Value-at-Risk modeling using the normal distribution

This procedure was, for many years, a calculation that major money center banks made at 4:15 in the afternoon on every business day, permitting the bank to adjust its hedge positions prior to the close of business in order to meet the capital requirement imposed by the calculation. The alert reader of earlier chapters will immediately see a flaw in VaR as it was implemented in its early stages: the assumption of normality. In Figure 9.2 the heavy-tailed outcome is superimposed over the normal with the amount of actual probability mass excluded from the normal highlighted in yellow on the right side of Figure 9.2.

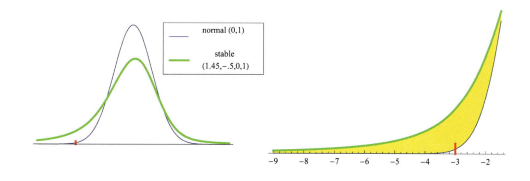

Figure 9.2. Value-at-Risk modeling using a non-normal distribution

9.3. The embarrassing problem with portfolios of real estate

Perhaps the most famous and useful maxim in investing is "don't put all your eggs in one basket", the principle of diversification. While the merits of diversification are valid and it is a powerful tool, there are practical limitations when it comes to real estate. The private real estate investor is not usually blessed with unlimited funds. Hence, forming portfolios of Tier II real property is at best not common and at worse impossible. Nonetheless, homage must be paid to the principle, not because so much theory has been developed around it but because the importance of it should never be far from an investor's mind if for no other reason than to adjust his return expectations if he wanders into a market where he cannot have it.

The problem VaR had with the assumption of normality was more easily overcome as the mathematics of heavy tails advanced. But it had another problem. It did not accomplish the major benefit of diversification which was to reduce risk by judiciously combining assets. The name given to this quality is "subadditivity" and means simply that the risk of holding two assets together was no more than the sum of the individual risks associated with the two assets. Ideally, the risk of the portfolio of two risky assets would be *less than* the sum of their separate risks, a central goal of diversification. But clearly the converse, risk of the combination is *more than* the individual risks, will not do.[7]

In the late 1990s ADEH defined what it meant for a risk measure to be what they termed "coherent". This gave rise to their "axioms of coherency", a set of rules that any risk measure must follow to qualify as coherent. Adopting the notation of Acerbi (2001, 2003), four axioms of coherency embody properties that any risk measure must exhibit: Consider a set of V real-valued random variables. A function $\rho: V \to \mathbb{R}$ is called a coherent risk measure if it is :[8]

$$\text{monotonic}: X, Y \in V, Y \geq X \Rightarrow \rho(Y) \leq \rho(X). \tag{9.1}$$

$$\text{sub-additive}: X, Y, X+Y \in V \Rightarrow \rho(X+Y) \leq \rho(X) + \rho(Y). \tag{9.2}$$

$$\text{positively homogeneous}: X \in V, h > 0, hX \in V \Rightarrow \rho(hX) = h\rho(X). \tag{9.3}$$

$$\text{translational invariant}: X \in V, a \in \mathbb{R} \Rightarrow \rho(X+a) = \rho(X) - a. \tag{9.4}$$

One observes that, in its original formulation, VaR is a tool that purports to describe how often a particular bad outcome could be expected, but is silent on how bad that bad outcome might be. Stated differently, in conventional use VaR tells a manager to stop before the point disaster may occur but not how big a disaster has been avoided or may become if one does not stop. To remedy this, Acerbi proposed a measure, most appropriate for assets held by institutions that trade in synchronous auction markets, which he termed "Expected Shortfall". Expected Shortfall (ES) satisfies the criteria in Equations 9.1 - 9.4. Thinking of the conventional VaR calculation as a point, Expected Shortfall is the average of a range, the mean of all the observations occurring after the VaR point (Figure 9.3).[9]

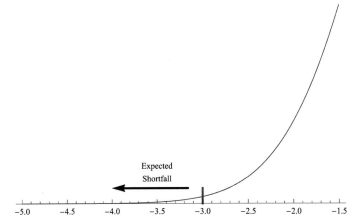

Figure 9.3. Expected shortfall as the mean of all observations beyond the VaR point

In addition to having the important subadditive quality, coherent risk measures have the appealing property that they are quantile measures, thus free of assumptions about the distribution. Accordingly, as they include the effect of extreme values, tail behavior is not ignored.

9.4. Spectral risk measure

Included in the class of coherent risk measures is a spectral risk measure (SRM), essentially a calculation arising from considering a spectrum of outcomes, sorted from worst to best, in the context of subjective risk aversion. Operationally, this is merely the weighted average (dot product) of a vector of sorted returns and a vector of weights produced by a suitably coherent risk aversion function, viz:

$$M_\phi(X) = -\int_0^1 \phi(p) F_X^{-}(p)\, dp \qquad (9.5)$$

Where M_ϕ is a coherent risk measure dependent on a set of weights produced by the subjective risk aversion function, $\phi:[0,1]\rightarrow\mathbb{R}$, known as a risk spectrum.[10] It is important to recognize that Equation 9.5, upon implementation, *will produce a number*. That number will be the spectral risk measure, a coherent measure that may be used to compare the risk of alternative investments.

Critical to this process is the selection of a qualifying risk aversion function, the principal property of which is that it is strictly non-increasing.[11] One can imagine a series of "families" of such functions, as depicted in Figure 9.4, progressing from linear to step functions to convex where weights are on the y-axis and sorted outcomes are on the x-axis.[12]

Equations 9.6 through 9.9 are qualified risk aversion functions, each illustrated in Figure 9.4. Note that all such functions have the properties that they are strictly non-increasing and all elements in the sequence total unity.

A convex (power) function

$$f(\gamma, n) = \left\{ \frac{(1+\gamma)^{n-1}}{\xi}, \frac{(1+\gamma)^{n-2}}{\xi}, \ldots, \frac{(1+\gamma)^0}{\xi} \right\}, \text{ where } \xi = \frac{(1+\gamma)^n - 1}{\gamma} \qquad (9.6)$$

When $\gamma = 0.1$ the first value in the sequence is 0.100153.

A linear (affine) function

$$f(a, b, n) = \left\{ \frac{a + b(n-1)}{.5\,n(2a - b + bn)}, \frac{a + b(n-2)}{.5\,n(2a - b + bn)}, \ldots, \frac{a + b(n-n)}{.5\,n(2a - b + bn)} \right\} \qquad (9.7)$$

When $a = b = 0.1$ the first value in the sequence is 0.0769231.

A single step function

$$f(\beta, \alpha, n) = \left\{ \frac{1}{\beta}, \frac{1}{\beta}, \ldots, \frac{1}{\beta} \right\}, \text{ where } 1 \leq \beta = \min \text{ integer} \geq \alpha n \leq n \qquad (9.8)$$

When $a = 0.1$ the first value in the sequence is 0.333333.

A double step function

$$f(\beta_1, \beta_2, \alpha_1, \alpha_2, n) = \left\{ \frac{2}{w\beta_1}, \frac{2}{w\beta_1}, ..., \frac{1}{w_{\beta_2-\beta_1}}, \frac{1}{w_{\beta_2-\beta_1}} \right\}, \text{ where } \begin{cases} w = \beta_1 + \beta_2; & 1 \leq \beta_2 = \min \text{integer} \geq \alpha_2 \, n \leq n \\ \alpha_2 \geq \alpha_1; & 1 \leq \beta_1 = \min \text{integer} \geq \alpha_1 \, n \leq n \end{cases} \quad (9.9)$$

When parameters are $\{0.1, 0.5\}$ the first value in the sequence is 0.125.

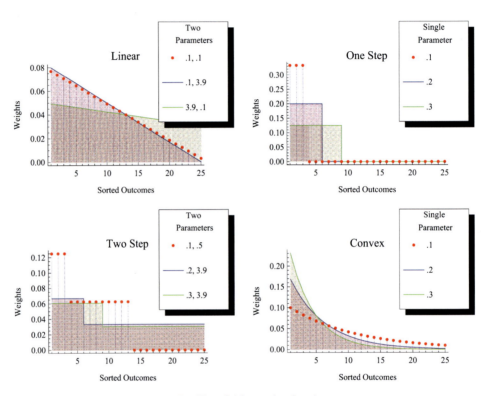

Figure 9.4. Families of risk aversion functions

There is ample support in economic theory for risk aversion functions having shapes as depicted in Figure 9.4. If the utility functions for *good* things have a non-decreasing shape, it is reasonable for a function describing something one wishes to avoid to have a non-increasing shape. The intuition is that one is increasingly risk averse across a particular spectrum of outcomes.

We have encountered the dot product in earlier chapters (Table 6.4). It is a matrix algebra concept that underlies the expectation for the discrete case. Suppose you have five possible payoffs and five associated probabilities. To find the expectation you merely multiply each probability times its payoff and total the products. Taking the dot product of the two vectors arrives at the same result. Here, in Table 9.1, is the example used to create Table 6.4:

payoff	probability
35	0.15
65	0.25
20	0.1
80	0.45
95	0.05

Table 9.1. Five outcome case for arbitrary subjective probabilities

Therefore the dot product of the two vectors in Table 9.1 is, as it was in Chapter 6

payoffs.probs

64.25

The computation anticipated by SRM is different in two ways. First, the probabilities in Table 9.1 are arbitrary. We either have some subjective belief in them or another way to create them. For SRM the probabilities must come from a suitably coherent risk aversion function with the properties that satisfy Equations 9.1 - 9.4. Also, the payoffs are not sorted in Table 9.1. Note that the expectation is not the same when the payoffs are sorted from least to most.

Sort[payoffs].probs

59.

For the probability spectrum let's choose a member of the family of power risk aversion functions having a shape as shown in the lower right quadrant of Figure 9.4 with a risk aversion parameter (convexity) of .3. Table 9.2 shows the new probabilities and the new arrangement of the payoffs, placing the vectors in a condition to be computed into an SRM. Note that order matters. Rearranging results in assigning the highest probability to the least desirable outcome through to the lowest probability assigned to the most desired outcome.

payoff	Convex (.3) probability
20	0.315832
35	0.242948
65	0.186883
80	0.143756
95	0.110582

Table 9.2. Sorted payoffs and suitable probabilities

Computing the SRM we have

Sort[payoffs].probsSRM

48.9729

One can visualize spectral measures with a bubble chart which scales the points (as bubbles) to match the degree of risk aversion. In Figure 9.5, consistent with requirements of SRM, returns are sorted from worst to best to create an ordered series. The weights are created from the risk aversion function with the greatest weight matched to the worst outcome and the least weight to the best. Thus bad outcomes are in the lower left quadrant and good outcomes are in the upper right quadrant. The dot product of these two vectors is the SRM. Figure 9.5 employs a power (convex) risk aversion function (Equation 9.6) with a risk aversion parameter of .5, displays the risk spectrum, reports the mean return and spectral measure. The graphic on the left uses normally distributed data. Data on the right are from a distribution where the stable parameter $\alpha = 1.46$. Tail behavior manifests itself in two ways: graphically we see (1) extreme values in the lower left corner not present in the normal version and (2) the gap between the mean and SRM differs between the two plots. Numerically, the SRM for the heavy-tailed data is an order of magnitude larger than the SRM for the normal data.[13]

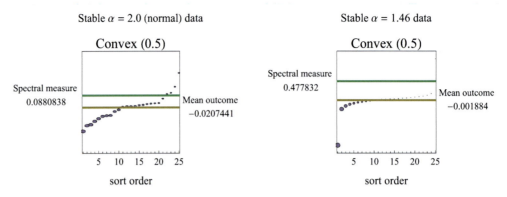

Figure 9.5. Bubble charts for SRM convex(.5) risk aversion function

9.5. Spectral risk measures for real estate investment

Among scholarly work to date several issues stand out as propitious for real estate. One is the application of risk measures across disciplines. While most of the work is in the banking area, SRM are appropriate for insurance and natural catastrophe settings. This breadth of applicability bodes well for including real estate. The second is the distinction between discrete and continuous measures (respectively Tail Conditional Expectation and Expected Shortfall) as real estate returns are, by their nature, viewed as discrete. Third is the recognition of a place for subjectivity, something familiar to real estate participants from the simple homeowner to the institutional risk manager. Finally, the cautions of Dowd, Cotter and Sorwar (2008) should be heeded as the choice of risk aversion function presents pitfalls that can lead to distorted risk evaluation.

Measuring risk is not easy; nor is deciding how to do it

A central message of Young and Graff (1995) was that asset-specific risk should not be ignored. Inherent in following that prescription is a measure of subjective risk evaluation. Real people operating real assets make *ad hoc* on-the-ground decisions based on their assessment of local economic forces. No database tells a shopping center owner to prefer a delicatessen over a beauty salon for its importance to the tenant mix. The law of large numbers applies most weakly, if at all, to the office building manager choosing a ground floor tenant for his building. Also, risk aversion, as it is viewed by the individual, changes over time. None of these realities blend well with traditional quantitative analysis. On the other hand, with the digitization of the industry, large numbers are for the first time plentiful for real estate and should not be ignored.

So, what's a portfolio manager to do?

Consider the following scenario for the CEO of a large institutional real estate firm facing a decision to expand or contract his holdings in a particular part of the country. He has a number of asset managers, segregated by regions.[14] He asks them for their best projection of performance of those properties under their control for the coming period.[15] They reply with a set of returns for each region, each element of which represents their analysis of local prospects for each property. Our CEO sorts these returns and, using a risk aversion function of his choosing based on his own preference for risk, he produces a set of weights, one each matching a return, and takes the dot product of the two vectors in each region. Supposing at least four regions in a country the size of the US, he can then rank the relative risk of the four regions and decide which should be favored with more investment and which should experience disinvestment.

9.6. Scenario analysis

9.6.1. Institutional data (NCREIF)

The first data are NCREIF returns by property type for the period 1978 (n = 226) through 2010 (n =2054), inclusive. Figure 9.6

shows three risk measures over that period, alpha (stable), spectral using a convex risk aversion function with a risk aversion parameter of .1, and standard deviation.[16]

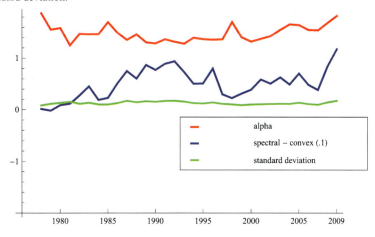

Figure 9.6. Comparison of three risk measures

Threshold conclusions one can take from Figure 9.6 is that the 32 years in question were much more volatile in the eyes of those using advanced risk metrics over those using standard deviation. Secondly, while alpha displays more volatility, spectral measure shows even more.[17]

A natural question might be: Given that SRM is preferred, how might it have been used had it been available over the period in question? Part of the answer to that question may be found in a comparison of volatility for different sectors over that time. Figure 9.7 shows SRM for the office, retail, industrial and apartment sectors over the same 32 years.

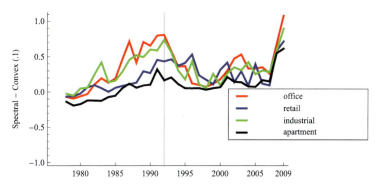

Figure 9.7. Spectral risk for different sectors

In Figure 9.7 we see that all four sectors enjoyed relative highs in volatility, as reflected by SRM, in the early 1990s. A manager of a portfolio of retail buildings might focus on this. Having noticed real estate's penchant for boom-bust cycles, a switch at that time is indicated.[18] The mean return on retail over the entire period studied is 8.15%. If the manager switched from retail to apartments in 1992 his 32 year return would have been 8.57%.

Thus far, these results are hardly startling. But they assume the manager's risk aversion remains the same over 32 years. Few people view risk as they approach the end of a quarter century the same way they did at the beginning. Changing the subjective risk aversion parameter introduces drama into the story. Suppose our manager, after surviving 13 terrifying years of retail operations critically examines the economic landscape, his product type, the maturity of his fund, his age and a host of other contributing factors. The result is a conversion. He decides the right course for the coming decade is not only a change in product type but far less risk tolerance. Recreating plots similar to Figure 9.5 in Figure 9.8 illustrates his current world view of retail (on the right) and (on the left) the one he adopted 15 years prior but applied to his expectation in the coming 17 years. At the 15 year point he weights bad outcomes heavier and notes, given constant expectation,[19] that his spectral risk is higher, making retail unsuitable going forward from 1992.

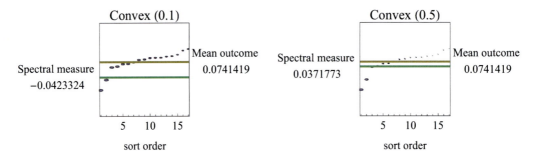

Figure 9.8. Change in risk tolerance

The change in suitability between the sectors is best illustrated in Figure 9.9. During the last seventeen years of the series the spectral risk, using his more risk averse parameter (.5) for retail, is .0372; for apartments it is .0281 as reflected on the left side of Figure 9.9. The right side shows the difference in the weighting based on the differing risk aversion parameters. This manifests itself by smoothing out the apartment curve. Comparing the right half of Figure 9.7 and the left plot of Figure 9.9 shows that, given his subjective stance toward risk, the apartment product has more suitable and lower stable SRM.[20]

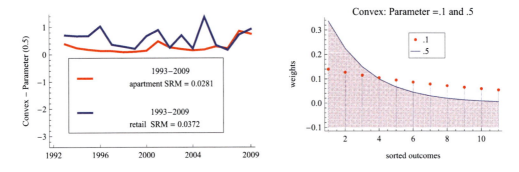

Figure 9.9. Spectral measures over time

Given a rich menu of choices of risk aversion functions enhanced by considerable fine-tuning via adjusting parameters, the possibilities for different outcomes are nearly infinite. This is not unlike a market for risk populated by millions of players all bidding against one another for property rights, each with a different attitude toward risk.

9.6.2. Non-institutional data (CoStar)

The second data are 23,123 repeat sales of multifamily properties of less than 100 units over the 15 year period Q1 1996 through Q1 2010. Returns are based solely on value change.[21] For these data we will focus on a time dimension. In hindsight it is easy to assert that the first ten years (13,058 observations) were comparatively good times, terminating in a bubble condition more pronounced in some markets than others; and the last five years (10,065 observations) were years following an abrupt full stop in market appreciation and subsequent decline (Figure 9.10).[22] Ignoring any change in subjective risk aversion which may have been warranted, we see how risk is higher during years in which a bubble is forming.

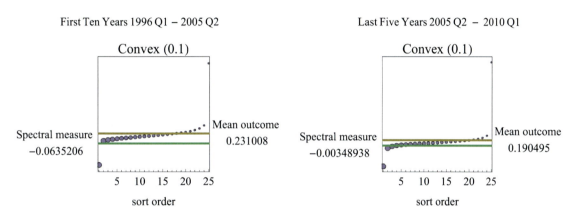

Figure 9.10. Spectral risk for non-institutional property

Another way to think about this is to look at investor risk tolerance and location over time in submarkets. Table 9.3 reflects the spectral measure for the two time periods in six large apartment markets. Using the convex risk aversion function with a parameter 0.1, risk is uniformly higher in each region after the market turns indicating more downside in the post-bubble period. An investor faces the following choice. He may change location (Denver for the first ten years is approximately equal to the next five years in San Diego) if he wishes to keep the same risk aversion parameter. In the alternative, should he wish to remain in place he must modify his risk tolerance.

	n	10 yrs Convex (0.1)	n	5 yrs Convex (0.1)	5 yrs Convex (0.5)
Los Angeles	3749	0.419064	2847	0.992975	1.39848
San Diego	976	0.103084	493	0.609911	1.09344
Chicago	938	0.450106	448	0.986965	1.26505
South Florida	756	0.43295	473	0.89015	1.23798
Denver	700	0.624495	483	0.987473	1.208
Phoenix	646	0.141387	335	0.757892	1.05993

Table 9.3. SRM, risk tolerance and location over time

9.7. Conclusion

The dissent of Young and Graff (1995) was the suggestion that forming portfolios of real estate assets to lower risk was less productive than investors are led to believe. This paper compounds that heresy by claiming that a search for the "right" probability distribution for real estate may also be misguided. Brown (2010) argues that an empirical distribution may be the only way to satisfy those wedded to classical statistics as a risk measurement tool for real estate. For those willing to depart the relative comfort of their former ways a spectral measure may provide a useful alternative.

For practitioners, spectral measures offer formal support for something they have been doing their entire careers: evaluating risk subjectively. The simple dot product of weights and ordered outcomes is an extension of the widely used "Best Case - Worse Case - Most Likely" methodology that has served professionals well for decades. Perhaps a by-product of spectral measures is to bring academics and field gladiators closer together.

If there is merit to a new way of thinking about risk independent of its implementation, real estate investment could benefit from that thinking. Among those who doubt that everything is "normal" are those that believe previous attempts to explain risk in real estate have fallen far short of the mark. The challenge to those still not satisfied by the spectral approach is to offer an alternative that represents both a departure from and an improvement of the old methods.

Endnotes

[1] People are more inclined to talk about their winnings. One hears the boasts of the "self-made man", sometimes forgetting that *everyone* is self-made. Only the successful ones admit it.

[2] "Basel" refers to the city in Switzerland where central bankers from a number of countries met to craft the agreements which became known as "The Basel Accords".

[3] See Bank for International Settlements website page "Monetary and financial Stability" subsection Basel III for more information. For a thorough and at times irreverent summary of these activities, see Dowd, et al., (2011)

[4] Several good books on this event exist (see references).

[5] A similar approach in insurance mathematics dates from Wang (1996).

[6] For banks this behavior was initially conceived as hedging foreign exchange risk. As the banks later generalized the model to cover all sorts of risky behavior, we take the same liberty here without dwelling on how misguided such an expansion might be.

[7] There are optimization routines that demonstrate the perverse outcome that can happen. Enough has been written about this elsewhere so we won't delve any deeper into it here. The term "Tail Conditional Expectation" (TCE) appears at this same time. TCE is also sometimes called "TailVaR" or Conditional VaR (CVaR) and may be viewed as a special case of Expected Shortfall in that it satisfies the axioms of coherency only for continuous distributions. In actuarial terms we also find two closely related but technically different terms, "mean excess function" and "worst conditional expectation". All deal with tail behavior and/or the effect of extreme events.

[8] An equivalent substitution for monotonicity is 9.1b - postive: $X \in V, X \geq 0 \Rightarrow \rho(X) \leq 0$.

[9] Clearly, equation 9.2 is the most important to the idea of diversification. The others are also necessary. The other equations deal with insuring that probability decreases as you move further away from the mean (Equation 9.1); with the case (Equation 9.4) when one's position is large relative to market depth (liquidity risk); and does not vary with different denominations of currency (Equation 9.3).

[10] The risk aversion function is based on a constant coefficient of absolute risk aversion.

[11] Dowd, Cotter and Sorwar (2008) point out that for certain functions in order not to produce bizarre results, this requirement must be strengthened to strictly decreasing.

[12] Note the use of the neutral term "outcome" rather than "return". The negative sign in Equation 9.5 converts what is typically negative (losses) to positive. Hence, increasing risk takes on an intuitive appearance in graphic representations. This can be confusing as returns may be either positive or negative. Also, some restrictions apply. The illustrations in Figure 9.4 are stylized. For example, in order to create the requisite shape for the Two Step function the second parameter must be larger than the first.

[13] Data for the right graphic in Figure 9.5 are actual real estate return data.

[14] They could be segregated by product type or some other reasonable method.

[15] Here we depart from the ADEH banking scenario which might contemplate an overnight holding period for a portfolio of foreign exchange options. This is real estate. Returns are expressed as annual returns and the projection period may cover several years.

[16] The remaining figures in this chapter were created using large proprietary datasets which could not be supplied. Therefore, the *Mathematica* code for the graphics is not included.

[17] Of course, alpha is not influenced by a subjective risk aversion parameter.

[18] Since the graph displays risk, lower plot involves less risk, the preferred condition.

[19] And assuming perfect foresight, which having the data we can do.

[20] One cannot help but observe in both Figures 9.6 and 9.7 risk rises dramatically across all sectors at the end of the series, representing the now widely understood bursting of the bubble. Heretofore, real estate bubbles tended to leak. The graphs indicate this was not so in 2005.

[21] Returns are computed as $r = \sqrt[n]{\frac{P_t}{P_{t-n}}} - 1$ where P_t is the most recent sale and P_{t-n} is the prior sale n periods in the past.

[22] Data were segmented by second sale date, hence some properties held for a long period of time may still have had gains when sold after 2005.

[23] This chapter benefits from graphics and programming enhanced by the very skilled and creative assistance the author received from Seth Chandler of the University of Houston Law Center.

References

Acerbi, Carlo. *Coherent Representations of Subjective Risk Aversion*. Abaxbank 2003.

Acerbi, Carlo. *Risk Aversion and Coherent Risk Measures: a Spectral Representation Theorem*. Abaxbank. July 10, 2001.

Acerbi, Carlo. *Spectral Measures of Risk: a Coherent Representation of Subjective Risk Aversion*. Journal of Banking and Finance. 2002; 26(7):1505-1518.

Acerbi, Carlo ; Nordio, Claudio, and Sirtori, Carlo. *Expected Shortfall as a Tool for Financial Risk Management*. Working Paper (Abaxbank, Italy). 10.

Acerbi, Carlo and Simonetti, P. *Portfolio Optimization with Spectral Measures of Risk*. Working Paper (Abaxbank, Italy).

Acerbi, Carlo and Tasche, Dirk. *Expected Shortfall: a natural coherent alternative to Value at Risk*. Economic Notes. 2002; 31(2):379-388.

---. *On the coherence of expected shortfall*. Journal of Banking and Finance. 2002; 26(7):1487-1503.

Adam, Alexandre; Houkara, Mohamed, and Laurent, Jean-Paul. *Spectral risk measures and portfolio selection*. BNP Paribas. Working Paper.

Adler, Robert J.; Feldman, Raisa E., and Taqqu, Murad S. A Practical Guide to Heavy Tails. Boston, MA: Birkhauser; 1998.

Albanese, Claudio and Lawi, Stephan. *Spectral Risk Measures for Credit Portfolios*. Journal of Economic Literature. 18.

Artzner, P.; Delbaen, F.; Eber, J. M., and Heath, D. *Coherent measures of risk*. Mathematica Finance. 1999; 9:203-228.

---. *Thinking Coherently*. Risk Magazine. 1997; 10(11):68-71.

Artzner, Philippe; Delbaen, Freddy; Eber, Jean-Marc; Heath, David, and Ku, Hyejin. *Coherent Multiperiod risk measurement*. RiskLab (ETH Zurich). February 2002.

Bradley, Brendan O. and Taqqu, Murad S. *Financial Risk and Heavy Tails*. Rachev, S. T., Editor. Handbook of Heavy Tailed Distributions in Finance. First ed. Amsterdam: Elsevier Science, B.V.; 2003; pp. 35-103.

Brown, Roger J. *Location, Location, Distribution*. Real Estate Review. 2010; **39**(4):3-8.

Brown, R. J., Young, M. S., "Coherent Risk Measures," *Journal of Property Investment & Finance*, **29**(4/5), 2011 pp. 479–490.

Cheng, Siwei; Liu, Yanhui, and Wang, Shouyang. *Progress in Risk Measurement*. Advanced Modelling and Optimization. 2004; 6(1):20.

Dowd, Kevin. *"Too Big to Fail"* Cato Institute Briefing Paper #52, September 23, 1999.

Dowd, Kevin; Cotter, John, and Sorwar, Ghulam. *Spectral Risk Measures: Properties and Limitations*. Social Science Research Network. 2008.

Dowd, Kevin; Hutchinson, Martin; Ashby, Simon; and Hinchliffe, Jimi M., *"Capital Inadequacies, the Dismal Failure of the Basel Regime of Bank Capital Regulation"*, Cato Institute Policy Analysis No. 681, July 29, 2011.

Embrechts, P.; Kluppelberg, C, and Mikosch, T. Modelling Extremal Events: for Insurance and Finance. New York: Springer; 1997.

Embrechts, Paul. *Extreme Value Theory: Potential Limitations as an Integrated Risk Management Tool*. Derivatives Use, Trading & Regulation. 2000; 6.

Lowenstein, R., When Genius Failed. New York: Random House; 2000.

Rockafellar, R. Tyrrel and Uryasev, Stanislav. *Optimization of conditional value-at-risk*. The Journal of Risk. Spring 2000; 2(3):21-41.

Wang, S. *Premium Calculation by Transforming the Layer Premium Density*. Astin Bulletin. 1996; 26:71-92.

Woo, Gordon. *Natural Catastrophe Probable Maximum Loss*. British Actuarial Journal. 2002; 8(V).

Problems

1. In the interactive graphic below, notice the default spectral risk measure, its distribution (normal[0,1]), risk aversion family (power) and number of observations or length (40). Although the stable distribution is not the default, its default parameters are shown (1.8, 0, 0.04, 0.4). Describe the direction of change in SRM you expect when you choose the stable distribution. Using the drop down menu for choosing the distribution, select stable and note the change in SRM. Did it move in the direction you predicted? Why or why not?

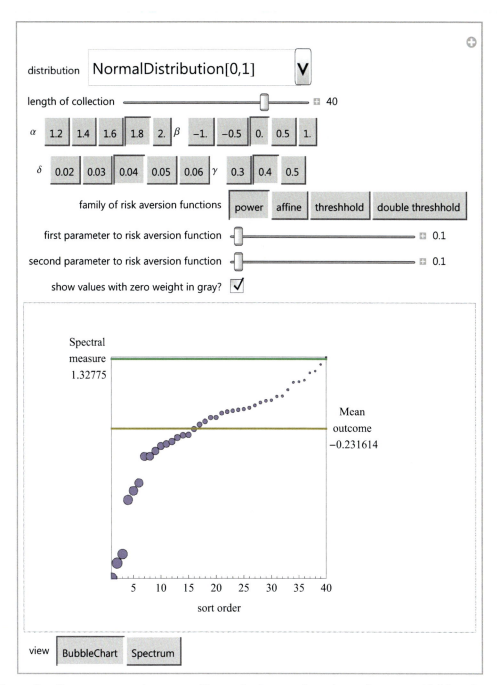

2. The text lists five reasons spectral measures offer promise for managing real estate investment risk. Name three of them.

3. Of the four axioms of coherency, which is most concerned with gains from diversification?

10

The Tax Deferred Exchange

"Anyone may arrange his affairs so that his taxes shall be as low as possible; he is not bound to choose that pattern which best pays the treasury. There is not even a patriotic duty to increase one's taxes. Over and over again the Courts have said that there is nothing sinister in so arranging affairs as to keep taxes as low as possible. Everyone does it, rich and poor alike and all do right, for nobody owes any public duty to pay more than the law demands. Taxes are enforced exactions, not voluntary contributions. To demand more in the name of morals is mere cant."

Judge Learned Hand in Helvering v. Gregory, 69F.2d 809

10.1. Introduction

In Chapter 8 we established that private real estate investors may add entrepreneurial labor to their capital investment. While this complicates the investment return calculation, it offers significant and often overlooked tax benefits. We provided some justification for studying the "labor-added" phenomenon as more than just a simple part time job. This chapter explores a particularly powerful strategy available to real estate investors who plan transactions in their properties carefully.

In this chapter we will:

- Explicitly model real estate investment to include the consequence of income taxes;
- Introduce the concept of a tax deferred exchange;
- Show in a series of examples the way exchanging may be incorporated into an investor's wealth building plan;
- Perform a cost-benefit analysis of exchanging
- Determine if exchanging may be viewed as a risk modifier; and
- Point out circumstances under which exchanging is ill advised.

10.1.1. Taxes are less certain for real estate investors

We hear often enough that two things in life are certain: death and taxes. For real estate investors the former is more certain than the latter. Real estate offers no relief from death but *does* provide an opportunity to reduce or perhaps even eliminate a substantial portion of one's capital gain taxes. Section 1031 of the IRS Code, as amended, provides that one may *realize* the benefits of a capital gain by disposing of a property, but not *recognize* the gain for tax purposes if, upon the sale of a real estate investment, one immediately (or nearly immediately) acquires a substitute property in what is known as a *tax deferred* exchange.[1] It is not our purpose here to go through the intricate details of how one actually conducts such a transaction, rather to demonstrate what economic benefits may accrue to one who does. We will also contrast the benefits of both a sell-and-repurchase strategy and a buy-and-hold strategy with the exchange strategy.

There are numerous advantages to structuring a transaction as a tax deferred exchange. The obvious one is that capital gains tax is delayed until some later point in time. This keeps capital working in one's investment portfolio and compounding, presumably at a high rate of return, a larger sum of money for a longer period of time than would be the case if taxes were paid at the point of each transaction. Virtually all who know and understand tax deferred exchanging focus on this aspect of the strategy. Such thinking is not wrong, merely incomplete. There are other, perhaps equally potent, reasons for a tax deferred exchange strategy. There are also situations in which an exchange is *not* recommended.

An important result of the "add labor" strategy is to convert human capital into non-human capital by building what is sometimes called "sweat equity". The right to repeat this in a new property without the payment of capital gain tax is a major benefit of the tax deferred exchange. Hence this chapter, in addition to illustrating the usual benefits of exchanging, will develop the tax ramifications of the add labor strategy. Finally, this chapter will demonstrate the value of exchanging as a *risk modifier strategy*.

Most of academic finance and economics "assumes away" the complication of income taxes. This can frustrate the reader who knows that taxes are a reality and usually affect one's decisions. In defense of academics, it should be noted that working with American income tax rates is a frustrating task. The code is a constantly changing, moving target. Working with graduated tax rates requires use of a step function, a rather inconvenient mathematical device. As this chapter deals directly with taxes we may not assume them away lest the entire subject disappear. However, some assumptions are necessary in the interest of simplicity. One of these is a flat tax rate. The determined reader will find a way to write *Mathematica* code that is more realistic, but our conclusions here will not change by relaxing the flat tax assumption.

There are lessons for readers outside the United States. First, Section 1031 has been in the US tax code since its inception. Congress intended citizens have the right to defer tax on gains when transferring from one location to another while remaining in the same business. This fosters important incentives that contribute to the development of society. Second, taxation policy affects behavior. The US tax code in its present form is not a work of art. Even the administration of Section 1031 transfers has become needlessly complicated under the guise of "simplification". Policymakers in other countries may wish to proceed with caution before following the US model. Recent amendments to Section 1031 have had unintended consequences that influence the market.

A primary justification for ignoring income taxes in other writings is that all economic agents operate in a common income tax environment. The marginal difference in tax brackets spanning different ranges of income certainly affects the accuracy of any particular calculation, but these may be viewed as *de minimus*. The central message of this chapter is that some capital gain taxes may be delayed and some *may actually be eliminated*. This is a more powerful effect than one of merely assuming all taxpayers are not taxed or taxed at the same rate. Indeed, the point of this chapter is that some taxpayers holding particular assets and transferring them in certain ways may reduce, delay or eliminate some taxes altogether.

Organized around a set of stylized examples, this chapter explores not only the obvious benefits of exchanging but some of the less obvious disadvantages of a poorly thought-out exchange strategy. We will take the usual approach of evaluating the costs and benefits to determine if the benefits exceed the costs.

Given that the investor has entrepreneurial abilities and tendencies we will look at:

- The value of tax deferral in nominal terms, as a percentage of the tax due, as a percentage of the capital gain tax due on a normal sale and as a percentage of the property to be acquired.
- The effect of tax deferral on risk.
- The cost of exchanging, not just the hard costs but implicit costs often overlooked.
- The alternatives of sale and repurchase, refinance or simply hold for a longer period.

This chapter introduces *Mathematica*'s modules, a particularly helpful and powerful feature. In a complex world it is important to be able to isolate the most important variables on which investment decisions rest. As we move through the exchange strategy we have to retain most of the burdensome minutiae that we labored over in earlier chapters. Since many of those calculations involve nothing new, after mastering them in earlier chapters it is now useful to put them out of view. For instance, real estate is usually financed with self-amortizing financing. There is no reason to have the loan amortization calculation in the forefront of these discussions. Exchange or no exchange, loans are a fact of life and their amortization is not mysterious. Thus the loan calculations - once the initial inputs are known - are pushed to the background and out of sight in the module. The same can be said for depreciation, sale proceeds and capital gain calculations. All of these are computed with fairly simple algebraic equations that need not be at center stage with the more important concept of the tax deferred exchange. Accordingly, the reader may take on faith that the ministerial calculations are being accurately made in the background and the important decision variables and questions are in the limelight.

10.1.2. Variable definitions

The examples here are similar to those in Chapter 4 describing basic investment analysis.[2] For pedagogical reasons we included a number of variables in Chapter 4 that are not needed here. For example, because operational variables prior to net operating income are mathematically trivial they have been ignored here so that all examples in this chapter begin with NOI. Also, having provided the full elaboration of many crucial real estate calculations in earlier chapters we will introduce in this chapter a method of placing many of these calculations in the background. *Mathematica* permits us to use all the critical variables, keeping track of them and the functions that flow from them in a "package" hidden from the user's view. The list of variables below has considerable overlap with that in Chapter 4. Variables in this chapter use *Mathematica*'s lowercaselongfilename convention. The idea is to make variable names easy to recognize when modifying *Mathematica* modules. Thus for example in Chapter 4 we used "*dp*" for down payment, here we use "downpayment".

downpayment	=	down payment, made at $t = 0$ and assumed to be Jan 1 of the acquisition year
capitalizationrateatpurchase	=	'going in' capitalization rate
capitalizationrateatsale	=	'going out' capitalization rate
investorrequiredrateofreturn	=	discount rate (when $npv = 0$ this is the internal rate of return)
monotonicgrowth	=	growth rate for cash flow, when monotonic
logisticconstant	=	logistic constant when using the modified logistic growth function
accelerationfactor	=	acceleration factor when using the modified logistic growth function
terminalyear	=	length of holding period (also year of sale, presumed to be on Dec 31) for each property held
initialnetoperatingincome	=	first year net operating income (debt free cash flow)
interestrate	=	interest rate (per payment period – monthly so that i = annual interest rate/12)
initialloanbalance	=	initial loan balance
totalamortizationperiod	=	number of years to fully amortize the loan
investorincometaxrate	=	income tax rate
landpercentofproperty	=	allocation of tax basis to land (as a percent of total value)
buildingdepreciationrate	=	depreciation rate on improvements
capitalgainrate	=	capital gain tax rate
recapturerate	=	tax rate for recapture of depreciation
sellingcostrate	=	sales cost rate
prepaymentpenalty	=	loan prepayment penalty

The use of modules eliminates definitions in Chapter 4 such as after tax cash flow (*atcf*), an output of one module, or loan balance (*bal[n]*) which is an interim calculation needed to produce an output. The reader is encouraged to take the variable values from the examples below and insert them into the templates in Chapter 4 to satisfy himself that the results are the same.

10.1.3. The structure of the examples

Business decisions are a complex fabric of competing goals. What follows represents a relatively small set of possible paths and outcomes for an investor. The reader may easily become frustrated with the presentation. Patience is advised for the real world offers greater challenges. While the companion Excel workbooks reflect the same results as the chapter displays, the difference in how the information is presented can be useful and instructive. As an exercise the reader is encouraged to locate the matching results and understand their interdependencies. The examples illustrating the ideas in this chapter are organized as follows.

1. An initial "base case" (base = purchase-hold-sell strategy) is examined to provide background and context. In the base case the investor merely purchases, holds for six years and sells a single property. During the holding period the value grows monotonically.

2. Example 1 (dataEG1= modifying the base case growth projection) deviates from the base case only by introducing the idea of growth at different rates over different time periods (the logistic growth idea introduced in Chapter 4) during the six year holding period.
3. Example 2 (dataEG2a and dataEG2b = tax deferred exchange strategy) involves two properties that are each held for three years in sequence. The second property is acquired via exchange of the first property. Thus, the ownership of the two properties span the same time period as Example 1. Each property grows in value under the same conditions as assumed for dataEG1.
4. The outcome of the exchange strategy is then contrasted with the results achieved via the *taxable* sale of the first property (dataEG2a) at the end of year three, the purchase of the second property (dataEG2c = the sale-and-repurchase strategy) with the after tax proceeds of the sale of the first, concluding with the taxable sale of the second property at the end of three more years (again a total of six). In this example we will consider tax deferral as a kind of risk modifier.
5. The sale-and-repurchase strategy portion of Example 2 is re-examined (dataEG2d and dataEG2e = the sale-and-*better*-repurchase strategy) using a lower price for the second purchase, presumed to be achieved with superior negotiation following the taxable sale of the first property. This addresses (a) the implied cost of exchanging and (b) the question of how much discount is needed on acquisition two to offset the value of tax deferral if exchanging is not an option.
6. In Example 3 (dataEG3a and dataEG3b = exchanging-versus-the-plodder) we repeat the same analysis as Example 2 but return to the monotonic growth of the base case. We then compare the exchange outcome with the sale and purchase alternative (dataEG3a and dataEG3c). Finally, we return to the base case assumptions to consider a longer term, 12 year buy and hold strategy of a single property.

Each example or variation illustrates a different strength or weakness of holding, selling, exchanging and/or reacquiring property.

10.2. The base case: Purchase - Hold - Sell

We retain as our base case a specific project similar to that in Chapter 4, the data for which are entered Table 10.1:

downpayment	360 000
initialnetoperatingincome	119 925
investorincometaxrate	0.35
buildingdepreciationrate	0.0363636
landpercentofproperty	0.3
capitalizationrateatsale	0.0971053
monotonicgrowth	0.03
logisticconstant	0
accelerationfactor	0
interestrate	0.00791667
initialloanbalance	875 000
totalamortizationperiod	360
investorrequiredrateofreturn	0.13
terminalyear	6
sellingcostrate	0.075
capitalgainrate	0.15
recapturerate	0.25
prepaymentpenalty	0
numberofunits	22

Table 10.1. Base case inputs

In Chapter 4 we computed the simple "rule of thumb" tests applied to first year performance. Here we employ our first *Mathematica* module to make these calculations. When a new module or function is introduced the Help Browser description is provided. That output is called with a question mark before the module or function name. The modules and functions perform calculations and create graphics. There are a number of popular software packages that produce the same output. It is your author's belief that the reader is far better off knowing how computations are made than depending on software. In fact, the act of creating software or reading its operating instructions such as are found in the Help Browser descriptions can deepen the user's understanding of the process. It is not expected that the majority of readers will become *Mathematica* users. It is hoped, however, that readers will reach a level of knowledge beyond that achieved by merely using Excel or some other muneric software package.

Because we ignore pre-NOI calculations, the GRM and expense ratio are excluded from the computations in Table 10.2.

? RulesOfThumb

RulesOfThumb[data] inputs a list of values as data and returns a list
  {Capitalization Rate, Price per unit, After Tax Cash on Cash Return, Debt Coverage Ratio
  and Loan to Value Ratio} of first year rule of thumb measures for an investment property.
RulesOfThumb[data,propertynumber,exData] inputs a list of values as data and returns a list {Capitalization
  Rate, Price per unit, Cash on Cash Return, Debt Coverage Ratio and Loan to Value Ratio} of first
  year rule of thumb measures for either of two properties in a series. If propertynumber=1 exData
  argument may be omitted. If propertynumber=2 exData must be the exchange dataset, the
  Exchange.m package must be loaded and the CarryoverBasis module must have been evaluated.

RulesOfThumb[base]

Capitalization Rate	0.0971053
Price Per Unit	56136.4
Cash on Cash Return	0.0824367
Debt Coverage Ratio	1.35831
Loan to Value Ratio	0.708502

Table 10.2. Base case rules of thumb

For the multi-year projection leading to discounted cash flow analysis we use the ATCF module to produce Table 10.3. One of the optional arguments for this function is propertynumber. As we will see later, this input is important due to the tax considerations of the exchange and how they affect the depreciation deduction allowed for the second property.

? ATCF

ATCF[data,year] inputs a list of values as data and returns a list {Net Operating Income, Debt Service, Depreciation,
  Income Tax and After Tax Cash Flow} of outcomes for the year specified. If year is terminal year that argument
  may be omitted. ATCF[data,year,propertynumber,exData] inputs a list of values as data, selects a year for output
  for a property acquired by exchange and returns a list {Net Operating Income, Debt Service, Depreciation,
  Income Tax and After Tax Cash Flow} of outcomes for the year specified for an exchange acquisition. If
  propertynumber=1 exData argument may be omitted. If propertynumber=2 exData must be the exchange
  dataset, the Exchange.m package must be loaded and the CarryoverBasis module must have been evaluated.

Net Operating Income	139026.
Debt Service	88289.7
Depreciation	31436.4
Income Tax	9785.96
After Tax Cash Flow	40950.3

Table 10.3. Terminal year operating performance

For the terminal year reversion in Table 10.4 we need calculations made at the time of sale, which we accomplish using the EquityReversion module.

? EquityReversion

EquityReversion[data] inputs a list of values as data and returns a list of terminalyear values {Sale Price, Beginning Loan Balance, Ending Loan Balance, Original Cost, Sale Costs, Accumulated Depreciation, Capital Gain, Capital Gain Tax, Pre–Tax Net Equity and After Tax Net Equity}for an investment property. EquityReversion[data1,data2,propertynumber,exData] inputs a list of values as data1 for the first property and data2 for a second property acquired in exchange for data1 property. It then computes a number of terminalyear values {Sale Price, Beginning Loan Balance, Ending Loan Balance, Original Cost, Sale Costs, Accumulated Depreciation, Capital Gain, Capital Gain Tax, Pre–Tax Net Equity and After Tax Net Equity} for the property acquired via an exchange. If propertynumber=1 only data1 is required and the other three arguments may be omitted. If propertynumber=2 exData must be the exchange dataset, the Exchange.m package must be loaded and the CarryoverBasis module must have been evaluated using data1 as its argument.

Sale Price	1,474,655.
Beginning Loan Balance	875,000
Ending Loan Balance	833,449.
Original Cost	1,235,000
Sale Costs	110,599.
Accumulated Depreciation	188,618.
Capital Gain	317,674.
Capital Gain Tax	66,512.9
Pre-Tax Net Equity	530,607.
After Tax Net Equity	464,094.

Table 10.4. Terminal year equity reversion

The *npv* and *irr* functions calculate the Net Present Value and IRR are shown in Table 10.5.

? NPV

NPV[data] inputs a list of values as data and computes net present value of an investment property.
NPV[data1,data2,propertynumber,exData] inputs two lists of values as data and computes net present value based on the aggregate results of two properties over sequential holding periods. If propertynumber=1 exData argument may be omitted. If propertynumber=2 exData must be the exchange dataset, the Exchange.m package must be loaded and the CarryoverBasis module must have been evaluated.

? IRR

IRR[data] inputs a list of values as data and computes the internal rate of return for an investment property.
IRR[data1,data2,propertynumber,exData] inputs two lists of values as data and computes the internal rate of return of a sequence of two properties if propertynumber =2. If propertynumber = 1 propertynumber and exData arguments may be omitted. If propertynumber=2 exData must be the exchange dataset, the Exchange.m package must be loaded and the CarryoverBasis module must have been evaluated.

NPV	557.32
IRR	13.0351%

Table 10.5. Base case net present value and internal rate of return

It is important to point out that, Table 10.5 shows the *after tax irr*. Below (AllocatePie) are the components of the sale proceeds in this, our base case. This sets the scene for the primary purpose of this chapter, which is to examine the ramifications of NOT having to pay capital gain tax.

? AllocatePie

AllocatePie[data] inputs a list of values as data, computes the portions of sales proceeds allocated to Loan Balance, Sales Costs, Captial Gain Tax and the Owner's Equity Reversion for an investment property, displaying these in a pie chart. AllocatePie[data1,data2,propertynumber,exData] inputs a list of values as data, computes the portions of sales proceeds allocated to Loan Balance,Sales Costs,Captial Gain Tax and the Owner's Equity Reversion for a second property acquired via tax deferred exchange, displaying these in a pie chart. If propertynumber=2 exData must be the exchange dataset, the Exchange.m package must be loaded and the CarryoverBasis module must have been evaluated.

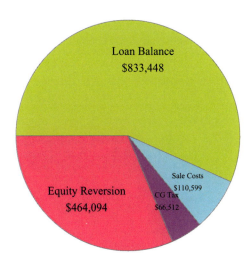

Figure 10.1. Taxable sale allocation

Another useful illustration shows how the benefits of continued ownership are configured in the coming year. One often needs to know if continuing to hold the property for another year is the most productive alternative. In Figure 10.2 (NextYearPie) we calculate the after tax cash flow to be derived from another year of ownership and the change in net equity at the end of another year, displaying the components in pie chart form. Of course, this change might also be negative but we model it here as positive. (One should exercise caution in all pie charts because *Mathematica* will not output a pie chart with a negative segment).

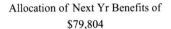
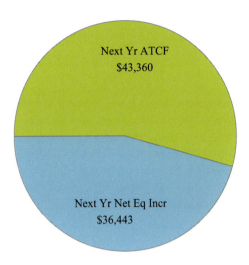

Figure 10.2. Benefit of another year of ownership

The base case represents a quite standard DCF analysis, implies monotonic growth over a fixed holding period terminating in a taxable sale. Using the modified logistic growth function described in Chapter 4 and the exchange strategy, we now relax these assumptions.

10.3. Example 1 - A modified growth projection over six years

First, we modify our data to reflect the entrepreneurial growth associated with an early transformation period. Note that in the base case data the variables for the logistic growth curve, *lc* and *af* were zero. Below, in Table 10.6 these variables take on non-zero values.

downpayment	360 000
initialnetoperatingincome	119 925
investorincometaxrate	0.35
buildingdepreciationrate	0.0363636
landpercentofproperty	0.3
capitalizationrateatsale	0.0971053
monotonicgrowth	0.03
logisticconstant	**1.5**
accelerationfactor	**2**
interestrate	0.00791667
initialloanbalance	875 000
totalamortizationperiod	360
investorrequiredrateofreturn	0.13
terminalyear	6
sellingcostrate	0.075
capitalgainrate	0.15
recapturerate	0.25
prepaymentpenalty	0
numberofunits	22

Table 10.6. Input dataEG1 for Example 1

The first year measures (rules of thumb) for this data are identical to the base case. The difference will appear in the "out" years.

Capitalization Rate	0.0971053	Capitalization Rate	0.0971053
Price Per Unit	56 136.4	Price Per Unit	56 136.4
Cash on Cash Return	0.0824367	Cash on Cash Return	0.0824367
Debt Coverage Ratio	1.35831	Debt Coverage Ratio	1.35831
Loan to Value Ratio	0.708502	Loan to Value Ratio	0.708502

There are considerable differences in terminal year outcomes arising from the meaningful difference in cash flows over time due to the entrepreneurial effort applied.

	Base Case CF	EG1 CF
1	29 677.2	29 677.2
2	31 828.3	71 039.4
3	34 031.	74 985.9
4	36 285.5	77 347.8
5	38 591.9	79 471.3
6	40 950.3	81 540.8

Table 10.7. Six year after tax cash flow comparison of base case with example 1

base		dataEG1	
Sale Price	1474655.	Sale Price	2074789.
Beginning Loan Balance	875000	Beginning Loan Balance	875000
Ending Loan Balance	833449.	Ending Loan Balance	833449.
Original Cost	1235000	Original Cost	1235000
Sale Costs	110599.	Sale Costs	155609.
Accumulated Depreciation	188618.	Accumulated Depreciation	188618.
Capital Gain	317674.	Capital Gain	872798.
Capital Gain Tax	66512.9	Capital Gain Tax	149781.
Pre-Tax Net Equity	530607.	Pre-Tax Net Equity	1085731.
After Tax Net Equity	464094.	After Tax Net Equity	935949.

Table 10.8. Terminal year comparison of base case with example 1

As usual, we are interested in the net present value and *irr* measures under these changed conditions. They are, understandably, superior to the base case.

Base NPV	$557.
dataEG1 NPV	$353,158.
Base IRR	13.0351%
dataEG1 IRR	29.8681%

Table 10.9. Base case and example 1 IRR and NPV comparisons

As the *irr* is so much above the required rate of return and the *npv* is so large, one might argue that, provided the required rate of return, r, was chosen appropriately for a "normal" real estate investment of this type - independent of its need for renovation - the *excess irr or the entire npv* represents the return due the investor for his entrepreneurial efforts. Be that as it may, just changing the way value increases has considerably increased the productivity of this investment (and the productivity of the investor's time). Here, in a bar chart is a comparison of the final sale results for the two programs.

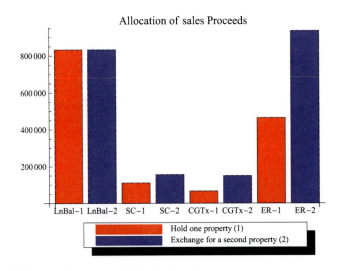

Figure 10.3 shows a pie chart in which the total outcome and relative size of the components are, as expected, considerably different.

CompareAllocate[data1,data2] renders two datasets as pie charts in the ratio of the size
of their equity reversions. Datasets should be entered in increasing size order of the output.

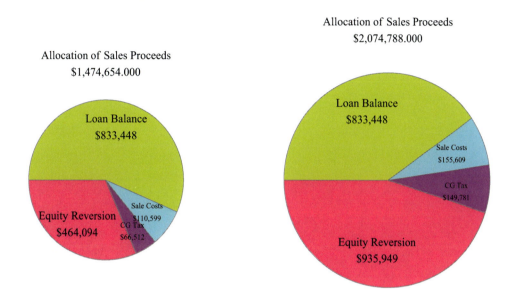

Figure 10.3. Allocation of sales proceeds for base case and Example 1

? AllocatePie

AllocatePie[data] inputs a list of values as data, computes the portions of sales proceeds allocated to Loan Balance, Sales Costs, Captial Gain Tax and the Owner's Equity Reversion for an investment property, displaying these in a pie chart. AllocatePie[data1,data2,propertynumber,exData] inputs a list of values as data, computes the portions of sales proceeds allocated to Loan Balance, Sales Costs, Captial Gain Tax and the Owner's Equity Reversion for a second property acquired via tax deferred exchange, displaying these in a pie chart. If propertynumber=2 exData must be the exchange dataset, the Exchange.m package must be loaded and the CarryoverBasis module must have been evaluated.

Note in both cases, regardless of how we illustrate it, meaningful capital goes to capital gains tax. Comparing the base example capital gain and tax with the same numbers for the second example in Table 10.10, not surprisingly we find a considerable difference.

	Cap Gain	CG Tax
Base	317674.	66513.
EG 1	872798.	149781.

Table 10.10. Base case and example 1 capital gain and tax comparisons

There are two points to be made here. One, the obvious, is that an investor has a greater incentive to defer taxes the larger the tax liability he faces. More importantly, if one accepts the proposition that the excess *irr* or the positive *npv* represents a return on his time *the act of deferring the tax on that portion of the gain represents an act of deferring taxes on compensation for the investor's efforts*. The benefit is analogous to that offered employees via corporate retirement and 401(k) plans. But in this case the outcome is more directly influenced by the investor's entrepreneurial management style. In the long run this homegrown deferred compensation plan amounts to a *pre-tax* conversion of human capital into non-human capital.

We are again interested in the configuration of the benefits flowing from an additional year of ownership. The first year of interest is the year following the period of high growth. As most of the growth takes place in the first three years, presumably the owner has "maximized" the investment/development opportunities at that point and contemplates settling in for "normal" growth. It at this point the investor begins to consider an exchange. The starting point for this decision is his present property and its prospects. Hence, in the fourth year the after tax cash flow and equity gain are divided as shown in Figure 10.4.

? NextYearPie

NextYearPie[data] inputs a list of values as data, computes the after tax cash flow
and equity reversion occurring in terminalyear for the data, displaying these in a pie chart.

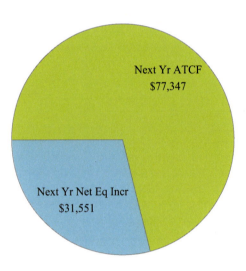

Figure 10.4. Fourth year Example 1 results

? CompareNextYear

CompareNextYear[data1,data2] renders two datasets reflecting a successive year's results as pie
charts in the ratio of their sizes. Datasets should be entered in increasing size order of the output.

At times, a comparison with the base case is useful. Here is the output of a function that does this, reflecting the fourth year of operations of the base case and Example1 (dataEG1)

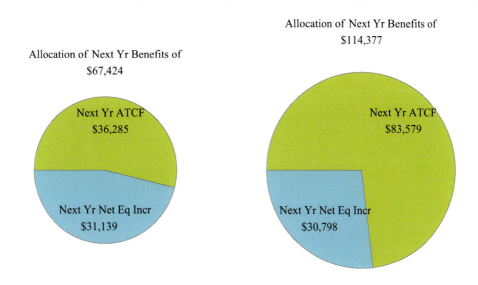

Figure 10.5. Comparing the next year benefits of two different datasets

10.4. Example 2 - The tax deferred exchange strategy

For the next step, we look at the same investment period, six years, during which, rather than hold a single property, we acquire two properties in sequence. Each will be held three years, each require entrepreneurial effort and each will undergo the early year rapid improvement in value due to those efforts. Thus, the entrepreneurial impact occurs twice, and the tax otherwise due on the gain attributable to that entrepreneurial effort will be deferred.

We will keep many of the same assumptions regarding growth rates, income tax rates, expense ratios and rules of thumb from the base case example. Thus, both properties in this example will be presumed to be acquired on approximately the same economic terms, the second property differing from the first only in scale and a slight difference in going out capitalization rate.

The data for the first property (dataEG2a) in Table 10.11 are the same as the data in Example 1 except for the shorter holding period, k, and slightly different cap rate at sale.

downpayment	360 000
initialnetoperatingincome	119 925
investorincometaxrate	0.35
buildingdepreciationrate	0.0363636
landpercentofproperty	0.3
capitalizationrateatsale	**0.10048**
monotonicgrowth	0.03
logisticconstant	1.5
accelerationfactor	2
interestrate	0.00791667
initialloanbalance	875 000
totalamortizationperiod	360
investorrequiredrateofreturn	0.13
terminalyear	**3**
sellingcostrate	0.075
capitalgainrate	0.15
recapturerate	0.25
prepaymentpenalty	0
numberofunits	22

Table 10.11. Data input dataEG2a for Example 2a

Hence, the acquisition standards for the first property, as represented by the rules of thumb, are the same. Here are equity reversion and rules of thumb results for the new data, the latter matching Table 10.2.

Sale Price	1959069.			
Beginning Loan Balance	875000			
Ending Loan Balance	857154.	Capitalization Rate	0.0971053
Original Cost	1235000	Price Per Unit	56136.4
Sale Costs	146930.	Cash on Cash Return	0.0824367
Accumulated Depreciation	94309.1	Debt Coverage Ratio	1.35831
Capital Gain	671448.	Loan to Value Ratio	0.708502
Capital Gain Tax	110148.		
Pre-Tax Net Equity	954986.		
After Tax Net Equity	844838.		

To make the comparison as fair as possible, for the second property we will replicate the acquisition standards from the first property. That is, we wish the first year rule of thumb ratios in the second property to be the same as those for the first property. The purpose of this is to hold constant a kind of risk standard, the assumption being that two properties with the same *ltv* and *dcr* expose the investor to approximately the same risk. While not perfect, this approach is useful in a stylized example such as this for reasons that will become apparent later. To accomplish this we will "back in to" some of the values in the second property in order to hold first year rule of thumb measures constant. One consequence of this is that some of the values may reflect unrealistic odd numbers which in practice would likely be rounded to the nearest one thousand dollars.

The ability to sell a property and defer payment of income taxes is indeed cause to celebrate. But there is a price attached. Any gain not recognized for tax purposes on disposition cannot be included in the tax basis of the newly acquired property and thus is not eligible for depreciation. The practical effect of this is to transfer the basis from the old property to the new, an accounting task known as an exchange basis adjustment. The exchange basis adjustment determines the depreciation deduction available for the second property.

Any complexity in the exchange basis adjustment arises from *partially* tax deferred, delayed or reverse exchanges. In the interest of simplicity we will assume the exchange is concurrent and fully tax deferred. Qualifying for this it is not difficult. One need only acquire a property with at least as much equity *and* at least as much debt as the property disposed. Stated differently, except as may be necessary to pay transaction costs, one may not take any money out of the transaction (such money, known as "boot received" must be zero) *and* one must not be relieved of debt when comparing the new property to the old (net loan relief must be zero).

10.4.1. Exchange variable definitions

newloan	=	new loan on acquired property
oldloan	=	loan on disposed property at time of disposition
mortgagerelief	=	mortgage relief in the exchange
totalboot	=	total boot received from the transaction
bootpaid	=	total boot paid into the transaction
acquiredequity = newequity	=	equity in acquired property (forced to be equal to the pre−tax sales proceeds from the prior property)
netmortgagerelief	=	net mortgage relief after credit for boot paid
accumulateddepreciation	=	the accumulated depreciation taken on the first property during holding period one
indicatedgain = potentialgain	=	indicated gain
recognizedgain	=	gain recognized for tax purposes
mewadjustedcostbasis	=	new adjusted cost basis in acquired property
newlandportion	=	new land allocation of acquired property
newbuildingportion	=	new building allocation of acquired property
newannualdepreciation	=	new depreciation allowance on acquired property

Some of the data for the exchange of tax basis into the second property comes from the *pre-tax* conclusion of holding the first property, provided in Table 10.12.

potentialgain	671 448.
originalcost	1 235 000
accumulateddepreciation	94 309.1
salecosts	146 930.
oldloan	857 154.
newvalue	3.27613×10^6
newequity	954 986.
bootpaid	0
totalboot	0
buildingdepreciationrate	0.0363636
newlandpercentofproperty	0.3

Table 10.12. Data for exchange of basis

The exchange of basis adjustment results in the new property having what is called a "carry-over basis" shown in Table 10.13. *Mathematica* performs this in the CarryoverBasis module using the exchData. Note that the last item on the list is the new annual depreciation deduction for the new property. *The nominal dollar amount of this deduction is smaller than it would be if a similar size property were purchased for cash.* This is a disadvantage of exchanging that must be overcome by some compensating benefit. One of our tasks here is to explore and quantify that benefit.

One comment about tax calculations, here or elsewhere, is appropriate at this point. Neither *Mathematica* nor Excel is necessary for any tax calculation associated with real estate investments. The mathematics of taxation barely exist. More accurately taxation is nothing more than arcane definitions and tedious arithmetic. The reader should not be taken aback by these calculations as anyone with a grade school education can compute them. The art, if any exists in this area, is knowing when to compute them and how to place upon them an economic value.

? CarryoverBasis

CarryoverBasis[exData] inputs a list of values from a tax deferred exchange transaction as data, makes the exchange of basis calculations that lead to depreciation deduction for the property acquired in the exchange.

New Loan	2321146.
Mortgage Relief	0
Net Mortgage Relief	0
Equity Acquired	954986.
Value Acquired	3276132.
Indicated Gain	671448.
Recognized Gain	0
New Adjusted Cost Basis	2604683.
New Land Allocation	781405.
New Building Allocation	1823278.
New Annual Depreciation	66301.

Table 10.13. Carryover basis for second property

Note that the equity reversion for the first property equals the equity acquired in the second property. The equity reversion for the first property is computed after the payment of mortgage balance and sales costs only *but before payment of income tax*.

First property equity reversion is $954,986.

Typical of a stylized example, we force the acquisition capitalization rate on the second property to equal to the acquisition capitalization rate on the original property

dataEG1[[6]][[2]]

0.0971053

Comparing the two in Table 10.14 we see many similarities. In fact the only differences are in the size of the property (in dollar value and number of units), the loan on the property and its income. We assume ratios, financing conditions, tax rates, land allocations and growth expectations are the same. Of course these may all be changed for sensitivity testing.

	dataEG2a	dataEG2b
downpayment	360 000	954 986.
initialnetoperatingincome	119 925	318 130.
investorincometaxrate	0.35	0.35
buildingdepreciationrate	0.0363636	0.0363636
landpercentofproperty	0.3	0.3
capitalizationrateatsale	0.10048	0.0971053
monotonicgrowth	0.03	0.03
logisticconstant	1.5	1.5
accelerationfactor	2	2
interestrate	0.00791667	0.00791667
initialloanbalance	875 000	2.32115×10^6
totalamortizationperiod	360	360
investorrequiredrateofreturn	0.13	0.13
terminalyear	3	3
sellingcostrate	0.075	0.075
capitalgainrate	0.15	0.15
recapturerate	0.25	0.25
prepaymentpenalty	0	0
numberofunits	22	37

Table 10.14. Example 2 input data for the 1st property (dataEG2a) and the 2nd property (dataEG2b) in an exchange

We assume the properties are located in the same area, thus making somewhat realistic the fact that the acquisition standards of the second property are similar to those of the first property. In any stylized example, one can find contradictions. The price per unit for both properties at the time of the exchange transaction (disposition of the first property and acquisition of the second property) has been forced to be approximately the same, but the capitalization rate for the acquired property is below the one sold (which means that $cri_{2b} < cro_{2a}$). An argument could be made for reversing these but because any such argument would rely on the introduction of specific facts, such argument is no better than the one that can be made for the data as presented.

Here is a summary of the second acquisition.

Value	3276132.
Initial loan	2321146.
Down Payment	954986.
NOI	318130.

The second property is acquired under the same general income/price conditions as the first property. We note that the rules of thumb for the two properties, except for price per unit (because the second property is acquired three years later) and After Tax Cash on Cash Return (because of the reduced depreciation in the carryover basis), are the same. *Important to our discussion later in this chapter, note that two risk variables, Loan to Value Ratio and Debt Coverage Ratio, are the same.*

dataEG2a		dataEG2b	
Capitalization Rate	0.0971053	Capitalization Rate	0.0971053
Price Per Unit	56136.4	Price Per Unit	88544.1
Cash on Cash Return	0.0824367	Cash on Cash Return	0.0761728
Debt Coverage Ratio	1.35831	Debt Coverage Ratio	1.35831
Loan to Value Ratio	0.708502	Loan to Value Ratio	0.708502

Table 10.15. Rule of thumb measures for two properties in an exchange sequence

The net effect is that, midway in our investor's six-year real estate investment he has sold a property the value of which he had maximized and acquired a property to which he will apply the same entrepreneurial effort. It is meaningful that the transfer of his maximized equity to a property in need of his talent has been done without the payment of income taxes (something that cannot be easily accomplished with financial assets).

The final step is to combine the performance of the two Example 2 properties (dataEG2a and dataEG2b) over a six year holding period and compare that outcome to Example 1 wherein a single property was held for six years. This information is shown in Figure 10.5 where the six year hold strategy is (1) and the two property in sequence with exchange is (2)

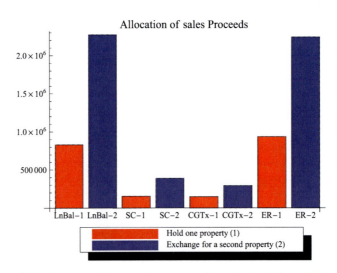

Figure 10.5. Sale proceeds comparison between Example 1 and Example 2

Here is the after tax cash flow and equity reversion data for the last year in the holding period for the second property.

		Sale Price	5196898.
		Beginning Loan Balance	2321146.
		Ending Loan Balance	2273804.
Net Operating Income	504646.	Original Cost	2604683.
Debt Service	234209.	Sale Costs	389767.
Depreciation	66301.	Accumulated Depreciation	293212.
Income Tax	77500.9	Capital Gain	2401351.
After Tax Cash Flow	192936.	Capital Gain Tax	389524.
		Pre-Tax Net Equity	2533327.
		After Tax Net Equity	2143803.

Next we look at the same information for the original property if held over the same aggregate time period (six years) as the two properties.

		Sale Price	2074789.
		Beginning Loan Balance	875000
Net Operating Income	201473.	Ending Loan Balance	833449.
Debt Service	88289.7	Original Cost	1235000
Depreciation	31436.4	Sale Costs	155609.
Income Tax	31642.4	Accumulated Depreciation	188618.
After Tax Cash Flow	81540.8	Capital Gain	872798.
		Capital Gain Tax	149781.
		Pre-Tax Net Equity	1085731.
		After Tax Net Equity	935949.

Clearly, the benefit of the tax deferred exchange is considerable.

For the *npv* and *irr* calculations over the entire six years for Example 2 we include the cash flows from both properties and the after tax equity reversion from the second property, which for simplicity we assume is disposed of in a taxable sale (although there is no reason one could not merely continue with another exchange). Table 10.16 compares this result with holding a single property for six years in Example 1.

NPV for Example 1	$353,158.
NPV for example 2	$1,039,897.
IRR for Example 1	0.298681%
IRR for Example 2	0.46205%

Table 10.16. Examples 1 and 2 performance comparison

Note that Mathematica will compute the *irr* for the second property only, which is 42.1506%, but there is a problem with this in that the equity reversion for property two includes the payment of tax on capital gains deferred from property one. This *irr* for only property two is calculated using a capital gain that arises in part from depreciation attributable to property one. But the calculation does not consider the associated benefit of property one cash flows. Thus, the *irr* solely for property two is not correct. To avoid this distortion, individual properties in a series of exchanges after the first one should only be evaluated on a pre-tax basis for *irr* and *npv* purposes.

The fact that after tax *irr*s should only be calculated on the cumulative and aggregate outcomes of all properties in a series underscores an important point from Chapter 8. The decision to acquire investment realty is often a lifestyle decision. The investment is long term not only from the standpoint of individual properties but from the length of time measured by a series of properties. In a way this introduces a different sort of "portfolio", one that includes a number of properties held sequentially rather than at the same time. Investors who put all their eggs in one basket and watch (also change and improve) that basket move their eggs from basket to basket tax free and measure the results of their portfolios at the end of the last investment after the outcome of a sequence of property investments is known.

There are ramifications for policymakers in countries where income tax laws for capital gains are being formulated. The early architects of the US tax code believed it was important to the development of society to keep capital in the hands of private entrepreneurs. The decision to permit tax deferred exchanging in a society has repercussions on the development of that society's built environment and long term investment.

We mentioned at the beginning that for some investors capital gain taxes may be completely eliminated. This happens if the sum of all holding periods exceeds the investor's remaining life because under present US estate tax law capital gain taxes are forgiven at death. The practical result of this is that the estate tax effectively takes the place of the capital gain tax. As estate tax rates may be more than capital gain rates care should be taken not to overuse the exchange strategy.[3]

10.4.2. The value of tax deferral

An interesting empirical question arises over whether investors, seeking tax deferral, pay more for property they acquire via an exchange than they would have if they had merely purchased the property. Some investors view the deferral of taxes as "an interest free loan from the government". This is questionable reasoning in that it assumes that investors have no money of their own but are merely custodians of the government's money. Regardless, the incentives are aligned to make tax deferral attractive and investors are tempted to pay extra to get it. One needs to know the value of tax deferral. Using the tools in this chapter we can explore this value.

We know that had property one been sold the capital gain of $671,448. would have been recognized and a capital gain tax of $110,148. would be due from the sale proceeds. We know the holding period of property two:

```
terminalyear /. dataEG2b

3
```

One representation of the value of the tax deferral is nothing more than the value (present or otherwise) of the earnings on the taxes unpaid on the sale of property one that become due upon the sale of property two. A critical choice is the rate of return used to calculate those earnings. If we assume the *irr* from these two properties is the investor's average return, the nominal dollar value of tax deferral is merely the result shown in Equation 10.1.

$$\text{Deferred Tax} * (1 + IRR)^{\text{holding period of property two}} - \text{Deferred Tax} \tag{10.1}$$

Knowing this we may also be interested in how the value of tax deferral compares to the tax itself. Additionally, we could be interested in how the value of tax deferral compares to the value of the property acquired.[4] The "ValueOfTxDef" module produces this information for Table 10.17.

```
? ValueOfTxDef
```

ValueOfTxDef[data1,data2,rate,term] returns a three element list. The elements are

(1) the marginal value in dollars of tax deferral associated with the property described as data1,

(2) the marginal value of tax deferral as a percentage of
    capital gain tax otherwise due on the sale of the property described as data1, and

(3) the marginal value of tax deferral as a percentage of the purchase price of the property
    acquired described as data2 using the rate at which equity invested in the acquired
    property is expected to compound (rate) and the length of time it will compound (term).

Value (IRR = 0.46205%, HP = 3)	234094.
Value as a percent of capital gains tax due	2.12527
Value as a percent of the acquisition price of the new property	0.0714544

Table 10.17. The value of tax deferral

Using the assumptions above we find that the value of the tax deferral is roughly twice the amount of the tax and about 7% of the value of the target acquisition property.[5] These two measures give us some sense of scale as to how important the tax benefits are in the big picture.[6]

The nominal dollar amount is considerable, but obviously sensitive to the compounding rate chosen. If a more modest return is used, as in Table 10.18, the value for the same holding period is less for each benchmark.

Value (IRR = 15% HP = 3)	57373.4
Value as a percent of capital gains tax due	0.520875
Value as a percent of the acquisition price of the new property	0.0175126

Table 10.18. The value of tax deferral if investment return alternatives are less

This reduction may be overcome by increasing the holding period as in Table 10.19. Deferring the tax for as long as possible is usually a good practice.

Value (IRR = 15% HP = 8.15 years)	233936.
Value as a percent of capital gains tax due	2.12383
Value as a percent of the acquisition price of the new property	0.0714062

Table 10.19. The value of tax deferral if investment return alternatives are less but property is held over a longer period

Below, in two plots one can see the way tax deferral value changes with the change in return (on left) and the change in holding period (right).

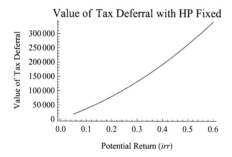
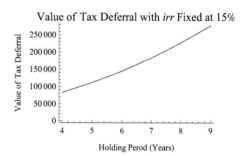

Figure 10.6, scaled to the taxes deferred and the time delay of dataEG2, demonstrates the power of this strategy as the return to one's entrepreneurial effort increases. Those with the ability to optimize opportunities, not surprisingly, benefit more from tax deferral, but so do those who hold the property longer even if the *irr* is moderate. Of course, the outcome is even more potent when high rates of return are combined over longer periods.

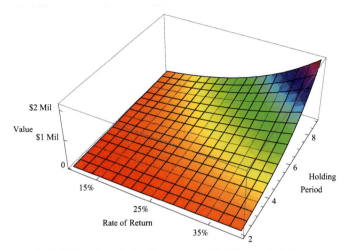

Figure 10.6. Value of tax deferral as return and holding period change

If one pays an additional "premium" to the seller to accommodate the exchange several things happen. Most importantly, the value of the deferral is reduced because the price of the second property is higher. There are ancillary effects, some of which ease the pain of the higher price. The basis is higher so the depreciation deduction is higher. Also, the gain on sale is less, thus capital gains taxes are reduced. Overpaying for the property does not necessarily entitle the buyer to gains on the overpayment so it is unreasonable to assume that nominal dollar growth will increase. Finally, paying a higher price involves either adding equity or debt, a decision that has its own set of ramifications.

The net of these effects can never be positive, thus never recommends paying a higher price. The moral of the story is the same as it has always been: It always cheaper to pay taxes than lose money. One should not make business decisions based on tax consequences even when those tax consequences are superficially as compelling as deferring the tax on a large capital gain.

10.4.3. Tax deferral as a risk modifier

Next, let us investigate just what affect tax deferral has on the final outcome as measured by the *npv* and *irr*. The way to approach this is first to calculate the outcome if the first property had been sold and a second property had been purchased with the after tax proceeds of property one. We begin by reviewing Table 10.11 or the middle column of Table 10.14, the data inputs that lead to the profile and outcome of the first property in Example2, dataEG2a. The three year operating history produces the annual cash flows and reversion shown in Table 10.20.

Year	CashFlow	Reversion	Total
1.	29677.		29677.
2.	71039.		71039.
3.	74986.	844838.	919823.

Table 10.20. Three year summary of first property in Example 2 (dataEG2a)

One consequence of the payment of capital gain tax is that the funds available for purchasing another property are less than they would have been if the first property was exchanged. A decision must be made regarding the size of the second property. One may either (a) purchase a smaller property using the same proportion of debt; (b) purchase the same size property by adding cash from other sources in the amount of the cash paid in taxes; (c) incur additional debt to increase the size of the purchase; or (d) combine the foregoing alternatives in various ways. For the moment we will assume that leverage approximates risk. So if we wish to hold risk constant we will employ no more leverage in our sale-and-repurchase strategy than we would have if we exchanged. This assumption leads to determining the size of the second property purchased by the loan to value ratio (*ltv*). Some algebraic rearrangement of the basic real estate valuation identities will convince you that one can produce the net operating income from capitalization rate, loan-to-value ratio and down payment, three variables that exist in dataEG2a.

$$noi = cr * \left(downpayment + \frac{down\ payment * ltv}{1 - ltv} \right) \quad (10.2)$$

A closer look at the last term in Equation 10.2 discloses that it is the initial loan balance expressed in terms of the *ltv* and down payment.

$$initial\ loan\ balance = \frac{down\ payment * ltv}{1 - ltv} \quad (10.3)$$

We will assume, as we have before, that the second property is purchased in the same geographic area as the first and has a similar capitalization rate. We will initially assume that the second property is acquired with the same percentage of debt (*ltv*) as both the first property and as the exchange property would have been. With these assumptions we begin to build a set of data inputs for a new second property which this time we will purchase rather than acquire by exchange. Recall the going out capitalization rate for property one (dataEG2a) in Table 10.11 is 0.10048. Using this capitalization rate, the after-tax equity reversion of property one as down payment and using the assumed debt ratio, net operating income for the second property becomes $291216. and the initial loan is $2,053,425.

Inserting this information into the dataset *using equations dependent on ltv* for the initial loan amount and net operating income we have inputs for a second, *this time purchased,* property two (dataEG2c). Using our assumed *ltv* we can produce the value of all the inputs for that property in Table 10.21:

downpayment	844838.
initialnetoperatingincome	291216.
investorincometaxrate	0.35
buildingdepreciationrate	0.0363636
landpercentofproperty	0.3
capitalizationrateatsale	0.103971
monotonicgrowth	0.03
logisticconstant	1.5
accelerationfactor	2
interestrate	0.00791667
initialloanbalance	2.05342×10^6
totalamortizationperiod	360
investorrequiredrateofreturn	0.13
terminalyear	3
sellingcostrate	0.075
capitalgainrate	0.15
recapturerate	0.25
prepaymentpenalty	0
numberofunits	33

Table 10.21. Data input dataEG2c for Example 2c

Adding down payment to initial loan gives the value of the purchased property two, $2,898,262.27, which we see is considerably less than the value of exchange-acquired property two (dataEG2b) of $3,276,131.65, resulting in a difference of $377869.

This difference is, therefore, unavailable to grow under the owner's entrepreneurial direction. Our interest is in learning how the absence of this capital affects the return after crediting back certain advantages of the purchase-and-sale strategy. One such advantage is the higher depreciation deduction. A *Mathematica* function automates the process and allows us further inquiry into the effect of tax deferral on the *irr* (the output of which can be reconciled Excel worksheet "ExchEG2c.xls") . [7]

```
? SaleRepurchase
```

> SaleRepurchase[data1,data2,loantovalueratio] inputs two lists of values as data for properties each presumed to be held and sold (propertynumber=1 in both cases) and computes the internal rate of return and net present value of the combined properties assuming the after-tax sale proceeds of the first property is reinvested in the purchase of the second property and the second property is disposed of in a taxable sale.

```
Internal Rate of Return is 44.7485%
Net Present Value is $957,920.
```

Recall the *irr* achieved under the exchange strategy (results match Excel file "ExchEG2.xls")

```
Internal Rate of Return for the exchange strategy is 46.205%
Net Present Value for the exchange strategy is $1,039,897.
```

Suppose we attempt to replicate the exchange *npv* and *irr* results in the sale and repurchase strategy by adding leverage. First recall the loan-to-value ratio for the last computations

```
ltvEG2c // N
```

0.708502

Some trial and error with the *ltv* argument leads us to an *irr* equal to that produced under the tax deferred exchange strategy (results match Excel file "ExchEG2c1.xls". Note that the *npv* will be different because the hurdle rate is pre-specified in the data for that computation and changing the amount of debt changes the cash flows).

```
SaleRepurchase[dataEG2a, dataEG2c, .7382]
Internal Rate of Return is 46.2053%
Net Present Value is $1,036,488.
```

This demonstrates that tax deferred exchanging can be viewed as a risk modifier because the *irr for the exchange strategy was achieved with less leverage than the irr for the sale and repurchase strategy*. Provided one accepts leverage as a measure of risk, the exchange strategy may be seen as involving less risk than the sale and repurchase strategy. Oddly this result imparts some credibility to the flawed "interest free loan from the government" idea. By exchanging the investor retains his capital in his investment free of tax. Therefore, he does not have to borrow the same funds from a lender to whom he would pay interest.

10.4.4. The sale-and-*better*-repurchase strategy: The cost of exchanging

Earlier we said that one should never make business decisions based on tax consequences. This is a corollary of a broader truism: It is cheaper to pay taxes than lose money, something that is always true when tax rates are less than 100%. Recall Table 10.18 showed that, given a moderate *irr* and a short holding period, the value of tax deferral as a percentage of the acquired property was a rather modest 1.751%.

Suppose that tax deferred exchanges carry additional transaction costs. They do in a real sense in that specially qualified brokers, attorneys, tax accountants and escrow holders are required, all of whom are aware of the tax benefit and how their special skills make tax deferral possible. Suppose further that some aspect of the exchange inconveniences the seller of the target property in that he is exposed to additional complexity, risk the transaction does not close and possible delays. Equally plausible is the fact that the seller is aware of that the buyer will enjoy tax benefits from the seller's accommodation of the exchange process, for which he would like to extract a premium price. All of these costs may be avoided if the buyer approaches the seller with a cash offer to purchase that is free of exchange complications.

With that in mind, let us equate these costs with "losing money" in the pursuit of tax deferral. Using our assumptions of a moderate *irr*, short holding period and a low rate of tax deferral value per dollar of acquisition price, let us calculate the overall results of a taxable sale followed by a "better" purchase. This would be a purchase characterized by savings - in the form of a lower price - at least equal to the value of the tax deferral. Taking the opposite perspective, we ask the question: What discount must be available as an offset in a case where tax deferral is not available?

Thus, the new property is purchased at a percentage discount equal to the value of tax deferral as a percentage of the new property, $3,171,147. Suppose further that all of the discount is applied to the downpayment, thus the down payment would be $850,001. The problem is that the after tax equity reversion from the sale of property 2a, $844,837.58, is less than this figure. Thus, we assume the down payment on the discounted property is the minimum of either (1) the amount that would have been invested less the discount or (2) the amount realized from the sale after taxes, in this case $844,837.58. This makes the initial loan balance at purchase $2,326,309. This completes the dataset needed for this example, dataEG2d, shown in Table 10.22.

downpayment	844838.
initialnetoperatingincome	318130.
investorincometaxrate	0.35
buildingdepreciationrate	0.0363636
landpercentofproperty	0.3
capitalizationrateatsale	0.103806
monotonicgrowth	0.03
logisticconstant	1.5
accelerationfactor	2
interestrate	0.00791667
initialloanbalance	2.32631×10^6
totalamortizationperiod	360
investorrequiredrateofreturn	0.13
terminalyear	3
sellingcostrate	0.075
capitalgainrate	0.15
recapturerate	0.25
prepaymentpenalty	0
numberofunits	33

Table 10.22. Data input dataEG2d for Example 2d

Taking the long approach to computing the combined *irr* for the combined six year holding period for the two properties (results match Excel file "ExchEG2d.xls". Note that this approach is needed as the SaleRepurchase module does not accommodate different growth rates in the separate properties)

```
IRR is 45.9464%
```

The *irr* we just calculated is 0.259% below, about one quarter of a percent, that which would have been achieved if the second property had been acquired at a higher price but with tax deferred exchange proceeds.

Ignoring the .0025 as trivial and assuming the true value is the lower price, the net effect of an exchange at a higher price is to employ untaxed dollars to pay the premium necessary to achieve tax deferral. In essence, this gives all the benefits of tax deferral to the seller. One must not lose sight of the fact that the taxes, even if deferred, are eventually due and must be paid (suggesting that taxes are inevitable). Also, recall that we made some assumptions about the amount of loan required. Computing the loan to value ratio for the property acquired without exchange produces 73.359%, a higher debt ratio, therefore higher risk. This is hard to treat as trivial.

All of this leads us to believe that while tax deferral is a powerful benefit, one cannot justify "paying" for tax deferral. *Only if the target property can be acquired via exchange under the same conditions as it would have been purchased outright can the acquisition be justified.* For the buyer-exchangor we have modeled here, we find that he must keep all the benefits of the exchange and not transfer any of them to the seller in the form of a higher price. Under these assumptions, the taxes remain due, are paid after a short deferral and the value of tax deferral is comparatively slight and must be protected.

One must keep in mind the effect of the alternative use of the funds and the holding period. As the potential *irr* available in the acquired property increases and/or the holding period for the acquired property increases, the importance of the conclusion just reached changes. But the conclusion itself never does. One can never gain by giving tax dollars both to the seller and a few years later to the government.

If the exchangor at the time of his taxable disposition of the last property can find a buyer with exchange motives from whom he can extract an offsetting benefit in the form of a higher price, he may recover, albeit delayed, all or part of any premium he may have paid at the time of his tax deferred acquisition. Everyone participating in such market activity contributes to a sort of "tax bubble" that will burst when Congress suddenly changes some part of the law that reduces or eliminates the tax benefit of exchanging.[8] The last buyer who paid for tax benefits in the form of a higher price finds no one when it is time to sell that is willing to pay an equivalent increment when the tax benefit is reduced or missing.

At the beginning of this chapter we said that we would avoid the many intricate details necessary to consummate a qualified tax deferred exchange. But we also alluded to one such matter in a passing reference to the delayed or so-called "Starker" exchange. This detail deserves special attention. When originally conceived, the qualified tax deferred exchange was conducted as a concurrent transfer of one property for another. The delayed technique grew out of a series of IRS court cases in the 1970s involving family members of T. J. Starker that lead to the authorization of a non-simultaneous exchange. But the authorization was uneven, some more permissive, some more restrictive, among the different districts of the US Tax Court. In 1986 Congress stepped in and codified procedures that became Treasury regulations in 1991. These procedures are intricate and should be carefully followed by anyone planning an exchange. There are important general caveats that must not be overlooked.

In order to conduct a non-simultaneous exchange and still qualify for tax deferral, among other things, one has 45 days after the close of his original disposition to *identify* the target acquisition property. The taxpayer then has the shorter of (a) and 180 days (which includes the 45 days) or (b) the close of the tax year, as evidenced by the filing of a tax return, to complete the acquistion. A common scenario goes like this: The seller lists his property and begins looking for a target acquisition. A buyer is located who for whatever reason must close the purchase on his own, shorter, time schedule (perhaps his 180 day period is about to expire). The seller is encouraged by his broker to close the sale promising that he will find the seller a replacement property within the 45 days. The seller may nominate no more than three potential properties to acquire and then actually acquire one of them in the time limit specified. Otherwise, the capital gain realized on the sale of the original property is recognized and taxable.

Only the naive will fail to see the opportunity for mischief here. This may be generally classified as "Starker risk", a kind of transaction risk that will be discussed below and may be completely avoided by the most sophisticated exchangors.

Assuming that the broker is diligent and does actually locate three properties, a series of practical difficulties arise. The pool of potential acquisitions is limited to those that are available between the time of closing and 45 days thereafter. Once selected, the three properties must represent the best of all possibilities. The seller - now buyer - can only make an offer on one property at a time.

While the other party is contemplating such an offer, owners of the other two properties find buyers. The pool of potential acquisitions shrinks to one. Is this not every seller's dream, to have a buyer whose *only permissible acquisition* is his property? Is there not a perverse incentive for the broker to delay a serious search for the target acquisition until the 44th day? Time is running throughout all of this. The passing days are a gun to the exchangor's head held there by the tax man.

Starker risk may be divided into three categories:

1. The misplaced motivation to purchase based on expiring tax benefits that leads to an unwise acquisition;
2. An adverse finding during the due diligence process that either eliminates the only permissible acquisition or, in a variation of #1 above, requires the exchangor to acquire a substandard property; or
3. A host of technical malfunctions such as the death or incapacity of the seller, lender inability to fund a loan or other procedural matter that delays the closing beyond the maximum permitted time allowed.

What alternatives exist for the careful investor? One is to select and qualify the target property well before the close of the sale of his property, allowing him to recover from a malfunction. Better yet, is to require the other parties to participate in an old-fashioned simultaneous exchange. This is anathema to the modern broker raised to repeat the mantra "Don't worry, we will find something in 45 days" and may reduce the pool of target acquisitions as brokers avoid an investor with difficult, albeit rational, objectives. Congress may have allowed the conduct of a deferred exchange but they did not outlaw the conduct of the alternative. The best brokers are ones who know this and are willing to conduct the exchange in the client's best interest.

A set of simple rules appear here: Do not enter into a contract to transfer your property unless the terms of the transaction are so beneficial that you can afford to pay the taxes on the sale. If this is not possible and a proposed sale is only justified if an exchange is involved, require that such an exchange be simultaneous. Failing to observe these rules implicitly leaves the investor open to violating the important advice to never make business decisions based on tax motives.

10.5. Example 3 - Exchanging and "The Plodder"

To this point we have focused on the way a tax deferral strategy affects the entrepreneurial type who adds labor to his investment to improve its value rapidly in the early years of ownership. There are other, perhaps more numerous, real estate investors who are "buy-and-hold" types. They rely on neighborhood or regional growth over time to increase the value of their investments, perhaps offsetting inflation better than financial assets would over the same period of time. To illustrate this type of investor we will return to the inputs from the base case for the first half of Example 3 (monotonic growth over a six year holding period) shown in Table 10.1 and the middle column of Table 10.25.

downpayment	360 000
initialnetoperatingincome	119 925
investorincometaxrate	0.35
buildingdepreciationrate	0.0363636
landpercentofproperty	0.3
capitalizationrateatsale	0.0971053
monotonicgrowth	0.03
logisticconstant	0
accelerationfactor	0
interestrate	0.00791667
initialloanbalance	875 000
totalamortizationperiod	360
investorrequiredrateofreturn	0.13
terminalyear	6
sellingcostrate	0.075
capitalgainrate	0.15
recapturerate	0.25
prepaymentpenalty	0
numberofunits	22

Table 10.23 shows a new set of exchange inputs to perform the basis carryover calculations

potentialgain	317 674.
originalcost	1 235 000
accumulateddepreciation	188 618.
salecosts	110 599.
oldloan	833 449.
newvalue	1.82028×10^6
newequity	530 607.
bootpaid	0
totalboot	0
buildingdepreciationrate	0.0363636
newlandpercentofproperty	0.3

Table 10.23. Data for base case exchange of basis

We will continue for the moment with our convention of using the capitalization rate for the property sold to value the property acquired, 0.09711%.

Table 10.24 provides the exchange of basis values for a new acquisition.

New Loan	1289670.
Mortgage Relief	0
Net Mortgage Relief	0
Equity Acquired	530607.
Value Acquired	1820277.
Indicated Gain	317674.
Recognized Gain	0
New Adjusted Cost Basis	1502603.
New Land Allocation	450781.
New Building Allocation	1051822.
New Annual Depreciation	38248.1

Table 10.24. Carryover basis for property acquired with base case property

The computation leading to the acquisition of the new property will, as before, depend on the sale of the first property, assume all proceeds are reinvested, new loans are at least as much in nominal amount as old loans and the exchange is fully tax deferred. Comparing the two in Table 10.25, note especially the size of each building based on the number of units.

	dataEG3a	dataEG3b
downpayment	360 000	530 607.
initialnetoperatingincome	119 925	176 759.
investorincometaxrate	0.35	0.35
buildingdepreciationrate	0.0363636	0.0363636
landpercentofproperty	0.3	0.3
capitalizationrateatsale	0.0971053	0.0971053
monotonicgrowth	0.03	0.03
logisticconstant	0	0
accelerationfactor	0	0
interestrate	0.00791667	0.00791667
initialloanbalance	875 000	1.28967×10^6
totalamortizationperiod	360	360
investorrequiredrateofreturn	0.13	0.13
terminalyear	6	6
sellingcostrate	0.075	0.075
capitalgainrate	0.15	0.15
recapturerate	0.25	0.25
prepaymentpenalty	0	0
numberofunits	22	27

Table 10.25. Example 3 input data for first property (dataEG3a) and second property (dataEG3b)

Final year operating and sale results are modestly profitable with net present value and *irr* meeting projections (results match Excel file "ExchEG3.xls") and a comparison of six- and twelve-year results appear to recommend the exchange undertaken.

NPV[dataEG3a, dataEG3b, 2, exchData3]

14 918.5

IRR[dataEG3a, dataEG3b, 2, exchData3]

0.135662

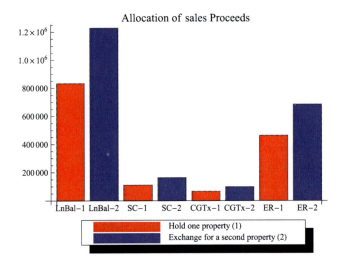

It is useful to note that in this stylized example the primary motivation for the exchange is to return to the original leverage. Since all other inputs are constant, one "buys" the extra increment of the larger property with the increased equity from the smaller property, employing the same loan-to-value ratio as used for the first acquisition. Due to sales costs this is an expensive approach. To accomplish the same objective one could refinance the original property back to its original debt ratio and use the net refinance proceeds to purchase another property with a like debt ratio. The two properties in the aggregate, ignoring the inconvenience of multiple locations, would then function at least financially the same as the larger property acquired via an exchange without having incurred the transaction costs.

We again measure the performance of the exchange strategy against the sale and repurchase strategy, using the net after tax proceeds to purchase the largest possible property with the same leverage. The new data inputs are, therefore:

downpayment	464 094.
initialnetoperatingincome	154 601.
investorincometaxrate	0.35
buildingdepreciationrate	0.0363636
landpercentofproperty	0.3
capitalizationrateatsale	0.0971053
monotonicgrowth	0.03
logisticconstant	0
accelerationfactor	0
interestrate	0.00791667
initialloanbalance	1.12801×10^6
totalamortizationperiod	360
investorrequiredrateofreturn	0.13
terminalyear	6
sellingcostrate	0.075
capitalgainrate	0.15
recapturerate	0.25
prepaymentpenalty	0
numberofunits	24

The *Mathematica* function computes the IRR for the sale and repurchase (results match Excel file "ExchEG3.xls").

ATCF[dataEG3c /. ltv → .708502]

Net Operating Income	179 225.
Debt Service	113 819.
Depreciation	40 526.2
Income Tax	12 615.6
After Tax Cash Flow	52 791.1

SaleRepurchase[dataEG3a, dataEG3c, .708502]

Internal Rate of Return is 13.0351%

Net Present Value is $902.482

Note how close the last calculations are to the *irr* of 13.5662% and the *npv* of $14,918. for the exchange strategy.

One might well conclude that the exchange has little value to the buy-and-hold investor if the acquisition input values and economics of the property and its neighborhood remain constant. Recall the fact that the property disposed of was 22 units and the property acquired was 27 units. Sales costs were incurred on 22 units just to acquire an extra 5 units. This inefficiency suggests that a minimum increased size requirement might be necessary to justify an exchange. An interesting empirical study would examine a number of exchanges to determine if perhaps one should not exchange unless one acquires a property at least 1.5 or 2 times the size of the disposed property.

Suppose our investor merely retained his original property for the same total time. Because he saves mid-holding period sales costs he has a higher return in both *irr* and *npv* terms (results match last page, "JustHold", of Excel file "ExchEG3c.xls").

Sale Price	1760815.
Beginning Loan Balance	875000
Ending Loan Balance	760139.
Original Cost	1235000
Sale Costs	132061.
Accumulated Depreciation	377236.
Capital Gain	770990.
Capital Gain Tax	153372.
Pre-Tax Net Equity	868614.
After Tax Net Equity	715242.

IRR for 12 year hold is 14.3232%

NPV for 12 year hold is $36,314.

Sale Price	2173505.
Beginning Loan Balance	1289670.
Ending Loan Balance	1228427.
Original Cost	1502603.
Sale Costs	163013.
Accumulated Depreciation	418107.
Capital Gain	737378.
Capital Gain Tax	152417.
Pre-Tax Net Equity	782066.
After Tax Net Equity	629649.

Note below that while total sales price in the two strategies is greater for the exchange strategy *the owner's share* is greater when no exchange takes place. We see that under these assumptions the primary beneficiary of the exchange is the broker. To show how a picture can be distorted change the scaling method to the one that benefits the owner.

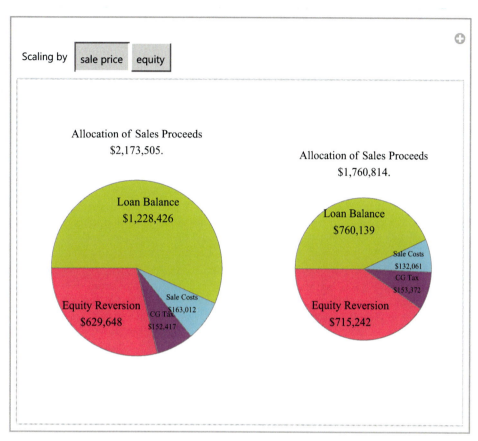

Figure 10.7. Allocations with and without exchanging

Several conclusions may be drawn from this. Once again we confirm the fact that pursuing tax objectives for their own sake is counterproductive. Another is that the primary beneficiaries of some exchanges are brokers. Commissions make up the majority of real estate transaction costs. In order to offset these transaction costs the investor must be able to achieve significant financial objectives. There is a limit to the benefits of re-leveraging via an exchange and these benefits may not be sufficient to offset transaction costs.

10.6. Data issues

Data providers sometimes included a binary (Y/N) field to answer the question: "Was an exchange involved". This is important when studying markets to determine how tax policy affects investor behavior. However, a refinement is necessary. For this data field to have its maximum value it is important to identify *how* the exchange fits into the transaction. If the sale involved an exchange in which the seller was the last in a series and did not further exchange his property there is a different effect than if the seller became an acquiring party in a subsequent exchange. Theoretically there should be a cumulative effect. The last seller who does not require an exchange may reap benefits from each party lower down in the chain, especially if the 45 day deadline is shorter with each successive transaction. There is no reason this must happen but it should increase pressure in the system as the number of exchanges in a series grows if the deadline does grow shorter. We leave the interesting study of this to the game theorists.

What we suggest is not a trivial task for data collectors. The result of any such effort would be to track transactions after the closing and tie multiple transactions together. This is not an appetizing assignment and one we do not expect to be completed soon. Until that is done we will have to rely on theory to study investor behavior in a tax environment that sometimes rewards exchanging over sale and repurchase.

10.7. Conclusion

After wading through a blizzard of numbers, sorting out complex sub-calculations dependent on other variables and running a variety of hypothetical situations, there is one conclusion that is neither a surprise or in doubt: The investor who adds entrepreneurial labor to increase his rate of return *and* delays his income tax for a long time is able to build terminal wealth faster.

For investors where entrepreneurial issues do not apply and annual returns are moderate the conclusions are less certain. Given the costs, explicit and implicit, the investor who merely plods along with the rest of the economy must be very careful when undertaking an exchange. Scale factors come into play. The size of the acquired property relative to the disposed property strongly influences whether the cost of an exchange can be justified.

In our continuing quest to understand real estate risk, exchanging plays a minor role. There is an analogy to the debate over double taxation of corporate dividends. A double taxation policy encourages borrowing leading to the additional risks in the securities market. For real estate a *sequential* taxation policy incrementally taxes each property in a series as it is sold. This encourages more borrowing either for non-taxable refinance and re-purchase strategies that reduce investor efficiency by adding multiple locations or for borrowing to keep ownership levels where they would have been if a tax deferred exchange strategy were available. Either of these, while good news for banks, is not good news for society in general if borrowing is seen as adding unnecessary risk to the system.

It has been observed by many that taxes are necessary to operate a civil society. In the debate over which taxes provide the most revenue and do the least harm to the market it is generally agreed that the best tax is the one that changes behavior the least. Income taxes have a poor record in this regard. Capital gains taxes probably fare no better. The study of real estate tax deferred exchanges is fertile ground for watching the contortions of investors bent on reducing their tax obligation.

A final note for policymakers may be in order. Section 1034 (applying to single family residences) and 1033 (applying to property subject to condemnation) provide different sets of rules for the sale and re-acquisition of property without the payment of taxes. There may be merit in the simplification of these various sections into a single set of rules that acknowledges the benefits to society that accrue from allowing land to remain untaxed in entrepreneurial and productive hands for as long as possible. For those countries in the beginning stages of formulating tax policy, the clean slate they start with might first recognize the perverse incentives in the US tax code as written and avoid expensive pitfalls.

If there is one conclusion that remains it is the idea that entrepreneurial effort adds value not only to the investor's terminal wealth but to society's built environment. The preservation of the nation's housing stock and the optimization of its commercial facilities depend on the wide dispersal of ownership among the most qualified investors. Keeping those assets in capable hands for as long as possible would seem to benefit society the most.

Endnotes

[1] While this chapter focuses on the most widely used IRS code section, Section 1031, there are numerous other opportunities to defer taxes in a real estate setting. The reader is encouraged to become familiar with transfers into and out of partnerships (Section 721), between individuals and corporations (Sections 333 and 351), tax deferral offered those who suffer a casualty loss (Section 1033), just to name a few. The particulars of each of these differ in important ways and competent tax counsel should be consulted before implementing any strategy involving these IRS code sections.

[2] With the important difference, that value is a function of a market rate of growth, not a function of both income growth and the capitalization rate.

[3] As the first edition of this book was being written the US Estate Tax Code was in a state of considerable uncertainty. The taxable portion of estates was dropping and the entire tax was due to expire in 2010, then a year later restored to the condition it was prior to the changes. Some of that happened, some did not. As the second edition is being written in late 2011 the

[4] public endures endless speculation about the future of tax policy in the United States. No one can predict the destination of this very political matter and current tax law should be consulted at the time plans are made.

[4] Taking the present value of any of these measures is of course possible and would reduce them all. This introduces the additional complexity of deciding what discount rate to use, something we leave for the reader's reflection and experimentation.

[5] Suspiciously close to the size of the transaction costs.

[6] There is an interesting policy issue we could address. It is claimed that reduction in capital gain rates actually increase tax revenue because more people are willing to sell and incur gains. The argument is that the increased number of taxable transactions offsets the lower rates. The answer to this question is beyond the scope of this chapter but one can see how the problem might be approached.

[7] The reader may find slight differences between the amounts produced by Mathematica and those produced by Excel. These differences may be traced to the different ways the two programs round decimals.

[8] Congress did just that as the first edition of this book was being written. Capital gains tax rates were lowered in 2003, reducing the benefit of exchanging incrementally. The admonitions of footnote 3 are repeated.

References

Allen, M. (1990). <u>Creative Real Estate Exchange: a Guide to Win-Win Strategies</u>. Chicago, IL: National Association of REALTORS.

Internal Revenue ServiceIRS Revenue Ruling 72-456. 26 CFR 1.1031(d)-1.

Sherrod, J. R., & Diggs, J. B.Merchantile Trust Company of Baltimore and Alexander C. Nelson, Trustees of the Estate of Charles D. Fisher v. Commissioner of Internal Revenue. <u>Merchantile Trust Company v. IRS</u>, Docket # 68338.

Tappan Jr. , W. T. (1989). <u>Real Estate Exchange and Acquisition Techniques</u> (2nd ed.). Englewood Cliffs, NJ: Prentice Hall.

Problems

1. The best exercise for the material in this section is for the reader to trace the narrative and outputs of this chapter throughout the companion Excel files which track the results almost exactly.

11
The Management Problem

"...all that can be required of a trustee is that he conduct himself faithfully and exercise sound discretion and observe how men of prudence, discretion and intelligence manage their own affairs-not in regard to speculation, but in regard to the permanent disposition of their funds, considering the probable income as well as the probable safety of the capital to be invested."

The Supreme Court of Massachusetts in Harvard College versus Amory (1830) articulating the Prudent Man Rule

11.1. Introduction

This chapter addresses what is known as "the agency problem", recognizing that when an agent holds someone else's capital the agent's objectives are often different from the owner's.

In this chapter we will

- Describe the optimization problem that faces any manager of properties in multiple locations;
- Describe the owner's problem showing how his objectives differ; and
- Illustrate the misalignment of incentives and compensation arrangements common to the business of managing small investment properties.

11.2. The unavoidable management issue

There is little debate that the ownership of real estate involves management. The debate is about (1) who shall do the management, (2) what management costs, (3) how one accounts for that cost and (4) what management arrangement is the most efficient. We observed in Chapter 8 that the owner may do his own management. If he does he adds to his investment with each hour of labor he applies to his rental property that he could have applied to other activities, profitable or otherwise. At a minimum, this has the effect of complicating the return calculation. Alternatively, to preserve both the integrity of the return calculation and the owner's peace of mind one may contract for management services with a third party whose fee becomes a part of the expense schedule. In this way management is charged against the property's income before the owner's return is calculated.

Things are rarely that simple. Property size and location play a significant role. There is a suspicion that so-called "professional" property management really isn't. Especially for small properties, the quality of property management can vary widely. A significant literature exists on the subject of agency, studying the separation of ownership and control. Our story is about the *combination* of ownership and control.

11.3. The property manager's dilemma

A company offering property management services, like any firm, wishes to maximize net profit by increasing revenue and lowering costs. The rule adopted to accomplish this is called the firm's "production function". To create this function we assume that the firm generates revenue as management fees, and incurs two broad classes of expenses. The first are in-house costs consisting primarily of accounting services rendered to owners. For simplicity these are assumed to be fixed. The second involves dispatching an employee to visit and inspect those properties under management. These latter costs are variable and will be generally referred to as "transaction costs" because each visit to a property involves a transaction that incurs, at a minimum, some travel expense (hence these may also be considered "transportation costs"). Important factors in these variable costs are the number of properties the manager chooses to manage, the size of those properties and the distance between them.

Initially we will assume that management fees *realized* are calculated as a rate per unit. In actual practice the fee is *charged* as a percentage of income, something we shall address later. For now realized fees are computed by multiplying a rate, g, times the number of units, u.

Therefore, the first net profit function, np, we will use is:

$$np = g\,u - ac - tc \qquad (11.1)$$

Where:

np = net profits
g = rate per unit at which fee income is realized
u = number of units managed
ac = accounting costs
tc = transaction (transportation) costs, a function of the number of locations, loc, a transportation rate, h, and distance, d, both between locations and from the office to various locations.

Transaction costs are modeled as an increasing function of location count and distance:

$$tc = \frac{h\,u\,e^{d\,loc}}{2} \qquad (11.2)$$

Where:

tc = transaction costs
h = a rate at which transaction costs are incurred
d = a remoteness factor to provide for distance of each property from the office
loc = number of locations
e = the base of the natural log

Illustrating a model with many variables requires reducing their number by fixing some of the variables at specific values. We use several datasets to facilitate this. Table 11-1 provides the datasets we will use in this chapter.

d1	d2	d3	d4	d5	d6	d7
ac → 10	ac → 10	ac → 10	ac → 10	ac → 10	fc → 50	ac → 10
g → 500	g → 500	g → 500	g → 500	h → 0.05	α → 1.25	h → 0.05
h → 0.05	h → 0.05	h → 0.05	h → 0.05	u → 50	β → 0.05	u → 50
u → 50	u → 50	d → 0.5	u → 50	d → 0.5	mgt → 0.1	d → 0.5
d → 0.6	d → 0.5		d → 0.5	loc → 3		loc → 15
			α → 1.25	α → 1.25		α → 1.25
			β → 0.05	β → 0.05		β → 0.05
				mgt → 0.1		mgt → 0.1

Table 11.1. Seven datasets for examples

The first two datasets, **d1** and **d2** differ only in the value we give to the distance factor, d. As one might expect, at different remoteness factors, d, the steepness of the *tc* function varies over different numbers of locations in a portfolio containing a fixed number of units as we see in Figure 11.1.

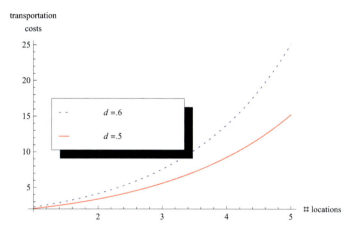

Figure 11.1. Transaction costs at two distance factors as the number of locations change

As a consequence, of course, net profit is a decreasing function of the number of locations and the distance factor.

In Figure 11.2 the distance factor creates the difference between the two plots of net profits as the number of locations increases, all else taking fixed values.

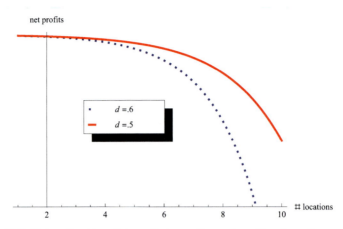

Figure 11.2. Net profits at two distance factors as the number of locations change

It may appear that what really matters is average building size. But does it? Suppose that *ac* is a fixed resource that places an upper bound on the total number of units that may be managed. The optimization problem becomes one of finding an appropriate size building, given the fixed number of units. This involves finding the optimal building size expressed as the ratio, $\frac{u}{loc}$. The optimal will always be the lowest number of locations. The perfect job may be managing one large building, but the market does not always accommodate that perfect outcome. Management usually involves multiple locations. Inserting the transaction cost function, Equation 11.2, directly into the manager's net profit, Equation 11.1, we have:

$$np = g\,u - ac - \frac{e^{d\,loc}\,h\,u}{2} \tag{11.3}$$

Providing fixed values for some of the inputs again, this time omitting a value for *u* which we wish to vary, we define a simpler function with real numbers and only the two arguments of interest, units and location:

$$500\,u - 10 - \frac{0.05\,e^{0.5\,loc}\,u}{2} \tag{11.4}$$

Our simplified story can be plotted in Figure 11.3 to show how net profit varies based solely on the number of units and locations, given fixed values for accounting costs, the fee per unit, distance and transaction rates from dataset **d3**.

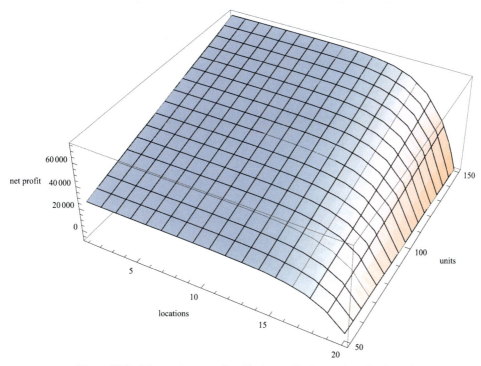

Figure 11.3. Manager's net profit with changes in the number of units and locations

11.3.1. Is building size really important?

We can define net profit a second way, *np2*, this time in terms of a new variable to represent building size, $size = \frac{u}{loc}$. Rearranging to express units in terms of this new size variable, $u = size\ loc$, we plot Equation 11.5 in Figure 11.4.

$$np2 = 500\ loc\ size - 10 - 0.025\ e^{0.5\ loc}\ loc\ size \tag{11.5}$$

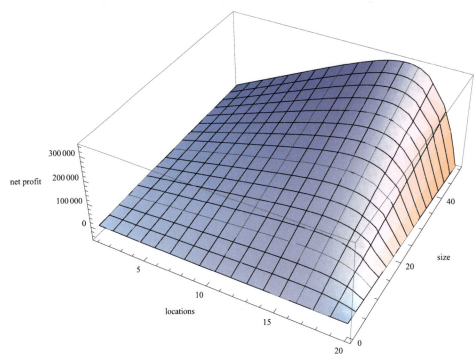

Figure 11.4. Net profit with changes in the number of locations and building size

The derivative with respect to location of this last net profit function demonstrates that the largest obtainable net profit, $np2_{max}$, is independent of building size. At first glance we note that $np2$ is dependent on size because size is in its derivative.

$$\frac{\partial np2}{\partial loc} = \left(500. + e^{0.5\,loc}(-0.025 - 0.0125\,loc)\right) size \tag{11.6}$$

While this is true, it is not true that $np2_{max}$ is dependent on size. Setting the derivative equal to zero and solving the implicit function, size and the constant -0.025 "divide out" leaving a function that has location as its only variable. Solving Equation 11.7 for *loc* gives 15 locations (rounded because you can't have a fractional location) as optimum under these conditions.

$$\frac{\partial np2}{\partial loc} = \left(500. + e^{0.5\,loc}(-0.025 - 0.0125\,loc)\right) size = 0 \tag{11.7}$$

The optimal number of locations is $15.4721 \cong 15$

We reach the surprising conclusion that under these conditions building size does not matter.[1]

We can show the relationship (always given the fixed inputs) of distance between properties and optimal number of locations. Optimal number of locations is found by multiplying a constant by the inverse of the distance factor.

$$\text{optimal locations}(d) = \frac{7.73603}{d} \tag{11.8}$$

When the distance between properties, d, increases, the number of optimal locations decreases as one might expect. The next result uses $d = .7$. Figure 11.5 shows the path of *optlocf* as distance increases. This suggests the intuitively satisfying result that dense urbanization offers more management efficiency than rural or sparsely urbanized areas, something we may have guessed from things we learned in Chapter 1.

When distance increases to .7 optimal locations falls to 11

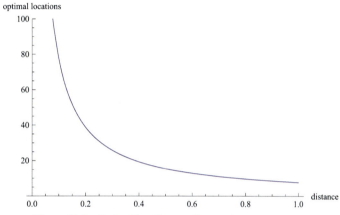

Figure 11.5. Optimal locations as distance increases

We set aside these insights for the moment to address the other party's problem.

11.4. The property owner's dilemma

Especially for small properties, management fees are calculated as a percentage of *effective gross income* (*egi*) collected from tenants. *Egi* is defined as the actual receipts after vacancy and credit losses. The manager has a fiduciary obligation to maximize the owner's *net* income. With management fees a percentage of the collected rent, the manager's fee income is maximized by collecting the most rent from tenants. This conflict introduces a perverse incentive because tenants paying the highest rent often subject the property to more intense use and often vacate after a short tenancy. While the manager shares in vacancy losses because his fee is based on *collected* income, increased expenses are borne solely by the owner. The net income of both manager and owner are affected by vacancy rates. But the owner's interest in maximizing net income considers expenses; the manager's interest in maximizing fee income does not.[2]

11.4.1. The "No vacancy rate" approach

For the moment we shall ignore the connection between higher rents and vacancy rates and deal only with the variable cost issue. Later we will include the vacancy factor to provide a more realistic result.

The owner's net operating income (*noi*) is:

$$noi = r - fc - vc \tag{11.9}$$

Where:

noi = net operating income
r = rent collected
fc = fixed costs (not related to occupancy such as taxes and insurance)
vc = variable costs (occupancy–driven costs such as maintenance which for now will include vacancy)

Variable costs, which include management fees, are modeled as an increasing function of rent:

$$vc = 100 \cdot \left(1 - e^{-0.025\,r}\right) + mgt\, r \qquad (11.10)$$

Where:

vc = variable costs
e = base of the natural log
mgt = management fee, a percentage of rent

Substituting Equation 11.9 into Equation 11.10 we have

$$noi = r - mgt\, r - fc - 100\left(1 - e^{-0.025\,r}\right) \qquad (11.11)$$

For the purposes of illustration we will use a 10% management fee. Figure 11.6 reveals that variable costs rise at a constant rate after an initial steep rise.

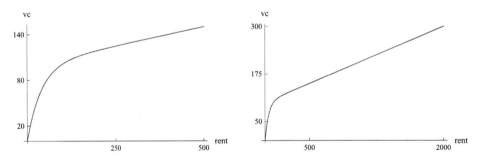

Figure 11.6. Variable costs as rent increases

Next we take the derivative of variable costs with respect to rent. Taking the limit of that term as *r* increases without bound, we notice that variable costs approach the management fee *rate*. We confirm this graphically by plotting the derivative against rent in Figure 11.7. This suggests that after some point, variable costs become a constant percent of rent. Stated differently, one could conclude that after some rent all variable costs other than management fee reach a maximum. When those non-management costs level out (as above) the only component of variable cost increase is the increase in management fees which are a direct function of rent.

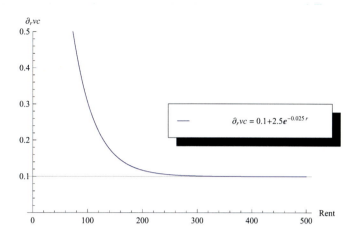

Figure 11.7. First derivative of vc with respect to r as rent increases

Another way of saying the same thing is from the perspective of net operating income. The limit and the plot of the derivative of *noi* with respect to rent, Equation 11.12, in Figure 11.8 both show that the change in *noi* becomes a constant 90% (100% - the 10% management fee) after a certain rent level.

$$\frac{\partial noi}{\delta r} = 0.9 - 2.5\, e^{-0.025\, r} \qquad (11.12)$$

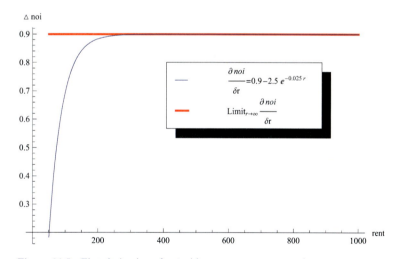

Figure 11.8. First derivative of *noi* with respect to rent as rent increases

This suggests that rents can be increased without bound and *noi* will continue to rise to infinity. While perhaps mathematically possible, economics intervene. At some rent there will be no tenants. More generally, fewer tenants are available as rent rises.

11.4.2. Enter the vacancy rate

We now introduce the idea of vacancy. Collected rent, *cr*, is a percentage of the (hoped for) scheduled market rent.

$$cr = sr(1 - vf) \tag{11.13}$$

The difference between scheduled rent and collected rent is the vacancy factor, *vf*. Rearranging Equation 11.13 we have

$$vf = 1 - \frac{cr}{sr} \tag{11.14}$$

Where:

vf = vacancy factor, $0 < vf < 1$
cr = collected rent
sr = scheduled rent

It is convenient for expository purposes to introduce the vacancy factor through a function for collected rent dependent on scheduled rent. Thus collected rent is scheduled rent scaled by the vacancy factor. In dollars, collected rent, *cr*, is what remains after schedule rent, *sr*, has been reduced by vacancy. Equation 11.13 may also be expressed as

$$cr = sr - vf(sr) \tag{11.15}$$

Therefore, if we say that

$$cr = sr + 1 - \alpha^{\beta\, sr} \tag{11.16}$$

the term $1-\alpha^{\beta\, sr}$ is the dollar amount of vacancy suffered. This term must be negative to make $cr < sr$. Therefore, $\alpha^{\beta\, sr}$ must be > 1. In equilibrium, a "normal" vacancy rate represents no more than the usual market frictions arising from tenant turnover. In healthy rental markets the vacancy rate should be around 5% due to these frictions. Clearly, the choice of α and β is important to achieve this result, but the size of *sr* is also involved. In our present model, the interplay between these variables results in either an unrealistic rent or an unrealistic vacancy factor.

The best model is the simplest model. While it might be possible to impose inequality constraints such that $0 \le sr \le 2000$ and $0 \le vf \le .05$ to improve realism, it would come at the expense of simplicity. The compromise is that the vacancy rate demonstrated in the illustration below is unrealistic. Alternatively, by manipulating α and β, one could produce a more "normal" vacancy factor. Doing so makes *sr* quite high, a result that is perhaps acceptable if one considers *sr* to be an aggregate rent for a large building, not just a single unit.

In the Appendix to this chapter we propose a "cure" for some of the unrealistic aspects discussed above. After reading it one wonders if the cure is worse than the disease.

11.5. Reconciling the two problems

How do both parties both optimize? The market sets rent under which both must operate and both parties benefit from the highest collected rent. Therefore, our procedure will be to first find the scheduled rent that results in the highest collected rent, given our definition of *cr*. We will then specify conditions under which each party optimizes their respective income at that scheduled rent. We plot Equation 11.16, a function for collected rent that both depends on the scheduled rent and considers vacancy.

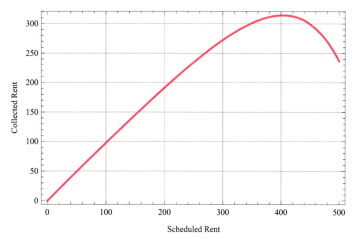

Figure 11.9. Plot of collected rent with change in scheduled rent

Using data **d4** to fix certain values in Equation 11.16 we set the partial derivative of *cr* with respect to scheduled rent to zero and find the optimum scheduled rent to be $402.94. Adding that information to **d4**, inserting it into Equation 11.16 and solving for *cr* provides $314.30, suggesting an unappetizing vacancy factor of 21.995%. Figure 11.10 shows the expected rise in vacancy factor with the rise in rent.

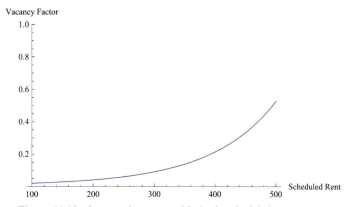

Figure 11.10. Increased vacancy with rise in scheduled rent

Returning to the property manager's problem, this time considering the vacancy factor by substituting *mgt cr* for *gu* in the original *np* function and substituting Equation 11.16 for *cr*, we construct a new net profit function *np3*.

$$np3 = mgt\, cr - ac - tc = mgt\left(1 + sr - \alpha^{sr\,\beta}\right) - ac - \frac{e^{d\,loc}\,h\,u}{2} \tag{11.17}$$

This time using data **d5** in Table 11.1, we compute the optimum scheduled rent in the same fashion as before, taking the partial derivative of *np3* with respect to scheduled rent, setting it equal to zero and solving. Optimal rent is $402.94, making the manager's profit under those same conditions positive ($15.83).

Figure 11.11 shows the new profit function for the manager we see it peaks at the same optimal rent.[3]

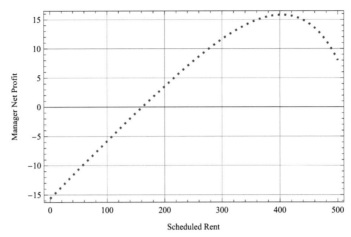

Figure 11.11. Plot of manager's net profit with change in scheduled rent

Finally, we look at how the owner's position is optimized. This time vacancy is separated and dealt with in *cr* so variable costs, *vc1*, and the new net operating income, *noi1*, are a function of *collected* rent (*egi*).

$$vc1 = 100\left(1 - e^{-.025\,cr}\right) + mgt\,cr \qquad (11.18)$$

$$noi1 = 1 - 100\left(1 - e^{-0.025\left(1+sr-\alpha^{sr\,\beta}\right)}\right) - fc + sr - \alpha^{sr\,\beta} - mgt\left(1 + sr - \alpha^{sr\,\beta}\right) \qquad (11.19)$$

Plotting, we see that optimal net operating income is again achieved at the same scheduled rent.

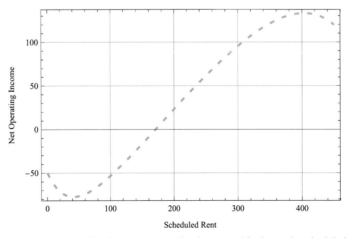

Figure 11.12. Plot of new net operating income with change in scheduled rent

Optimal rent (the same $402.94) and the owner's net operating income at that rent is computed to show owner's *noi* is also positive.

```
sr_noi1max = FindRoot[Evaluate[∂_sr (noi1 /.d6) == 0], {sr, 400}][[1]]
(noi1 /. sr_noi1max) /. d6
```

sr → 402.94

132.919

The importance of this exercise is to place both the owner and the manager problems at the same rent level set by tenants who demand space. Plotting Equations 11.16, 11.18 and 11.19 on the same graph in Figure 11.13 combines the perspectives to show collected rent, the manager's net profit and the owners net operating income all optimized when scheduled rent is $402.94.

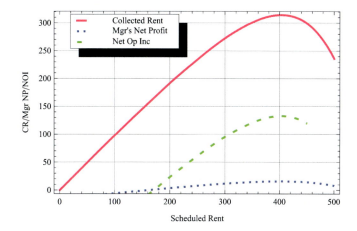

Figure 11.13. Combined plots of collected rent, manager's profit and owner's net income with change in scheduled rent

But there is a problem. Recall that we solved Equation 11.7 using data **d3** to conclude that the optimal number of locations is 15. But using data **d5** to produce the plot above from Equation 11.17 we had to restrict the number of locations to 3 for profit to be positive. In a plot of *np3* using data **d7** in which the location parameter is set at the optimal 15, Figure 11.14 shows us that the manager does, indeed, maximize his net profit at the optimal rent but at no scheduled rent are profits positive. In fact, for this model, management is unprofitable at any number of locations above 3. Under these conditions the manager and the owner *cannot simultaneously optimize their respective net incomes under the incentive framework currently in use by the industry.*

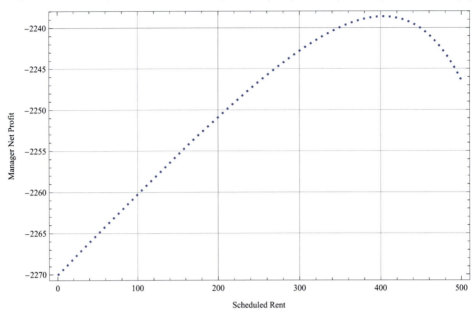

Figure 11.14. Manager's net profit when locations = 15

To justify management of small properties in many locations one must either combine it with the rewards of ownership or management efforts must complement and enhance income from other sources. Indeed, management is sometimes merely an accommodation brokers offer owners. Responsible real estate professionals who do both are careful to maintain a separation between the two activities to prevent the kinds of conflicts discussed above.

11.6. Data issues

This chapter leads to a bleak conclusion, something we might loosely call the Impossibility Theorem of small investment property management. An earlier sage remarked "If you want something done right, do it yourself". One asks, Is there no middle ground? Perhaps there is and perhaps data can assist. The key is to manage the manager. The owner must institute supervision policies to keep the manager alert and aware of his duties and the owner's objectives. One method of supervision is monitor utility consumption.

A building occupied by residential tenants is usually plumbed such that the owner pays for water consumption. Such a utility can be used as a canary in the mine shaft. Tracking water consumption and noticing when it changes is an early warning of the need for owner inquiry. Most municipalities render a water bill showing the prior and current meter reading used to compute the charge for the time period. The meter measures gallons or hundreds of cubic feet (742 gallons - 1 HCF). Some owners have the water bill sent to them rather than to the manager, giving the owner the earliest opportunity to receive and use the information.

Water consumption should follow some sort of distribution. In this case the assumption that it is normal is reasonable. Thus the standard z table can be used as the red flag. High z-score readings mean an observation far from the mean and therefore unlikely. When a high z-score occurs the owner should look into the matter to see if additional non-permitted occupants have moved in, excess lawn irrigation is taking place, the tenants have started a car washing business or there is a leak in the building. While not a sure thing, the change in water consumption indicates that some sort of change has taken place at the site. Such changes should be of interest to the alert owner and may not (although one can argue that they should) come to the attention of the manager.

We use a database of actual water consumption on a small residential property over approximately twelve years. In each record the first element is the meter reading for hundreds of cubic feet consumed and the second is the number of days between meter readings. It is sometimes easier to think in terms of gallons per day, a simple conversion.

The mean (451.805) and standard deviation (228.941) of gallons consumed per day give us some idea of what to expect. If the data are distributed normally, 95% of all observations should be within 1.645 standard deviations of the mean (we only care about one tail). Those above that should be considered 'suspicious'. So, consumption in excess of 828.41 gallons per day should be considered not normal. In 70 meter readings, 9 exceed 828.41 gallons per day and should be investigated.

Suspicious meter readings

844.516
872.667
851.569
1044.620
880.710
978.154
965.161
914.222
1019.010

Picking out the "spikes" in the series, we see the 9 occasions upon which the owner should have made a personal inspection to determine why the water consumption for that period was above the critical value.

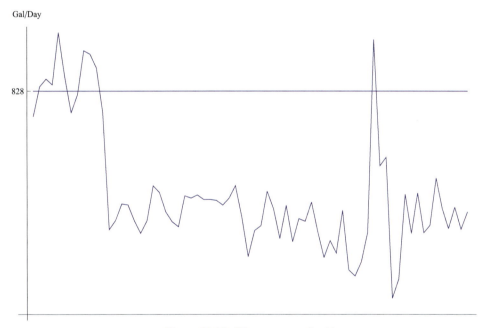

Figure 11.15. Water consumption history

11.7. Conclusion

To place the subject in the positive, as building size increases the compensation available for managers increases and the possibility of retaining capable people rises because they are more highly compensated. Also, larger properties and portfolios of large properties often attract managers who understand complex compensation arrangements. An obvious solution to the conflict described in our model is to make the manager's compensation dependent on net rather than gross income. By industry convention, this procedure is uncommon for small properties. One reason for this might be that the owners of these properties have non-uniform maintenance procedures making managers unwilling to base their compensation on something that is out of their control. Or, it may be that small property management is simply not very lucrative so the added expense of administrating complex compensation arrangements is just not justified. Regardless, the smaller the property, the more likely the compensation will be a percentage of collected rent and incentive arrangements will be inefficient.

The successful Tier II investor is a hands-on owner. If he is not there is reason to suspect his tenure will be short. In addition to the perverse incentives described in the model some brokers use their management (or lack of it) to obtain listings on properties. Real estate brokerage is often more profitable than management and brokers find that if they have control of the management of the property they can influence or participate in sales when the owner becomes frustrated with the process. Unscrupulous managers may manipulate the situation to steer the owner toward a sale in order to claim a brokerage commission. To eliminate this temptation, the astute Tier II investor who does use a management firm may wish to delete the standard clause in many management agreements that calls for the manager to be the broker or be paid a commission in the event the owner wishes to sell. Separate from the incentive problem, one can make an argument that the skill sets required to be an excellent manager and those required to be an excellent broker are quite different. The two are different specialties, having very different compensation arrangements and attracting very different kind of people. One wonders if it is likely that someone who is a good property manager is also a good broker. Surely such people exist but it seems they might be in the minority.

Finally, one must consider who has the greatest incentive to see that all goes well. Returning to "the building as the firm" metaphor, the owner's compensation is the residual claim to whatever remains after all others have been satisfied. It is the owner who has the global view of his objectives, the market and his property. Ultimately, he is the manager regardless of who he hires to execute specific tasks.

In real property ownership the buck stops at the owner. Denying this is folly.

Endnotes

[1] This is not to say that larger buildings do not produce more net profit, something clearly evident from the plot in Figure 11-4. The plot shows that for all sized buildings, given that they are all the same as they are in our stylized example, the optimum number of locations is 15. The effect is more pronounced in larger buildings.

[2] There is an even more perverse incentive in some management contracts that pay the manager a fixed fee when tenants turnover. The problems this engenders are too obvious to address at any length here.

[3] To keep the profit positive in the rent range for our example it is necessary to constrain locations to 3, and accounting costs to 10. More about this later.

References

Institute of Real Estate Management. (1991). <u>Principles of Real Estate Management</u>. Chicago, IL: Institute of Real Estate Management.

Jensen, M. C., & Meckling, W. H. (1976). Theory of the Firm: Managerial Behavior, Agency Costs and Ownership Structure. <u>Journal of Financial Economics, 3</u>, 305-360.

Wei, J. (1975). Least Square Fitting of an Elephant. CHEMTECH, 5(2), 128-129.

Problems

1. Using Equation 11.8 compute the optimal locations when d = 1.4
2. Using the format of Table 11.1 create a dataset with different variables and compute the owner and the manager's separate optimal scheduled rent. How does your result differ from those shown in this chapter? To what do you attribute the difference?

Appendix: A caution on the use of data to construct theories

The model in this chapter has some deficiencies. This Appendix is designed to propose a correction but at the same time make a point about how far one may go to mathematically model a process.

Making vacancy and rental rates reasonable

Recall that we complained of the requirement to have either unrealistic vacancy rates or unrealistic scheduled rent, at least on a per unit basis. Let's see what it takes to repair this problem.

Defining a new function for collected rent, *crOpt*, one can use Equation 11.20 and its derivative Equation 11.21 to demonstrate optimum rent at a so-called "market vacancy rate". This involves fixing a value for α and finding roots for the remaining variables, β and scheduled rent. Below is an example of the sort of thing one can do, however ill-advised, with *Mathematica*.

$$crOpt = sr + 1 - \alpha^{(\beta\, sr)^6} \tag{11.20}$$

$$\frac{\partial\, crOpt}{\partial\, sr} = 1 - 6\, sr^5\, \alpha^{sr^6 \beta^6}\, \beta^6\, Log[\alpha] \tag{11.21}$$

Fixing $\alpha = 1.3$, at 5% vacancy we have optimal scheduled rent at just under $500 per month.

Optimal scheduled rent at 5% vacancy is $469.21

Figure 11.16 shows how the 95% occupancy line intersects the crOpt function at its apex under these conditions.

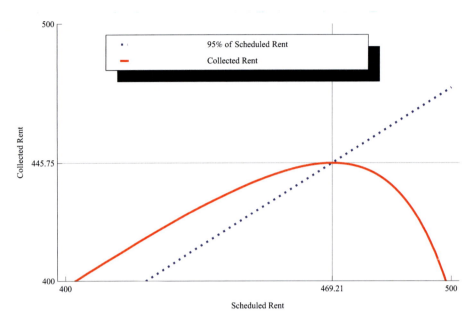

Figure 11.16. Optimized collected rent with a 6th order function for vacancy

The procedure above requires a sixth order function, something unlikely to exist in nature. The interaction of market forces that produce market vacancy is a complex process. Our purpose was not to solve a general equilibrium problem for the housing market here. Thus, hearing Sir Occam sharpening his razor in the background, we assert without proof that empirical results elsewhere indicate that scheduled rent is optimized in the area where vacancy is around 5% and return to the model in the chapter.

The model to end all models

We have made the point on several occasions that one can get in trouble with simplifying assumptions. Examples include: assuming that there is a linear relationship between variables or that data are distributed normally. At the other extreme, one must be careful not to overcomplicate. *Mathematica* is often the perfect tool to explain a complex process but one may, while not taxing *Mathematica* in the least, still strain credulity. One must exercise care in "back-fitting" a pet theory to data. In the hands of one who is inclined to "prove anything with numbers" *Mathematica* is a powerful and perhaps dangerous tool.

Suppose we are presented with the 27 observations of paired data in Table 11.2 representing as the first element in each pair the predictions of market returns made by economists; and as the second element the actual outcomes.

Predicted	Actual
0.0509461	0.282387
0.0727802	0.449782
0.131004	0.503639
0.343523	0.521106
0.537118	0.508006
0.710335	0.475983
0.826783	0.490539
0.921397	0.474527
0.967977	0.393013
0.959243	0.152838
0.935953	0.151383
0.922853	0.305677
0.921397	0.224163
0.908297	0.259098
0.845706	0.279476
0.815138	0.317322
0.809316	0.0320233
0.714702	0.0320233
0.694323	0.213974
0.57933	0.212518
0.286754	0.253275
0.215429	0.200873
0.174672	0.0349345
0.0873362	0.0393013
0.0917031	0.270742
0.0800582	0.379913
0.0509461	0.283843

Table 11.2. Economists' prediction and actual realizations

We wonder if there is a correlation and calculate the Person correlation to get -0.0368665. The correlation appears non-existent. How can this be? There must be SOME relationship between what economists say and what happens. Undaunted, we plot the data. LO AND BEHOLD!! What do we see in Figure 11.17? A PATTERN!!

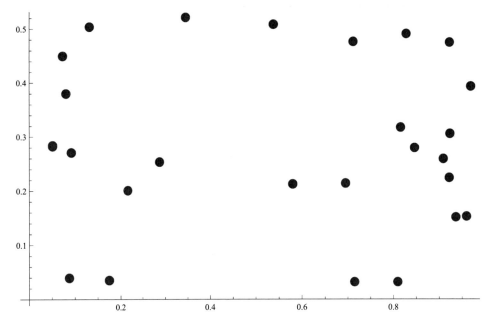

Figure 11.17. Plot of economists' prediction and actual outcomes.

We wish heartily that our data support a "theory" that there is some functional relationship between what economists say and what actually happens.

Mathematica is equal to the task. The Interpolation function fits polynomial curves between successive data points. A table is then created that increases the number of points, all equally spaced. The choice of InterpolationOrder = 1 avoids filtering by the Interpolation process and ensures that all the new points fall on the lines created by connecting the original points.

In Figure 11.18 we can plot these new points (the left) and connect them (the right) to better see the pattern in the data.

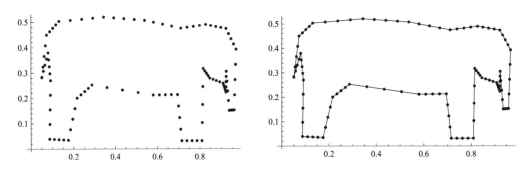

Figure 11.18. A more fine-grained look at economists' prediction and actual outcomes

James Wei (1975) observed that there is a least square Fourier sine series that will fit these coordinates, the equations for which are

$$x(t) = a_o + \sum_i a_i \sin \frac{it\pi}{36} \tag{11.22}$$

$$y(t) = b_o + \sum_i b_i \sin \frac{it\pi}{36} \tag{11.23}$$

Professor Wei claimed that the minimum number of terms in the Fourier expansion was 30. *Mathematica* makes this quite easy.

The question becomes one of finding a sufficient number of terms, beginning with an offset term, a_o, the remainder each with a constant coefficient, to create a shape that fits the data. In the *Mathematica* statement below we test with five and find that the fit of the data to our model is not too impressive...

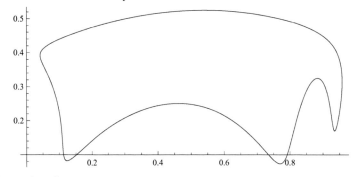

...but 9 terms is an improvement...

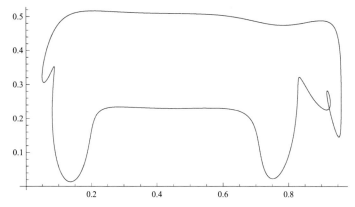

...and fifteen makes the fit a very close one.

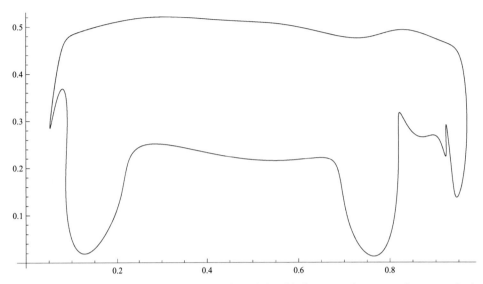

The conclusion is that there is a 15 term Fourier sine series relationship between what economists say and what actually happens! Or, more likely, the correlation value generated at the outset tells a simpler, more accurate (if less flattering to economists) story - there is no relationship between the two variables.

As Professor Wei's elephant had an eye, it is only fair to add the five more points to improve our elephant's vision if not appearance. Figure 11.19 lets you "elephant walk" through the number of points required. The message becomes: If you want this elephant to have feathers, *Mathematica* can include them in the fit. Have you have found a theory in your data? No. Is your client impressed? Perhaps, if your client is Disney Studios.

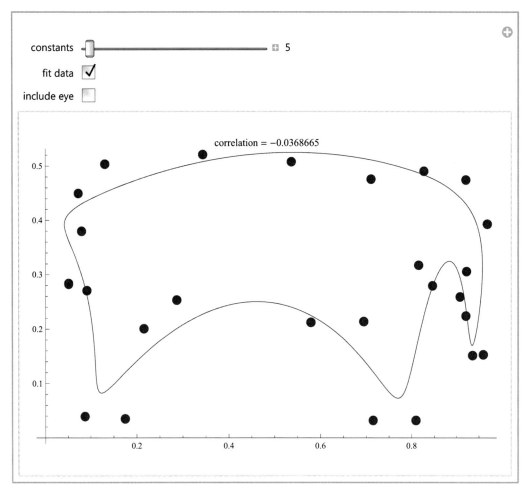

Figure 11.19. How many constants do you *really* need to fit an elephant?

12

The Lender's Dilemma

"Neither a borrower nor a lender be."

Polonius giving advice to his son Laertes in Hamlet Act 1, Scene 3

12.1. Introduction

In the typical real estate acquisition the lender often has more money in the property than the borrower. Hence, the Golden Rule,[1] gives the lender a say in various aspects of the investment.

In this chapter we will:

- Discuss different lender appraisal techniques and how they can affect buyers and the transaction;
- Examine due diligence standards for various property sizes;
- Develop the beginnings of a Bubble Theory based on the connection between the loan-to-value ratio (*ltv*), the debt coverage ratio (*dcr*) and the capitalization rate; and
- Explore how data on capitalization rate trends can guide lenders and borrowers to better decisions.

12.1.1. Lenders and their rules

The lender influences the transaction in the way he grants the loan on the property. The buyer's interest in the property at any given price is often dependent on certain loan terms. When the loan terms change the buyer's interest in purchasing the property changes, which can lead to a price change.

Included in the lender's offer is a particular loan amount. This can be based on a percentage of the property's value, the loan-to-value (*ltv*) ratio, or on the basis of how much the property's income exceeds the payments on the loan, the debt coverage ratio (*dcr*).

We mentioned these two lender rules of thumb in Chapter 3 but left until now a close examination of them. These two are risk management tools. There is nothing mysterious or particularly difficult about these rules. Like the other rules of thumb, they are simple linear relationships. What is interesting is how they relate to each other and what happens in the market as the lender moves from one to the other.[2]

Work in this chapter involves considerable manipulation of industry standard loan amortization equations. While mathematically trivial, there is considerable tedium involved which can be relieved in a number of ways. As of version 8 *Mathematica* provides functions which perform all the computations of standard Ellwood tables that are programmed into Excel or any financial calculator.[3]

We will rely on these heavily as we have elsewhere in this book and keep unnecessary minutiae as much in the background as possible

12.2. Appraisal techniques

The lender typically requires the buyer to furnish an appraisal or completes an appraisal in-house. The decision to grant the loan, how much loan to offer and the terms of the loan are all dependent on this appraisal. Appraisal standards have evolved over many years. To provide background and context we will focus on two of these standards and how they apply to the income approach to value.

12.2.1. The capitalization rate approach vs. the mortgage equity approach

The traditional, older, capitalization rate appraisal approach values the property as a whole, as if purchased by the investor for cash, free and clear of debt. It ignores the effect of debt financing.

The mortgage-equity approach parallels discounted cash flow analysis (DCF) dealt with in Chapter 4, valuing the equity separate from the debt then adding the two together to arrive at the value of the entire property. A significant benefit of the more modern mortgage-equity approach is that it explicitly allows for variation in future income. Through the multi-period cash flow model an appraiser can model variation in the cash flows due to variation in the economic forecast. This represents an improvement because it overcomes one of the three bad assumptions of cap rate mentioned in Chapter 3, the assumption that income never changes.

Borrowing money to purchase investment realty has the potential to confer two benefits on the buyer:

1. If the interest rate on the loan is less than the capitalization rate the borrower enjoys positive financial leverage in the form of cash flow in excess of debt service; and
2. If the owner experiences a period of inflation unanticipated by the lender (especially if the loan is granted at a fixed rate of interest) he will reap leveraged equity growth as the appreciation of the entire property value is credited to his equity.

Of course, these benefits come at the expense of risk because leverage magnifies both profits and losses.

The choice of how much debt to use often discloses a difference of opinion between borrowers and lenders about inflation expectations. When borrowers view inflation expectations differently than lenders they place a different value on the property. This results, given fixed *noi*, in borrower capitalization rates differing from lender capitalization rates.

Some rearranging of the identities for *ltv*, *dcr* and value will convince you that market value may be represented as either of the two identities in equation (12.1)

$$\frac{noi}{cr} = mv = \frac{noi}{12 * constant * dcr * ltv} \qquad (12.1)$$

Where "*constant*" is the ratio of monthly installment payments required on the loan to the loan balance.

Setting the two expressions for *mv* equal to each other and solving for *cr* produces equation (12.2).

$$cr = 12 * const * dcr * ltv \qquad (12.2)$$

Although lenders have some say in setting interest rates, due to competition and the influence of the Federal Reserve Bank, the lender's discretion is across such a narrow range that it may be ignored for our purposes. Thus, using an amortization period of 360 months and exogenously determined interest rates, we assume that the choice of constant is essentially out of the control of the parties to the loan contract. (This is not to preclude the borrower from electing a shorter amortization term to retire debt faster, something he can do without agreeing to a shorter loan provided prepayment is allowed.)

We pointed out in Chapter 3 that, if one does not model individual cash flows separately as part of an economic forecast, discounted cash flow analysis adds nothing of value to capitalization rate. Indeed, a primary benefit of using DCF analysis is to be able to vary cash flows as part of arriving at value. The lender that fixes *both* the *ltv* and the *dcr* is in effect dictating the use of capitalization rate

to the buyer. Two important consequences follow:
1. It forces the buyer to use an inferior valuation tool; and
2. It requires that the buyer to accept the lender's inflation expectations.

12.2.2. The lender's perspective

To illustrate we will analyze a sale of a property that has been arranged at a price of $1,000,000. The property has $100,000 of net operating income, thus the buyer's capitalization rate is 10%. The buyer requires an 80% loan to complete the transaction.

Assume that 30 year loans are available at 8% interest. The monthly loan constant is 0.007338

The lender's underwriting policy provides that the loan may not exceed 80% of appraised value (ltv = .8) and net income must exceed debt service by 50% (dcr = 1.5). These are admittedly stringent standards to make our point.

Using the right side of equation (12.1) we find that the lender's value is $946,413.15, which is below the buyer's value. Thus, the lender places a higher capitalization rate on the property of 0.105662. So the loan approved of $757,130.52 satisfies both the ltv and the dcr requirement, but is insufficient for the buyer's needs, falling short by $53,586.85. This is because the lender employs a valuation technique that depends on annual noi, the constant, and BOTH a fixed pre-determined dcr and ltv. The lender's cap rate produces a different value than the buyer agreed to pay and that difference can be significant. In this case it is 5.359% less than the borrower thinks the property is worth.

12.2.3. The borrower's perspective

The buyer's approach to value is different. By agreeing to pay $1,000,000 for the property and to borrow $800,000 at market rates and terms, the borrower is saying that the equity is worth $200,000 *to him*. Thus, he has examined the present and anticipated cash flows in light of his chosen discount rate and, *after considering payments on an $800,000 loan*, makes the following calculation using Equation 3.9 from Chapter 3.

$$200\,000 = \sum_{n=1}^{t} \frac{atcf_n}{(1+d)^n} + \frac{ater_t}{(1+d)^t}$$

The connection between the difference in the parties' opinion of value and the differences in their inflation expectations is found in their differing opinions of g in Equation 3.12 of Chapter 3.

Regardless, the lender's capitalization rate, produced by his fixed *ltv and dcr*, is higher than the buyer's. The lender believes that the buyer has over-valued the property. Assuming both are rational and in possession of the same information set regarding the current business climate, which is correct?

Only time will answer this question. In order for the parties to agree to disagree and continue in the loan transaction something has to give.

The lender may either:

1. Decline the loan. If there are other, less restrictive, lenders in the market who can attract this loan the borrower goes elsewhere, or
2. Relax one, either *ltv* or *dcr*, of his underwriting standards in order to acquire this loan.

If this is a desirable loan to a qualified borrower the second alternative is preferable. Over time the quality of the lender's portfolio is influenced by the quality of borrowers he attracts. Better qualified borrowers use modern valuation techniques that attempt to forecast changing income over time. The converse, if one believes that lower quality buyers use outmoded valuation techniques, is that over time the lender who fixes both *ltv* and *dcr* suffers from adverse selection as his loan underwriting standards attract weaker borrowers.

Thus, in order to use a mortgage-equity appraisal method for lending decisions that aligns with the borrower's use of discounted cash flow analysis for purchasing decisions, either *ltv* or *dcr* must be allowed to vary.

What remains are the questions of whether the borrower is better qualified to make a forecast or if his forecasts are better than the lender's. There is also the matter of which loan standard to allow to vary. It is to those critical questions that we turn next.

12.3. Irrational exuberance and the madness of crowds

Let's step back a moment and consider the lender's concern that the buyer is overpaying. Suppose that for a period of time buyers gradually abandon the use of better analysis tools in favor of short cuts. This sort of behavior is met with lender restraint, a sort of benign paternalism. The manifestation of that restraint is in the lender's choice of underwriting tool.

Acquisition standards and criteria for Tier I and Tier III property differ as much as the participants in these two markets. The level of due diligence, analysis techniques, appraisal standards and negotiating prowess all increase with a move from the one-to-four unit Tier I property to institutional grade property. Hence, due diligence might be a function of property size. If we restrict our argument to the these extremes, a graph of this claim looks like Figure 12.1.

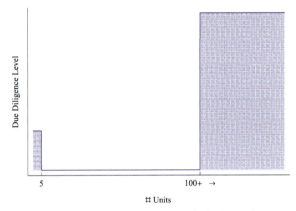

Figure 12.1. Due Diligence in the Tier I and Tier III markets

The focus of this book is on the property in the middle, Tier II property. One wonders if the move in sophistication is continuous across all sized properties. Thus, retaining the Tier concept but concentrating on Tier II, we ask if due diligence increases continuously with size? If so, Tier I represents a minimum level of due diligence and Tier III the maximum. If we claim that due diligence quality is linear in size one would expect an increase in due diligence across Tier II as property size increases, as shown in Figure 12.2:

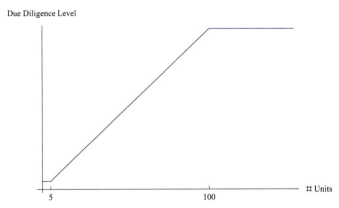

Figure 12.2. Tier II constantly increasing due diligence by size

Figure 12.2 illustrates a "static" model, a snapshot of reality at any given moment. Whatever we believe about how investors approach the acquisition process, it is likely that such a process changes over time. Thus, it is a dynamic process. The acquisition standards of 2002 are probably not the same as those of 2012. Acquisition standards themselves should be viewed as cyclical, responding to changes in the surrounding environment.

Investors in a hurry resort to rules of thumb (ROT) to quickly evaluate whether a property is worth a closer look. The use of a rule of thumb *for acquisition* is a different matter. It represents a reduced level of due diligence over more sophisticated methods such as discounted cash flow techniques. The Tier I market rarely uses DCF, more often using the rule of thumb known as gross rent multiplier (*grm*). At the lowest size of Tier I, the single-family rental, value is perhaps, say, 100 times its monthly rent. Some apply that to duplexes, triplexes and four-plexes. Somewhere along the line monthly *grm* is abandoned in favor of annual *grm*. This is hardly a rise in sophistication because the annual *grm* is just the monthly *grm* divided by 12. Few, if any, Tier III acquisitions are made on the basis of *grm*. The question is: at what size property do *grm*s drop out completely in favor of DCF and other sophisticated methods? Is it 20 units? 50 units? 90 units? Also, wherever the drop-out point, does the drop-out point change at different times in different markets? Perhaps most importantly, why does it change?

In very strong seller's markets an often asked but seldom answered question is: When will it end? Or, where is the top? One way to approach that question is to ask when do the simple rules of thumb measures that *shouldn't* be relied upon for decision-making creep into the larger buildings populated by what should be the more sophisticated investors? A 20 unit building made up of 2 BR units renting for $1,000 per month, sold for $100,000 per unit, is purchased at the 100 times gross monthly income rule that once applied to houses. What that says is that the housing consumer is paying the same in rent-to-benefit terms for an apartment as he once paid to rent a house. Apartments don't have yards, apartment renters have to share walls with neighbors who may not be good neighbors. The question of "How high is up?" becomes more urgent when house economics, ratios and standards begin to drive investment decisions.

An interesting empirical question might ask if there is a relationship between the top of the market and a time when rules of thumb dominate appraisal and acquisition standards at the larger property levels? Figure 12.3 illustrates such an idea.

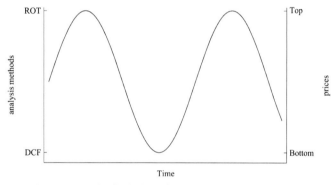

Figure 12.3. Cyclical view of due diligence methods

The essence of the rules of thumb is to impound future events implicitly into one simple measure, a kind of short cut. By contrast, the central value of forward projection methods is to allow the analyst to *explicitly* consider the effect of changing future events on the expected outcome. Departing from more complete methods in favor of the rules of thumb basically says either "I don't care what the future brings" or "The future will be just like the present". These sentiments are usually counterproductive over the long run.

This is the converse of the problem we had when examining the lender's and the buyer's perspective earlier. Then the borrower was negotiating with the lender to allow an underwriting restriction to vary in order to improve both parties' analysis and decision making. In the present case the lender finds his borrowers failing to use or failing to appreciate the value of forward projection methods. His reaction, to impose restraint on what he sees as irrational exuberance, is to modify his loan underwriting standards. This does not necessarily mean that he fixes both *ltv* and *dcr* (although that can be the case), rather it means he choose wisely between them.

To get to the bottom of this we return to the earlier comment that the lender and borrower disagree on *g* in Equation 3.12. In Chapter 7 we mentioned the three-way relationship between capitalization rates, interest rates and inflation. When inflation expectations increase interest rates rise as lenders build inflation expectations into their rates. Since capitalization rates include the cost of funds (interest rates), one would expect capitalization rates to increase also. That this is not always true is an anomaly. Buyers of income property, anticipating higher future income, bid up prices causing capitalization rates to *fall*. Tension is created by this anomaly because everyone knows that it cannot continue forever. Price inflation traceable to this anomaly introduces concern about a bubble in the market. Much has been written about the difference between expected and unexpected inflation. Our interest is about how two parties to a transaction behave when their separate opinions differ in these areas.

12.4. Bubble theory - How high is up?

Markets are cyclical. It is widely accepted that timing is everything. Easy to say and hard to implement, knowing when to get out is very often the key to investment success. If we accept the argument of the prior section that rules of thumb, as decision tools, dominate as the market approaches a peak, we can take advantage of that to examine the interaction of these rules with an eye toward discovering if and when the lender-borrower difference of opinion about the future suggests the market has gone as high as it can be expected to.

Lenders operate as a sort of governor, acting out the unpopular role of guarding the punch bowl, adding just enough joy juice (easy credit) to keep the party interesting but not enough to allow it to become unruly. This restriction manifests itself as lender underwriting moves from loan-to-value ratio to debt coverage ratio.

12.4.1. Positive leverage

To further develop this story we need to look closely at the idea of positive leverage. This is simply the "buy-low-sell-high" maxim at work in financing terms. One hopes to borrow money at one rate and re-invest it at a higher rate. Indeed if this is not accomplished, the long run outcome is as disastrous as a policy of buy-high-sell-low.

The expression of positive leverage has two versions:

- For some, positive leverage occurs when the capitalization rate exceeds the interest rate; alternatively
- Positive leverage means that the capitalization rate exceeds all debt service including principal payments.

We will have to choose between these eventually but a short review of why each has merit is useful.

The first version is appropriate in cases where the loan contract requires only interest payments or if one wishes to compare pure yield rates. It also offers the benefit of simplicity, allowing us to work with annual rates and not have to deal with monthly amortization.

The second version is more appealing to lenders interested in knowing that the property generates enough net income to meet all its obligations. In the interest of realism and to accommodate the investor-lender conflict we will gravitate toward this second version. The loan constant is the division of the loan payment by the loan balance. This number only remains truly constant in the case of "interest only" financing. In the case of self-amortizing debt it changes with each payment, offering the bizarre result of not being constant at all. Because our story will unfold using only first year measures, we will deal only with the <u>initial</u> loan constant, meaning the initial loan payment divided by the initial balance.

We make three further simplifying assumptions to facilitate the discussion.

First, we will assume away tax consequences and deal with only pre-tax measures. This is justified for a variety of reasons. Investors purchasing even moderately sized real estate usually must have substantial financial resources making them eligible for the higher - and flat - income tax brackets. Investors are thus presumed to have substantially similar after-tax motives. Also, since tax returns are confidential, as we have noted earlier, tax benefits are not observable so empirical verification of after-tax results is essentially unavailable.

Second, we will momentarily assume away principal payment, using the interest-only version of positive leverage. This simplification is easily dropped later. We begin this way in order to keep the equation as simple as possible. The preponderance of debt service in the first year goes to interest. So the effect of principal payments on first year cash flow is minimal and may be ignored at the outset.

Third we assume that interest rates, at least for the first year, are fixed.

The simplest expression of pre-tax cash-on-cash return is the division of before tax cash flow (*btcf*) by the equity down payment as shown in Equation 12.3.

$$\text{simple } cc = \frac{btcf}{equity} \quad (12.3)$$

Recalling that value = $\frac{noi}{cr}$ and $btcf = noi$ - debt service, the numerator of Equation 12.3 can be expressed in terms of *noi*, cap rate, loan-to-value ratio and interest rate. The denominator can also be expressed with the same terms omitting the interest rate, creating Equation 12.4 By ignoring principal payment at this stage, *i* indicates that the debt service (the constant) is merely the interest rate.

$$\text{simple } cc = \frac{noi - \left(\frac{noi}{cr} ltv\, i\right)}{\frac{noi}{cr}(1 - ltv)} \quad (12.4)$$

We rearrange Equation 12.4 to obtain Equation 12.5 in which *noi* cancels out.

$$simplecc = \frac{btcf}{equity} = \frac{noi - \left(\frac{noi}{cr} ltv\, i\right)}{\frac{noi}{cr}(1 - ltv)} = \frac{i*ltv - cr}{ltv - 1} \quad (12.5)$$

Let's look at the classic benefit of positive leverage. Using plausible, so-called "normal market" numbers (ltv = 75%, cap rate = 9%, interest rate = 8%) in which investors enjoy positive leverage with a "normal" spread we compute the simple cash-on-cash return, "*simplecc*":

simplecc /. {ltv → .75, i → .08, cr → .09}

0.12

Note that these equations are devoid of a variable for appreciation. To this point one obtains enough return in the capitalization rate to service debt and have funds left over in the first year to reward down payment capital in double digits without any appreciation assumption. The *simplecc* rate above becomes 12% because one earns 9% on the down payment equity which represents 25% of the total investment PLUS a 1% "override" on reinvesting the lender's funds (which represent 75% of the total investment). As the lender's money is exactly 3 times the borrower's that 1% override is multiplied three times and added to the 9% the investor received on his equity for a total of 12%.

As our interest is in price bubbles, let's see what happens to positive leverage as prices rise. When capitalization rates drop to the point where they equal interest rates the override is eliminated.

simplecc /. {ltv → .75, i → .08, cr → .08}

0.08

As leverage is now "breakeven", the investor receives a cash-on-cash return equal to the capitalization rate with no "override". There is no first year benefit from leverage under these conditions. Investors must look elsewhere to justify borrowing. That elsewhere is future appreciation in value.

Before continuing we will complicate Equation 12.5 to introduce the reality of monthly payments and principal amortization into the story. Most real estate loans amortize, most real estate lenders use the full principal and interest payment in their *dcr* computations, and borrowers calculate before tax cash flow using all lender payments in the debt service part of the equation. To accommodate these realities we must replace interest (*i*) with debt service (*ds*). Debt service involves not only the interest rate (*i*) but a second variable, term (*t*). The equation for the amount required to retire a $1 loan produces the constant. As most real estate loans are based on 30 year amortization with monthly payments, we will use $t = 360$ as the number of months in the debt service for Equation 12.6

$$ds = 12\left(\frac{i}{1 - \frac{1}{(1+i)^{360}}}\right) \tag{12.6}$$

Substituting debt service (*ds*) for interest rate (*i*) in Equation 12.5 and rearranging, we obtain Equation 12.7 noting that *noi* has once again canceled out. This equation expresses cash-on-cash return, "*cc*", for an investment using amortizing debt.

$$cc := \frac{cr\left(1 - \frac{12\,i\,ltv}{cr\left(1 - \frac{1}{(1+i)^{360}}\right)}\right)}{1 - ltv} \tag{12.7}$$

Using the same plausible inputs from our first example with positive leverage, we can again compute a cash-on-cash return. Note two differences from the *simplecc*. First we must input the interest rate as a monthly variable because the *ds* calculation computes monthly payments and multiplies them by 12 to arrive at the annual debt service. Second, because of the reduction of cash flow due to principal payments, the *cc* result we obtain is smaller.[4]

```
cc /. {ltv → .75, i → .08 / 12, cr → .09}

0.0958448
```

Figure 12.4, a three dimensional plot of our *cc* function with debt service in place of interest rate, illustrates the obvious, which is that cash-on-cash returns rise as debt service, a function of interest rates, falls and capitalization rates rise. Note the negative cash on cash outcomes below the intersection with the zero cash on cash plane in the front right quadrant.

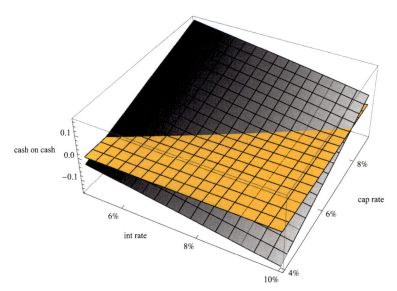

Figure 12.4. Cash-on-cash return as a function of capitalization and interest rates

Obvious as the above may seem, it leads us to an important and useful observation. The lender's *dcr* is about whether and by how much the property income exceeds the loan payments. The dollar amount of any excess is the same as the borrower's before tax cash flow.

12.4.2. The lender as governor

Assume that lenders' opinion of value lags those of borrowers'. As the difference widens, borrowers find that they apply for a loan that is 75% of the *purchase price* and get a loan that is 75% of the lender's *appraised value*, a loan amount that is, perhaps, only 70% of the purchase price.[5] If buyers still want to buy and sellers remain inflexible on price, demanding cash, buyers must add more down payment to make up the difference. Lagging appraised values indicate a *defacto* change in the lender's risk management strategy from *ltv* to *dcr*.

Why does the buyer make the concession of placing more of his own money in the deal despite the absence of a current year reward in the form of positive cash flow? What is it that the buyer is willing to pay for that the lender is unwilling to finance? This question is similar to asking why a buyer accepts breakeven leverage. He gives up the current year override in the expectation of future growth (*g*) in rent and value. In Equation 3.13 in Chapter 3 we concluded that introducing monotonic growth to the multi-period discounted cash flow method of valuation converged in the limit to Equation 12.8, using *noi* for *cf* in Equation 3.13.

$$v_s = \frac{noi}{d - g} \quad (12.8)$$

This merely redefines cap rate as the difference between the discount rate (*d*) the investor demanded and the growth rate (*g*) the investor expects will produce part of the return that the discount rate represents.[6]

The expectation of future growth explains why investors permit their down payments to rise as cash-on-cash returns fall. The introduction of *g* into the capitalization rate equation essentially impounds those out-year rewards into the computation of first year return. One might argue that making return dependent on higher cash flows *to be received in the future* looks more like speculation than investing.[7]

Lenders agree with this assessment and refuse to finance buyers' speculative behavior. Their reaction, as unofficial governors of the market, is to constrain loan amounts, thus the loan-to-sale price ratio, to those supported by past sales that they can actually see, not sales that *may* happen based on projected higher income that *may* be collected. Imperfect a restraint that it might be, this behavior represents the lenders' refusal to *fully participate* in a bubble economy. The term "fully participate" is carefully chosen. It may be that the immediate prior sales that the lender can see and does base its present loan on were part of the bubble. Also because of the pressure of deposit cost and the competition for loans some portion of the lender's portfolio is carried into at least the early stages of price euphoria. However, if sanity is to prevail, lenders, by lowering *ltv*s, avoid participating in the last expansion of the bubble. We name Equation 12.9 "ccg" for c̲ash-on-c̲ash with g̲rowth assumption", which after rearrangement and simplification bears some similarity to Equation 12.7.

$$ccg = \frac{(d - g)\left(1 - \frac{12\, i\, ltv}{(d-g)\left(1 - \frac{1}{(i+1)^{360}}\right)}\right)}{1 - ltv} \quad (12.9)$$

12.4.3. Resolving the conflict

Using Equation 12.9 we begin to see the connection between the borrower's cash-on-cash return and the lender's debt coverage ratio. Restating Equation 12.3 and expanding its numerator, we have

$$simple\ cc = \frac{noi - ds}{equity} \quad (12.10)$$

The lender's debt coverage ratio is:

$$dcr = \frac{noi}{ds} \quad (12.11)$$

Declining *ltv*s follow adjusting *dcr*s upward as the disagreement between lenders and borrowers widens over what the future holds. The lender's change from *ltv* to *dcr* as an underwriting tool affects how risk is distributed between the lender's senior claim and the borrower's subordinate claim. The investor/borrower is in the first lost position. When the bubble deflates (the slow movement of real estate means price bubbles don't often burst) the lender wants the buyer to take the loss.

It is not news when buyers/borrowers are more optimistic than lenders. Let us adopt 1.0 as the least stringent *dcr*, meaning that the property has exactly enough income to make its loan payments with nothing left over. We can define the lender's margin of safety, the extent to which *noi* exceeds the loan payments, as "excess *dcr*" in Equation 12.12:

$$\text{excess } dcr = dcr - 1 = \frac{noi}{ds} - 1 \geq 0 \quad (12.12)$$

When excess *dcr* is zero, *btcf* is zero and cash-on-cash return is zero. Investors partially, though reluctantly, concur with their lenders, accepting zero as the minimum cash-on-cash return. It is possible to accept the negative cash flow that comes with negative leverage but that is beyond the scope of our effort here (borrowers otherwise willing are often restrained from doing so by lenders prohibiting it as a condition of granting the loan). Again the words "partially concur" are carefully chosen. Borrowers express their disagreement with the lenders by increasing their equity investment. This is exactly what the lenders had in mind. If the borrowers are going to reap the benefit of higher future cash flows the borrowers should finance that risk (if the loan is at a fixed rate the lender receives none of the higher future income and even with variable interest rates the full benefit is usually not captured by the lender).

So, as *cc* and *excess dcr* are both pushed to zero any additional price increase must be financed by the buyer. With values rising and acquisition *noi* constant the dynamic that keeps *excess dcr* at zero is reduction of percentage of sales price represented by the loan amount. The top of the bubble asks: How much additional buyer equity investment is too much to support the seller's promise of growth in income?

At this point an uptick in interest rates, given the delicate balance of *excess dcr* and *cc* at zero, deflates the bubble. At low interest rates buyers feel that the expected growth portion of the discount rate is sufficient to justify their additional investment. If interest rates remain low, and if they actually increase income during their ownership they may find yet another buyer with even more optimism and even more cash, given lender constraints on *ltv*. This continues through the last "greater fool", the moment that interest rates rise, at which time the bubble deflates and the party is over.

12.4.4. Three 2D illustrations

Defining *xdcr* in Equation 12.13 we can create a series of illustrations of this phenomenon, each in two dimensions.

$$xdcr := \frac{(d-g)\left(1 - \frac{1}{(1+i)^{360}}\right)}{12\, i\, ltv} - 1 \quad (12.13)$$

Figure 12.5 shows plots of excess debt coverage ratio and cash on cash, each as a function of interest rates that range from 5% to 15%. Panel (a) uses two discount rates, 16% and 18%, but assumes that growth expectations are constant at 4%. An important point is near the origin where *xdcr* and *ccg* both approach zero and the difference in discount rates no longer matter. Panel (b) reflects two growth rates but assumes that discount rates are constant at 16%. Again, the two curves coincide close to the origin. Expected growth no longer matters at that point as neither lender nor investor have a margin for error. This suggests that the maximum expansion of the bubble is near. Panel (c) has constant discount rate (16%) and growth rate (4%) rates over the same range of interest rate change but with different loan to value ratios. Naturally, the lower *ltv* produces higher *xdcr*.

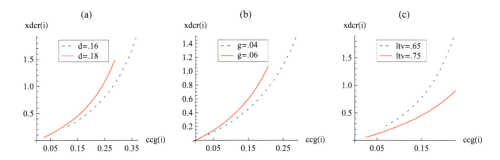

Figure 12.5. 2D illustrations of the lender-borrower conflict

12.4.5. A challenge in three dimensions

The advantage of two dimensional plots is that they are easy to interpret. Three dimensional parametric plots allow us to show more variables at the same time but are harder to interpret. This will frustrate some readers. But the world of investments is complex and often more than two variables are needed to explain a phenomenon. Straining to visualize what follows gives insight into how successful investors think. To prosper in business one must often keep many balls in the air at once. The graphics below, still limited to three dimensions, do only a portion of that but offer a significant increase over the limitations of two dimensions.

Figure 12.6 is a 3D plot showing the effect of rising interest on the both lender's and the investor's safety margin. Remember that, measured in dollars, the investor's *btcf* is exactly the same as the lender's excess debt coverage. What makes them seem different at first glance is the fact that they are usually expressed as rates. The investor scales his *btcf* against his equity investment and the lender scales his excess debt coverage against the property's income. Naturally, when interest rates are at their lowest, both investor and lender have comfortable margins. The highest (upper rear) corner in Figure 12.6 shows this happy condition. As interest rates rise (along the lower front edge of the "floor" of the graphic), margins of error are squeezed for both parties as values fall along the *ccg(i)* and *xdcr(i)* axes. Note that *ccg(i)* declines as you approach the upper left forward corner and *xdcr(i)* declines as you approach the lower left forward corner.

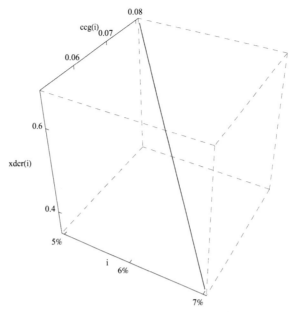

Figure 12.6. 3D parametric plot of *ccg(i)*, *xdcr(i)* and interest rate

One can take the plot of the diagonal line in Figure 12.6 and projects it onto the sides of the 3D "box" formed by joining the axes. Note that the box in Figure 12.7 is slightly larger than the one in Figure 12.6. For this reason the diagonal plot does not reach the corners in Figure 12.7. The scale of the labeled axes is the same in both graphics. With the addition of gridlines on the sides one can read the change in the parametric function with respect to pairs of variables. The best way to view it is to find three different origins and focus on the pairs of variable that form the plane for which that origin constitutes a corner.

1. The "floor" is the {*i*, *ccg(i)*} plane showing that as interest rates rise cash-on-cash with growth falls. (Move the *ccg(i)* tick marks straight down to the lower edge of the west wall and use the lower front left corner as the origin to visualize it.)
2. The "back wall" is the {*i*, *xdcr(i)*} plane showing that as interest rates rise excess debt coverage falls. (Move the both sets of tick marks straight back to the lower and left rear edges and use the lower rear left corner as the origin to visualize it.)
3. The "west wall", is the {*xdcr(i)*,*ccg(i)*} plane, shows how the two margins of error fall together. (If you are viewing this chapter as a CDF, rotate the graphic so that the upper left corner is as one normally sees Cartesian coordinates with the origin to the lower left. Note also that values on what is then the *x* axis are falling as you move away from the origin rather than rising as they are usually shown.)

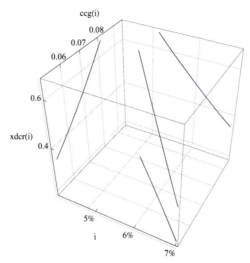

Figure 12.7. 3D parametric plot of *ccg(i)*, *xdcr(i)* and interest rate projected against the sides of the enclosure.

12.4.6. Endgame

Recall that Equation 12.13 has (*d* - *g*) in its numerator. But the difference between discount rate and growth, *d* - *g*, is just capitalization rate. Making that substitution creates Equation 12.14. This combines two named variables in to one to permit maximum use of 3D graphics in Figure 12.8.

$$xdcr1 = \frac{cr\left(1 - \frac{1}{(1+i)^{360}}\right)}{12 * i * ltv} - 1 \qquad (12.14)$$

Mathematica's 3D contour plot displays the surface implicitly defined by *xdcr1* = 0 (unless other contours are directed). The Shadow feature allows us to see a plane projected on the wall of the graphic's perimeter. In Figure 12.8 what are gridlines on 2D plots become "gridplanes". While the ticks are labeled on only one edge there are a total of four edges at which they might be placed preserving the same values. Thus, for instance the values for *ltv* (0.5,0.6,0.7,0.8) are at the top of the north wall in Figure 12.8 but could be at the lower rear edge where the floor meets the north wall. The shadows are projected onto only three walls assuming the source of light is perpendicular to the plane on which the shadow appears. Thus the only planes of interest are the west wall, the north wall and the floor. Gridlines also appear only on these three walls. By moving the ticks to the appropriate edge pairs of gridlines may be combined in three different ways. The combination of any adjoining pair of gridlines defines a plane of constant value of the remaining variable, which has its axis perpendicular to the plane.

Let's examine each of these three walls one at a time.

1. The projected shadow on the west wall shows the range of the values of *i* and *cr* as *ltv* moves through its specified range, all while *xdcr* = 0. We illustrate a reasonable range of capitalization rate as 0.06 to 0.11. The picture changes if the capitalization rate range changes. There is one and only one point in the west wall shadow for each possible value of *ltv*. We can view the side-by-side aggregation of *ltv*s as being opportunities for fewer or more transactions. No transactions are possible in the white areas, given the constraint that *xdcr* = 0 and the specified limits of *i*, *ltv* and *cr*. Of course, lenders are always happy to allow transactions to take place where *xdcr* > 0 but we assume buyers have pushed prices to the point where those transactions do not occur. In order to keep their down payments to a minimum while paying high prices, borrowers apply for the maximum loan allowed, one with a payment that fully exhausts *noi*. The shadow has the shape of a truncated triangle with the truncated end nearing the floor. The smaller area of the shadow nearer the floor shows lenders phasing themselves out of deals as interest rates rise and

capitalization rates fall because fewer values of *ltv* are possible in those ranges of interest and capitalization rates when *xdcr* is zero.

2. The same applies to the north wall where the shadow plot shows all the combinations of *ltv* and *cr* as *i* moves over its specified range. As the triangle narrows traveling west the number of possible transactions shrink with higher interest rates.

3. Finally, the floor shows all possible values of *i* and *ltv* as *cr* moves through it's specified range. While the same effect is happening in the westward direction, the smaller truncated end of the triangle on the floor takes on additional meaning when one recalls that $cr = d - g$. Here we get a clue to the possible breaking point.

Expanding our earlier question of how much added equity is too much, we now wonder about the composition of the last permissible capitalization rate? Is it weighted toward the discount rate (*d*) or growth (*g*)? While we cannot know the answer to this question, we can speculate that the limit of growth expectations has been reached. There is an upper limit to how high buyers believe the sky is. It would seem that the cost of capital influences that upper limit. During the last expansion of a bubble, buyer expectations are maintained solely by low interest rates.

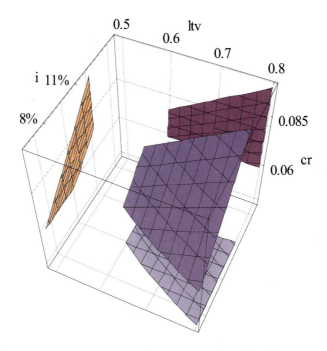

Figure 12.8. 3D contour plot of *ltv*, interest and capitalization rates

One observation to be made at this point is that the main plot in the center and all three projected triangles have truncated smaller ends (brought about by the way we have restricted the range of the variables). This means, for example, at the lowest (60%) *ltv* transactions can occur across a smaller range of lower capitalization and interest rates. We should emphasize that larger loans (with higher debt service) permit zero or greater cash flow if interest rates are low or capitalization rates are high. We rule out the latter because that implies falling prices, the opposite of what we observe in a bubble market. As prices rise one is moved to ask: Where is the compensation for the (ever higher) down payments funds?

Some experimentation with the ranges of the three variables in the plot (always keeping *xdcr* = 0) produces different shapes as one would expect.

This game ends when the variables are "tuned" such that the combination of *ltv*s, capitalization and interest rates are balanced on the only permissible *xdcr* = 0 point (the red point at the lower right corner of the center triangle in Figure 12.9) in such a way that transactions may only take place at that point. An increase in interest rates produces an impermissible drop in *xdcr* below zero that can only be avoided by an increase in capitalization rate. If net income does not change this means prices must fall.

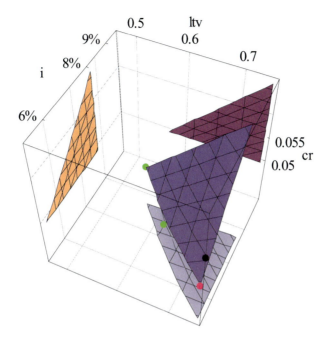

Figure 12.9. 3D contour plot where *xdcr* = 0

Significant negative leverage (higher interest rates at the same fixed capitalization rate as shown by the green points on the center triangle in Figure 12.9) may be accommodated by smaller *ltv*s. The consequence of this is that buyers put more of their own money into the acquisition *and* depend even more on rising values to offset that negative leverage and provide a long term positive overall return. By adding cash buyers neutralize lender restraint. The farthest extension of this is that buyers completely abandon debt financing altogether, purchasing property for all cash at values that do not relate to current income in any way. The green points represent the path to this unlikely outcome. At some point the buyers refuse to finance higher prices that implicitly require more speculative growth to support them.

With any rise in capitalization rate higher *ltv*s again become permissible at higher interest rates (black point on Figure 12.9). As prices fall the lender will continue to rely on *dcr* as his primary loan underwriting tool. Only when net income actually rises do lenders return to *ltv*. The lender uses *ltv* when increasing values offer the most protection; and uses *dcr* when net income offers the most protection. The lender's dilemma is in two parts. He must know how the selection of risk management tool affects the quality of his portfolio; and he must know when to change from one to the other.

Returning to an earlier perspective, the plots in Figure 12.10 illustrate the effect of changing *ltv*. Each plots *xdcr* against the same range of interest and capitalization rates. Both show a plane where *xdcr* is zero. Both show that higher positive before tax cash flow rises to the rear where the highest capitalization rates and lowest interest rates are combined. Transactions may only occur where the curved plane is above the flat *xdcr* = 0 plane. Those combinations that are below the surface of the flat plane cannot take place.

Of particular interest is the line at the intersection of the two planes in Figure 12.10. On the left, when lenders offer relatively high *ltv*s over a broad range of capitalization rates the line constituting the intersection of the two planes is fairly long, indicating that many transactions may occur. On the right, because more of the curved plane is "above water", it appears that more transactions can take place. But the combination of lower *ltv*s and capitalization rates make the intersection line much shorter. Since buyers have pushed prices higher, transactions do not occur at the higher capitalization rates. With the lower *ltv* on the right we are left with a range of transactions only at lower interest rates, generally showing up only along the west portion of the front edge of the curved plot.

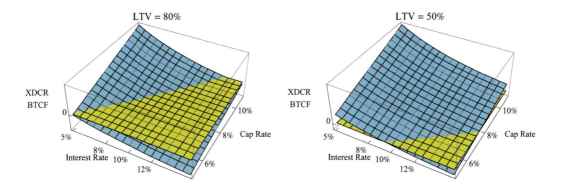

Figure 12.10. Plot of *xdcr* against interest and capitalization rates at two *ltv*s

The investor who buys in a "normal" market with positive leverage (cap rate > interest rate on loan) and positive cash flow is compensated *in the acquisition year* for committing his down payment funds. As prices and speculative fever rise, cash flows are pushed to zero. The only thing justifying investment is future increased income with its associated increase in value. Such compensation is delayed and therefore subject to a discount that considers both the cost of waiting and the risk. The bubble reaches its maximum size when demand stops. This occurs when there are no more dollars to chase property. The money dries up when two things happen. The lenders refuse to finance speculative behavior and investors, refusing to discount future rents further, will not risk larger down payments.

12.5. Data issues

Now that we have some feel for what happens during times when borrower and lender inflation expectations differ, we will consider the data implications.[8]

We use data on 542 repeat sales of Tier II apartment buildings (between 5 and 20 units) over a 21-year period from 1970 to 1990, inclusive.

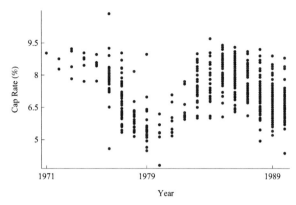

Figure 12.11. Capitalization rates for Tier II property sales

Figure 12.11 shows some fairly wide swings of capitalization rates over 21 years. Recall Figure 12.3 shows the theoretical path of analysis techniques over time. Testing our theory with our data (adjusting the axes labels for the inverse relationship between cap rates and prices) shows a similar appearance in Figure 12.12.[9]

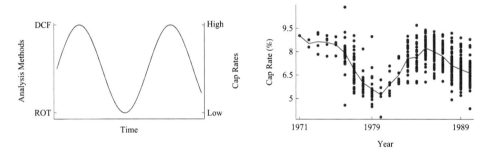

Figure 12.12. Theory and practice

As we have said, given that the lender must choose between *ltv* and *dcr*, when does he use one and when the other? Intuition suggests that *ltv* is preferable when values are rising because the lender is protected by the owner's growing equity. When prices are falling *dcr* insures there are sufficient funds to cover payments regardless of value. But *what really matters is how income is moving in relation to value*. The trend of the capitalization rate tells us something about that.

Capitalization rate, as the ratio of income to value, is rising when income rises faster than value and is falling when value is rising faster than income.[10]

Clues to the direction of capitalization rates might be found in unexpected places. Let's take a look at investor holding period. Assume that investors must work or incur risk to increase income. Therefore they *earn* any increase in value that is attributable to rent raises. But when value is rising faster than rent (capitalization rates are falling) owners receive a windfall in the form of an unearned increment. When the next investor bids up value without an increase in income the seller is rewarded for doing nothing. It makes sense that he would ride that wave as long as possible. Thus, when cap rates are falling one would expect holding periods to increase.

Of the 542 observations, 68.08% of owners waited to sell until the going out rate was lower than the going in rate. The average holding period was 1,720 days.

Like many theories for which empirical support may be found, the implementation may be difficult. In order to know when to change from *ltv* to *dcr* lenders don't need to know when cap rate direction changed in the past, they need to know when it will change in the future. Whether watching investor holding period is the best signal for this is unclear. There could be a number of signposts along the road, some better than others. The main point is that the use of real estate data, once again, can supplement sound theory and good intuition.

Having spent a good deal of time with the normative approach, a reality check involves looking at what lenders actually do. Below are data on the leveraged sale of 5331 US office buildings that took place between January, 1997 and February, 2003. This was a period of strong recovery for real estate in general following the recession of the mid-1990s and the stock market decline of the late 1990s. The average capitalization rate and *ltv* has been computed for each year and is reflected in Table 12.1.

year	ltv	cr
1997	0.734687	0.100004
1998	0.728563	0.0932465
1999	0.726625	0.0954574
2000	0.718316	0.0952261
2001	0.715686	0.0927814
2002	0.715507	0.089094
2003	0.701955	0.0832

Table 12.1. Average annual *ltv* and capitalization rates for office buildings

The plot of the two indicate that lenders do appear to lower *ltv*s as capitalization rates fall.

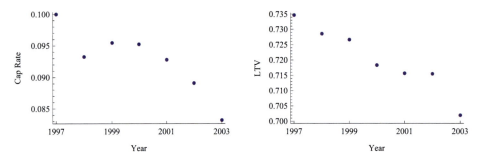

Figure 12.13. Plot of office building *ltv*s and capitalization rates over time

12.6. Conclusion

Institutional lenders may conclude two things from this chapter. One is that they should be alert to changes in the direction of capitalization rates when setting loan underwriting policy. The other is that changes in underwriting standards affect both the quality of loan portfolio and market transaction prices.

Investors should recognize the best entry and exit points, noting how the direction of capitalization rates affects their final results. Perhaps the most astute investors in any market refuse to be carried along with the crowd, sit out bubble markets and avoid auction environments. Greater fools eventually become sellers. Wise real estate entrepreneurs know that profits are *made* on the purchase of a property, they are only *collected* at the sale.

The most radical claim we might make is that Tier II investor activity predicts a wave of inflation. Having left until later the answer to the question of who is better prepared to make that forecast, only anecdotal evidence supports this claim at present. Real estate, like other hard assets (gold, rare coins, art, etc.), are considered safe harbors when financial markets are weak. There is evidence that they also tend to perform well in inflationary environments. If Tier II investors are particularly sensitive to this they might be an early warning system for inflation expectations.

Events surrounding the sub-prime mortgage melt down blur the boundaries of what may be called "investment". The genesis of those problems was political as lawmakers, in the interest of broadening home ownership (actually just a vote-buying scheme), sought to force lenders to make loans to people of questionable creditworthiness. The single family residence is in the Tier I real estate class and for our purposes not considered an "investment". However, securitization "packaged" poor quality loans into investments that received high ratings from agencies that were also drawn into the morass. The lending mindset which lowered underwriting standards crept into the entire real estate market. Indeed, the so-called "credit freeze" that followed the bankruptcy of Lehman Brothers affected all parts of global economy. This supports the admonition that we are all in the market together and connections between players must not be ignored.

Endnotes

[1] He who has the Gold makes the Rules.

[2] There is a difference like night and day between the lender environment that existed at the time of the first edition of this book (2005) and the time the second edition was in final editing (late 2011). The former may be considered somewhat "normal" times; the latter unlike any time in memory. Endnote 1 in Chapter 4 informs the reader that over a long period of time many things change. The lender environment is no different. Some rules apply universally and it is in the spirit of those rules this book has been created.

[3] L. W. "Pete" Ellwood was a somewhat iconic figure in real estate history. He was an appraiser who, before the advent of computers, laboriously produced a book of tables which permitted one to look up various results we now take for granted. For those with an interest in such things, among the electronic files for this chapter is an Excel version of Ellwood's tables and a package, Ellwood.m which, while obsolete due to version 8 functions, provides the curious reader with the underlying equations. There are numerous internet sites that now make these calculations.

[4] Some would argue that this reduction is unimportant because the retirement of debt merely shifts items in the balance sheet between cash and equity. This argument is compelling in other settings, but does not serve our purpose here.

[5] This points to another subject, long discussed but never resolved, the price-value dichotomy. It is not our task to resolve that here.

[6] Also from Chapter 3 we know that d and g must be different and d must be larger than g.

[7] An elaboration of this idea involving the partition of the *irr* is contained in the electronic supplement to Chapter 5 and at www.mathestate.com.

[8] Actual dataset is included with the electronic files for this chapter.

[9] This is the sort of satisfying outcome that accompanies the prudent use of data. The downside is that such efforts often lead to other questions, For instance, one wonders if rules of thumb dominated acquisition criteria in the late 1970s and 1980s.

[10] Other combinations can produce rises and falls in capitalization rates, but the ones mentioned are the most common.

References

Brueggeman, W. B., & Fisher, J. D.. *Real Estate Finance and Investments*, 11th ed. New York, NY, McGraw-Hill Irwin, 2001.

Ellwood, L.W. *Ellwood Tables for Real Estate Appraising and Financing,* 4th ed., Chicago, Il American Institute of Real Estate Appraisers, 1977.

Lusht, Kenneth M., *Real Estate Valuation, Principles and Applications,* State College, PA, 2001.

Problems

1. The graphic below animates the dynamics of the lender's dilemma. Moving the slider bar, discuss how the number of closed loans become more dependent on low interest rates as *dcr* and *ltv* change.

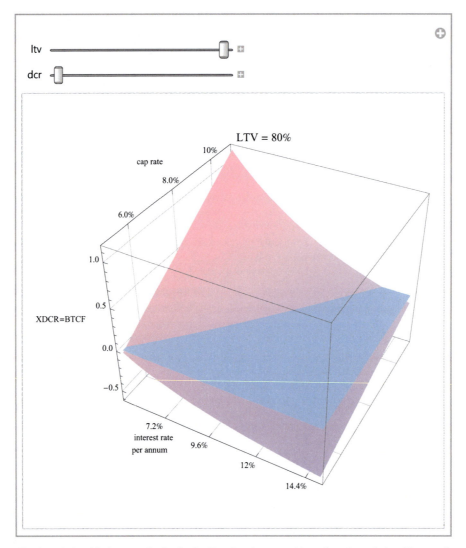

2. Describe the relationship between *btcf* and *xdcr*. To what degree and how does that relationship contribute to the formation of a bubble?

13

The Private Lender

"The contemplation of difficult mathematics, Wolfskehl realized, was far more rewarding than the love of a difficult woman."

Paul Hoffman <u>The Man Who Loved Only Numbers</u> p. 209

13.1. Introduction

The two most common ways the private real estate investor becomes a lender are:

1. Originate or purchase a loan for cash; or
2. As the seller of investment property, provide a buyer with financing for a portion of the purchase price by taking a note rather than cash in partial payment.

There are many ramifications to either strategy. They may also be combined, an example being a loan made as part of a sale is then purchased by a private investor. Like many real estate opportunities, the permutations are numerous.

In this chapter we will:

- Examine motives of private investors who choose to become lenders;
- Discuss the difference between aggressive and conservative lending policies;
- Measure the true economic cost of private funds;
- Describe specific loan provisions that accomplish tax objectives; and
- Warn against a few of the "traps for the unwary" that exist in the tax code.

Lending is a process requiring a host of special skills. Local laws govern many of the conditions under which loans are made. This book is not about those details. Rather, it is about the economic, financial and tax ramifications these activities.

13.2. The "hard money" loan vs. the "purchase money" loan

A loan secured by real property made directly to a borrower via a cash advance from the lender is known as a "hard money" loan. Loans granted to buyers by the seller as part of a sale are referred to as "purchase money" loans. While this is our convention, the language is imprecise. Some states consider cash loans from third parties "purchase money" simply because the proceeds of the loan constitute part of the purchase price. A common misconception is that because cash was paid for a hard money loan it should be held to some sort of higher standard. This is not true. A loan is a loan. Lenders, regardless of how they came by the instrument, usually want to be paid and want good security that will redeem the debt in the event of borrower default. Nonetheless, sellers sometimes make desirable loans to induce buyers to purchase, perhaps at a higher price. This will be taken up in detail later.

As hard money lenders, institutions put borrowers and their property through a rigorous and time consuming examination prior to granting the loan. Borrowers and properties that do not meet their standards are declined. Borrowers often seek out private parties because the loan can be made faster with fewer formalities. This is not to say that private loans are or should be poorly thought out or that private lending is a casual matter. A few simple rules can successfully guide the real estate investor who wishes to make loans. The fact that these rules are simple does not make them any less effective.

13.2.1. The diversification problem

Although it is possible for a private investor to own a portfolio of loans, real estate lending involves an entry cost close to that required for the purchase of a parcel of real property. Because most private investors have relatively small amounts to invest they cannot achieve the same diversification benefits a large lending institution can. For this reason, the first rule of private real estate lending must always be observed:

Rule 1: Never make a loan on a property you are unwilling or unable to own.

This rule opens the discussion on just what it is that a private lender obtains when he makes a real estate loan. Of course, the textbook legal answer is that he gets a security interest in the property. Perhaps. A financial or risk management view is that he faces some probability that he will own the property sometime in the future. The most common remedy for a lender who does not receive payment is foreclosure.[1] Thus, the lender must view his situation as having made a loan to the property for in many jurisdictions it is the property, not the borrower, that is expected to repay the loan. Many states do not permit a lender to collect funds from the borrower in excess of the amount collected from the sale of the property.

The private investor should make the loan as if he were buying the property at some unspecified time in the future under economic and physical conditions that are less rosy than the day the loan was made. After all, why does a buyer default? Why is no one else willing to rescue the buyer and obtain the property? If these questions cast a chill on the reader's enthusiasm to be a real estate lender that is understandable.

If lending is a deferred ownership opportunity, to deal with the "opportunity" portion one need only follow the acquisition analysis standards set forth elsewhere in this book. To deal with the "deferred" portion one need only choose the loan to value or debt coverage ratios carefully.

Underwriting ratios are meant to prevent the lender from ever becoming the owner. The second rule of private real estate lending is:

Rule 2: Never make a loan at a loan to value ratio that will permit you to become the owner of the property.

Following those two simple rules (and some other technical rules of documentation) should prevent most real estate lending problems and result in timely payments. On the few occasions when borrowers get in trouble someone else will enter the picture to cure the problem in return for the opportunity to obtain the property, perhaps at a discounted value.

13.2.2. Other possibilities

Good rules are boring (and make short chapters). There are some interesting quirks of real estate lending that can take us in a very different - but still useful - direction. Suppose the investor sees the market in a bubble condition as discussed in Chapter 12. He can wait until those buyers stumble and have to sell or he can loan to those buyers with the knowledge that they might stumble into foreclosure. This is a case where only the first rule of private lending is being observed. Such an investor views the possibility of obtaining the property in foreclosure as a valuable option to acquire a property at a price below the last round of appreciation (or the last puff of inflation into the bubble).

This strategy has its own difficulties. One never knows what the borrower may do when trouble calls.

- He may gather his resources and see the problem through. In this case the lender should receive a high return, presuming that the loan was made at a higher interest rate than other alternatives at least in part because the loan to value ratio was higher.
- He may file bankruptcy, delaying the foreclosure process and increasing its cost.
- He may find a financially stronger third party to purchase his interest at a discount but at a price that is still greater than the loan balance.

- He may neglect the property through a long period of decline before and during the foreclosure process, reducing its value to below the loan balance.

13.2.3. Did we make a loan or did we buy the property?

The line between lending and owning blurs as the interest rate charged on the loan rises. Let's examine this statement closely and see why it may be true. Imagine a lender who is indifferent about whether the loan obligations are met. Such a lender might even welcome the opportunity to own the property.

Regardless of the laws of man, economic laws dictate that the lender's ultimate source of repayment is the property. As the loan is presumably for a term of years, it is important to know the property's value at various times such as the loan funding date, the maturity date, the date the buyer defaults and the date the lender takes possession in a foreclosure. Let's begin by defining a simple compound interest function that will govern the property's value over time.

$$fv = pv(1+g)^t \qquad (13.1)$$

Where:

pv = present value
fv = future value
g = growth (may be negative)
t = time

This function anticipates a simple monotonic increase of a certain percent per year ($g > 0$) and is compared in Figure 13.1 with a flat value over time ($g = 0$).

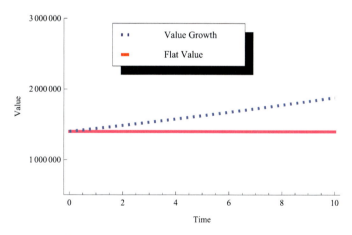

Figure 13.1. Value over time with and without growth

High interest rates should accompany high loan to value ratios. Figure 13.2 shows the loan balance over time *assuming that interest is accrued and added to principal* at a relatively high interest rate (r). This is a simplifying but realistic assumption. It is entirely possible that a borrower may take out a loan on vacant land calling for annual payments and then, unable to make even the first payment, default. The result is a foreclosure that may take a year or more, at which point the lender then has invested his original principal plus interest accrued up until he is able to take title and sell the property.

The borrower's equity in the property is the difference between the property's value at any given time and the loan balance at that same time. At the point the loan balance is equal to the value, the borrower has no equity and is only nominally the owner. That is, he may be in title but he has no economic interest in the property. From an economic standpoint, the lender is the *de facto* owner of the property.[2] Thus, we are interested in when the two plots meet. Given a fixed set of loan terms but two different possible property values (one flat, one increasing), we have two possible breakeven points (*bept*). Note that the first of these (*bept1*) is a little more than two years after the loan is made and the second (*bept2*) is a longer time, slightly less than 3 years following the funding of the loan. The reason for this, of course, is that the increase in property value in the second instance delays the time when the borrower's equity is exhausted.

The first breakeven point in Figure 13.2 is: 2.19557 years. Breakeven point #2 is: 2.83516 years.

This can be demonstrated by combining two plots. After studying Figure 13.2, imagine what happens to the breakeven point if the value of the property falls ($g < 0$) after the loan is made.

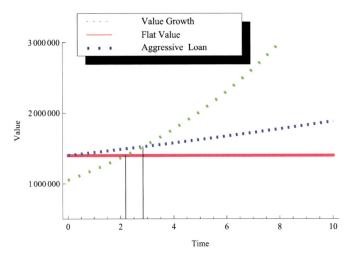

Figure 13.2. An aggressive loan with and without growth in property value

This carries an additional lesson in property rights. A well established legal concept warns: "The Law abhors a forfeiture". Courts frown on predetermined penalties in contracts. Most states provide for minimum periods of reinstatement or redemption during a foreclosure or after a borrower loses his property in foreclosure. This gives the borrower an opportunity to avoid having his equity unceremoniously "captured" by a lender who may have had a hidden agenda or superior bargaining position when the loan was made. High loan-to-value loans combined with restrictions on lenders' foreclosure rights mean the borrower can at least "live out" his remaining equity during the time (including redemption time) it takes the lender to foreclose, obtain possession and clear title.

By playing with the variables in our example one concludes that whatever "blurring" there is of the line between lending and owning, it is dependent (a) on the loan to value ratio, (b) the interest rate on the loan, (c) the change in property value during the period of any default and (d) the time involved in foreclosure.

Now let's change the situation to reflect the more conservative loan made by a lender whose only motive is lending. This lender observes *both* fundamental rules of private lending. Rather than loaning 75% he only loans 60%. With this improved security the borrower is entitled to a lower rate, say 10% per annum. Note the change in the breakeven points in Figure 13.3 to more than five years if the property does not increase in value and nearly 8 years if it goes up slightly.

The first breakeven point in Figure 13.3 is: 5.35961 years. Breakeven point #2 is: 7.76905 years.

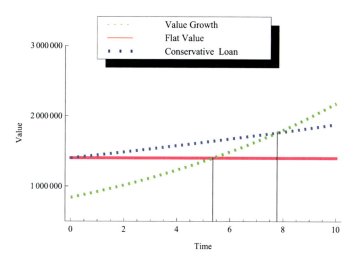

Figure 13.3. A conservative loan

We now turn to the subject of a purchase money loan. In keeping with our wish to consider the twists and turns in the process that make life interesting, we will examine a private loan with tax deferral benefits for the lender.

13.3. The installment sale

While every sale transaction requires at least a buyer and a seller, for most transactions a third party lender is also required. We have noted that institutional lenders impose expensive and burdensome requirements in connection with making loans. Many of these requirements are appropriate for any lender but some are peculiar to how a lending institution does business. A private lender may elect to suspend or waive certain requirements, making the financing process easier and less expensive for the borrower.

Separate from underwriting standards, a third party lender introduces its own profit motive. When the seller agrees to be the lender, profits from the transaction that would have gone to a third party lender remain to be shared by the buyer and seller. This section is about that allocation.

Here we combine several of the ideas we have covered thus far. In Chapter 5 we learned that maximizing terminal wealth leads to maximum utility. Chapter 8 discussed how adding labor influences returns. Chapter 10 showed that tax deferral is a good thing, and that timing the exchange closing is critical. Chapter 15 will discuss the value of options. Private lending involves all of these. What will unfold in this section is an intricate weaving of economic interests and property rights in a transaction involving only two parties. As in Chapter 10 we will plumb the murky depths of the US tax system to discover how parties modify their behavior to accomplish after-tax investment objectives.

We will examine alternatives from the standpoint of each party. Conflicting interests abound in this area. Reconciling these is the art of real estate brokerage. Placing numerical values on the tradeoffs is the science.

13.3.1. The data inputs

We will continue the example begun in Chapter 4 and further developed in Chapter 10 by reproducing below exchData2 from Table 10.13.

New Loan	2321146.
Mortgage Relief	0
Net Mortgage Relief	0
Equity Acquired	954986.
Value Acquired	3276132.
Indicated Gain	671448.
Recognized Gain	0
New Adjusted Cost Basis	2604683.
New Land Allocation	781405.
New Building Allocation	1823278.
New Annual Depreciation	66301.

13.3.2. The client status

For reference, our exchange-buyer client in Chapter 10 expected or had achieved (depending on whether one is projecting forward or looking back at the exchange acquisition) the results shown in Table 13.1.

Terminal year cash flow data ($)

Net Operating Income	504646.
Debt Service	234209.
Depreciation	66301.
Income Tax	77501.
After Tax Cash Flow	192936.

Net present value = $1,039,897.

Equity reversion data ($)

Sale Price	5196898.
Beginning Loan Balance	2321146.
Ending Loan Balance	2273804.
Original Cost	2604683.
Sale Costs	389767.
Accumulated Depreciation	293212.
Capital Gain	2401351.
Capital Gain Tax	389524.
Pre–Tax Net Equity	2533327.
After Tax Net Equity	2143803.

IRR = 46.205%

Table 13.1. Client status

13.4. The motivation of the parties

To maximize terminal wealth, one must control costs. The cost of financing is the buyer's concern. The seller keeps a watchful eye on taxes. For each party there are both long- and short-term considerations.

13.4.1. The buyer

Until now we have been silent on the source of financing, merely assuming that buyers obtain loans from conventional lenders. These lenders offer financing at market rates and terms that include origination costs. We ignored these costs for simplicity thus far but now wish to look at them closely. Suffice it to say that if the exchange-buyer in Chapter 10 can avoid these costs he is better off. Also, if he can obtain a below market interest rate, that is in his best interests. Suppose an institutional lender charges 2.5% of the initial loan for origination. If the seller is willing to provide the financing these costs are reduced considerably. They are not reduced to zero because there are always some costs in documenting a real estate loan. We will assume the seller could provide financing at .5% of the initial loan, a savings of 2 'points' or approximately $50,000. (2% of the initial loan balance is $46,422.92).

There are four ramifications of this:

1. The buyer and seller would both like to capture these savings. The seller's position to the buyer is "But, you were going to pay it anyway." The buyer replies "You were not going to get it if I did pay it."
2. Should the buyer and seller agree on how to divide the loan cost savings the natural way for the seller to receive his share is in the form of a price increase. This has tax ramifications for both parties. The seller has a higher capital gain but under the doctrine that after-tax money is better than no money, he does not complain. The buyer has a higher basis resulting in a higher depreciation deduction and lower future capital gain. But as it is cheaper to pay taxes than lose money, deductions are small consolation.
3. As part of reaching agreement on the division of the financing cost savings the question arises as to the *form* of payment. The buyer can (a) increase his down payment, effectively paying the seller in cash, (b) increase the amount of the loan the seller will carry, effectively financing the cost, or (c) pay the amount in any combination of cash and higher loan balance.
4. The decision required in #3 introduces secondary considerations having to do with underwriting risk, interest deductions, amortization period, etc.

Using the tools provided in prior chapters we can calculate the effect of many of the above decisions, or a combination of them, on either party. The advanced mathematics of game theory and matrices in multiple dimensions of Euclidian space might suggest a global optimum for both parties. Such an effort, while interesting, is beyond the scope of this work. In practice the parties depend on the bargaining and negotiating abilities of their respective agents to reach an acceptable agreement.

It is easier for us. We make assumptions.

13.4.2. The seller

Before looking at the seller's position we will make some assumptions about his circumstances. We will assume he is a mature investor whose property represents the latest in a series of exchanges. Along the way he has added labor as discussed in Chapter 8 but now has reached the point where his effective return on his real estate has dropped due to his lack of time, interest or ability to continue to actively manage his property. The combination of long holding periods, a set of sequential exchanges and the addition of costless (from a tax standpoint) labor means that he faces a large capital gain tax upon sale. Although he may be able to retire on the after tax cash proceeds, he is intrigued at the opportunity to continue in a real estate lending capacity that is passive - or relatively so - and one that offers continued tax deferral.

The foregoing qualitative assumptions lead to the requirement of specific information about the seller's tax basis, cost of sale and loan balance. Table 13.2 provides this information and the calculations for two capital gain reporting methods.

Under the above assumptions the seller of the second property in Example 2 of Chapter 10 (dataEG2b) must take $24806 from other sources in order to close the sale and pay his taxes. This is clearly an unappetizing result. Fortunately, Section 453 of the US tax code provides for the reporting of a capital gain under the Installment Sale method. By this rule the gain is divided into two parts, the recognized (cash) portion and the non-recognized (promissory note) portion. The result, in the right column of Table 13.2, is to tax only the cash received at the time of sale and defer remaining taxes until the seller receives cash payment of any principal due under the terms of the note.

	Without installment sale ($)	With installment sale ($)
Seller adjusted basis	300,000.	300,000.
Seller sale costs	156,908.	156,908.
Seller loan balance	300,000.	300,000.
Capital gain tax rate	0.15	0.15
Recapture Rate	0.25	0.25
Seller accrued depreciation	250,000.	250,000.
Sale Price	3,276,132.	3,276,132.
Down Payment	954,986.	954,986.
Loan from seller	2,321,146.	2,321,146.
Seller Capital Gain	2,819,224.	2,819,224.
Seller recognized gain	2,819,224.	954,986.
Seller CG Tax	522,884.	168,248.
Seller Net Proceeds	(24,806.)	329,830.

Table 13.2. Net proceeds with and without installment sale reporting

Using the Installment Sale method of reporting the capital gain we overcome the negative net proceeds problem. But several other repercussions must be considered:

1. The seller, having deferred a portion of his gain into the buyer's installment note has retained investment dollars that would have otherwise gone to the payment of taxes;
2. The retained investment dollars are not only larger in nominal amount than the after tax figure, they probably earn an interest rate higher than what might have been obtained in fixed interest passive securities (of course there may also be a higher risk);
3. The seller should compare, in nominal dollar form, his interest earnings from the installment obligation to those that might be obtained from re-investing *the after tax* proceeds from the outright cash sale in alternate investments;
4. The seller, after making a series of calculations may find that his *primary* motive in selling is to obtain an installment sale and that cash offers will not be entertained;
5. In order to induce buyers to make offers that suit the seller's tax motives the seller may offer loan terms slightly more attractive than conventional lenders presently offer;
6. As a lender, the seller bears responsibility for all the underwriting, management, servicing costs and potential foreclosure risks any other lender would face;
7. Depending on whether any existing loan can be assumed, the seller may be able to choose between carrying a smaller second loan behind the existing first loan or retiring the existing loan and receiving a larger installment note from the buyer secured by a first mortgage;
8. The documentation of the loan, known in the law as "perfecting the security", is a technical process requiring careful attention to detail and some documentation costs.
9. Once the installment obligation has been incurred the seller's tax fate lies in the hands of the buyer/borrower who, if he is allowed to, may pre-pay the note at any time, triggering full payment of the remainder of the seller's taxes;
10. The buyer knows all of the above and has an interest in capitalizing on each of them for his own benefit.

While each item on the list above may be quantified in some fashion, there are a number of qualitative issues that we will dispense with by making some reasonable assumptions. We will assume the seller is still healthy and active enough to retake title if foreclosure is necessary, is technically qualified to document and manage any loan, is sufficiently familiar with his own property and its surrounding environment to be able to appropriately price the loan by selecting an interest rate consistent with its risk. The seller prefers to hold a first mortgage rather than a second so will use a portion of the cash proceeds to retire the existing loan. This will leave the buyer's down payment unchanged and the seller with a loan that is approximately 70% of the sale price of the property.

13.5. The installment sale transaction

To construct an actual transaction some quantitative assumptions are also needed. We will assume the interest rates on intermediate term government bonds are 7%. The buyer, having a projected time horizon of ten years has agreed to a so-called "lock-in" provision prohibiting prepayment of any principal during the first seven years of the loan. In return the seller has offered 10% interest, one percent below the market rate. The buyer has agreed to increase the purchase price by an amount approximately equal to the origination costs (2.5% of the loan amount ≈ $60,000) by increasing the amount of the loan. The seller will pay for all cost of documentation.

In the foregoing paragraph there are a number of tradeoffs. The buyer must retain the property subject to the loan in its present form for seven years regardless of changes in the lending market. Should he decide to sell before seven years he must do so with the loan in place. Thus, the lock-in prohibits valuable options. The question becomes: Is the total value of the seller's concession package (lower interest rate, financed documentation cost) worth more or less than the buyer's concessions (higher purchase price, locked in loan)?

13.5.1. Is the seller's financing a good deal for the buyer?

In the interests of brevity we will make a point only about how much one can "afford" to pay for below-market financing terms. The choice is between two financing methods, each producing a different set of cash flows and final reversion. We cautioned earlier against paying for tax benefits. This is similar in that the buyer must be sure he will actually receive any private financing benefits he "purchases" from the seller. There are several ways to analyze these benefits.

1. We can test *npv* for the seller financing alternative to insure that it exceeds the conventional loan alternative.
2. We can perform the same test using *irr*.
3. Ignoring the tax implications, we can calculate the point in time when the higher price is recovered by interest rate savings.

To begin we use dataEG2b from Chapter 10 (Table 10.14) as the starting point.[3] To evaluate the seller financing we need the terminal year to be variable. Thus the only difference between dataEG2b and dataEG4a in Table 13.3 is the fixed terminalyear value is replaced with "tyear".

downpayment	954986.
initialnetoperatingincome	318130.
investorincometaxrate	0.35
buildingdepreciationrate	0.0363636
landpercentofproperty	0.3
capitalizationrateatpurchase	0.0936
monotonicgrowth	0.03
logisticconstant	1.5
accelerationfactor	2
interestrate	0.00791667
initialloanbalance	2321146.
totalamortizationperiod	360
investorrequiredrateofreturn	0.13
terminalyear	tyear
sellingcostrate	0.075
capitalgainrate	0.15
recapturerate	0.25
prepaymentpenalty	0
numberofunits	37

Table 13.3. Data input from dataEG4a

13.5.2. An *npv* test

For the seller financing plan we create a second Example 4 dataset, dataEG4b, for which we make the variable "tyear" substitution in dataEG2b but we also adjust the interest rate down from 9.5% to 8.5% and initial loan balance up $60,000 to reflect the benefits and costs of the seller's financing, all shown in Table 13.4.

downpayment	954986.
initialnetoperatingincome	318130.
investorincometaxrate	0.35
buildingdepreciationrate	0.0363636
landpercentofproperty	0.3
capitalizationrateatpurchase	0.0936
monotonicgrowth	0.03
logisticconstant	1.5
accelerationfactor	2
interestrate	0.00708333
initialloanbalance	2381146.
totalamortizationperiod	360
investorrequiredrateofreturn	0.13
terminalyear	tyear
sellingcostrate	0.075
capitalgainrate	0.15
recapturerate	0.25
prepaymentpenalty	0
numberofunits	37

Table 13.4. Data input from dataEG4b

The larger purchase price and larger loan requires the Exchange of Basis reflect this additional consideration. For this we define exchData3 by making the appropriate substitutions into exchData2 and show it in Table 13.5.

potentialgain	671448.
originalcost	1235000
accumulateddepreciation	94309.1
salecosts	146930.
oldloan	857154.
newvalue	3336132.
newequity	954986.
bootpaid	0
totalboot	0
buildingdepreciationrate	0.0363636
newlandpercentofproperty	0.3

Table 13.5. Data for exchange of tax basis

Plotting the different *npv* for each terminal year, the seller-financed alternative consistently plots above conventional financing. The seller financing, notwithstanding the increased price, is preferred.

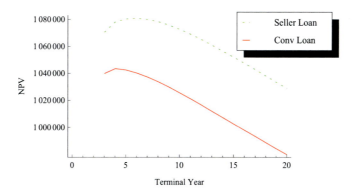

Figure 13.4. *npv* for various holding periods with and without seller financing

We can pick a specific time horizon from the Figure 13.4 and subtract the two points to determine, for that holding period, how much the seller financing enhances *npv*.

npv at ten years		
dataEG4a	dataEG4b	Difference
1,072,698.	1,025,696.	47,002.

Another way to look at it is to plot the difference between the two *npv* outcomes at each point in time. The difference levels off at the end of 20 years. Longer time horizons such as these are only important if the seller financing is very long term. Beyond 27.5 years the depreciation deduction ends, something the present level of *Mathematica* real estate programming does not support.

13.5.3. An *irr* test

Using *irr* we reach similar conclusions. In Figure 13.5 the seller financing consistently plots above the conventional lender alternative and the difference shows it growing throughout the seller's time horizon.

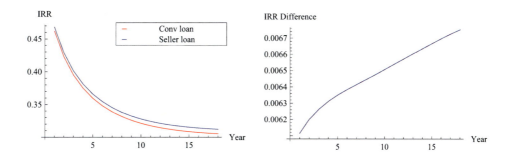

Figure 13.5. *irr* outcomes with and without seller financing

13.5.4. A simple "tax blind" test

There is a simple test used in any refinance decision that may be applied in this case. It ignores the tax issues and requires knowing when, if payments were the same, the amortization schedules of the two arrangements cross.

Figure 13.6 plots of amortization based on the loan terms from a conventional lender (dataEG4a before the seller's offer of financing) and using the seller's financing in dataEG4b. We see how a loan with a lower interest rate and lower payments but a higher initial balance would amortize over 30 years. Given the same 30-year amortization period for the non-seller financing, the plots cross at a particular point but they merge at the end for they both must reach zero at the same time.

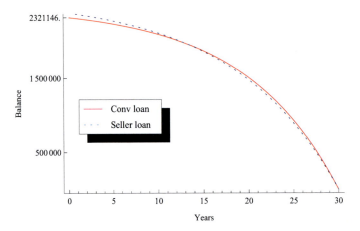

Figure 13.6. Loan amortization with and without seller financing.

On the surface this would question the value of the seller financing. If one pays more for the property to get the seller's financing and it takes more than 13 years to recover to the same point as the old loan, why use the seller's loan if your intent is to hold the property less than 13 years?

The problem with this approach is that we are not making a fair comparison. Lower payments at the lower interest rate loan and the higher cash flows they generate are not considered.

A better comparison applies the excess cash available from the lower payment to principal so that the loan retires faster. Suppose that the buyer made the same monthly payment required for the conventional loan on the larger loan to the seller carrying the lower interest rate. Admittedly, this requires ignoring the seller's desire to delay payment of principal. And, this may not be the borrower's preference. But it does bring the two situations into conformance for the purpose of comparing them.

Several steps are necessary for this analysis. First, we need to determine when the higher loan amount would be fully retired using the old payment schedule. Using Equation 13.2 we can determine the period required to fully amortize by solving for *n* in the payment equation.

$$n = -\frac{Log\left[1 - \frac{bal\ interestrate}{pmt}\right]}{Log[1 + interestrate]} \quad (13.2)$$

Substituting our data into Equation 13.2, we can obtain the amortization period for the seller financing given the payment schedule of the conventional financing. It takes 283 months to fully amortize the loan.

Second, we need to plot a function that represents the amortization period for the seller loan under the accelerated payment schedule. Figure 13.7 shows that the buyer recovers the extra cost (in the form of higher purchase price) of the seller's loan in the first three years of ownership.

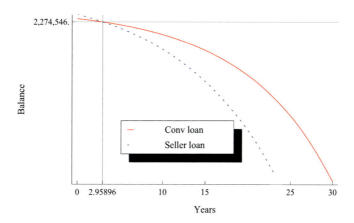

Figure 13.7. Loan amortization with and without seller financing using a conventional financing payment schedule for both loans.

It appears that the buyer is justified in accepting the seller's financing offer provided either (a) he cares little about the lock-in provision and (b) he intends to own the property more than 3 years.

13.6. A prepayment penalty

We have examined the seller's financing alternative from the standpoint of the buyer, learning that he has excess *npv* available under the fact situation presented. In the last section we asked if the value of the seller's package was worth more or less than the buyer concessions. Our analysis showed that the interest rate reduction and financed origination costs left about $50,000 of excess *npv* at the buyer's ten year time horizon. We assumed that this adequately compensates the buyer for the lost option inherent in the lock-in provision. Such a determination is largely subjective, composed of the seller's expectation of gain early in the holding period and/or his beliefs about the direction of interest rates.

In this section we will assume that the buyer feels the option to prepay is worth *more* than $50,000. If the seller is unwilling to further reduce the price or interest rate we would appear to have no deal. But there is yet another alternative. The seller may permit early repayment if prepayment is accompanied by a bonus in the form of a prepayment penalty or fee.

There are many ways to structure a prepayment penalty. We shall consider just two of these. The first is a rather standard provision used in residential lending, the second is more common to commercial lending.

1. Any prepayment in any loan year in excess of 20% of the remaining outstanding balance must be accompanied by an additional payment equal to six months interest on the excess amount prepaid.
2. Any prepayment received will be charged a prepayment penalty based on a sliding scale beginning with a 7% prepayment penalty in the first year and declining 1% per year thereafter. Prepayments after year 7 shall be without penalty.

For simplicity we will assume that all prepayments occur at the end of the year. Table 13.6 shows penalties for each of the first ten years. If one wishes to add subjective probabilities to each year and discount the products of the penalties and their probabilities one could place an expected dollar value on this alternative.

The second prepayment arrangement is more expensive in the early years and less expensive in the later years, falling to zero after year seven. Comparing these two alternatives in Figure 13.8, the buyer would be wise to assess the probability of holding the property longer or shorter than the breakeven point at just over four years.

Year	PPmt1	PPmt2
1	80 346.9	161 478.
2	79 680.8	137 466.
3	78 955.8	113 690.
4	78 166.8	90 191.7
5	77 307.9	67 016.8
6	76 373.2	44 218.4
7	75 355.8	21 856.7
8	74 248.5	0
9	73 043.4	0
10	71 731.7	0

Table 13.6. Prepayment penalties under different schedules

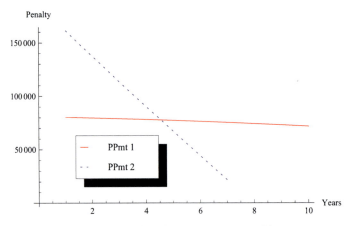

Figure 13.8. Two prepayment penalties

From the seller's standpoint, the capital gain deferred into the buyer's installment obligation is the difference between the entire capital gain and the portion recognized in the sale. The amount deferred times the capital gain tax rate produces the tax due upon payment in full of the note.[4]

Capital gains tax (at 15%) due upon full payment of note is $279,635.69. At issue are the earnings on this sum. Ignoring the risk difference, these earnings may be calculated by applying the spread between the intermediate term government bond yield and the interest rate available on the installment obligation. We will assume this spread is 3%. The annual earnings on the unpaid taxes are $8,389.07. Also, for simplicity, we will ignore the small amount of taxable annual principal payments made on the note each year. Using the buyer's discount rate (the choice of discount rate is arbitrary), the pre-tax present value of these payments is $38,286.

At issue are the earnings on this sum. Ignoring the risk difference, these earnings may be calculated by applying the spread between the intermediate term government bond yield and the interest rate available on the installment obligation. We will assume this spread is 3%.

The seller would like to keep the loan outstanding as long as possible.[5] The prepayment penalty discourages early payment. If interest rates for conventional financing remain above the interest rate on the seller financing, this will also discourage refinancing. But after the buyer adds his entrepreneurial effort in the early years, maximizes the property and arranges a sale, his buyer likely will require new financing in a different amount. To continue his tax deferral, the seller, if willing and able, should standby to assist the next buyer with appropriate adjustments in the rates and terms. He may even add cash to increase the loan amount.

As the years progress the seller realizes the extra income year-by-year. Each year the present value of the remaining income to be earned on the tax deferred gain drops in a nearly linear fashion (Figure 13.9), assuming full payment at year 7 is unavoidable.

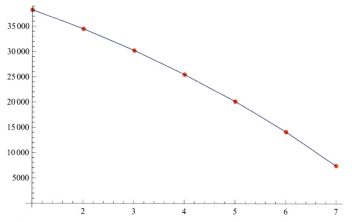

Figure 13.9. Decline over time in present value of income from tax deferral

Indefinite deferral may be possible via restructuring the debt for a sequence of buyers, adding value to each sale. Each time the loan is recast the seller should go through another underwriting analysis, assess his objectives, survey the market for alternate investments and reconsider anew the opportunity to finance the property.

Alternatively, should a particularly good relationship develop between the borrower and lender, the lender may be able to preserve his installment sale by transferring the note to another property owned by the borrower. In this way the borrower's wealth building program is enhanced by a sympathetic lender who "moves" with the borrower through his series of exchanges.

13.7. Conclusion

The loans illustrated in this chapter are just a few examples of the many alternatives and opportunities in real estate lending. With endless permutations a careful planner can tailor transactions to suit the parties' level of risk aversion, expectations, financial objectives and tax position.

In the installment sale we see another example of how tax laws influence behavior. The benefits of further tax deferral are clear to most investors. The use of the installment sale technique has merit but must not be abused. There are traps for the unwary that require investors to carefully consult with competent tax counsel.

It is tempting to combine the benefits of exchanging and the installment sale in one transaction. This is not impossible but must be handled carefully. Problems arise in the case where a seller receives a note on a property that came to him in the exchange but is then immediately resold. To qualify for a tax deferred exchange the acquired property must be held for the same purpose as the disposed property. Assuming that the disposed property was held for investment, the acquired property - having been immediately resold to the buyer who executed the note - was *not* held for investment. Thus, even though such a sale would otherwise qualify as an installment sale, the gain is triggered on the exchange. Therefore, there is no benefit to the installment sale structure as no gain is deferred into the acquired property.

Interest rate is negatively related to price. In the US interest is taxable at a higher tax rate than gain. The natural inclination is to lower the rate of interest to induce the buyer to pay a higher price. Ignoring the buyer ramifications (which are substantial), why not just lower the interest rate to zero and raise the price so that the buyer/borrower principal only payments are the same as they would have been for a normal loan? The IRS has also thought of that and has an "imputed interest rule" that recalculates the loan using market interest terms in order to properly show the interest that is implicitly included in the payments.

Family members, especially between generations, can make good use of these tools. It is common for a parent to sell to his child reporting the gain as an installment sale. But the IRS has "related party" rules that must be carefully followed.

The issues touched on briefly in this chapter each may be interpreted differently in different fact situations. It is for this reason that readers of material such as this are always urged to consult with competent legal and tax counsel about the specifics of their transaction prior to taking action.

More than once we have mentioned the need for "competent" counsel. "Competent" is a term of art having many meanings to many people. Very often specialists become very competent in narrow fields and lack an essential ability to see the big picture. Tax and legal are two of those fields. Some accountants and fewer lawyers are also good at evaluating economic issues that are not specifically legal or tax questions. But very often a third "generalist" is needed to make certain the combination of legal and tax planning also makes good financial sense. An investor can easily become frustrated shuttling between advisors, obtaining different and sometimes conflicting advice. Such an experience is a by-product of our complex society. Careful, well-intentioned advisors are invaluable. The best approach may be to collect them all into one conference room and require them to coordinate their agreements and sort out their differences.

Endnotes

[1] These laws are complex and many exceptions apply. Since the first edition of this book the subprime mortgage "crisis" precipitated a very large number of federal and state consumer protection laws which contain a host of traps for the unwary. Especially in the Tier I market a private lender must exercise great caution lest he fail to perfect the security or give proper disclosures and open himself up to a number of defenses the borrower may assert.

[2] This is the condition that in 2008 became popularized in the press as being "under water". In 2011 as the second edition was being edited it was estimated that as many as seven million homes in the US were in this situation.

[3] The full dataset and all intermediate computations are provided in Excel format among the electronic files for this chapter

[4] This assumes all recapture was paid at the time of sale so the only remaining gain is real gain taxed at capital gain rates.

[5] as a practical matter the parties may agree on "interest only" payments, something that maximizes the tax deferral for the seller and increases the buyer's cash flow slightly.

References

IRS publication 537, Installment Sales.

Pope, Thomas R., Anderson, Kenneth E., Kramer, John L. Prentice Hall's Federal Taxation 2012 Comprehensive, 25/E. Old Tappan, NJ, Prentice Hall/Pearson Education, 2012.

Problems

1. Using the graphic below, assume that the distance between the two vertical lines represents a margin of safety for the lender, change the growth and interest rates such that the safety becomes more, then less. What do you conclude about the effect of interest rates on the security of the loan?
2. The graphic below has two points were lines cross. Change the inputs such that there is only one crossover point and note the value of the inputs that produce that result. What does this say about the security of the loan?

3. Is there ever a case when the crossover points in the graphic below are reversed in order? In the default condition the value crosses the flat (initial balance) red line first, then the loan balance if there is growth. Do you think these could be reversed? What could cause it and what is the effect on lenders and borrowers?

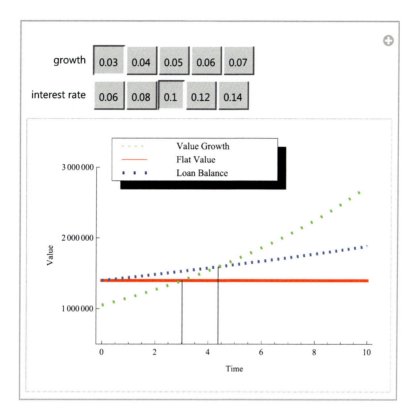

14

The Life Estate as Financing

"In the long run we are all dead"

John Maynard Keynes, A tract on monetary reform. London, Macmillan, 1923. vol. 4, p. 65

14.1. Introduction

"Creative financing" is an overused term. It is also poorly defined, meaning anything from a simple second mortgage on a house to a corporation's use of exotic hedge positions. Everyone wants to call what they do "creative" to distinguish their activities from the common or humdrum. Most real estate financing alternatives have been used before, so true creativity is hard to come by.

In this chapter we will

- Establish a new and broader definition for creative financing based on intra-family arrangements;
- Discuss how the idea of a Life Estate and a Zero Coupon Bond may be employed to solve problems of housing in retirement;
- Consider how conventional arrangements or reverse annuity mortgages either solve the problem or fall short;
- Examine the retiree's housing dilemma from two standpoints, discretionary income or house size; and
- Compute investment returns for the Remainderman who provides financing for the retiree's living arrangements.

14.1.1. Retirement and creative financing

One broad definition of creative financing is merely financing provided by individuals rather than by institutions. Oddly, this was the only kind of financing in earlier times before the establishment of banking systems, thus if "creative" means "new", private financing hardly qualifies. In our attempt to blaze a trail in financing, we will stretch the definition further to include any specific rearrangement of property rights that simply moves benefits between investors and consumers in a unique way. With the increase in retiring baby boomers and a (hoped for) concomitant maturity and success of their progeny, an opportunity exists to consider ways in which one generation can finance the other. For those who have financed their children for many years this version of creative financing may be a pleasant enough turnabout.

In 1988 Congress authorized a mortgage instrument known as a Home Equity Conversion Mortgage (HECM), more generally known as a reverse annuity mortgage because it operates exactly the opposite of the usual loan arrangement. Under an HECM seniors can turn a portion of their home equity into an annuity to overcome a "house-rich, cash-poor" condition. Rather than receiving a lump sum and making payments back to the lender for a number of years, the borrower under an HECM signs all the loan documents but receives no large lump sum initially. Instead, monthly payments are sent him by the lender for a period of time.

At the end, usually when the house is sold following the departure or death of the borrower, the lender gets a lump sum re-payment that includes accrued interest. Although we will cover some of the mechanics of the HECM, the main idea of this chapter is to bypass the institution to structure an intra-family investment that provides economic benefits to two family members in the same transaction.

Suppose that one contemplating retirement would like to move to a different region where home prices are higher but so is appreciation. A common move of this sort is from the colder climes to the sunbelt, often motivated by health reasons, personal lifestyle or to be closer to grown children. We will assume our retiree owns a debt-free home of modest value in a Midwestern state. Suppose further that a younger family member, perhaps living in a warmer climate to which the retiree would like to move, is interested in an investment that supports both the retirement and estate planning goals of his senior family member.

Two concepts must be defined before proceeding. The first is a Life Estate and the second is a Zero Coupon Bond.

14.1.2. A life estate

One normally thinks of owning property in perpetuity. Thus, one has the right to devise one's property to others at death via a will or trust arrangement. Those who inherit then have a similar right, and so on, in perpetuity. In the US it is legally possible to divide such a perpetuity into two time periods, a Life Estate and a Remainder. A Life Estate is a specific form of ownership of real property. It is different in that the rights to the property are limited in time by a human life. It can be any life but for simplicity we will assume it is the life of the party who occupies the house, in this case our retiree. Thus, if our senior family member owns a life estate in a house he has legal ownership and all that entails (possession, control, etc.) for the remainder of his life. He can even sell his interest but he only sells the life estate. Any buyer then has the same rights in the property but subject to a time limit measured by the retiree's life. For this reason life estates are rarely sold and are not very liquid. Upon the death of the holder of the life estate, the life estate "falls" to the Remainderman who owns the remainder in perpetuity. The encumbrance represented by the life estate is extinguished upon the death of the retiree leaving his Remainderman with the complete bundle of rights to do with as he sees fit without restriction just as in the usual case of fee simple ownership. Rather than get tangled up in what happens if the retiree vacates the house prior to death, we will further assume that he occupies the house until his death.

14.1.3. A zero coupon bond

The usual form of a Zero Coupon Bond is a long-term bond generally issued by a government. It pays no interest until maturity. The purchase price, naturally, is less than the payment at the end. We have encountered means elsewhere in this book to compute the yield on such an investment. Important to the usual Zero is that the payoff date is certain, a feature our program will lack.

Our goal in the analysis that follows is to make this as economically viable a transaction as possible. This will not be easy. To avoid gift implications we assume that the junior family member (investor) is not an heir of the retiree. We purposely use a family member as the investor/lender for reasons that will become clear later.

14.2. The retiree's dilemma

We assume that the choice variables are either (a) living in a larger house (or its economic equivalent) for the remainder of one's life and leaving no bequest to heirs or (b) living in a small house and leaving a bequest. For this we will need to define a number of terms:

le	=	number of years the retiree will occupy the house represented by his life expectancy
v	=	value at purchase of the house to be occupied, a proxy for size
oc	=	operating cost of the property (taxes, insurance, maintenance), a function of the size of the property
b	=	bequest at death
g	=	growth in value over time
inc	=	income of the retiree, a constraint on the size of the loan and therefore on the value of a purchased house that can be financed
pti	=	payment-to-income ratio, a maximum imposed by a lender
dp	=	down payment on the retirement home, sometimes assumed to be equal to the value of the prior residence
loan	=	loan acquired for purchase or refinance of the house
i	=	interest rate on any mortgage, expressed monthly
t	=	total amortization period (in months) of any mortgage obtained
pv	=	present value of any income stream obtained or foregone

To place the analysis in some perspective, before examining the life estate we will consider two conventional alternatives. One is the simple ownership of the property with a loan on it; the other is the reverse annuity mortgage. The situations differ substantially from each other in that the simple ownership illustration employs a fact situation that constrains the retiree to a smaller house possibly in an unsuitable location. On the other hand, the reverse annuity mortgage usually involves a large home already owned for some time that now has little or no debt.

For the reverse amortization mortgage we also define:

val	=	value of a house to be encumbered with a reverse amortization mortgage
pmt	=	payment due from lender to borrower under a reverse amortization mortgage
ltv	=	lender's maximum loan-to-value ratio under a reverse amortization mortgage

14.2.1. The conventional arrangement

Let us begin with a conventional arrangement in which one sells his existing debt free home of modest size and value and uses the proceeds as a down payment for the purchase of a new house. He lives in this house until he dies and leaves the house to his heirs.

The manner in which loan payments are calculated is no mystery, thus it is easy to solve for a loan balance that can be supported by a payment of a certain size. Our retiree may borrow at interest rate, *i*, an amount, *loan*, that a portion of his income, *inc*, represented by a lender imposed maximum payment-to-income ratio, *pti*, can repay over a full amortization period, *t*.[1]

$$loan = \frac{(1+i)^{-t}(-1+(1+i)^{t}) \, inc \, pti}{i} \quad (14.1)$$

The maximum value of the house he can purchase, *v*, is equal to the amount he can borrow, plus the value of his old residence used as a down payment, *dp*.

$$v = dp + \frac{(1+i)^{-t}(-1+(1+i)^{t}) \, inc \, pti}{i} \quad (14.2)$$

The balance of the loan, *balance(n)*, at the end of any particular year, *n*, is a function of the interest rate, term and the initial loan.[2]

$$\text{balance}(n) = \frac{-(1+i)^{12n} + (1+i)^t}{-1 + (1+i)^t} \text{loan} \tag{14.3}$$

The sale price, s, at death is the value, v, increased by growth, g, compounded over the life expectancy, le

$$s = (1+g)^{le}\left(dp + \frac{\left(1 - \frac{1}{(1+i)^t}\right)\text{inc pti}}{i}\right) \tag{14.4}$$

The bequest, b, is then merely the remaining equity, the difference between the value at sale and the loan balance.

$$b = \frac{(-1 + (1+i)^{12\,le-t})\text{inc pti}}{i} + (1+g)^{le}\left(dp + \frac{(1 - (1+i)^{-t})\text{inc pti}}{i}\right) \tag{14.5}$$

Table 14.1 shows three datasets to be used for the examples in this chapter. The second and third datasets are used only in the Reverse Amortization Mortgage section and only differ in life expectancy, growth rate and loan to value ratios. Note that the variable for value, v, provided in Equation 14.2 is a computed value and *val* in the datasets is a fixed given value.

		data1	data2	data3
Down payment	*dp*	135 000	135 000	135 000
Growth	*g*	0.04	0	0.04
Interest rate (monthly)	*i*	0.005	0.005	0.005
Term of loan	*t*	360	360	360
Life Expectancy	*le*	6	8	7
Operating Cost	*oc*	0.04	0.04	0.04
Income	*inc*	3750	3750	3750
Payment–to–income ratio	*pti*	0.4	0.4	0.4
Value	*val*	300 000	300 000	300 000
Loan–to–value ratio	*ltv*	0.6	0.6	0.4
Payment	*pmt*	1500	1500	1500

Table 14.1. Three datasets

Table 14.2 provides the output obtained when applying Equations 14.1 - 14.5 to the three datasets. The first column of data (**data1**) reflects values for what we are calling "the conventional arrangement."

	data1	data2	data3
Value	385 187.	385 187.	385 187.
Down Payment	135 000	135 000	135 000
Loan	250 187.	250 187.	250 187.
Sale Price	487 385.	385 187.	506 880.
Loan Balance	228 666.	219 595.	224 266.
Bequest	258 719.	165 592.	282 614.

Table 14.2. Values produced by the three datasets

Our illustration ignores the fact that operating costs for the house may increase but also ignores the fact that retirement income may be indexed. In the interest of simplicity, these are assumed to cancel.

14.2.2. The reverse amortization mortgage

We now consider a retiree who owns a larger house free of debt and wishes to generate monthly income from his home equity without selling the home. The lender will grant the loan based on his life expectancy, *le*, the value of the house, *val*, interest rate, *i*, and payment amount, *pmt*. Elwood table #2 handles the way a dollar added each period at interest grows. The lender sets a maximum the loan can grow to based on the loan to value ratio, *ltv*. Equation 14.6 becomes a choice, the minimum of which is selected.

$$hecmbal(n) = Min\left[\frac{(1+i)^{12n} - 1}{i} pmt, \; ltv \, val \, (1+g)^n\right] \quad (14.6)$$

Thus, given the data, we can compute the balance the loan will have grown to at life expectancy and the value of the home at that same time. As we assume growth in **data1**, the home value is greater, so the retiree receives payments throughout his full life expectancy.

Loan balance at life expectancy	Home value at life expectancy
129 613.	227 757.

By incorporating growth into the model ($g > 0$) we assume that the lender is willing to lend against future increases in value. Should that not be the case ($g = 0$) the loan reaches its maximum (*ltv* * initial value) at 94.24 months and payments stop.

From a lender's risk perspective, the imposition of a cap is an essential underwriting decision. How the cap is computed is also important. It can be based, as in **data2**, on a fixed property value and permit a larger initial *ltv* or it can allow for growth in value but allow a lower *ltv* as in **data3**. Clearly the lender does not want the loan balance to exceed the property value. Because the loan documents are a contract, the lender must perform by making payments regardless of the change in value. Thus, different assumptions impose different burdens and benefits, respectively, on the lender and borrower. In **data3** we permit the growth assumption but reduce the loan-to-value ratio with the result that in 85.02 months the loan balance will be $158,440 and payments will stop.

Under this arrangement payments would stop at a certain point regardless of life expectancy. If the dollar amount of appreciation in house value grows faster than the balance of the loan, it is possible that the house could once again "afford" more payments and payments would resume.[3]

The sample amounts are not represented to be any sort of standard, they are arbitrary and merely serve as an illustration. Figure 14.1 demonstrates the importance to both parties of estimating life expectancy correctly, obviously not an easy task. The type of loan contract most desirable differs depending on how long one expects to need the income.

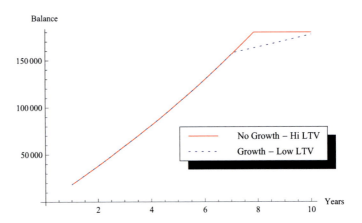

Figure 14.1. Reverse Amortization mortgages under different growth assumptions

Using Equation 14.7, one can approach it from the standpoint of the maximum payment allowed under the three scenarios in Table 14.1, each requiring one to know life expectancy exactly.

$$mopmt(n) = \frac{i}{(1+i)^{12n} - 1} \, ltv \, val \, (1+g)^n \qquad (14.7)$$

	Maximum payment
data1	2635.81
data2	1465.46
data3	1517.3

Table 14.3. Maximum payment under different assumptions

We see in the Figure 14.2 that for the choice between a plan with a larger loan to value ratio but no growth assumption (**data2**) and one with a growth assumption but a smaller *ltv* (**data3**) the decision changes when one's life expectancy is about ten years or more. Not surprisingly, the most permissive arrangement (allowance for growth *and* high *ltv*) in the original dataset (**data1**) provides the highest payment regardless of life expectancy.

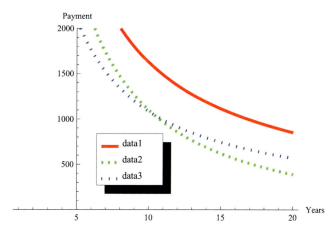

Figure 14.2. Payment under different sets of assumptions

14.3. Intra-family alternatives

The above examples represent ways to approach the problem using institutional lenders. We now turn to intra-family methods where economics only partially control. We shall focus on modifications to conventional arrangements. That is, we shall assume the reverse annuity mortgage option is not available because the retiree does not own a home of sufficient size to produce the desired results.[4] There are two ways to approach such a financing scheme.

1. Should someone be willing to purchase a house for our retiree to live in for his lifetime but with no right to devise by will, the retiree would have an additional $1,000 per month discretionary income. This, which we will call *The Income Viewpoint*, considerably enhances his retirement lifestyle.
2. Alternatively, the retiree could live in a house he could not otherwise afford if he is unconstrained by the loan qualifying payment-to-income ratio. We will call this *The Larger House Viewpoint*. This variation is just a special case of lifestyle enhancement in which the larger residence is how one elects to apply larger disposable income arising from the life estate arrangement.

14.3.1. The income viewpoint

In the conventional example, our retiree essentially "purchases" the satisfaction of leaving a bequest by incurring the obligation to make loan payments and forgoing the benefits associated with more discretionary income he would have had during his lifetime if he did not have loan payments to make. The income viewpoint amounts to "selling" that satisfaction in return for the enhanced present income. The interesting question is: how much of one is the other worth?

The trade off is between leaving a bequest, b, and income, *inc*.[5] A rational retiree chooses based on his calculation of the greater of these two. Such a calculation involves assumptions that can, at times be uncomfortable to make.

Using Equation 14.5 or consulting Table 14.2, we know the value of the bequest for **data1** is $258,719.

To make a fair comparison we need to know the present value of the income foregone in order that a bequest may be left. If our retiree is able to live in a house without paying loan payments he enjoys that income for the remainder of his life. The present value of this income is computed using Equation 14.8.

$$pv = \frac{(1+i)^{-t}\left(1-(1+i)^{-12\,le}\right)(-1+(1+i)^t)\,inc\,pti}{i(1-(1+i)^{-t})} \tag{14.8}$$

If we value that income at the same interest rate as the bank and accurately predict life expectancy (recall we said some uncomfortable assumptions would be necessary) the present value of those payments is $90,509.

Using **data1**, if one takes the simple (too simple!) position that the investor chooses the largest of these, he buys a house, makes payments and leaves a bequest. As the bequest is larger than the present value of the foregone income, his choice is clear.

Max[b, pv] /. data1

258 719.

Why is this too simple? It is naive to equate the value of money left to someone else in the future with the present value of dollars one may personally consume. Merely incorporating the time value of money and using the same rate as the bank, a present value calculation performed on the bequest seems at least reasonable. The decision rule becomes equation 14.9.

$$Max\left[\frac{b}{(1+i)^{12\,le}}, pv\right]$$ (14.9)

But under **data1**, using bank interest rates for the discount, this retiree still buys a house and leaves a bequest because the maximum under Equation 14.9 favors that strategy.

Max[b/(1 + i)^(12 le), pv] /. data1

180 664.

Present value may imperfectly adjust for the difference between the value our retiree places on his own consumption and the value he places on financing the future consumption of others. One way to deal with this is to increase the discount rate on the bequest. Suppose we arbitrarily value bequest dollars considerably less than present consumption dollars by making the discount rate three times the interest rate. Now, for our example, the value of the bequest is much lower. Using an 18% discount rate the bequest is $88,567.

Thus, our retiree opts to have someone else buy him a house, someone who will receive the house at his death.[6]

Max[b/(1 + .18/12)^(12 le), pv] /. data1

90 509.3

So for the income viewpoint and given **data1**, the decision turns on how dollars the retiree may consume are valued vs. how he values dollars he leaves behind. This means the retiree carefully selects a discount rate that adjusts future dollars others to receive to equal the value of dollars he may otherwise consume.

14.3.2. The larger house viewpoint

One point illustrates how this may, indeed, be creative financing. An institutional lender evaluates risk based on the probability of repayment taking place over the investor's lifetime. As there is a cap on his dollar return (all interest payments plus the principal), the lender makes a loan governed by the realities of (a) the income the retiree has during his lifetime to make payments and/or, (b) the liquidation value of the property needed to retire any balance remaining at the retiree's death. The Remainderman as lender has a different perspective. Since he captures the entire (uncertain) value of the property at death the Remainderman's payoff prospects are different. Also, it is possible that an older relative's care of a larger property for the Remainderman can produce positive results for the Remainderman included in these computations.

Let us begin by noting how the retiree will approach the possibility of a larger house. Remember that "larger" is just a metaphor for "better" in some tangible way. The house may be better located, newer, have a better view or otherwise in some sense be more desirable than the house the retiree might purchase. Or it might be larger. We assume that all of these desirable attributes will be captured in a higher price making possible the *measurement* of "larger" or "better".

Suppose that the retiree's self-imposed limit on the portion of his income he will spend on housing is the same fraction a lender will allow. That is, he wishes to have the most house he can support, paying in operating costs, *oc*, the same amount as his loan payment would have been had he purchased the property. The point is that our retiree has a housing budget that is a self-imposed constraint on the size of house he is willing to "support" whether that support is in the form of loan payments, upkeep or some combination of the two. Clearly, "bigger" or "better" is more feasible without loan payments. We will suppose that annual operating costs on an expensive residence run 4% of its purchase price. Thus, he can "carry" a house the value of which is equal the ratio of his annual housing budget to operating costs as shown in Equation 14.10.

$$lg\ hse = \frac{12\ inc\ pti}{oc} \qquad (14.10)$$

Clearly, using **data1**, our retiree acquires a much larger house valued at $450,000.

If we assume, naively, that the utility of different houses is represented by the difference in their values, the retiree chooses the greater of this difference or the bequest, again requiring an "appropriate" discount, which we have arbitrarily set at three times the bank interest rate for the purposes of Equation 14.11.

$$Max\left[lghse - v,\ \frac{b}{\left(1 + \frac{.18}{12}\right)^{12\ le}}\right] \qquad (14.11)$$

For **data1** our retiree still leaves a bequest because the value of the bequest exceeds the difference between the value he places on the larger house and the value his house will achieve during his life.

$$\frac{b}{\left(1 + \frac{.18}{12}\right)^{12\ le}}\ /.\ \text{data1}$$

88 567.2

lghse - v /. data1

64 812.6

$$\text{Max}\left[\text{lghse} - v,\ \frac{b}{\left(1 + \frac{.18}{12}\right)^{12\ le}}\right]\ /.\ \text{data1}$$

88 567.2

Equation 14.11 is a choice between two equations. Setting them equal to each other and solving for *pti* we locate an indifference point based on the portion of the retiree's income he is willing to devote to housing. Using $35,000 for down payment and $2,500 per month for income and **data1** for the other values, if all else is equal and the retiree is willing to use only 17.73% of his income for housing rather than the 40% the lender would allow, he is indifferent between the large house and the bequest. This provides planning flexibility in that under these circumstances the retiree may choose to use an additional 22.27% of his income for housing or for other retirement comforts.

The qualifier "if all else is equal" is important. Combining the variables using different values provides an infinite number of permutations. For instance, using lowering the bank interest rate 1.5% produces a *pti* indifference point of 42.26%, re-emphasizing the importance of the discount rate selection. The case shown here is a template for further reflection following some simulation using either *Mathematica* or the Excel workbook that accompanies this chapter.

14.4. The remainderman's position

The Remainderman's position is conceptually much simpler. He may be viewed as buying a zero coupon bond with an uncertain payoff date and amount. We assume that the Remainderman buys the house for its value, v, and concurrently sells a life estate to the retiree for the amount the retiree realizes from the sale of his old residence, dp. In that way the Remainderman really is providing financing, creative or not, for he takes the place of the lender. His investment is the amount of the loan, *loan*. The payoff is sale price of the property, an unknown amount, at the death of the retiree, on an unknown date.

14.4.1. The income case

Given **data1** his investment would be $250,187.42 upon which, using Equation 14.12, he obtains an annual return of 11.114%

$$retInc = \frac{Log[\frac{s}{loan}]}{le} \tag{14.12}$$

Return is negatively related to life expectancy. The choice of relative to stand in as lender is critical. One does not want to create a perverse incentive in such an arrangement. Measuring the utility our Remainderman gains from his relations' longevity (or lack of it!) is at best an unsavory task that even an economist would not relish. Figure 14.3 shows that although return is negatively related to life expectancy it is positively related to growth. In the reasonable ranges shown below the difference is most apparent in the early years.

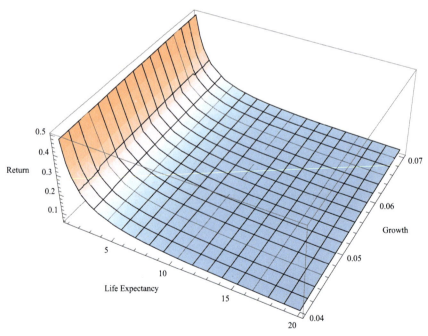

Figure 14.3. Return as a function of growth and life expectancy

14.4.2. The larger house case

The larger house alternative may be less attractive for the younger member (Equation 14.13). One reason is that in our example the retiree's purchase price for the life estate is limited to the value of his former residence used as a down payment. So even though the growth takes place on a bigger number, unless the larger house comes with a larger growth rate, because of the larger investment this alternative yields less, just under 10% for **data1**.

$$retLghse = \frac{Log\left[\frac{lghse\,(1+g)^{le}}{lghse - dp}\right]}{le} \tag{14.13}$$

The longer the arrangement continues, the lower the yield. At 20 years it drops to 5.705%.

The return is again negatively related to life expectancy but the decline is not quite so precipitous for **data1**. And if larger house comes with higher growth the return is respectable across the likely range of the investment time horizon as we see in Figure 14.4.

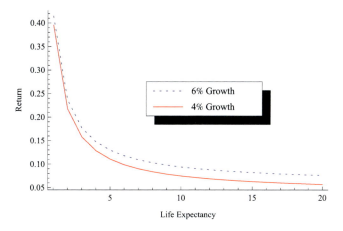

Figure 14.4. Remainderman returns with different growth rates

14.5. Conclusion

We have been rather cavalier about assuming a fixed value for life expectancy. One must be cautioned about using the mortality tables for inputs in the equations above. Mortality tables are based on a large pool of people and report the portion of those that can be expected to die during or survive until the end of any one year. For individuals the "expectation" is far less precise, variance from expectation can be considerable and dependent on a host of personal factors that may or may not be representative of actuarial results in a large pool.

This analysis could stand for the reason many seniors rent. The complexities of this chapter are bewildering enough to anyone not dealing with the challenges of aging. There are even more alternatives that approach the task differently. A shared appreciation mortgage or simple joint tenancy, are just two other possibilities that can achieve similar goals. The important general point is that the US has an economic system capable of precisely describing a large variety of property rights that can be combined in very specific ways. A talented estate planning attorney and a careful real estate analyst can craft an ownership arrangement tailored to individual needs.

Through this entire chapter we have deliberately ignored taxes. This should not be done when a transaction of this type is contemplated. The usual income tax questions include who gets the deduction for paying property taxes. There is a property tax/valuation question in states that re-assess on transfer of title. Estate tax questions hinge on the size of the estate, the size of the exemption and other factors. Finally, the capital gains taxes must not be ignored. Under present US tax law, when the life estate falls the Remainderman can move into the property for a short time, establishing it as his primary residence, and then sell it with no tax due on gains up to $500,000 ($250,000 if filing single). These are powerful benefits and costs that should be included in the decision.

Due to personal considerations, there are usually non-economic issues at work here. Hopefully these are positive. Numerous family benefits may be realized when older relations are close by (although opposite results can occur). It is assumed that this sort of transaction only takes place among stable, harmonious relations. If so, benefits not measured in dollars could enhance the financial decision in ways not available via conventional lending arrangements. Nonetheless, if the transaction is framed in economics offering a baseline of reasonable financial merit, family members can proceed in a way that minimizes the possibility of one becoming the dependent of the other.

Endnotes

[1] In the interest of simplicity, we ignore other home ownership operating costs at this stage.

[2] Note that this is NOT the equation for Ellwood table #5.

[3] This is not an appetizing loan servicing task for the lender.

[4] Or the retiree and his family do not want to enrich financial institutions. Reverse amortization loans are considered very expensive. Much of what appears in the remainder of this chapter assumes that there will be appreciation. As of late 2011 when the second edition was being edited it had been many years since homes had appreciated. Everyone presumes that some form of "normalcy" will return to the real estate market and prices will rise once again.

[5] This has been popularized by the bumper sticker adorning many recreational vehicles that proclaims "We're spending our children's inheritance!"

[6] We are reminded that we assumed the "someone" who buys the retiree a house is *not* his heir. If this were not the case the retiree would be, in a sense, merely deciding the form of the bequest.

References

Brown, R. J., Zhang, Y., *Senior Housing "An Intergenerational Solution",* Journal of Housing for the Elderly, Vol. 20, No.1/2, 2006.

Capozza, Dennis R. and Megbolugbe, Isaac F., editors. Journal of the American Real Estate and Urban Economics Association. Vol. 22, 1994.

Case, Bradford and Schnare, Anne B. Preliminary Evaluation of the HECM Reverse Mortgage Program. Journal of the American Real Estate and Urban Economics Association. 1994; 22 (2):301-46.

Crossman, Sharyn M. Mortgage and Lending Instruments Designed for the Elderly. Journal of Housing for the Elderly. 1984 Summer; 2(2):27-40.

DiVenti, Theressa R. and Herzog, Thomas N. Modeling Home Equity Conversion Mortgages. Actuarial Research Clearing House. 1990; 2.

Fratantoni, Michael C. Homeownership, committed expenditure risk, and the stockholding puzzle. Oxford Economic Papers. 2001; 53:241-259.

---. Reverse Mortgage Choices: A Theoretical and Empirical Analysis of the Borrowing Decisions of Elderly Homeowners. Journal of Housing Research. 1999; 10(2):189-208.

Keynes, J. M. A Tract on Monetary Reform. London: Macmilan; 1923.

Pastalan, Leon A. Home Equity Conversion: A Performance Comparison with Other Housing Options. Journal of Housing for the Elderly. 1983 Fall; 1(2):83-90.

Phillips, William A. and Gwin, Stephen B. Reverse Mortgages. Transactions of the Society of Actuaries. 1992; 44:289-323.

Rasmussen, David W.; Megbolugbe, Isaac F, and Morgan, Barbara A. The Reverse Mortgage as an Asset Management Tool. Housing Policy Debate. 1997; 8(1):173-194.

---. Using 1990 Public Use Microdata Sample to Estimate Potential Demand for Reverse Mortgage Products. Journal of Housing Research. 1995; 6(1):1-23.

Venti, Steven F. and Wise, David A. Aging, Moving and Housing Wealth. Wise, David, Editor. The Economics of Aging. University of Chicago Press; 1989; pp. 9-48.

---. But They Don't Want to Reduce Housing Equity. Wise, David A., Editor. Issues in the Economics of Aging. Chicago, IL: The University of Chicago Press; 1990; pp. 13-32.

---. Moving and Housing Expenditure: Transaction costs and disequilibrium. Journal of Public Economics. 1984; 23(1/2):207-43.

Weinrobe, Maurice D. Consumer Safeguards for Financial Instruments Unlocking Home Equity for the Aged. Journal of Housing for the Elderly. 1984 Summer; 2(2):55-71.

Problems

1. The graphic below, based on Figure 14.1, permits you to change the growth and *ltv* ratio for a reverse mortgage. Change the growth to zero and note how the shape of the plot changes. Leaving growth at zero change the *ltv*. What can you conclude from this as to how growth expectations affect the risk of the transactions to the different parties?

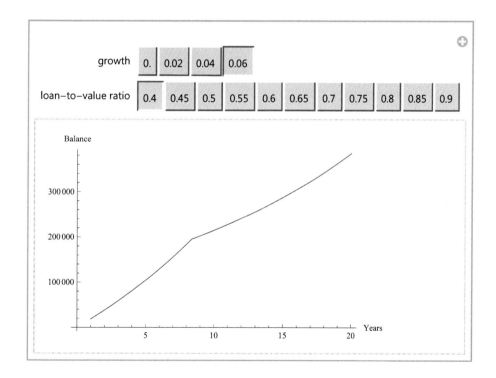

2. The graphic below, based on Figure 14.2, allows the same changes but plots the amount of the payment one may receive from a reverse mortgage. Arbitrarily the payment for a duration of ten years is also shown. Change the *ltv* input several times and notice what changes. Then change the growth input and notice the change. Choosing a combination of any two pairs (a growth value and a value for *ltv*) with another pair, notice the difference in payment amounts produced for each set of pairs. What risk does the borrower take and how does it differ between the two alternatives you chose?

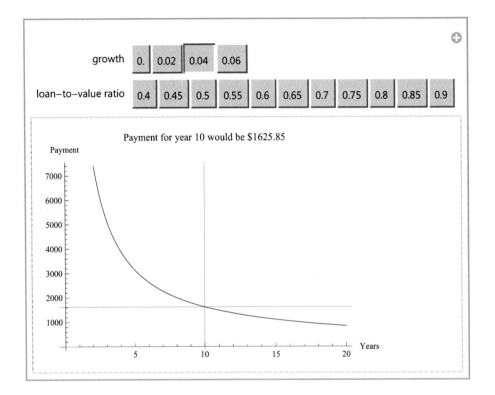

15

Real Options

"Do nothing"

George M. Shultz, as Secretary of the Treasury responding to a subordinate's request for direction following receipt of the "enemies list", a list of people President Nixon wished the IRS to audit. Secretary Shultz has been quoted as saying these were the two most important words he ever spoke as a public official.

15.1. Introduction

Option value theory is highly developed in the market for financial assets. As a result, a large international market exists in which one can buy and sell options to purchase various "futures" on stock, interest rates etc. When the underlying asset is real property such instruments are known as real options and, as one might expect, they are very different from their financial equivalent. In fact, one may argue that they are really not equivalent at all.

In this chapter we will:

- Compare and contrast financial and real options;
- Discuss how option value adds to whatever value is determined by *npv*;
- Distinguish options to take no action, to develop and to re-develop; and
- Lay the tentative groundwork for a complete theory of real options.

15.1.1. Real options are *different*

Several things distinguish real from financial options. Perhaps the most important is that when one buys or sells an option on a share of stock that action does not change the way the company that issued the stock does business. A financial option is essentially a "side bet" about how the value of stock in the secondary market might change over specific points in time. Not so with real estate where an option ties up a specific asset at a *specific place* in addition to covering specific prices and points in time. The act of optioning real estate often changes the behavior of the operators of that real estate.

Financial options are fungible. Every parcel of real property is unique.

The <u>exercise</u> of a financial option is again neutral as it relates to the company involved (this is less true in the case of warrants issued by US corporations where new stock issued on exercise does increase the supply). Because of the long life of real estate improvements, certain options such as the option to develop or the option to develop one type of improvement rather than another dramatically changes the underlying asset and may significantly change the supply of that product in the local market. Unlike financial options, *a real option may not have an expiration date and may exist even without another party or an option contract.* One may perceive the owner of a property having the perpetual option to do or not do certain things such as demolish, develop or abandon. In states where personal liability for real estate secured debt is uncommon or unenforceable a borrower has an option, actually a sequence of options, to "put" the property on the lender at the current balance of the loan at any time by ceasing to make loan payments.

The exercise of a real option is essentially *irreversible* or can only be reversed at prohibitive cost. Buildings, once built, last for decades and one must find a way to amortize the sunk cost in order to redeem one's investment.

Real estate's inexact pricing affects the problem of valuing real options. In valuing an option on a publicly traded stock one need only look in the newspaper or on the Internet to learn the value of the underlying asset. For real estate, opinions of the value of the underlying asset can vary widely. This leads to a major difference between the widely used Black-Scholes-Merton (BSM) model and any similar method for valuing real estate options. Also, BSM assumes trading takes place in continuous time with continuous price updates taking the form of Brownian motion. Clearly this cannot be maintained in real estate markets. (Childs, Ott and Riddiough (2002) take on the inexact pricing problem under the appropriate title "Noisy Real Assets.")

All of that said, there are still important things to be learned from examining the option value of real estate investments. Borrowing from the financial theory on options that does apply, we uncover a significant weakness of net present value theory: *npv* analysis overlooks option value.

For all purposes - financial and real - options are defined generally as the right without the obligation to obtain something of value upon the payment or giving up of something else of value. The "without the obligation" part is what gives rise to the unique aspects of options in that "one-way" outcomes are possible.

Because of the fact that the outcome is bounded below at zero (one need not exercise the option) a plot of the result is sometimes called a "hockey stick outcome" because of the shape of the payoff function. In Figure 15.1 we show the two common situations, the Call Option in which you have the right to *buy* an asset at a fixed price, called the "strike" price and the Put Option in which you have a right to *sell* an asset at a fixed price.

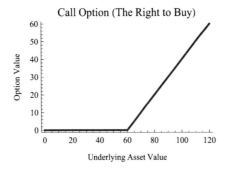 

Figure 15.1. Option payoff profiles approaching expiration

For simplicity we focus on the Call Option and assume we are dealing with a piece of vacant land eligible for development. We will ignore the cost of the option for the moment and assume that one may exercise the option to develop by constructing a building at a cost, k, which becomes the exercise or strike price. Net present value teaches us that when the sum of the present value of net projected rents for the project exceeds k the project should be built. However, most real estate parcels carry something called "embedded optionality". Exercising the option to build any one project closes the door to other, perhaps more profitable options such as waiting until conditions change and uncertainty is resolved. Similarly, the exercise of the option to devote the land to a certain type project, like a shopping center, forecloses the option to build on the same land a perhaps more productive structure, such as an office building. For that reason, we define the "option premium" as *the difference between the total value of the property employed in its most productive use and the npv of any particular use.* As long as there is uncertainty about the property's most productive use, the total (option and investment) value "floats" above the payoff function. Because no action is *required*, and inaction results in a zero outcome, the option premium portion of value is always non-negative.

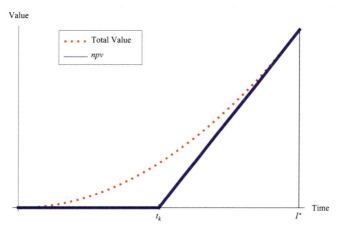

Figure 15.2. Real options including the option to wait

In Figure 15.2, the curved line represents the total payoff value including a premium associated with the option to wait. Point-in-time t_k represents the *npv* decision rule in action while I^* is the optimal time to build based on either the expiration of the option or resolving uncertainties associated with alternate improvements which may be built. The usefulness of all of this depends on three characteristics:

1. There must be time available to wait. That is, the option must not be at the expiration point. In addition to the expiration of an actual option contract, examples of events that would qualify as an implicit expiration are a zoning change that would forever prohibit a particular use, the expiration of a loan commitment or another nearby property owner's decision to build, changing the supply;
2. There must be a range of uncertain outcomes in the future; and
3. The final action must be irreversible (or begin a very long period before other options are again possible).

15.2. A two-outcome example

A simple two-outcome example demonstrates option value. The net present value function is Equation 15.1

$$npv := yr1rent + \left(\sum_{n=1}^{\infty} \frac{hi\,(p) + lo\,(1-p)}{(1+r)^n} \right) - k \tag{15.1}$$

Where

hi = upper = best case	=	the most optimistic year 2 rent (assumed to continue forever thereafter)
lo = lower = worst case	=	the most pessimistic year 2 rent (assumed to continue forever thereafter)
p	=	the probability of the highest outcome (hence 1–p = the probability of the alternative)
yr 1 rent	=	rent in first year (assumed to be paid in advance)
k	=	construction cost of a new building
r	=	discount rate

Table 15.1 provides a dataset of fixed values that helps with later illustrations.

	data1	data2
yr1rent	100 000	0
hi	150 000	150 000
lo	50 000	0
r	0.1	0.1
p	0.5	0.5
k	1 000 000	1 000 000

Table 15.1. Real option example input data

We assume that (a) first year rent is known, (b) there will be a one-time increase or decrease in rent based on uncertain economic conditions that will be only known at the beginning of period two and (c) that rent will continue thereafter forever. Our Equation 15.1 *npv* is positive indicating that we should proceed and build the project.

```
npv /. data1
```

100 000.

If we consider the option to delay we get a different answer. Waiting requires us to give up the known and certain first year income. The trade-off is that we reserve the right to make a different decision once a subsequent period yields more information.

We assume during the delay period construction costs rise at *r* but we earn interest at *r* on the unexpended construction funds, so these cancel out (however unrealistic this may be the results below do not change). Since the pessimistic outcome does not get built because its *npv* is always negative, for option value total, *ovt* in Equation 15.2, we focus only on the optimistic outcome and its probability.

As we must wait one year, the entire outcome is discounted at *r*. Using Equation 15.2, the option value of *ovt* is $295,455, higher than the build it now net present value of $100,000.

$$ovt = \frac{p}{(1+r)} \left(\left(\sum_{n=0}^{\infty} \frac{hi}{(1+r)^n} \right) - k \right) \tag{15.2}$$

15.2.1. The effect of bad news

The combination of the one-sided outcome and the arrival of new information produces an interesting result. The decision to go forward is determined only by bad news. This was first observed by Cukierman (1980) and then elaborated by Bernanke (1983).

We only complete the project if the high income alternative materializes. When the low income alternative occurs we abandon or wait.

Let's define Equation 15.3, *npv1*, allowing for either up or down movement in the initial income, inc_0. For simplicity we will fix the discount rate at 10%.

$$npv1 = inc_0 + p \sum_{n=1}^{\infty} \frac{(1+u)\,inc_0}{(1+.1)^n} + (1-p) \sum_{n=1}^{\infty} \frac{(1-d)\,inc_0}{(1+.1)^n} - k \tag{15.3}$$

Waiting, as before, means the option is reserved to choose, at t = 1, between doing and not doing the project depending on how matters develop. Thus the discounted present value of the two possible outcomes, each having a choice between zero and the alternatives, is shown in Equation 15.4.

$$npv2 = \frac{1}{1+0.1} (p \, Max[0, (1+u) \, inc_0 - k] + (1-p) \, Max[0, (1-d) \, inc_0 - k]) \qquad (15.4)$$

Because the second term on the right hand side always produces zero, Equation 15.4 simplifies to Equation 15.5

$$npv2 = \frac{p}{1+.1} (11(1+u) \, inc_0 - k) \qquad (15.5)$$

The critical point is when the two approaches produce the same answer. At that point we are indifferent between acting and not acting. Less and we wait; more and we build. Setting these two equal to each other and solving for inc_0 discloses that the decision is dependent only on the downside alternative and its probability $(1-p)$ which simplifies to Equation 15.6

$$k \frac{0.1}{1.1} \frac{0.1 + (1-p)}{0.1 + (1-p)(1-d)} \qquad (15.6)$$

To get to Equation 15.6 requires a fixed value for r. As shown in Equation 15.7, when r is symbolic u remains in the equation.

$$npv3 = \frac{-kr + inc_0 (1 + d(-1+p) + r + pu)}{r} \qquad (15.7)$$

$$npv4 = \frac{p(-k + 10 \, inc_0 (1+r)(1+u))}{1+r} \qquad (15.8)$$

When we set npv equal to npv and solve for inc_0 we have

$$inc_0 \to -\frac{k(-1+p-r)r}{(1+r)(1+d(-1+p)+r+p(u-10r(1+u)))}$$

15.2.2. Defining "now"

When discussing options one must be careful defining "now". The npv convention of Chapter 4 assumes the initial investment is made at $t = 0$ and all income is collected at the end of the first year, effectively $t = 1$. Thus the series index in Chapter 4 is from $n = 1$ to infinity. Equation 15.1 recognizes the reality that the first year's rent is collected at time zero (rent is paid in advance) and assumes construction costs are all paid at time zero. Thus neither first year rent nor construction costs are discounted in Equation 15.1. However, the result of the initial investment (building the structure at time zero) is the collection of the second year rent of (hi (p) + lo $(1-p)$) at the end of period 1. Therefore the second term of Equation 15.1 is an infinite series that uses conventional npv discounting and when evaluated converges to the equation for value via the capitalization rate. Since the two outcome case involves the expectation of rent, npv reduces to (a) first year rent plus (b) the *expected* infinite income capitalized at r beginning at $t = 0$; minus construction cost, k.

Recall that in the limit, as $n \to \infty$, the infinite series converges to simple capitalization rate if n begins at 1, thus:

$$\sum_{n=1}^{\infty} \text{Evaluate}\left[\frac{hi}{(1+r)^n}\right]$$

$$\frac{hi}{r}$$

However, note what happens in the "Evaluate" term for Equation 15.1 when *Mathematica* evaluates it. The result of using $n = 0$ as the beginning point is to compound the numerator one more period.

$$\sum_{n=0}^{\infty} \text{Evaluate}\left[\frac{hi}{(1+r)^n}\right]$$

$$\frac{hi(1+r)}{r}$$

This effect *is removed* by pre-multiplying by $\frac{1}{(1+r)}$ as shown here (for this illustration we have ignored p in the numerator)

$$\frac{1}{(1+r)}\left(\sum_{n=0}^{\infty} \text{Evaluate}\left[\frac{hi}{(1+r)^n}\right]\right)$$

$$\frac{hi}{r}$$

Thus, if we remove k from Equation 15.1 either of the following produce the same result (note the beginning index point)...

$$\frac{p}{(1+r)}\left(\sum_{n=0}^{\infty} \text{Evaluate}\left[\frac{hi}{(1+r)^n}\right]\right) == p\left(\sum_{n=1}^{\infty} \text{Evaluate}\left[\frac{hi}{(1+r)^n}\right]\right)$$

True

...and we can produce the same answer a third way by adding 1 to the index inside the Evaluated term and omitting the premultiplication by $\frac{1}{(1+r)}$.

$$\frac{p}{(1+r)}\left(\sum_{n=0}^{\infty} \text{Evaluate}\left[\frac{hi}{(1+r)^n}\right]\right) ==$$

$$p\left(\sum_{n=1}^{\infty} \text{Evaluate}\left[\frac{hi}{(1+r)^n}\right]\right) == p\left(\sum_{n=0}^{\infty} \text{Evaluate}\left[\frac{hi}{(1+r)^{n+1}}\right]\right)$$

True

15.2.3. The discount and expectation process

Construction cost, k, is removed from Equation 15.1 for the exercise described just above. So what remains when k is restored, should one discount the construction costs? The answer is "yes" because the option to wait, if exercised, delays not just the expenditure but the entire process. At first glance, this would appear to conflict with the statement, above, *"We assume during the delay period construction costs rise at r but we earn interest at r on the unexpended construction funds, so these cancel out."* But that statement only permits the value of k to remain the same in both examples, notwithstanding the fact that the funds are spent at different times. It is still necessary to discount the entire consequence of the exercise of the option back one period to retain parity between the two examples.

One may justifiably ask why p is applied to construction costs? After all, in the two-outcome, equi-probable example this seems to suggest that the decision to delay a year comes with the implied benefit that construction costs will decline by 50%. It is certainly true that...

```
Expand[p (a + b)]
```

a p + b p

...so that taking a as $\sum_{n=0}^{\infty}\left[\frac{hi}{(1+r)^n}\right]$ and b as k one can argue that p in Equation 15.8 is being applied to the construction costs. But the idea is that the probability is being applied to the *net outcome*, however it may be composed. Construction costs may rise or fall and may be offset by movement in the opposite direction of the high outcome so long as the net result of the high outcome after construction is what is realized. It is upon that net outcome, however composed, that p is applied.

Taking one's reservations on Equation 15.1 a step further, it could be said that our argument really depends on *the joint probability* of the high outcome *and* construction costs both occurring to achieve option value. Such a discussion has merit but exceeds the scope of this chapter.

15.2.4. Option value and the *npv* rule

Returning to the question at hand, do the two different answers, *npv* and *ovt* given **data1** and **data2** respectively, invalidate the *npv* rule? No, it just illustrates the fact that timing matters. *npv* does not require one to blindly accept *all positive npv projects*, rather one chooses the projects with the highest *npv* so as to maximize terminal wealth. In the case above we can view the choice as between the "build it now" project and the "build it later" project. This is the same project but the separation in time and probable outcomes at different times offer the opportunity to make different decisions.

We can make this calculation for any arbitrary period of waiting by creating a value function, Equation 15.9, dependent on the delay time, *delay*. Suppose, for instance, that we wait ten years. Although it becomes harder to maintain that construction cost increases are equal to r over a long time, we still have a value that exceeds *npv*

$$ov(delay) = \left(p\left(\left(\sum_{n=delay+1}^{\infty}\frac{hi}{(1+r)^{n-1}}\right) - \frac{k}{(1+r)^{delay}}\right)\right) \quad (15.9)$$

We are mathematically consistent when we make the delay zero, which is essentially the decision to build now. But from the standpoint of our example there are problems. The decision to build now implies that we have resolved the uncertainty about the future rent. Hence, why apply probability factors? Then there is the matter of the first year rent. It doesn't appear in Equation 15.4 but it exists in the example if one builds now. We accept some practical difficulties with *ov[0]* relating to our example as being trivial in the larger context.

```
ov[0] /. data2
```

325 000.

```
npvnow = (p ((∑_{n=1}^{∞} Evaluate[hi/(1 + r)^{n-1}]) - k)) /. data2
```

325 000.

```
TrueQ[(ov[0] /. data2) == npvnow]
```

True

The plot below appears to show the option value falling the longer we delay.

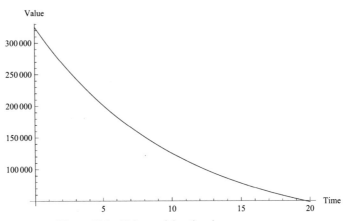

Figure 15.3. Value as delay time increases

The reason for this can be traced to the discounting of the expected future rent, which if delayed without offset by other income becomes smaller with longer delays. If the property produces income during the waiting period (discussed below), the effect of repeatedly collecting and banking rent until the exercise of the option would change the outcome. But more important is that the result above is counterintuitive. The *reason* we delay is that we believe that things might deteriorate. Keeping "*hi*" constant over time is artificial at best. It is also likely that we will revise our probabilities over time.

Our decision at each point in time in the two outcome case is really about a best case (*bc*) and worst case (*wc*) outcome and their related probabilities. We delay until the earlier of (a) the time when the expectation of those outcomes exceeds the *npv*, or (b) the expiration of the option due to some exogenous condition. Table 15.2 defines two new input datasets

	data3	data4
r	0.1	0.1
wc	200 000	200 000
bc	800 000	800 000

Table 15.2. Real option example input data

Equation 15.10 defines the function, *pnv*, to compute probable net value.

$$pnv = \frac{p\, bc + (1-p)\, wc}{(1+r)^{delay}} \quad (15.10)$$

Provided the "do nothing" decision is valued at $325,000, in Figure 15.4 we can plot the option value over two dimensions: delay time, *delay*, and probability of best case, *p*.

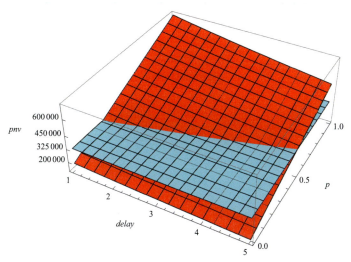

Figure 15.4. Probable net value as a function of delay time and probability

Analogous to the two dimensional "hockey stick" portrayal, in Figure 15.5 we can eliminate suboptimal outcomes below the fixed *npv* and focus only on the maximum of the two possibilities, obtaining a three dimensional version of the "hockey stick" shape.

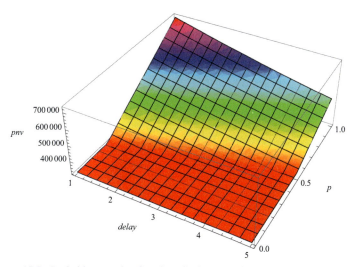

Figure 15.5. Probable net value function eliminating sub-optimal outcomes

Plotting *pnv* in Figure 15.6, we can look at what happens when the probability of the best case changes with the passing of time. The dotted line reflects what happens when the monotonic change in relative probabilities in the numerator - making *pnv* larger - reaches a point where it does not fully offset the increase in the denominator (making it smaller) brought about by the increase in *delay*. While initially comforting because it appears to offer an optimum point, the validity of this representation depends on justifying static outcomes over time, a questionable approach.

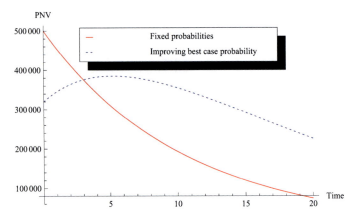

Figure 15.6. Probable net value function eliminating sub-optimal outcomes

15.3. The option to redevelop

Many political jurisdictions in the US currently embrace planning goals with trendy names such as "Smart Growth" or "City of Villages". The practical meaning of these is a promotion of increased density in the urban core in order to prevent sprawl. The market consequence of this is to favor what are known as "infill projects". These involve demolishing and/or remodeling an older building, recycling the land into a different use. Practitioners in the field view these as *redevelopment* opportunities.

The option to redevelop, Equation 15.11, introduces another factor: rent to be obtained on existing buildings prior to demolition. Provided things remain the same such that the year-to-year "build now vs. wait" decision parameters do not change, we repeatedly collect and bank (at rate *r*) the *yr1rent* until the exercise of the option. Over a long delay this can compound to a tidy sum. This sum together with the expected rent at the time of the exercise of the option is all discounted back to the present with *n = delay*.

$$npvd = \frac{1}{(1+r)^{delay}} \left(yr1rent \left(\frac{(1+r)^{delay-1} - 1}{r} \right) + \left(\sum_{n=delay+1}^{\infty} \frac{hi\, p + lo\,(1-p)}{(1+r)^n} \right) - k \right) \quad (15.11)$$

Table 15.3 provides input data for Figure 15.7.

yr1rent	100 000
hi	150 000
lo	50 000
r	0.1
p	0.6
k	1 000 000

Table 15.3. Redevelopment option example input data

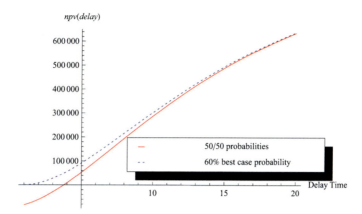

Figure 15.7. Redevelopment as a function of delay time

Note above that if best and worst case are equiprobable there are negative *npvd* values in the early years. However, with a slight increase in the best case probability all values are positive. The outcomes converge late in the series. This merely shows that adjusting probabilities changes the payoff profile over time. Clearly, there are many other permutations of the two outcome model that offer opportunities for further analysis. But we need to move on to a more general model.

15.4. Toward a more complete real option pricing model

The two outcome solution, however illustrative of the process, is too simplistic to be of practical value. BSM (1973) provides a method that may be implemented for financial assets but imposes conditions that real estate markets cannot fulfill. BSM claim that Brownian motion characterizes the movement of stock prices. This produces functions that are not continuously differentiable requiring stochastic calculus to reach the BSM solution. What we need for real property markets is a mid-point between the oversimplification of the two outcome illustration and the extreme and, for real estate, unrealistic complexities of the BSM.

In 1965 Paul Samuelson and Henry McKean suggested a formula that, while not perfect, offers advantages that bear discussing.[1] The Samuelson/McKean formula requires knowing (1) the risk-free rate of interest, something easily observed in government securities, (2) the current cash flow of the built property, something fairly easy to project and (3) the volatility of the built property's value. This last item is much harder to estimate for real estate and at times requires a leap of faith to arrive at a specific number. Nonetheless, no one will argue that future values fluctuate. Thus, while there is merit to the theory as a thought experiment, caution is advised when applying it.

Samuelson and McKean define an "option elasticity" measure, η, as

$$\eta = \frac{1}{var}\left(cfrt - rf + \frac{var}{2} + \sqrt{\left(rf - cfrt - \frac{var}{2}\right)^2 + 2\,rf\,var}\right) \qquad (15.12)$$

Where

rf = the risk free rate of interest

$cfrt$ = current cash flow rate of the property $\left(\frac{cf0}{equity}\right)$

var = variance in value as a measure of volatility

An elasticity measure reports the percentage change in the value of something per 1% change the value of something else. It also has the useful quality of being independent of scale. Here η describes the percentage change in vacant land value when the values of built properties change 1%

	data5	data6	data7
rf	0.05	0.05	0.05
$cfrt$	0.0975	0.08	0.05×1.05^t
var	0.04	0.0225	0.04
k_t		800 000	$800\,000 \times 1.02^t$

Table 15.4. Input data for general option value

Table 15.4 provides data for the examples that follow. We are interested in the point in time that development is optimal. This would be the critical point when the land value including the option value using the *ovt* rule equals the land value without the option value using the *npv* rule. To illustrate this we define

V = the value of the newly developed property using the npv rule

V^* = the 'hurdle value' or 'critical value' of the developed property below which the
land should be held undeveloped (this will appear as '*optV*' in *Mathematica* syntax below)

L = land value under the *ovt* rule

V^* is derived from the equation $\frac{V^*}{k} = \frac{\eta}{(\eta-1)} \iff V^* = k\frac{\eta}{(\eta-1)}$ which says that the ratio of the optimal developed property value to its construction cost (of improvements only without the land value) is equal to a "hurdle benefit/cost ratio", $\frac{\eta}{(\eta-1)}$.

We can now define the equation for land value

$$L = (V^* - k)\left(\frac{V}{V^*}\right)^\eta \tag{15.13}$$

and compare this value to those values produced by conventional *npv* analysis.

```
optV := k  η
          ─────
          (η - 1)

              ⎛  V  ⎞ η
L := (optV - k) ⎜─────⎟
              ⎝ optV ⎠

ov1 = optV /. data6

1.02056 × 10⁶
```

```
η /. data6
```
```
4.62718
```

If we standardize a unit of construction cost at $1 and use fixed inputs for the other variables we can, under those conditions produce an optimal land value *per dollar of construction cost* at any particular finished built value. For this to be so, L must become a linear function of k, something that is only so if *optV* is first calculated, and its value then used in the calculation of L. This is useful because the hurdle benefit/cost ratio is a scale independent ratio that can be applied to any construction cost to derive optimal value of a proposed project.

Applying this result to construction cost produces a land value that considers the embedded option.

If the proposed building had a finished market value of $1,000,000 based on *npv*, and if construction costs (including developer profit) were $800,000, then the land - by the residual method - is worth $200,000. The answer above indicates that the entire value including the option is

```
L /. V → 1 000 000 /. data6
```
```
200 738.
```

Thus, the value of the option is $200,738 - 200,000 = $738.

To plot this we need a nominal value function, *nv*, that picks all the positive possible *npv* values over a range.

$$nv = Max[0, (V - k)] \qquad (15.14)$$

Dropping the assumption that we know the finished market value of the property we assume the finished market value is V^*. When there is no difference between the optimal value and the finished market value the land value is, as expected, merely the difference between finished market value and its cost of construction. The insight here is that only when the *value of a completed development* reaches that V^* should the land be developed.

```
nv /. V → optV /. data6
```
```
220 557.
```

A plot of the three functions show them all meeting at the optimal land value. (Note the general similarity between Figure 15.2 and Figure 15.8.)

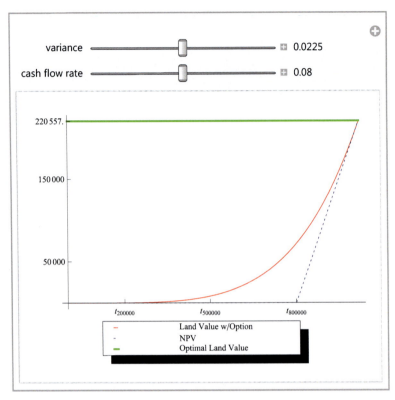

Figure 15.8. Three functions converging to optimal land value

Making some further assumptions about how cash flow and construction costs change at different rates over time, we can illustrate how the optimal time to exercise changes under these conditions. Note that the compounding rates are fixed for Figure 15.9. Changing these rates can yield dramatically different results.[2]

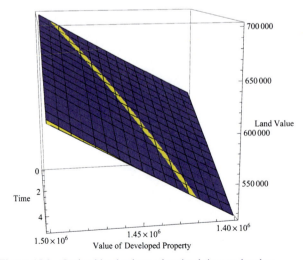

Figure 15.9. Optimal land value and optimal time to develop

15.5. Conclusion

Two oft-repeated sentiments are: "Timing is everything" and "It is good to have options". This chapter provides a look at the intersection of these two pearls. We have extended the *npv* rule beyond *which* project to select to include the question of *when* to select the optimal project.

The implications should be clear enough from the examples here but the practical difficulties of implementing some of these ideas are considerable. The best advice may be to employ this material as a philosophy to be used in negotiation rather than a technique to be honed to a precise numerical output. The imposition of restrictive assumptions, some of which may be hard to replicate in the field, has been a key to specific results in this chapter.

There are numerous real estate situations in which an option-value mindset produces useful insights. In an application involving government regulation, Titman (1985), in a form similar to the two-outcome model here, showed how land use restriction might actually accelerate development activity. The electronic version of this chapter contains an Excel file of that illustration.

Endnotes

[1] The author is indebted to Geltner and Miller (2001) for this observation. Some of the examples below are from Chapter 28 of their excellent text on Commercial Real Estate.

[2] Note that a slight distortion (1.0000005 Evaluate... in the code) of *ptv* is provided to highlight the point of tangency between the two plots, one of which - the yellow one with just an edge showing from beneath at the southwest corner - is almost entirely below the blue one.

References

Black, Fischer and Myron S. Scholes (1972) *The valuation of option contracts and a test of market efficiency*, Journal of Finance, 27 (2), 399–418.

Childs, Paul D., Ott, Steven H., Riddiough, Timothy J., *Optimal Valuation of Claims on Noisy Real Assets: Theory and an Application*, Real Estate Economics Volume 30, Issue 3, pages 415–443, Fall 2002

Dixit, A. K., & Pindyck, R. S. (1994). Investment Under Uncertainty. Princeton, NJ: Princeton University Press.

Geltner, David M., Miller, Norman G., Clayton, J., Eichholtz, P. Commercial Real Estate Analysis and Investments 2nd ed., 2006.

Samuelson, P.A., *Rational Theory of Warrant Pricing*, Industrial Management Review, vol. 6, pp. 13–31, 1965. Appendix by H. P. McKean, pp. 32–39.

Titman, S. (1985). Urban Land Prices Under Uncertainty. American Economic Review, 75(3), 505-514.

Problems

1. The option to redevelop involves the collection of rent on the existing structures prior to demolition. Equation 15.11 describes *npvd*, the net present value based on the delay time prior to recycling the land. An older structure may have maintenance issues during a longer than expected holding period. What part of Equation 15.11 would be affected by such events?

2. Figure 15.8 permits the reader to adjust variance and cash flow rates. Adjust each to the opposite extremes and describe how option value is affected.

16

The Economics of Leasing

"When we examine the modeling literature, its most striking aspect is the predominance of 'flat' linear models...On mathematical grounds we should certainly not expect to see them put forth as credible representations of reality."

John L. Casti, Five Golden Rules, p.123

16.1. Introduction

In Chapter 15 we examined an important developer tool, the option. In this chapter we take a close look at a developer financing tool, the ground lease.

In this chapter we will:

- Note how ground leases are a kind of financing;
- Emphasize the magnitude and importance of long term ground leases vs. short term commercial spaces leases;
- Discuss the ways in which property rights are created by leases;
- Model cyclical growth rates; and
- Illustrate the way options go in and out of the money.

16.2. The "Extreme lease"

Taking a wider view, one may generalize beyond the example in this chapter to a number of other lease situations. There are many analogs to shorter leases involving smaller parts of the real estate puzzle. The ground lease may be viewed as an extreme circumstance. The long term, the often large size of the parcel and the capital committed to building a structure all require very careful financial calculations and thoughtful legal analysis. While the principals can survive most economic or legal errors or regrets in a 5 year shop lease of a 1,000 square foot in-line retail space, this is less true of very long leases.

A ground lease is an interesting bundle of property rights, having both qualities of ownership when the tenant builds a building on another's land and leasehold qualities with respect to the land itself. As a financing tool the lease revenue stream mimics that of a loan but its enforcement remedies are quite different. In jurisdictions where real estate lending is non-recourse, the use of a lease as a financing tool exposes the lessee to bankruptcy costs not present in conventional financing.

Powerful tool that the ground lease is, complex legal and economic challenges limit its use to special cases.

16.2.1. The parties

There are usually two, three or four major players in the ground lease transaction.

1. A property owner who does not wish to sell but desires a secure, passive and indexed income. This is the ground lessor (landlord).
2. A lessee (tenant) who desires to lease the land and construct a building on it. This may be a developer or the development arm of a major credit tenant.
3. (Possibly) a developer, who actually builds the building for a tenant-user (usually a major credit tenant) and to whom he subleases the building.
4. (Possibly) a lender, providing financing for the building.

The structure of the developer/tenant arrangement may result in these roles being blurred or combined. Thus, while the owner of the ground and the lender are usually separate and distinct, parties #2 and #3 in the list above may be combined in a variety of ways. This sets up a difficult choice as to how to present the material in this chapter. If there is a separate ground lessee/developer, the landlord-tenant relationships for three of them are as shown in Figure 16.1. It is useful to think of the parties in the same vertical positions in the transaction as they are in Figure 16.1. The land owner of the land is on the bottom, embedded (not buried!) safely in his land. The landowner leases the land only to the developer/tenant who in turn leases it again under a sublease to a tenant/occupant who builds his building on top of the land.

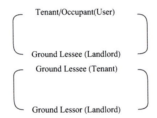

Figure 16.1. Ground lease participants

In Figure 16.1 the ground lessee/developer is in what is called the "sandwich" position because he is sandwiched in between the owner of the ground and the occupant-user. Developers typically lease ground from the landowner for $x, build out the site and lease the improvements for an amount greater than $x that provides recovery of the cost of construction plus a profit. For ease of exposition and to avoid confusion in presenting a multi-layered situation we will merge the financial interests of the developer/user. This just means that the developer ground rent in our example will be equal to the user space rent, something that can happen in practice but is usually not what the developer prefers.

We could just assume the tenant-user works directly with the landowner, eliminating the developer altogether. This simplification comes with a price. When there is a sandwiched party - a common occurrence - there are very interesting consequences. Thus, we will initially assume the unusual situation of a zero-profit development at lease inception and complicate the story later in the lease term to take advantage of the implications when there is a party in the middle of the sandwich.

We should note that under the ground lease any improvements remaining at expiration become the property of the landowner. For this reason the ground lease term is usually longer. This permits time to fully amortize the cost of any improvements constructed by the tenant.

16.3. A typical ground lease transaction

The developer leases the property for 99 years from the landowner. Lease payments will begin at a rate (the capitalization rate) based on the nature and value of the property and its proposed use. Leases are the real estate equivalent of bonds. Because ground leases are usually designed for major tenants, advantageous (to the ground lessee) terms relating to increases in rent (escalations) are often negotiated. Unfortunate for the ground lessor that this may be, the benefit is high security, especially if the ground lease is senior to any financing. In our example lease payments will be constant for five years and then increase by a fixed percentage (*rentgrowth*) at the beginning of each successive five year period. The examples below assume annual rent payments. The practical reality of monthly lease payments does not change the generality of what follows.

An important and distinguishing feature of this type of transaction is the bargaining power of a third party who is not a lender. Normally, negotiations are between buyer and seller or landlord and tenant, often influenced by a lender. In the ground lease case the major tenant end-user imposes constraints on the other parties, affecting how those parties negotiate.

16.3.1. The subordination issue

Viewing the ground lease as primary financing *for the land*, there are two ways the building may be financed. One way has the major user provide its own money and build the building with internal financing. The second way, usually the case if a developer is involved, requires a construction loan to build the building.

If there is a lender involved a second set of choices becomes critical. The lender may grant a loan secured <u>only</u> by the building, in which case the ground lease is <u>unsubordinated</u> and the lender may look only to the building and its owner for repayment. The implication is that the lender under the terms of an unsubordinated ground lease will, in the event the borrower defaults, find it necessary to make the ground lease payments to protect its interest. In the alternative, the lender may require both the land and the building as security, necessitating the lessor to <u>subordinate</u> his lease to the loan. In this case, in order to protect his interest the land, the ground lessor will have to make the payments on the loan in the event of default by the ground lessee.

There are important ramifications to the subordination issue requiring careful measurement of the risks involved. Normally there is a pricing consideration in that loans granted with a first priority (the ground lease is subordinate) will have a lower interest rate than those subordinate to the ground lease.

In the absence of default and ignoring the interest rate differential, the computations that follow are unaffected.

16.3.2. The option issue

The situation becomes more complex when an option to purchase is involved. The right to exercise the option may be delayed for a number of years, often related to the age of the ground lessor so that exercise occurs after his death. A dilemma arises over how the option price is computed. The developer/lessee/buyer under the option prefers a fixed capitalization rate for deciding value arguing that rent increases called for in the lease "index" the option price. But low escalation provisions characterize most major tenant leases. Should the market value of the land unencumbered by the lease rise faster than the market value of the land based on the contract rent called for in the lease the ground lessor suffers a declining *irr*. If, on the other hand, the ground lessor requires a fixed *irr* the lessee must accept a declining capitalization rate.

To model some of these outcomes we need a step function to handle the unique payment structure of the ground lease in which compounding occurs periodically but infrequently, resulting in multi-year periods of "flat rent" between adjustments. We assume increases only at the end of each fifth period. (For all of the examples in this chapter we use small nominal values. The reader may add his own zeros.)

By solving for *r* in Equation 16.1 we can determine the continuous compounding equivalent rate necessary to equal the same rent level achieved by the step function.

$$e^{rn} = rent_n \qquad (16.1)$$

Where:

e = the base of the natural log
n = final escalation period of the lease
$rent_n$ = rent for the final escalation period of the lease, achieved via contractual escalations in the lease

Assuming a 95 year lease with 8% rent escalations every five years, the continuous compounding increase is 1.454%. The profile of rent looks like Figure 16.2

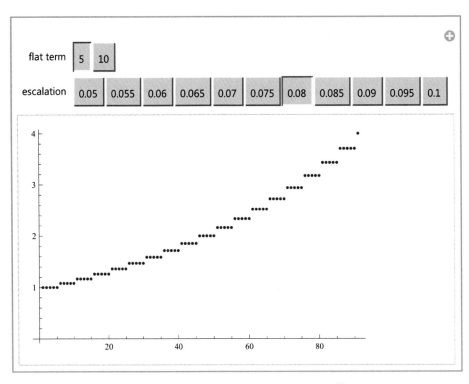

Figure 16.2. Typical ground lease rent profile

16.3.3. The cap rate - *irr* conflict

A capitalization rate is merely the inverse of the price one is willing to pay for a dollar of perpetual income. For natural persons 99 years is the practical equivalent of perpetuity. One reason ground leases are used is that the parties can't agree on price for that dollar of perpetual income in the present. (Taxes are another reason but we ignore that for now.) Different expectations about the future permit the parties to agree on a price at a later, usually much later, date. In the example below the owner believes his property is worth $11.11 today. The developer is not willing to pay that price, believing that the property is worth $10.53. But he is willing to pay $1 per year plus escalations *for possession of the property today*. The acquisition may be completed much later upon exercise of an option. The developer obtains possession of the property today for a present lease rate that capitalizes income at a rate of 8.5% ($\frac{\$1}{\$11.77}$) in the landowner's mind. In the developer's mind he is paying for the use of the land a price that capitalizes income at a rate of 9% ($\frac{\$1}{\$11.11}$). Notice that the rent for both is the same. Under an option the developer obtains *the right (but not the obligation) today* to pay $\frac{\text{then market rent}}{cr_{\text{tenant}}}$ some time in the future.

In our example we assume the option may not be exercised for the first 30 years. The landlord agrees to a fixed capitalization rate, $cr_1 = 8.5\%$, and requires that current market income be used to compute value. In order to have an *irr* we need an initial investment, *initinv*. This is the capitalized value of the first rent payment. Here we normalize rent at $1, and use slightly higher capitalization rate (the ground lessor's 9%) for the starting value than the capitalization rate (cr_{tenant}) to compute exercise price.

Equation 16.2 is present value function, *pv1*, for the market outcome wherein the first term discounts the equity reversion. This value is based on the income achieved in the lease at the time the option is exercised increased by any *actual* growth (*realgrowth*) which is presumed to be in excess of the contractual escalations in lease rent. The second term sums *n* discounted individual annual cash flows received under the lease over *t* years. This is a pre-tax, debt-free present value. Assuming no debt is realistic because these investments are often owned free and clear. Ignoring income tax is for convenience. We assume the actual annual growth in both market rent and value is 1.2% in excess of the growth in rent called for under the ground lease escalations.

$$pv1 = \frac{rent_1(1 + realgrowth)^n}{cr_1(1 + k)^n} + \sum_{t=1}^{n}\left(\frac{rent_t}{(1 + k)^t}\right); \qquad (16.2)$$

Where:

$rent_1$	=	initial rent
$realgrowth$	=	continuous compounding equivalent rent based on escalations in the lease plus some additional growth factor based on economic expectations
cr_1	=	capitalization rate
k	=	irr computed for the last period of the lease
n	=	lease periods of five year increments

When excess growth combined with the continuous compounding rate we found for the lease we have a total that approximates the change in value we found over a long period of time in the Los Angeles data at the end of Chapter 7. For our present example, real growth is 2.65371%

When excess growth is combined with the continuous compounding rate we found for the lease we have a total that approximates the change in value we found over a long period of time in the Los Angeles data at the end of Chapter 7. For our present example, real growth is 2.65371%

Assuming that the option is exercised after 30 but before 90 years, we pick several 5-year increments at which to measure the *irr* achieved at that point in time. The plot of these *irr*s in Figure 16.3 shows how they decline over time. The practical consequence of this is that the longer the investment is held, the lower the return, something rather unappetizing to most investors.

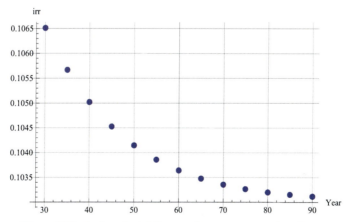

Figure 16.3. *irr* for selected five year increments over a long lease term

In the alternative, suppose the landowner requires the *irr* to remain constant at its initial value, the highest in the series that produced Figure 16.3. What happens to capitalization rate? It declines rather steeply over time in Figure 16.4, something unappetizing to buyers. Due to the fact that the option may not be exercised during the first 30 years under this arrangement, the option may never be worth exercising.

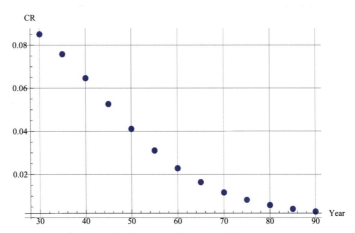

Figure 16.4. Corresponding capitalization rates for selected five year increments over a long lease term

Central to this conflict is the disagreement over the price, as reflected in the capitalization rate, at different points in time. A different set of *irr*s is produced when the same (9%) capitalization rate is used for both capitalizing the initial lease rate and determining the option price.

Plotting the two *irr* series shows that they both decline but at different rates, converging at about year 80 in this case.

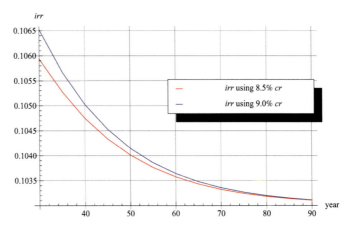

Figure 16.5. Plot of *irr* using different capitalization rates for selected five year increments

If we fix the *irr* at the value close to that achieved in the 60th (near convergence) year the capitalization rate rises during the early years in which the option may be exercised as seen in Figure 16.6. This works as an incentive for the ground lessee to exercise the option soon after he is allowed to do so.

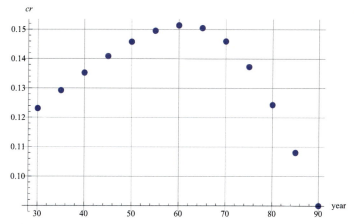

Figure 16.6. Capitalization rates using a fixed *irr* for selected five year increments

So we see that there are practically an unlimited number of combinations of lease terms, option terms and related assumptions that one can make in the area of ground leases. Each combination produces a different set of benefits. This makes modeling difficult for academic presentation but provides a wide range of possibilities in the field that may be tailored to individual situations.

16.3.4. When the option is "in the money"

Because we have assumed away the developer's spread at the outset of the lease, the developer's profit, if any, is concentrated in the option.

Like all options, there may be times when it is "in the money". In our transaction this arises when the market value based on economic rent exceeds the market value based on contract (lease) rent. The developer is betting that market rent will rise more than the artificial growth in rent called for in the major tenant's lease. If he is correct (often the case in urban areas with expanding population and fixed land supply) he realizes his profit from selling the property based on a price calculated by applying *market* capitalization rate to *market* rent, a value higher than the option price derived by dividing the artificial rent (whatever it is at the time) by the artificial (cr_1) cap rate set forth in the option.

What makes ground leased land different from bonds is that, unlike bonds, over a long period of time the value is likely to rise *in someone's hands*. The developer wants it to be in his by his option price moving farther into the money before expiration. The landowner wants to have it be in his by having a desirable capitalization rate as far out at possible. All of this is complicated further by the possessory interest of the tenant user whose lease terms may hold value down for a period of time.

To illustrate this we define a new present value function, *pvicr* (*p*resent *v*alue *i*ncrementing the *c*ap *r*ate), with an indexed capitalization rate.

$$pvicr = \left(\frac{rent_1(1 + realgrowth)^n}{(cr + dr\,n)(1 + k_n)^n} + \sum_{t=1}^{n}\left(\frac{rent_t}{(1 + k_n)^t} \right) \right) \qquad (16.3)$$

Where all is as was true for Equation 16.2 and:

dr = small increments of change in the rate, *cr*

Note that the difference between *pv1* and *pvicr* is that in *pvicr* the capitalization rate is incremented by *dr n*, essentially making the capitalization rate an increasing function of time. However unrealistic this may be, it serves to illustrate the conditions under which the option may be "in the money" only in certain years based on movement in the capitalization rate. Here *dr* represents an arbitrary fractional unit of the capitalization rate. We plot present value over time with the third dimension (cap rate Δ) representing a small range of *dr*.

The flat plane in Figure 16.7 is the initial investment. The intersection is where they are equal (*npv* = 0), above which the net present value is positive. [For readers of the electronic version of this chapter who have CDF Player installed in their browser, rotating the plot may be useful at this stage]. Note that when cap rates rise over time (values are falling, not a happy circumstance) if the option price is equal to the initial investment it is important to exercise the option early.

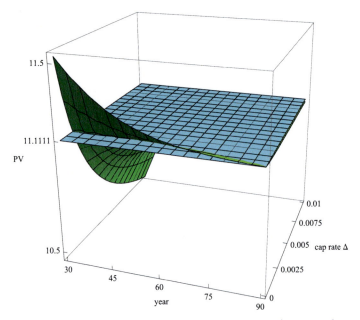

Figure 16.7. Incremented capitalization rates, year and present value

Even with 3D graphics a limitation is that we run out of axes at three. Two of our axes are used for *n* and the value of the function, leaving one to represent another variable. If we prefer to increment discount rate we can approach it with Equation 16.4, *pvik* (*p*resent *v*alue *i*ncrementing *k*), that assume capitalization rate remains constant over time. This produces a much wider set of PV outcomes shown in Figure 16.8.

$$pvik = \frac{rent_1\,(1 + realgrowth)^n}{cr\,(1 + k_n + dr\,n))^n} + \sum_{t=1}^{n}\left(\frac{rent_t}{(1 + (k_n + dr\,n))^t}\right) \qquad (16.4)$$

Where all is as was true for Equation 16.3 except:

dr = small increments of change in the rate, *k*

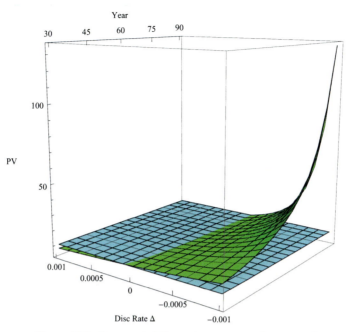

Figure 16.8. Incremented discount rates, year and present value

Several times we have warned against linear models, monotonic growth and other simplistic views of the real world. In Chapter 4 we introduced a special growth function, the modified logistic, to allow for growth of different rates at different points in time. We would be remiss if we did not consider still another possibility, the reality that growth is not always positive.

Indexing the discount rate such that it increases monotonically is unrealistic as rates fluctuate both up and down. This can be illustrated by modeling the discount rate change increment, *dra*, as a sine function.[1] The value of this approach is to note that the option moves in and out of the money over time depending on how discount rates change. The dark blue plane in Figure 16.9 is again initial investment. Again, rotation of the plot may be helpful.

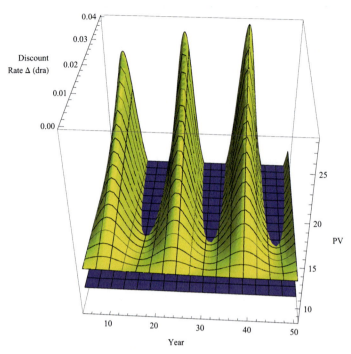

Figure 16.9. Fluctuating discount rates, year and present value

16.4. Lease termination

The limitation of 99 years for a ground lease arises from a law that imposes a "rule against perpetuities". This law is complex and will not be covered here but may be viewed as social policy that encourages title to change hands (its origin, not surprisingly, is in the desire of British authorities to tax estates of decedents). Very often economics intervene to make the actual term of the lease different from the term written in the contract. Put simply, few 99 year leases are fully performed through their stated expiration. Something happens to cause early termination. Examples are: Someone dies, the market changes and the ground lessee makes the landlord an offer that is too good to pass up, the user moves out leaving the property vacant, the lessee defaults. Sometimes a combination of these events occur. Essentially all possible outcomes can be summarized under three general scenarios:

1. The lease is fully performed and expires or renews via negotiation or exercise of renewal option;

2. The tenant defaults; or

3. The parties agree to early lease termination, perhaps accompanied by a payment from one party to the other.

To make the example manageable we will concentrate on the first 25 years of the ground lease during which a major single tenant has possession under a 25 year lease with an option to extend for another five years. In keeping with the simplification mentioned at earlier, for convenience rent under the user lease is the same as the ground lease. In practice the ground lessee/developer attempts to sublease to the user tenant at a higher rate from the beginning. Some of the risk of developing is that this may not happen.

The ground tenant's fortunes usually rise and fall on the economic health of his major subtenant-user. Therefore, events in the sublease very often influence events in the ground lease.

As we consider how the prospect of early termination affects the parties we find that real growth in value based on *market* rent is what matters. More particularly, we are interested in the *difference* between the actual market value and the value produced by capitalizing rent in the lease contract.

Assume that (a) original income was at market, (b) capitalization rates are a constant 8.5% and (c) real growth exceeds the ground lease escalations by the amount previously assumed so realgrowth is 1.454% plus 1.2% for a total of 2.654%. For simplicity we will continue to normalize rent at $1. Rent grows in accordance with Equation 16.5.

$$rg = \frac{(1 + realgrowth)^n}{cr} \tag{16.5}$$

Thus, at the end of 30 years rent has grown to $25.81 while the value based on capitalizing lease income and assuming a fixed capitalization rate is $18.67

Thus, at the end of 30 years value based on market rent has grown to $25.81 while the value based on capitalizing lease income and assuming a fixed capitalization rate is $18.67

This result shows that nominal real value in 30 years is more than the value reached by capitalizing lease income. Of course, 30 years is a long way off. Applying a discount factor to each would keep the relationship the same provided the discount rate was the same. However, there is good reason to use a smaller discount rate for the ground lease because of its senior claim. From the developer's standpoint, his interest is satisfied only after that of the ground lessor so he might well discount his value at a higher rate. It is left as an exercise for the reader to explore this iteration.

In Figure 16.10 we show the capitalized value of the property for the first 30 years based on ground rent escalating as a step function and the real value of the property based on a fixed, monotonic real increase in rent. The real growth, larger than the artificial growth of lease payments, quickly pulls the real value higher.

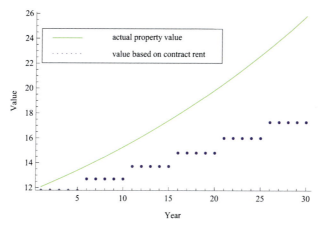

Figure 16.10. Actual value and value based on contract rent

During the first 30 years of the ground lease the sublease is a burden as the real value exceeds the capitalized value of the lease income. But the user lease terminates or renews at market eventually. At that time the lid is off the value and the developer realizes his profit through an increased income stream or the sale of the project.

Once again calling on the sine function for Figure 16.11, this time applying it to rent, we will add realism by specifying an oscillating growth pattern under which value rises and falls but generally trends upward over the long term. Notice that with the frequency and amplitude of the oscillations provided by this particular sine function in the early years, the variation intersects both the continuous function, Equation 16.5, and the step function for rent only. In the second half of the ground lease term all variation takes place above the step function representing the ground lease rent.

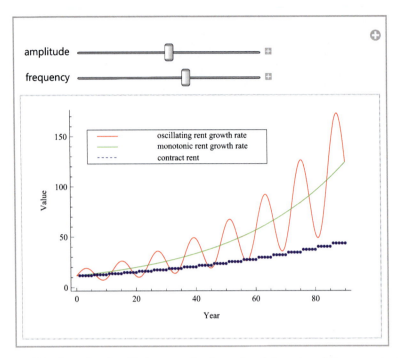

Figure 16.11. Smooth and oscillating rates of real growth and the rent escalations as a step function

Figure 16.12 shows five extreme points, A, B, C, D, and E occurring during the first 30 years of the ground lease. In the illustrations that follow we represent the end of the user sublease as year 27 to consider the uncertainty inherent in the option.

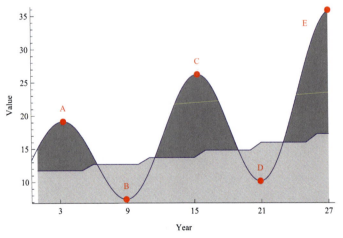

Figure 16.12. First 27 years with dramatic rent fluctuations

The difference between lease-driven value and market value are reported in Table 16.1.

	Value based on market	Value based on lease rent	Difference
A	19.1614	11.7647	7.39665
B	7.43668	12.7059	−5.2692
C	26.2375	13.7224	12.5151
D	10.183	16.0058	−5.82277
E	35.9267	17.2862	18.6405

Table 16.1. Difference between market and lease-driven values as critical points

We can reasonably expect that opportunities for lease termination exist at each extreme point. Since points A and B occur early on in the lease and represent relatively smaller differences between lease-driven value and market value, the points of most interest are C, D and E. Because E is the putative termination point, C and D represent useful opposing illustrations of typical events.

These two points in time represent an application of option theory discussed in Chapter 15. When the market value of the property exceeds the lease-driven value at point C the lease is an asset to the tenant and a liability to the owner. The opposite is true at point D. If bankruptcy costs are severe for the tenant the landlord is provided a "floor" in value during bad economic times (such as at points B and D).

Note that the parties do not know that point C is a high point. Considering the decline that follows, the ground lessee/developer may be ill-advised to buy out the tenant's position. But if he did the tenant would realize his maximum price. Reversing the parties, at point D, the tenant may be tempted to buy out the remainder of the lease obligation to escape further performance. The ground lessee/developer may be disinclined because he is giving up the floor the tenant lease represents but his optimum point to accept payment for lease termination would appear to be at point D. To include the tenant's bankruptcy alternatives one may wish to take a game-theoretic approach to consider how the tenant's threat of bankruptcy affects negotiations at point D.

Present value, based on the ground lease rent schedule of the property through year 27 assuming a capitalization rate of 8.5% and a discount rate of 12%, is $9.46. Present value, based on a real growth function, of the property through year 27 assuming a capitalization rate of .085 and a discount rate of .12 is $12.24. The difference, then, is the present net value of the option, $2.78.

A reasonable criticism at this stage is that we have held capitalization rates stable through a quarter century of fluctuating values. This is of course unlikely. One of the reasons that values change is that capitalization rates change to consider different expectations based on foreseeable market risk. Capitalization rates are inversely related to value so our stylized example could model capitalization rates oscillating opposite to value over the same period.

The resulting path of values in Figure 16.13 under the different regimes (good markets or bad depending on whether you are a buyer or seller) show divergence in the later years as one might expect. This is just one of an infinite number of permutations possible using the tools of this chapter.

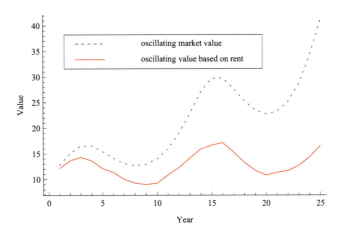

Figure 16.13. Fluctuating rent-based value and real value

16.5. Conclusion

One can make a lease look and act very much like a purchase. Indeed, there are some cases when the practical effect of leasing is to transfer possession under conditions that are nearly the same as those in a sale. When the lease covers non-depreciable ground the yearly operational tax consequences of lease payments and interest payments are identical to both parties. The main difference is that the lease is for a finite time and the lessee, absent an option, has no reversion. One must not trivialize the lack of a reversion because it is so far away. It is true that the long distance in time discounts its value close to zero but many years of appreciation over that same time offsets some or all of the discount. The trivial case is one in which present value is unchanged when discount rates and growth rates are identical over any number of years. When the discount rate is higher than the growth rate, as is usually the case, the present value does indeed drop, dropping close to zero as the difference between the two rates widens.

For smaller and shorter leases the stakes may appear less but the same dynamics apply. Tenants make improvements in scale with their commitment to the land. Restaurants and other capital intensive uses in retail space have an embedded interest in the land. The law is very protective of those rights and can punish a landlord who abuses them. When a tenant desires to sell his business and assign the lease many jurisdictions restrict the landlord's approval rights to protect the tenant's sale. If the tenant negotiates a favorable lease and the conditions of Point C in Figure 16.12 exist at the time the tenant wishes to assign the lease the tenant has an asset to sell to his buyer. A wise landlord treads lightly through the minefield of those circumstances lest he be accused of attempting to terminate the lease prematurely by refusing to permit assignment.

Ground leases are often motivated by tax deferral. As there is no sale, no gain is recognized. In Chapter 13 we discussed another tax deferral technique, the installment sale, that provides some of the benefits described in this chapter.

Ground leases often come into play when there is no other way to acquire the land. Development may be thought of as the most intense example of the labor-added ideas discussed in Chapter 8. The developer who has no other prospects may choose the ground lease deal to keep his organization active during times when he is searching for acquisitions. There are many markets when a small ground lease deal is better than no deal.

From the ground lessor's standpoint the merits of an unsubordinated ground lease are clear. The downside is reduced participation in appreciation and little opportunity for gain. In essence, the owner is barred from adding the entrepreneurial labor discussed in Chapter 8. Thus, ground leases become an estate planning tool late in the investor's career.

Let's end with a comment about seeing the forest and not the trees. We have jumped through a number of hoops in this chapter to model variation. Three different change variables (rent, capitalization rate and discount rate) are in the equations for this chapter. *Mathematica* may be equal to the task of displaying outcomes in which allow for change, indeed different types (monotonic, oscillating, step functions) of change for any of them or any combination of them. Further discussion of the minutiae note that sine functions have an infinite number of combinations of frequency, amplitude and drift.

All of these exercises are attempts to model change in a way that we hope enhances our ability to anticipate the future. In Chapter 7 we raised the notion that some uncertainty is essentially unmanageable. All efforts to predict the future are imperfect. This does not mean we should just blindly plow forward without making a reasonable attempt at modeling. It means we should view all models with a healthy suspicion.

The contortions of this chapter reminds us that the phrase "location, location, location" has real meaning. Given a good location the ground lessor, ground lessee and end user share an embarrassment of riches as they divide a set of alternatives, all of which are positive.

Endnotes

[1] No claim is made that rates fluctuate in accordance with a sine wave, either. But few would argue that they fluctuate.

References

le Moigne, Cecile; La, Eric Viveiros, *Private Real Estate as an Inflation Hedge: An Updated Look with a Global Perspective.* Journal of Real Estate Portfolio Management. Vol 14. No. 4, 2008 p. 263-286.

Pretorius, Frederick; Walker, Anthony; Chau, K. W., *Exploitation, Expropriation and Capital Assets: The Economics of Commercial Real Estate Leases.* Journal of Real Estate Literature. Vol 11. No. 1, 2003 p. 1-34.

Benjamin, John D.; Katkish, John; Losey, Robert L., *Irvine Hill Business Park: a Case Study in the Valuation of Real Property having Brownfield Issues.* Journal of Real Estate Practice and Education. Vol 5. No. 1, 2002, p. 57-76.

Problems

1. Figure 16.2 shows a step function that models the way contractual rent changes over the term of a lease. The default is 8% escalation every 5 years. Change the escalation percent to a different rate and explain why the other party would or would not counter with a request to change the flat term.
2. Figure 16.11 permits the reader to change the way value fluctuates over time. Fluctuation is modeled as a sine wave which has frequency and amplitude. Using the slider bars, change the plot and describe how the parties to the contract might change their behavior under different variation schemes.
3. Figure 16.12 shows 5 points. For each, name the party that considers the lease an asset and the party who considers the lease a liability.
4. In the figure below the two dimensional slider permits you to choose a combination of rate and frequency of lease escalation, appearing as "escalaction %" and "escalation period" below the plot. Change the setting to 5.75% and 3 years and note the effect on IRR.

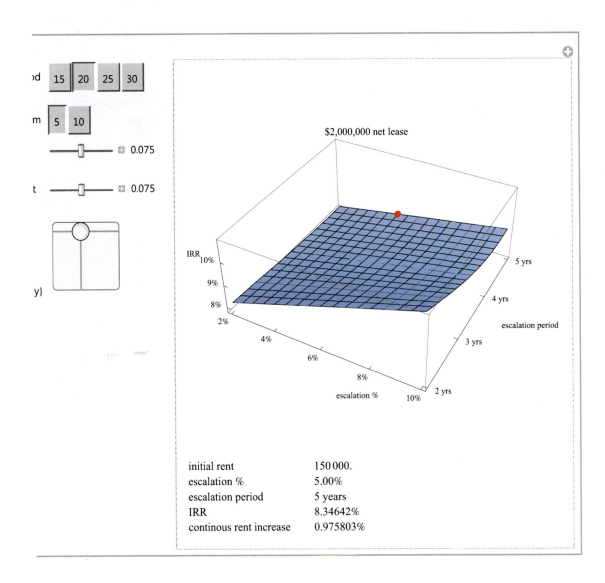

EPILOG

You have now survived <u>Private Real Estate Investment</u>. Ten years after I wrote the Preface to the first edition much about the world and the author has changed. As I revised and expanded the second edition in the Brave New World of government bailouts on a scale never imagined, I am even more convinced that all of what we consider solid is to be found in real estate. The scale of the numbers may have changed but the computations have not.

Technology has moved publishing into a phase as new and different as the era ushered in by Johannes Gutenberg. It is moving so fast you may have this in print or electronic form before the interactive version is available. Check www.mathestate.com for updates on versions, errata and other useful tools that will be developed to enhance this effort.

My librarian wife will scold me for not providing an index for the print version. In the Old Media days an index was the hallmark of a quality book. The second edition was written primarily to be an electronic book. Searchable e-books make an index a thing of the past. The print version suffers accordingly but *Mathematica* does not support the easy creation of an index, for which Wolfram Research and I beg forgiveness.

Two themes, important since long before even Gutenberg, dominate the message in this text. They are fundamental principles that every real estate investor, indeed every informed citizen of a free society should always have in mind. The study of real estate in an advanced secular society may be described as the search for the answer to two questions:

1. <u>**What is it that we value?**</u> The answer to this is NOT the bricks and mortar or the land and buildings. The thing we value is the *right to use the land*. Property rights are the foundation of every other right in society. Without a place where you can exclude others, the right to privacy has no meaning. Without a place to stand and speak where you are undisturbed, the right to free speech is meaningless. One can find analogs between property rights and all other rights in a civil society.

2. <u>**How do we value these things?**</u> In order for the things we value to have meaning we must agree on a method to compare them to other things. That method is unquestionably mathematical. The failure to precisely measure the benefit of ownership of property rights may be found at the base of a host of financial problems at the personal and national level.

The conclusion of this book, following most of half a century in the field, naturally comes near the end of my career. It has been a great run. My only regret is that I don't have another 40 or 50 years to do it again.

RJB

Made in the USA
Middletown, DE
03 December 2016